Fundamentals of Songwriting

Essential Tools and Techniques for Serious Songwriters

by Jeremy Siskind

Engraving by Kim Groves Brand

Cover & Design by Kelly DiBernardo Rupert

ISBN: 979-8-9874806-9-4

Visit Jeremy Siskind online at
www.jeremysiskind.com

Table of Contents

From the Author

In almost every age of human history, songs have been used to teach our children, make our friends laugh, bring families closer together, express our most intense emotions, woo lovers, worship, help communities celebrate or grieve, and protest unjust political regimes.

Still, despite centuries of songwriting, songs remain deeply mysterious. In the best songs, the alchemy of music and words produces a new creation possessing a magic that no music theorist could fully explain.

This book approaches songwriting with humility, recognizing that the creative process is more profound than a book can explain. Learning the information presented in this book won't transform you into Bob Dylan or Irving Berlin, Paul McCartney or Taylor Swift. It will, however, help you hone what songwriters call *the craft*, the practical skills that can be learned through hard work and study. Craft helps songwriters organize and shape raw inspiration into lines that rhyme, musical forms that fit together, and chord progressions that guide the listener on a journey through tension and release.

Fundamentals of Songwriting focuses on three foundational elements that make up a song – lyrics, melody, and harmony – while recognizing that other skills are useful for the modern songwriter. Even though vocal performance, piano/guitar arranging, digital production, and visual-based skills like costuming, dancing, and video editing can help transform a good song into an unforgettable artistic statement, they are, unfortunately, beyond the scope of what a single book can cover.

Allow me to leave you with a final thought, with apologies for the grandiosity: writing songs pushes us to meaningfully reflect on our deepest emotions, to explore the caverns of our soul that we don't often investigate during the chaos of daily life. When we transform our feelings into lyrics and music, we don't just express ourselves, we often come to understand and accept ourselves. In this way, songwriting isn't just fun, sexy, or satisfying – it's actually therapeutic. Every note, chord, and word that you write brings a small measure of healing to a world that sorely needs to be healed.

Please enjoy the book and thank you for writing songs!

Jeremy Siskind

How to Use This Book

Fundamentals of Songwriting presents a wealth of material – perhaps more than a songwriter could reasonably absorb in a single lifetime! As the author, my nightmare is that a young songwriter feels the need to master every form, term, and exercise before writing a single note. In fact, I worry that readers will use the significant length of the book as a crutch to avoid the vulnerable, intimidating work of putting pen to paper.

Please know this: the best way to learn songwriting is to write songs.

With that said, I hope that every page offers practical ideas, tools, and guidance to support you along the way. My greatest wish is that this book helps liberate you from writer's block, offers alternatives to your limiting writing habits, and pushes you to write songs you never thought you were capable of writing!

Although *Fundamentals of Songwriting* is carefully sequenced to move from essential concepts to more advanced ideas, it doesn't need to be read in order. Feel free to graze "buffet-style" through the chapters, seeking the material that will most help you in the moment. Maybe you need help writing better melodies: skip to Chapter 12 ("Melody"). Or if your lyrics feel cliché, try Chapter 8 ("The Lyricist's Toolbox"). Or you may want to focus exclusively on the "Practice" sections at the end of each chapter, which are designed to push your writing in new directions.

Each chapter about a specific song form is followed by a supplementary chapter, indicated with an "a" (such as Chapter 5a or Chapter 9a). These are my favorite chapters! Each of these chapters guides you through writing a song in a particular form while demonstrating the process step by step. If you want to start writing right away, skip to these chapters and write alongside me.

A QR code is included in the header of each chapter. Scan the QR code to access the chapter webpage, where you can find recordings of the songs referenced, sample "answers" to the written exercises, and other resources.

If QR code scanning isn't for you, you can bookmark the book's main page using the following link, which links to all of the chapter pages:

https://www.jeremysiskind.com/fundamentals-of-songwriting/

The main page can also be accessed by scanning the QR code on the right-hand side of this page.

Enjoy exploring these pages. I hope each page includes something that deepens your love of writing songs.

Scan Here
for Home Page

Chord Symbol Chart

This book uses common chord symbols to notate harmony. The following chart can be used as a reference to help you decipher any unfamiliar chord symbols.

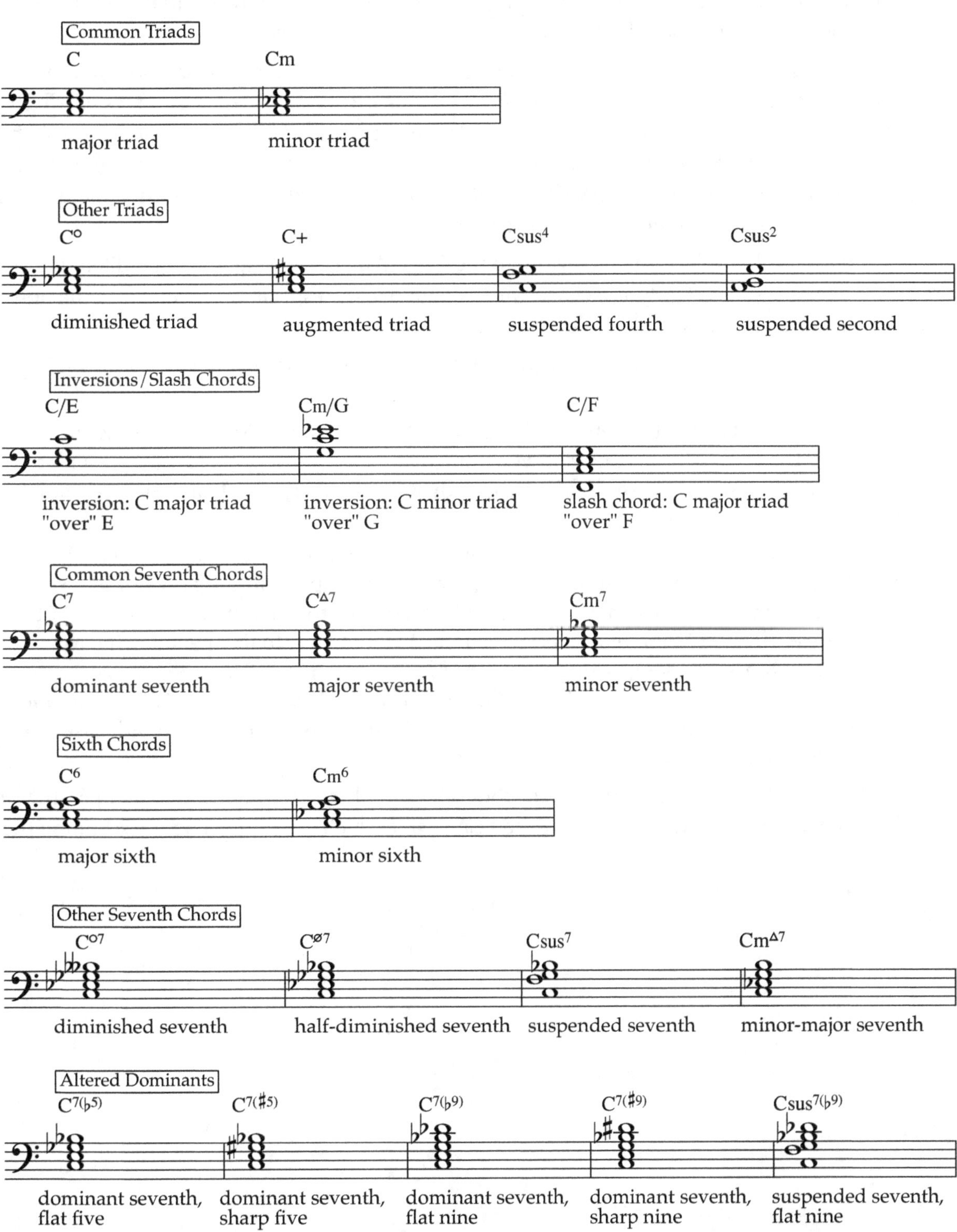

About the Songs

There are countless great songs that could have been used for examples in this text, and it's an impossible task to represent the entirety of the songwriting tradition. Unfortunately, odds are that I omitted your favorite artist and highlighted songs by an artist you can't stand. I'm sorry!

I chose songs with the goal of providing clear, familiar examples that represent a wide array of musical genres and eras. I frequently referenced the 2024 *Rolling Stone* list "The 500 Greatest Songs of All Time" in order to choose songs that are established as songwriting masterpieces. However, in some cases, I chose a song simply because it provided a great example of a lyrical or musical concept, even though it might not be as commonly known. In other sections of the book, copyright considerations played a role, and I intentionally chose songs that have entered the public domain.

Attributing songs was also difficult. For songs from the Great American Songbook, I credited the songwriter(s). However, for songs clearly associated with a single artist – especially big hits from the pop or rock world – I credited the artist who made the song famous.

Yes, it *does* feel sacrilegious not to credit the writers of a song in a songwriting book. But my logic goes as follows:

- Readers need to be able to immediately identify the song, and it is helpful to associate a song with the artist who performs it. We immediately know the song "Like a Virgin" by Madonna, but don't recognize "Like a Virgin" by Billy Steinberg and Tom Kelly, the actual songwriters.
- Many modern pop songs are written by large teams of writers and producers who share legal ownership of the song. In many cases, it can be disruptive to the flow of the text to include all of them. For instance, if I wanted to correctly attribute the writers of the 2014 Mark Ronson/Bruno Mars song "Uptown Funk," I would have to list the following eleven individuals who share songwriting rights: *Mark Ronson, Bruno Mars, Philip Lawrence, Jeff Bhasker, Nicholaus Williams, Devon Gallaspy, Charles Wilson, Robert Wilson, Ronnie Wilson, Rudolph Taylor, and Lonnie Simmons.* Unfortunately, such a list doesn't easily fit into the text of an instructional book.

If you're interested in the full songwriting credits for each example song, I've included them on the web page for the chapter in which the song appears. You can visit each chapter's web page by scanning the QR code next to the title.

1. Getting Started

How is a song born? Does it start with a feeling in your gut? With a dictionary opened wide? With a magic chord on the piano?

Many students would love a defined entry point that would make songwriting organized, process-oriented, and predictable. However, for many artists, the opposite is true. Songwriting can be messy, lengthy, unpredictable, and meandering.

Paul Simon is one artist for whom the process of writing a song is a journey of discovery. In an interview, Simon compares writing a song to "wandering down a path and you don't know what the destination is. Somewhere, toward the end, you can sort of see what the destination is, and you can understand what the journey is about. At which point, if I want, I can go alter some of the things that occurred to set it up. But usually, I don't. It usually just goes along as a story that I'm telling, and I'm a listener, and at a certain point I say, 'Oh! That's what it's about.'"

Simon also has advice on how a young songwriter can find their way along a winding path. In his song, "Song About the Moon," Simon offers helpful advice while honoring the intuitive and deeply personal nature of songwriting.

> *If you want to write a song about the moon*
> *Walk along the craters in the afternoon*

Simon's lyric invites us to consider that songs often begin with personal experience and encourages young songwriters to seek out adventure and experience that can be celebrated in a song. Or maybe, a songwriter need not literally experience the subject matter but can imagine the world of the song. The lyric takes a new turn in the next verse:

> *If you want to write a song about the heart*
> *Think about the moon before you start*

Although the playful lyric resists easy interpretation, these lines suggest that great songs bring a novel perspective. Writing a song only about "the heart" risks being boring, predictable, or derivative. Introducing an unexpected entry point like relating love to the moon can open unanticipated avenues.

In the final verse, Simon shares the following:

> *If you want to write a song about a face*
> *Think about the photograph*
> *That you really can't remember but you can't erase*
> *Wash your hands and dreams in lightning*
> *Cut off your hair and whatever is frightening*

Although this passage leans more towards imagery than instruction, its lyrics offer clues into where inspiration can be found. Those insights include:

- Write about something that you really care about (something that "you can't erase")
- Stay open to unexplained and unexpected bursts of insight ("wash your hands and dreams in lightning")
- Don't let your ego stand in the way of the truth; be vulnerable ("cut off your hair and whatever is frightening")

Simon is telling us that there is mystery, joy, and discovery in the process of songwriting. It makes sense that songwriting is so non-linear. After all, songs combine diverse elements: melody, harmony, poetry, form, production, arrangement, performance, and more. In modern times, songs are often combined with visuals and/or dance. Combining these diverse artforms into a three-minute masterpiece that captures the human experience requires something more akin to emotional conjuring than mechanical process.

Habits of Successful Songwriters

1. **Keep a Journal:** Whenever you have an idea for a concept, a rhyme, a chord, or a word to include in a song, write it down. That way, when you go to write, you won't be starting from scratch.

2. **Record Voice Memos:** Maintain a library of melodic fragments, chord progressions, and grooves, so that you will always have raw material to draw from when inspiration strikes.

3. **Write Consistently:** The only way to become a songwriter is to actually sit down and write. Have a strict writing schedule, ideally daily, and put words on paper. Don't wait for the perfect idea to come. If you force yourself to write ten ideas, one of them is bound to be good.

4. **Don't Judge:** You can't be a critic and an artist at the same time. Suspend judgment throughout the writing process so that you have space for inspiration. You might be surprised that ideas that might be dismissed as cheesy or cliché ultimately sound great in a final draft.

5. **Finish Songs:** Although it is okay to abandon a song without finishing, don't let it become a habit. Give yourself deadlines and finish songs on time, even if the end product is not yet satisfactory. Writing complete songs brings fulfillment and pleasure. Plus, only by completing songs can songwriters learn about form and pacing.

6. **Collaborate:** Having bandmates, cowriters, or a circle of songwriters helps keep you accountable, inspired, and moving forward. Attend an open mic in your area, join a writers' group, or call up your talented friend to help you find chords for your melody.

7. **Edit Ruthlessly:** Rarely does a song come out perfect the first time. Editing is how songwriters spend most of their time. It has been widely reported, for instance, that Leonard Cohen wrote more than 80 verses to "Hallelujah" in order to find a handful he liked for his recording.

8. **Listen:** Listening to and performing great songs by other writers is the best way to gain an intuitive sense of what a song should sound and feel like. Bob Dylan said, "Anyone who wants to be a songwriter should listen to as much folk music as they can, study the form and structure of stuff that has been around for 100 years." Grow a repertoire of songs that you know from memory.

9. **Read:** Songwriters love words and lots of great words have been written. Reading novels, short stories, and poetry deepens your vocabulary, offers narrative inspiration, and fuels your imagination.

10. **Pay Attention:** To an artist, anything can be inspiration. Imagine the life of the person walking across the street and take note of the smell wafting from the bakery you're walking by. Don't dismiss anything as being unworthy of a song. The creative impulse starts with constantly looking at the world and saying, "This is interesting; this matters."

30 Ideas for How to Start a Song

Even with the best habits, a songwriter needs a place to start.

One of the most common questions asked in songwriting workshops is: should you start with music or words? The answer to this question depends completely on the songwriter and the specific song. Great songwriters throughout history have differing opinions. Paul Simon starts with the music, whereas Bob Dylan starts with the words. As a songwriter myself, I have started songs from both angles and, although the entry point changed the character of the song, I have found that either method can create a powerful song.

As a teacher, I suggest that students explore multiple entry points. Because different processes yield different types of songs, good songwriters evolve by updating their process from song to song and from project to project.

And, besides, beyond simply music or words, there are so many ways to start a song. Each of the following thirty ideas offers a unique entry point. Some of these ideas might feel very familiar whereas others might surprise you. Find something familiar and something new in this list and start brainstorming ideas for a new song.

Musical Elements

1. **Melody** – Sing or play a melody on your instrument as the first idea in your song. If you need help making a melody interesting, look at the "Melody" chapter of this book.

2. **Chord progression** – Create a chord progression on your instrument. Chord progressions don't need to be complicated to be effective. For some chordal inspiration, examine the "Harmony" sections of this book.

3. **Bassline** – Sing or play a bassline on your instrument as the germ of your song. Think about great basslines like "Another One Bites the Dust" (Queen) or "Billie Jean" (Michael Jackson).

4. **Riff** – Find a guitar or piano riff that makes a great accompaniment. Think about a riff like "Beat It" (Michael Jackson) or "(I Can't Get No) Satisfaction" (The Rolling Stones). Come up with six ideas and then pick your favorite one as the start of your song.

5. **Hook** – Can you imagine the part of your song when everyone's singing along? That's called the hook. Hum ten catchy phrases into your voice memos, then choose your favorite. That catchy phrase can be the start of a smash hit.

6. **Sound** – Is there a specific kind of guitar sound or synthesizer patch you want to include? Maybe an unconventional instrument you plan to use? Brainstorm a unique sonic texture and write with that sound image in mind.

7. **Groove** – What kind of beat do you imagine? Michael Jackson wrote a lot of songs by first layering "mouth sounds" on a recording to create an original groove. Listen to recordings specifically to find a groove that matches your vision, then write to match the groove.

Musical Inspiration

8. **Harmonic Concept** – Learning about a new way to write chords, like secondary dominants or modal interchange? Use the concept to inspire a new chord progression, written more intellectually than aurally.

9. **Bridge First** – Some songwriters like to write the bridge, the middle section, where the music shifts to a new area. It can be an interesting starting point because it's the most adventurous musical section.

10. **Melodic Rhythm** – How will your melody flow? Speak a rhythm using nonsense syllables like "tat" and "doo" while imagining the underlying groove. Record it and start experimenting with words that fit the rhythm.

11. **Form** – Decide on a musical form for your song (you can read about Strophic, Verse-Chorus, AABA, and ABAC forms in this book). What do you want the overall shape of the music to be? Maybe you want to do something really unconventional with many sections like "Bohemian Rhapsody" or borrow a form, like the Rondo, from classical music.

12. **Old Chords, New Melody** – Take the chord progression of a preexisting song and write a new melody that fits with the chord progression. Once the melody is complete, you can either use the chord progression you "borrowed" or invent a different chord progression to fit the melody.

13. **Scale or Mode** – Do you know your scales like your harmonic minor and melodic minor or your modes like dorian, phrygian, lydian, etc.? Write a song using one of these less-expected sounds (a good example is John Mayer's "Home Life," written in the mixolydian mode).

14. **Preexisting Words** – Write a new melody to preexisting words, like a poem or a lyric to someone else's song. Then, replace the words you used with your own original words while maintaining your melody.

15. **Vamp and Sing** – Invent a four-chord vamp, that is, a repeated progression. Record the vamp or loop it live, improvising different ideas over the progression until something sticks.

Playing with Words

16. **Rhymes** – Keep a journal of interesting rhymes. Choose your favorite and decide how the rhyming words could fit together into a song.

17. **Repeated Sounds** – Brainstorm words with repeated sounds, for instance, "love," "leave," and "veil" all have "v" and "l" sounds. Use these words to start a lyrical line and continue writing the lyric with the mood and story of that first line in mind.

18. **Vowels** – Sing a melody with vowels that come naturally to your voice ("ooh," "ahh," etc.). Record your singing and find words that match the vowels you sang. Justin Vernon (Bon Iver) talks about creating lyrics in this way.

19. **Imitation** – Take a poem or song you like and "rewrite" it line by line, replacing the artist's words with similar words, almost like a "Mad Libs" exercise. For instance, if the original document has the phrase "riding a wild wave," you might write "watching a lovely cloud."

20. **Poetic Rhythm** – Challenge yourself to write in a specific poetic rhythm (iambic pentameter, for instance). Write 20 lines about a chosen subject in the given meter and use the best phrases that you wrote as the basis for a lyric.

21. **Parts of Speech** – Brainstorm interesting words from different categories like proper nouns, nouns, action verbs, adjectives, and adverbs, and see if two or more could combine to form the basis of a story or description.

Poetic Inspiration

22. **Idiom** – Look up some idioms, common phrases like "turn the tables" or "break a leg." Choose one that speaks to you and use it as the basis of a song by imagining how the phrase might fit into a story.

23. **Visual** – Imagine your song idea as a movie and consider how you would shoot it. Then, describe in your lyric what is happening on screen.

24. **Journaling** – Strive to fill three pages with an honest, unfiltered journal of your feelings in this moment. Then, look back at the journal to find the two or three interesting phrases or ideas. These phrases can become the basis of your song.

25. **Historical** – Imagine yourself as a character from history. Write a song about how you're feeling during a dramatic moment in your life.

26. **Memories** – Choose a lasting memory from your life and write down everything that you remember about it. Write a song describing the memory and how it affected you.

27. **Simplify** – Take a difficult concept from philosophy, literature, or art, and simplify it into poetry that can be sung. For instance, write about Zeno's idea that you can "never step into the same river twice."

28. **Dramatize** – Think of an important moral lesson or question and imagine a story that brings the concept to life. For instance, take the saying, "more money, more problems" and write a story of someone experiencing that phrase firsthand.

29. **Paint a Picture** – Not all songs need to tell a story. Think of a time and place that you want others to experience and describe it in detail.

30. **Senses** – As you think about your song, describe how it looks, sounds, feels, tastes, and smells. Some of these senses might be more relevant than others, but together, they can create a world that your listeners can vividly experience.

These ideas can serve as springboards. Use them as a jumping off point and follow your original ideas as far as they can take you.

Common Stumbling Blocks

It's common for aspiring songwriters to get stuck on their journey. The next section presents common anxieties faced by songwriters along with practical solutions.

1. **"I often start songs but struggle to finish them."**

   Possible solutions:
   - Find an accountability partner and set a deadline to finish and share your songs.
   - Decide on the form beforehand to create a roadmap with a clear destination.
   - Make a plan to go to an open mic event or share your song online on a particular day so that you have a built-in "deadline."

2. **"My songs are so personal that I end up feeling embarrassed or like I might offend someone I know."**

   Possible solutions:
   - Write songs from someone else's perspective, such as a historical figure or character in a novel.
   - Write about your own feelings but change the setting so it feels less familiar (maybe you're on a tropical island or writing during the Renaissance).
   - Write about yourself, but change perspectives, for instance, write in the third person ("he," "she") or the second person ("you").

3. **"All my songs end up sounding kind of the same."**

   Possible solutions:
   - Change your writing process, especially your first step. For instance, start by writing chords first rather than melody first.
   - Write with a partner, especially someone who has different strengths than you.
   - Pretend that you are writing a song to be performed by a famous artist and strive to capture their voice.

4. **"I don't know what style to write in."**

   Possible solutions:
   - Keep experimenting without judgment. Many artists cover a wide range of styles, even on a single album. Others arrive at their signature sound by combining their diverse influences.
   - Imagine the character who is speaking your lyric and what style of music fits their "voice" the best.
   - Write for a specific event or venue. If you are performing at a coffee shop, maybe you want to have a song in a more "folk-y," acoustic style whereas if you are performing at a jazz club, you potentially want to have something in a swing style.

5. **"My songs don't sound very good."**

Possible solutions:

- Keep writing! Songwriting is like a muscle that can be trained and grown through repetition.
- Read this book and do the practice exercises. They are all designed to train your songwriting skills.
- Work on your performing by taking vocal lessons and/or lessons on your instrument. Sometimes good songs are missing a good performance.

Writing songs can be scary and vulnerable and self-doubt is part of the process. Don't give into all of the voices telling you to quit. Instead, work with purpose, forge new paths around your obstacles, and remind yourself of why you write songs.

Takeaways

1. Songwriting is mysterious, experiential, and non-linear. Though we must approach it with intention, it can't be perfectly calibrated or automated.

2. There is no "right way" to write a song. Different songwriters start from different places. The best songwriters experiment and evolve with each new song they write.

3. Good habits are essential. Keep folders of raw materials, write consistently, and regularly finish songs.

4. Experiment with different starting points, such as melody, harmony, sound, rhyme, story, form, or even a personal experience.

5. You don't have to write about yourself. Try taking the perspective of a character from a book, show, movie, or a figure from history.

Practice

1. Circle three ideas that you like from the thirty presented in this chapter. For each one, brainstorm an initial concept for a song. For example, if you like idea #26, "Paint a "Picture," decide what image you're going to portray of and brainstorm details that you want to include.

2. Choose three songwriters you admire and search for information about how they like to write their songs.

3. Write a weekly schedule identifying the time that you will dedicate to songwriting.

2. Text Setting

Sing each of the following phrases to the tune of the opening phrase of "Happy Birthday." Instead of "Happy birthday to you," sing:

- Have you seen her today
- I'm a lover of cheese
- Cheddar cheese is the best

These all fit pretty well with the melody, at least to my ear. Sing the next three phrases to the same tune:

- Happy Easter also
- Of course you are a fool
- Haven't you heard she's gone

For me, this set feels awkward. For instance, I want to put the emphasis on the "al" of "also," but the melody holds on the "so." It feels clunky. Now, sing the last set:

- It's undeniable
- My birthday is stupid
- Birthday fun is coming for you

These three clash more strongly with the melody. In fact, the final option is way too long for the number of notes we have for the given melody.

Why do some of these phrases feel natural and others don't? The answer lies in **text setting**, the relationship between music and text. Even a song with imaginative lyrics and a beautiful melody can fall flat if the words and music aren't aligned.

Syllables and Notation

To understand how lyrics interact with melody, we first need to understand how language itself generates rhythm. It all starts with the building block of language, the syllable. A **syllable** is a portion of a word that represents a single rhythmic utterance. Every syllable includes a single vowel sound and associated consonants.

Words with only one syllable are classified as **monosyllabic** whereas words with multiple syllables are called **polysyllabic**. The next list shows examples of monosyllabic words expanded into polysyllabic words:

Monosyllabic words: cat, hang, pout, sort, sum, find, pill

Polysyllabic words: cattle, hangout, pouting, sortable, finder, pillbox

Usually, exactly one syllable is sung for one musical note. Whereas monosyllabic words are simply written beneath the noteheads, polysyllabic words are divided into their component syllables using hyphens, with each syllable placed beneath its corresponding note. When dividing a word into syllables, strive to reflect the typical pronunciation of the word to help the singer pronounce it naturally. For instance, divide "twinkle" as "twin-kle" rather than "tw-inkle." When notating syllables beneath a melody, text always goes beneath the staff.

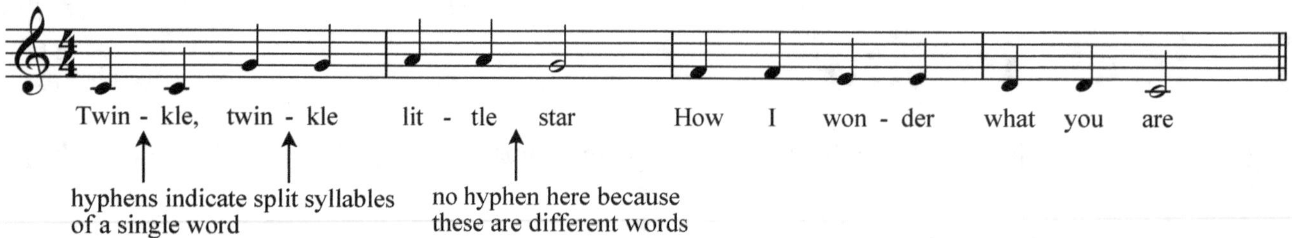

When one syllable is sung across multiple notes, it is called a **melisma**. A style of singing in which syllables are regularly stretched over multiple notes can be called **melismatic**. Christina Aguilera and Mariah Carey can be referred to as "melismatic" singers. Melismas are indicated by a solid line when the stretched syllable is the final (or only) syllable of the word and with a dashed line when the stretched syllable falls in the middle of a word.

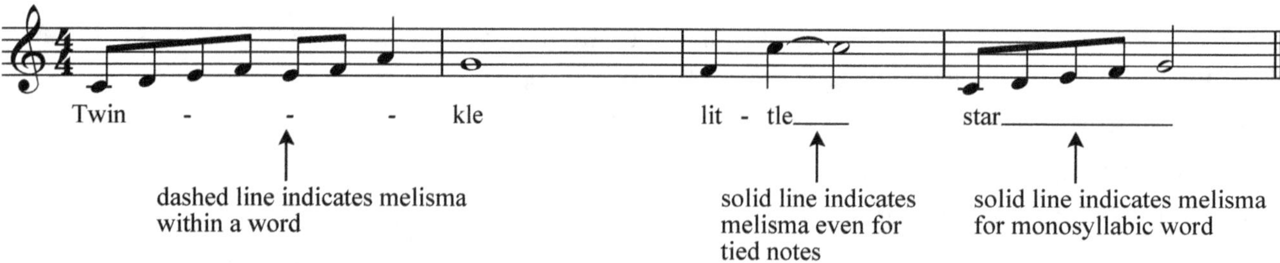

It is impossible to place two syllables on one note because each syllable indicates a new rhythmic impulse. However, it is possible to shorten words using **elision** by replacing a vowel with an apostrophe. For instance, instead of pronouncing "every" with three syllables, a songwriter can elide the middle vowel to create the two-syllable elision, "ev'ry". Instead of using the word "meandering" with four syllables, a songwriter could elide the "e" and create the three-syllable elision, "meand'ring".

The next example contains elisions in every phrase.

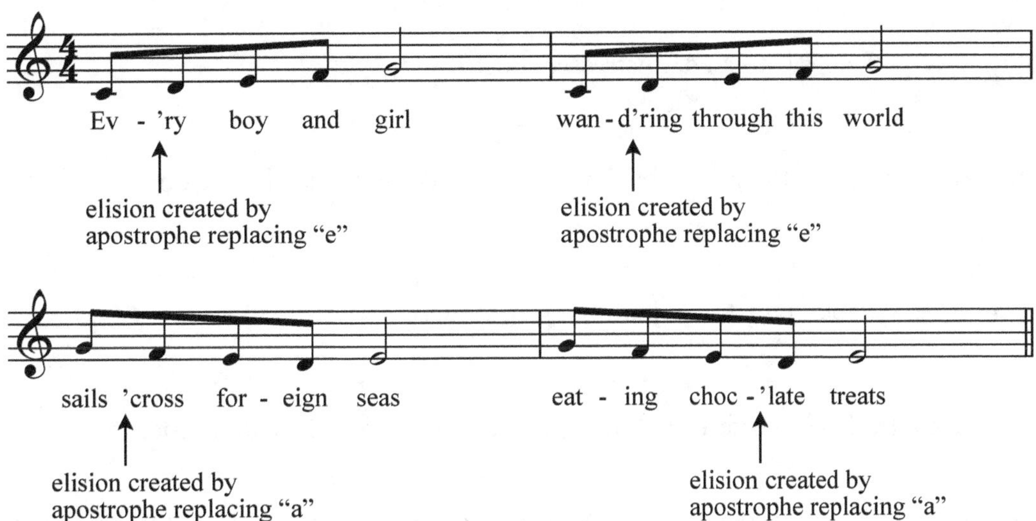

Although, at first glance, elision can seem poetic or formal, elision frequently reflects the rhythms of casual speech. There are many common words for which English speakers frequently don't enunciate every syllable. For instance, rarely do people pronounce all three syllables of "every" or "chocolate." In musical styles that mimic casual conversation, like pop, folk, and singer-songwriter, it makes sense to curtail commonly shortened words.

Stresses and Unstressed Syllables

All polysyllabic words have at least one **stressed syllable**, the part of the word that carries rhythmic emphasis. **Prosody** is the study of stressed and unstressed syllables in poems and songs. In prosody, stressed syllables are indicated with **a slash** (/) or a **dash** (-). Most polysyllabic words also have **unstressed syllables**, those that do not carry the rhythmic weight. Unstressed syllables are indicated with an **"x"** or a **u shape** (˘). Although English speakers mostly agree on stressed and unstressed syllables, there is some room for interpretation when determining which syllables should be stressed.

Poetic feet, also known as **metrical feet**, are building-block units combining stressed and unstressed syllables. The four most common poetic feet in English are:

1. **Trochee**

   Pattern: two syllables | stressed, unstressed

   / ˘   / ˘   / ˘   / ˘   / ˘   / ˘

   Examples: pattern | curtain | rebound | laughter | that one | leave me

2. **Iamb**

   Pattern: two syllables | unstressed, stressed

   ˘ /   ˘ /   ˘ /   ˘ /   ˘ /   ˘ /

   Examples: amount | terrain | believe | depend | a plane | the sun

3. **Dactyl**

Pattern: three syllables | stressed, unstressed, unstressed

Examples: caravan | pottery | terrible | mentioning | come to me | live again

4. **Anapest**

Pattern: three syllables | unstressed, unstressed, stressed

Examples: contradict | interfere | volunteer | entertain | in a while | after lunch

When determining stress for multiple shorter words, notice how you naturally want to speak the words. In general, nouns, verbs, and adjectives are stressed over connective words like articles, pronouns, prepositions, and conjunctions. However, stress can fluctuate based on meaning and context. Changes in stress can shade the meaning of a sentence. "LOOK at him" means something slightly different than "Look AT him" or "Look at HIM." These changes in meaning should be kept in mind when determining which syllables should receive a musical stress.

Matching Lyrical Stress and Musical Emphasis

Although poetic feet are essential in poetry, they play a smaller role in songwriting. Poets create rhythm by repeating a single metrical foot, but song lyrics vary their rhythm to match the music. The rhythm of the melody determines which words are held longer and which are sung more quickly. In general, lyrics are only written in repeated poetic meters when the melodic rhythm remains constant.

So how do songwriters synchronize music and words? Songwriters match stressed syllables with melody notes that receive **musical emphasis**. Musical emphasis is generally determined by three factors: strong rhythmic placement, longer hold, and higher pitch. Although not every stressed syllable will align with all three methods of musical emphasis, employing a combination of these devices creates a natural, speech-like fit between music and lyrics.

Method 1: Strong Rhythmic Placement

Rhythmic placement is the most important tool for effective text setting. Traditionally, stressed and unstressed syllables are mapped onto the melody's stronger and weaker beats. Stressed syllables are placed on relatively stronger beats and unstressed syllables are placed on relatively weaker beats.

Rhythmic Hierarchy

In music, **measures** indicate a hierarchy of stronger and weaker rhythmic positions. A note's placement within the measure is the most powerful indication of whether it receives emphasis. The next section shows common hierarchies for the three most common musical meters: four-four (4/4), three-four (3/4), and six-eight (6/8).

Four-four (4/4)

Four-four (4/4) is by far the most common meter in Western music. Most pop and rock songs are written in four-four. The time signature indicates that there are four beats in a measure, and a quarter note represents one beat. The next example shows a breakdown of the different rhythmic positions within a four-four measure:

{ Most emphasis: the **strong beats**, beats one and three

Some emphasis: the **weak beats**, beats two and four

Least emphasis: the **offbeats**, the "ands"

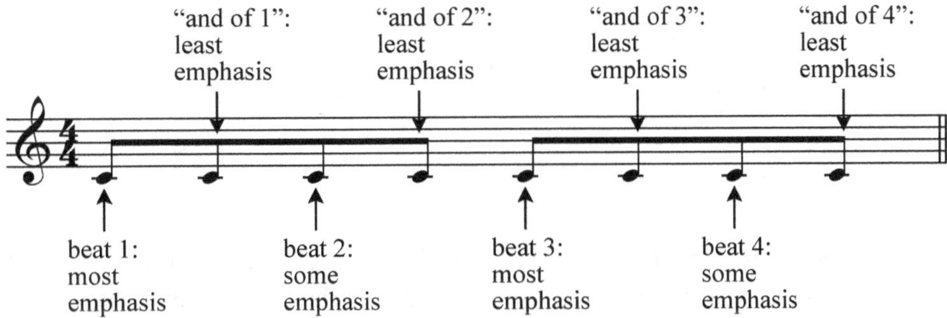

If there are shorter notes, such as sixteenth notes or eighth-note triplets, they receive the least emphasis, less emphasis than notes on the beats or on the "ands."

Three-four (3/4)

Three-four (3/4) meter is associated with waltzes like "The Tennessee Waltz" and lilting ballads like "Piano Man." Three-four meter indicates that there are three beats in a measure, with a quarter note representing one beat. The next example shows a breakdown of the different rhythmic positions within a three-four measure:

{ Most emphasis: the **strong beat**, beats one

Some emphasis: the **weak beats**, beats two and three

Least emphasis: the **offbeats**, the "ands"

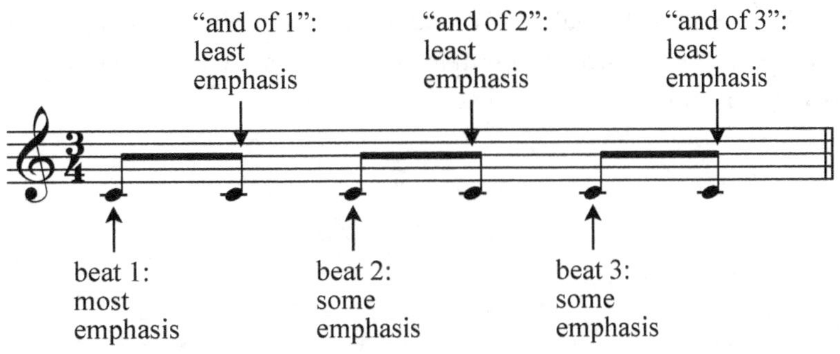

Six-eight (6/8)

Six-eight (6/8) is the final common meter for Western music. Songs in six-eight time, like the Beatles' "Oh! Darling" and Leonard Cohen's "Hallelujah" generally have a gentle sway. It indicates that there are six beats in a measure, with an eighth note representing one beat. The grouping of a six-eight meter indicates two sets of three eighth notes. (ONE-two-three-FOUR-five six). The next example shows a breakdown of the different rhythmic positions within a six-eight measure:

Most emphasis: the **strong beats**, beats one and four (the first and fourth eighth notes)

Least emphasis: all other beats, 2, 3, 5 and 6

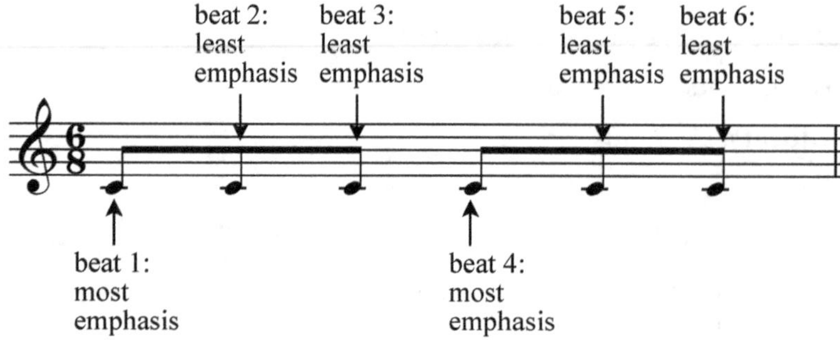

Syncopation

Syncopation, placing emphasis on offbeats, is common in all genres derived from African traditions, which includes rock, jazz, R&B, and pop. Syncopation disrupts the clear relationship between strong and weak beats by shifting emphasis to weaker beats. Notice the way the notes of "Twinkle, Twinkle, Little Star" are shifted to the offbeats to create syncopation in the next example.

When setting text to a melody with syncopation, consider where each melody *would* fall *if* it were placed on the beat. It might be necessary to "restore" the melody to an unsyncopated version in order to determine how the rhythmic hierarchy functions.

Method 2: Longer Hold

Stressed syllables are placed on relatively longer notes while unstressed syllables are placed on shorter notes. For "Twinkle, Twinkle, Little Star," the lyric would be analyzed as follows:

/ ˘ / ˘ / ˘ /
Twinkle, twinkle, little star

/ ˘ / ˘ / ˘ /
How I wonder what you are

/ ˘ / ˘ / ˘ /
Up above the world so high

/ ˘ / ˘ / ˘ /
Like a diamond in the sky

Sing the song to yourself and consider where the long notes are placed. All of the long notes occur on stressed syllables at the end of the line: "star," "are," "high," and "sky." Try singing an altered version of "Twinkle, Twinkle" in which you hold out the penultimate (second to last) syllable of each verse ("lit-tleeeeeeeeeee star"). The text setting suddenly sounds awkward both because of the distorted note lengths and because the displaced last syllable no longer lands on a strong beat.

Method 3: Higher Pitch

In natural speech, we often emphasize words by modulating pitch slightly upwards. Melodies often reflect this tendency as well and higher pitches often indicate musical emphasis.

This is especially noticeable in modern pop and sung rap, where melodies often use just a few repeated notes. In these styles, unstressed syllables are sung on a single, low pitch and stressed syllables are sung on higher notes for emphasis and variety.

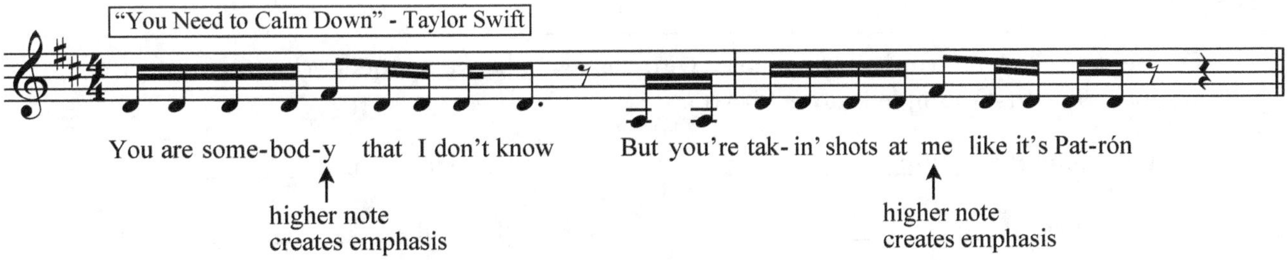

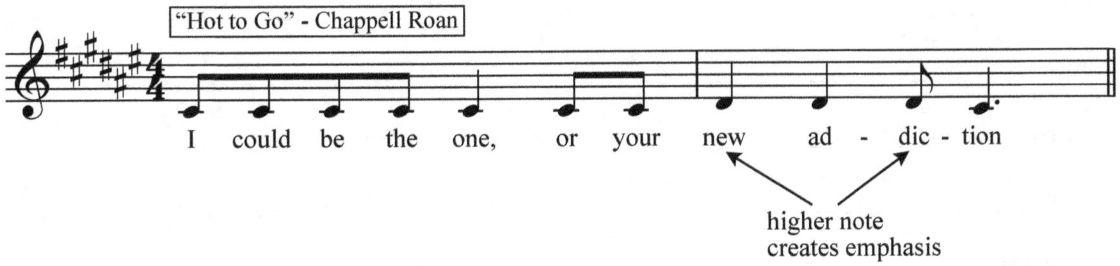

When stressed syllables align emphasized melody notes using strong rhythmic placement, longer holds, and higher pitch, lyrics naturally fit the melody. When songwriters execute these strategies well, their songs have the feeling of speech: comprehensible, personable, and honest. Good text-setting is especially important in musical theater, where the audience absolutely needs to understand the lyrics in order to understand the story.

However, not every songwriter wants their songs to sound like speech. Purposefully mismatching lyrical and musical emphasis can make a lyric memorable, funky, or personal. For instance, in the previous example, Taylor Swift musically emphasizes the final syllable ("dy") of "somebody" instead of stressing the expected first syllable ("some"). She also changes the emphasis on "Patrón" by placing the "Pa" of "Patrón" on the strong beat even though the stress should clearly go on "rón" (as indicated by the tilde). The unexpected accents are not an accident. Swift frequently "mismatches" musical and lyrical accents as part of her signature style. Leaning into these kinds of misalignments can pique the listener's interest and make a song more memorable.

Takeaways

1. A syllable is a single rhythmic unit. Place one syllable on each note, connecting syllables within a word using hyphens.

2. Melisma is a term for stretching one syllable over multiple notes. "Elision" is a term for shortening the number of syllables in a word by omitting a vowel.

3. Syllabic stress refers to what part of a word receives rhythmic emphasis. Poetic feet are common patterns of syllabic stress.

4. Aligning musical and lyrical emphasis creates an intuitive fit that makes a lyric feel like natural speech. Three ways to achieve musical emphasis are: strong rhythmic position, longer hold, and higher pitch.

5. Not all songwriters want their text setting to sound speech-like. Working against normal speech patterns can help make a song memorable, especially in pop music and rap.

Practice

1. Divide the following words into syllables with dashes in between, then write the number of syllables. The first example is done for you.

    A. Trombone *trom-bone, 2*

    B. Zither _______________

    C. Violin _______________

    D. Piano _______________

    E. Accordion_______________

    F. Organ _______________

    G. Mandolin _______________

    H. Orchestra _______________

    I. Harmonica _______________

    J. Tuba _______________

    K. Lute_______________

    L. Piccolo _______________

    M. Harmonium _______________

    N. Contrabassoon _______________

    O. Banjo_______________

2. Apply the boxed text to the musical passage below it. Syllables that use melismas indicate the number of notes the melisma should last. For instance, "Love (x3)" means to stretch the word "love" for three notes.

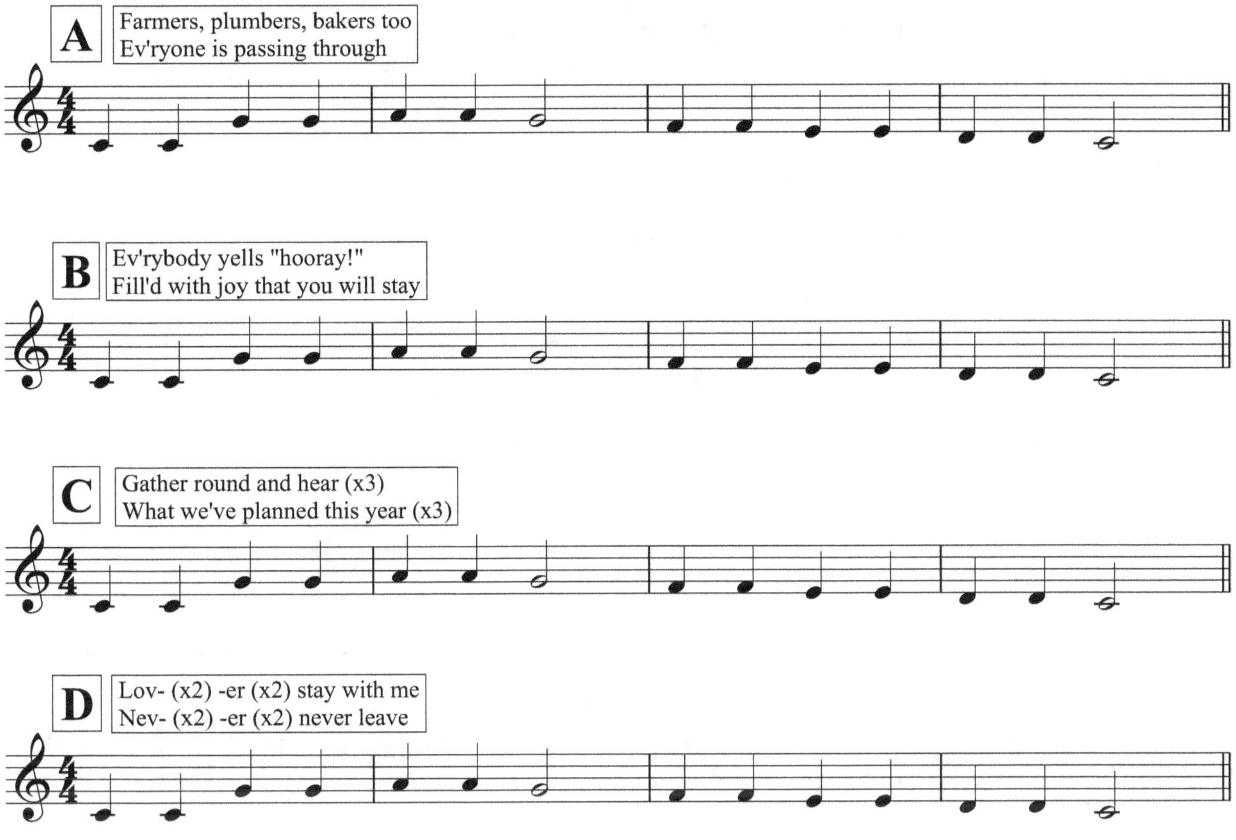

3. Write in the stressed (/) and unstressed (˘) syllables above these words/phrases and determine whether they are trochees, iambs, dactyls, or anapests. The first one is done for you.

A. announce   iamb

B. mystified   _____________

C. delicate   _____________

D. peanuts   _____________

E. nunnery   _____________

F. delay   _____________

G. disappear   _____________

H. at a glance   _____________

I. a ghost   _____________

J. get a car   _____________

K. laugh with me_____________

L. shoot me   _____________

M. of course   _____________

N. do it   _____________

O. look at him   _____________

P. stop him   _____________

4. Write a lyric about the arrival of winter that precisely matches each of the suggested meters:

   Example: / ˘ / ˘ / ˘ / ˘ / ˘

   5 Trochees: Falling branches scare me when I'm driving

   4 Anapests ______________________________

   6 Iambs ______________________________

   3 Dactyls ______________________________

   4 Trochees ______________________________

   3 Iambs + 3 Trochees ______________________________

   3 Anapests + 3 Dactyls ______________________________

5. Speak the lyrics of "Mary Had a Little Lamb" along with a metronome. Experiment with different rhythms, moving faster and slower, holding out some syllables, and changing pace for different lines.

6. Write three different lyrics to the melody of "Twinkle, Twinkle, Little Star" reflecting the musical emphasis of the original melody.

   Writing suggestion: A student explains to their teacher why they were late to class.

7. Analyze the accent pattern of the verse of "Lucy in the Sky with Diamonds" then write two different lyrics replicating the accent pattern. Replicating the accent pattern will create a new lyric that matches the original melody.

Writing suggestion: A therapy patient tries to avoid talking about her parents.

Picture yourself in a boat on a river

With tangerine trees and marmalade skies

Somebody calls you, you answer quite slowly

A girl with kaleidoscope eyes

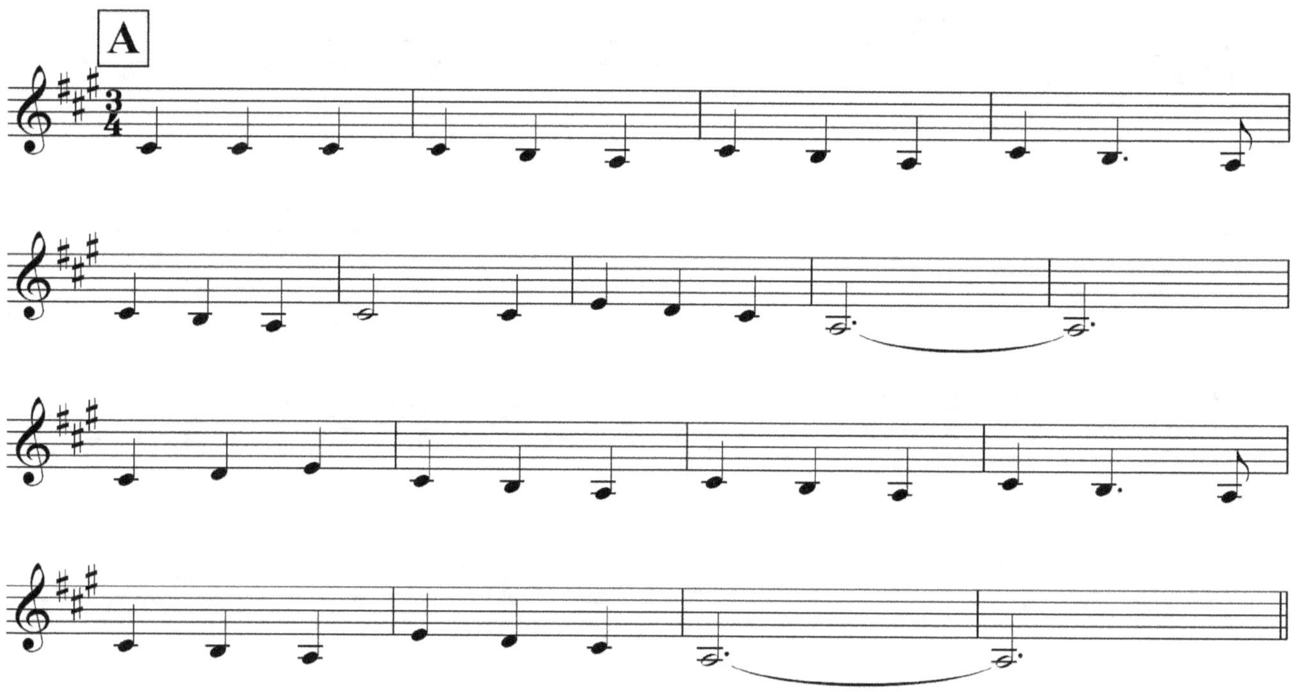

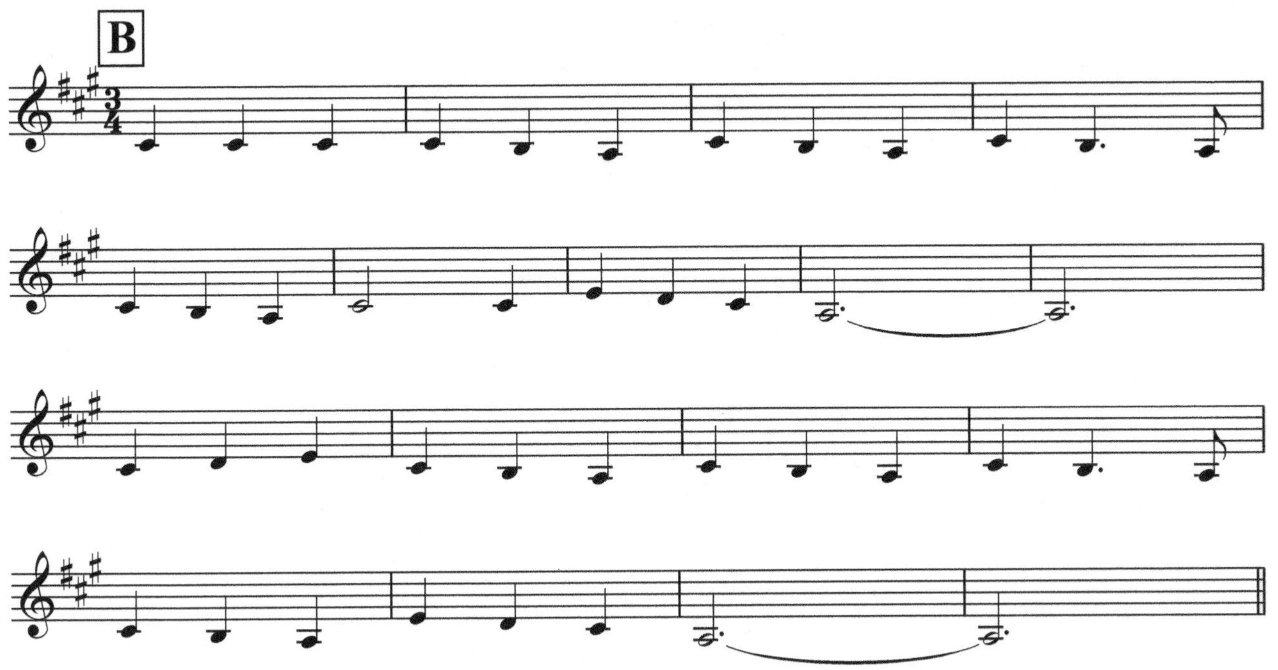

8. Analyze the stressed and unstressed syllables of the following lyric and then create three different melodies for the lyric, each one focusing on a different aspect of musical stress.

Will you carve me a cathedral

Out of clouds and wind and air?

Will you make me spires and archways

Everywhere, everywhere?

3. Rhyme

In a 2010 *60 Minutes* interview, journalist Anderson Cooper asks rapper Eminem if he constantly thinks about rhyming. "All day," Eminem replies. "I actually drive myself insane with it." He shows Cooper physical evidence of his obsession – boxes of wrinkled notebook paper and hotel notepads jam-packed with rhyme ideas.

In the same interview, he explains that it frustrates him that people say that nothing rhymes with *orange*. The trick to rhyming, he says, is in how you pronounce the word, divide the syllables, and enunciate it. To demonstrate his point, he performs a short rap, rhyming "orange" six times in a single sentence:

> *"I put my orange four-inch door hinge in storage and ate porridge with Ge-orge."*

The interview reveals two important aspects of rhyme: first, rhyming takes work and discipline. Great rhymers strive to expand their vocabularies, practice rhyming constantly, and persevere until they find the perfect word. Second, rhyming isn't straightforward. Words that seem unrhymable at first glance might accommodate thought-provoking, delightfully surprising rhymes if the songwriter approaches the task with imagination and ingenuity.

As an audience member, it's thrilling to watch Eminem rhyme with *orange*. There's something very human about appreciating a good rhyme. We pack children's books with rhymes, laugh at accidental rhymes in conversation, and remember aphorisms better when they rhyme (like "no pain, no gain" or "you snooze, you lose"). In songs, rhymes help listeners form expectations and give them a little burst of dopamine when that expectation is met or, better yet, cleverly subverted. Rhymes organize the listener's experience of the song and help them understand the lyric.

But make no mistake: rhymes are not just for the listeners. Structuring writing around rhymes helps songwriters brainstorm new ideas and pushes them into unexpected lyrical terrain. The pursuit of rhyme shapes a lyric's direction, guides word choice, and sparks surprising images and details.

The Spectrum of Rhyme

So, what is rhyme? **Rhyme** refers to pairing words that share similar sounds, especially at the ends of lines or phrases. Although you probably feel like you have an intuitive sense of which words rhyme and which words don't, the mechanics of rhyme are actually quite intricate and surprising. In fact, rhyme should be thought of as a spectrum of sound similarity rather than a yes-or-no binary.

Rhyme is determined by a word's final stressed syllable. Two words can be said to rhyme when their final stressed syllables share either a vowel sound, a final consonant sound, or both.

Pure rhyme is the strongest kind of rhyme. In a pure rhyme, both the vowel sound and final consonant sound are identical in the final stressed syllable. Note that rhyme is based on how a word sounds, not how it's spelled. For instance, "where" and "bear" have the same vowel sound even though the vowel is spelled differently.

The following chart shows a breakdown of pure rhymes, broken down by sound:

Words	Vowel Sound	Final Consonant Sound	Explanation
bar/car	"ah"	"r"	The final sounds of the words match exactly
womb/gloom	"oo"	"m"	Although these words are spelled quite differently, their sounds are identical
pain/entertain	"ay"	"n"	Because "tain" is the final stressed syllable of "entertain," it's the syllable that needs to rhyme
spree/we	"ee"	Ø	Both words have no final consonant sound

Pure rhyme is especially important in musical theater and children's songs because these genres prioritize making the lyric both easily understood and irrepressibly catchy. Pure rhymes are also found commonly in hip hop and rap because the rhyme is often the focus of the lyric.

Assonant rhyme is the next most common kind of rhyme. To achieve assonant rhyme, match the vowel sounds of two words' final stressed syllables but do not match the final consonant sounds.

The next chart shows examples of assonant rhyme:

Words	Vowel Sound	Final Consonant Sound	Explanation
ban/cat	"a"	"n"/"t"	The vowel sounds match exactly even though the final consonant sounds do not
mutt/rough	"uh"	"t"/"ff"	Although the vowels are spelled differently, their sounds are identical
entail/lame	"ay"	"l"/"m"	Because "tail" is the final stressed syllable of "entail," it is the syllable that needs to rhyme
tree/steam	"ee"	Ø/"m"	"Tree" has no final consonant sound, whereas "steam" does have a final consonant sound

Assonant rhymes are common in pop and singer-songwriter genres because they establish pleasant sonic relationships between words without sounding as clear and precise as pure rhymes.

Consonant rhyme is subtler than pure or assonant rhyme. Listeners may or may not process consonant rhymes as obviously "rhyming." To achieve consonant rhyme, match the final consonant sounds of two words' final stressed syllables but do not match the vowel sounds. While consonant rhyme is the least common type of rhyme, it can be found in the singer-songwriter, rap, and pop genres, which value self-expression more than immediate clarity.

The next chart breaks down the mechanics of consonant rhyme:

Words	Vowel Sound	Final Consonant Sound	Explanation
man/done	"a"/"uh"	"n"	
graph/tiff	"a"/"i"	"f"	Although the final consonant sound is spelled differently, the sound still matches
abstain/boon	"ay"/"oo"	"n"	Because "stain" is the final stressed syllable of "abstain," it is the syllable that needs to rhyme
foe/bee	"oh"/"ee"	Ø	Neither word has a final consonant sound

Bob Dylan Demonstrates Three Types of Rhyme

Bob Dylan's masterful lyrics utilize all three types of rhymes – pure, assonant, and consonant – to shape some of his most famous songs. Observe the different kinds of rhymes in the following examples:

Pure Rhyme (from "Simple Twist of Fate")

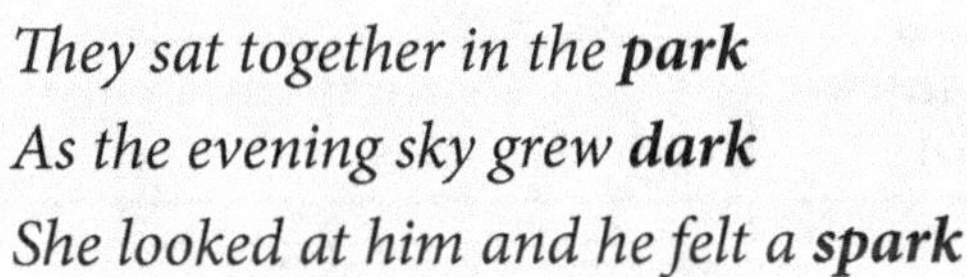

> *They sat together in the **park***
> *As the evening sky grew **dark***
> *She looked at him and he felt a **spark***
>
> *And wished that he'd gone **straight***
> *And watched out for a simple twist of **fate***

Words	Vowel Sound	Final Consonant Sound	Explanation
park/dark/spark	"ah"	"rk"	
straight/fate	"ay"	"t"	Even though the vowels are spelled differently, their sound is the same

Assonant Rhyme (from "Blowin' in the Wind")

> *How many roads must a man walk down*
> *Before you call him a **man**?*
> *How many seas must a white dove sail*
> *Before she sleeps in the **sand**?*
>
> *And how many ears must one man have*
> *Before he can hear people **cry**?*
> *Yes, and how many deaths will it take 'til he knows*
> *That too many people have **died**?*

Words	Vowel Sound	Final Consonant Sound	Explanation
man/sand	"a"	"n"/"nd"	Although the final consonant sounds are quite similar, they are not exactly the same
cry/died	"i"	Ø/"d"	"Cry" has no final consonant sound; the two vowels are spelled differently, but sound the same

Consonant Rhyme (from "Simple Twist of Fate" and "Blowin' in the Wind")

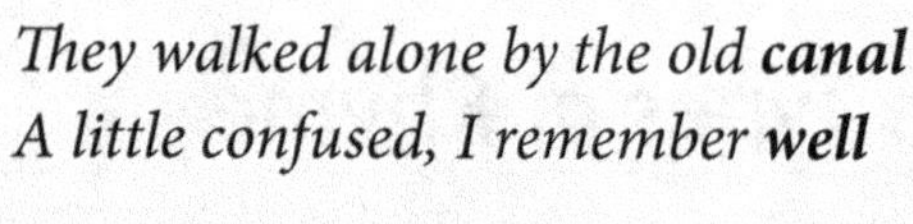

> *They walked alone by the old **canal***
> *A little confused, I remember **well***
>
> *The answer my **friend***
> *Is blowin' in the **wind***

Words	Vowel Sound	Final Consonant Sound	Explanation
canal/well	"a"/"eh"	"l"	"nal" is the final stressed syllable of "canal"
friend/wind	"eh"/"i"	"nd"	Although these vowel sounds are similar, they are not identical. The words might be considered an "off rhyme" or a "near rhyme"

Even within each category (pure, assonant, consonant), some rhymes are more obvious or more subtle than others because some sounds are more closely related. Notice that "friend" and "wind," from the previous example, almost rhyme because "eh" and "i" are similar vowel sounds, whereas "friend" and "hound" sound further apart.

Consonants can sound closer or further than others, often reflecting how our mouth shapes the sound. For instance, words ending with "m" and "n" or "s" and "z" might sound almost indistinguishable whereas words ending "l" and "k," for instance, might sound unrelated. Combinations of two consonants ("st," for example) often sound close to words that use just one of those consonants ("s" or "t"). "Last" and "lass" sound almost identical. The two words are separated only by a small motion of the tongue against the teeth at the end of the word.

Although your ear will likely tell you which consonants are close, you can also reference the following list of similar consonant and vowel sounds:

- "m" and "n"
- "s" and "z"
- "f" and "v"
- "p" and "b"
- "r" and "l"

- "ee" and "ay" (like "beet" and "bait")
- "ay" and "eh" (like "bait" and "bet")
- "eh" and "i" (like "friend" and "wind")
- "ah" and "uh" (like "bot" and "butt")

Off rhyme and **near rhyme**, terms often used interchangeably, describe two words that almost rhyme but fall short due to slight mismatches. Although these terms could refer to any assonant or consonant rhyme, they are especially relevant when words have similar sounds but *just* miss being a pure rhyme due to slight sonic differences. Consider pairs like breeze/peace, mate/fret, and wrong/frond.

Masculine and Feminine Rhyme

Recall that rhyming words must match the *final stressed* syllable. In all of the earlier examples, the final stressed syllable of each multisyllable word is the final syllable. When rhyming words are monosyllabic or have the stress on their final syllable, they create a **masculine rhyme**.

Words in which the final syllable is unstressed produce **feminine rhyme**, which requires rhyming the final stressed syllable plus all subsequent syllables. Usually, the unstressed syllables following the stress match exactly between the two rhyming words, putting the focus squarely on the stressed syllable. Because feminine rhymes rhyme two or more syllables, they are inherently **multisyllabic rhymes**.

Let's examine how to create feminine rhymes:

Word: laughter

Stress Analysis: stress + unstressed ["laugh" (stressed) + "ter" (unstressed)]
How to Rhyme: rhyme with "laugh," rhyme or repeat "ter"
Possible Rhymes: after, rafter, draft her

Word: honey

Stress Analysis: stress + unstressed ["hon" (stressed) + "ey" (unstressed)]
How to Rhyme: rhyme with "hon," rhyme or repeat "ey"
Possible Rhymes: money, bunny, sunny, funny, sun me

Word: pottery

Stress Analysis: stress + unstressed + unstressed ["pot" (stressed) + "er" (unstressed) + "y" (unstressed)]
How to Rhyme: rhyme with "pot," rhyme or repeat "tery"
Possible Rhymes: lottery, watery, not hurry

Syllables preceding the final stressed syllable have no bearing on the rhyme. For instance, "steering" rhymes with "commandeering" even though "commandeering" has more syllables before its final stressed syllable. Only the final stressed syllable and the subsequent syllables are involved in the rhyme.

Feminine Rhymes and Off Rhyme

Because of the inherent complexity of rhyming multiple syllables, many feminine rhymes are pure rhymes, including all of the rhymes presented in the previous section. However, feminine rhymes can be assonant or consonant rhymes if the final stressed syllable of both words share either their vowel or final consonant sounds. For example:

Words: honey/yummy
Rhyme Type: assonant rhyme (feminine)
Explanation: the final stressed syllables ("hon"/"yum") have identical vowel sounds; the final syllables ("y") sound identical

Words: honey/phony
Rhyme Type: consonant rhyme (feminine)
Explanation: the final stressed syllables ("hon"/"phon") have identical final consonant sounds but different vowel sounds; the final syllables ("y") sound identical

Words: pottery/mockery
Rhyme Type: assonant rhyme (feminine)
Explanation: the final stressed syllables ("pot"/"mock") have identical vowel sounds but different final consonant sounds; the final syllables ("ery") sound identical

Words: pottery/buttery
Rhyme Type: consonant rhyme (feminine)
Explanation: the final stressed syllables ("pot"/"butt") have identical final consonant sounds but different vowel sounds; the final syllables ("ery") sound identical

These examples illustrate how songwriters can think expansively about rhyme and uncover unexpected rhyming opportunities even within multisyllabic words.

Feminine Rhyme Examples

The next examples show examples of feminine rhymes from songs drawn from the Great American Songbook, the singer-songwriter tradition, and pop music.

Feminine Rhymes: Pure Rhymes

> How glad the many **millions** of Annabels
> and **Lillians** would be to capture me.
>
> —"I've Got a Crush on You,"
> George Gershwin/Ira Gershwin

> Your looks are **laughable,**
> **unphotographable**
>
> — "My Funny Valentine,"
> Richard Rodgers/Lorenz Hart

> Your faith was strong but you needed proof
> You saw her bathing on the roof
> Her beauty in the moonlight **overthrew ya**
> She tied you to the kitchen chair
> She broke your throne and she cut your hair
> And from your lips she drew the **Hallelujah**
>
> — "Hallelujah," Leonard Cohen

Feminine Rhymes: Off Rhymes

> 'Cause honey your soul could never grow old, it's **evergreen**
> And baby, your smile's forever in my mind and **memory**
>
> — "Thinking Out Loud," Ed Sheeran

> You didn't see my **valentine?**
> I sent it via **pantomime**
>
> — "Valentine," Fiona Apple

> You got exactly what you **asked for**
> Running out of pages in your **passport**
>
> — "Hotline Bling," Drake

> There's something so **wretched** about this
> Something so **precious** about this
> Honey, I'm so **broken** about this
> I might be **hoping** about this.
>
> — "From Eden," Hozier

Internal Rhyme

Where a rhyme appears in a phrase determines whether and how listeners will perceive it. Rhymes usually occur on the final stressed syllable before a musical pause or hold, often indicated by the end of a lyrical line. However, songwriters sometimes include **internal rhymes**, rhymes placed within a line or between two lines and are not followed by a musical pause. There are three main types of internal rhymes:

1. Intra-Line Rhyme

These rhymes place two rhyming words in the same poetic line or musical phrase. Because of their proximity, they create a sense of rhythmic propulsion.

> *Where one **relaxes** on the **axis***
> *of the wheel of life*
>
> *That used to **be there** you could **see***
> *where they'd been washed away*
>
> — both from "Lush Life,"
> Billy Strayhorn

> *Oh you know, you know, you know*
> *I'd never ask you to change*
> *If **perfect's** what you're **searching** for*
> *Then just stay the same*
>
> — "Just the Way You Are,"
> Bruno Mars

> *You said fusion was the broken heart that's **lonely's only** thought*
>
> — "The Temptation of Adam," Josh Ritter

2. Inter-line Rhyme

These rhymes include two rhyming words in the middle of two different lines or musical phrases. Inter-line rhyme creates a recognition of lyrical intentionality and the pleasure of sound repetition.

> *Life is **lonely** again*
> *And **only** last year everything seemed so sure*
>
> *Now life is **awful** again*
> *A **troughful** of hearts could only be a bore*
>
> — both from "Lush Life," Billy Strayhorn

> *Under miles of **stone**, the dried fig of his heart*
> *Under scarab and **bone** starts back to its beating*
>
> — "The Curse," Josh Ritter

> *Now I'm **falling** asleep*
> *And she's **calling** a cab*
>
> — "Mr. Brightside,"
> The Killers

> *It used to be so **easy** living here with you*
> *You were light and **breezy** and I knew just what to do*
>
> — "It's Too Late," Carole King

3. Mixed Placement Rhyme

The third type of internal rhyme combines an internal rhyming word with a word at the end of a line. It is the hardest type to perceive, yet gives the listener a sense of satisfaction at the end of the line

> *Romance is **mush***
> ***Stif**ling those who **strive***
> *I'll live a **lush life***
> *In some small **dive***
> — "Lush Life,"
> Billy Strayhorn

> *Although he may not be*
> *The **man some** girls think of as **handsome***
> *To my heart, he carries the key*
> — "Someone to Watch Over Me,"
> George Gershwin/Ira Gershwin

Internal rhyme is especially prevalent in musical theater, children's music, and hip hop because it makes a song sound clever, well-crafted, and rhythmic. A high density of internal rhyme gives the sense of a virtuosic lyricist at the top of their craft. When used unexpectedly, it generates rhythmic propulsion and inspires delight in the listener.

Rhyme Scheme

Songwriters get to decide when and how often their lyrics rhyme. The pattern of when lyrics rhyme is called a **rhyme scheme**. Traditionally, repeated musical phrases follow the same rhyme schemes, so once a rhyme scheme is established, it is replicated for equivalent musical sections. Repeating a rhyme scheme forms expectations in the listener's mind, which the songwriter can meet or subvert to satisfy and delight them.

Rhyme schemes are analyzed using letters. Each new rhyme is labeled with a new letter, proceeding from A to Z. Once a rhyme is established, its designated letter continues to identify that rhyme. The letters track only the rhymes at the ends of lyrical lines, not internal rhymes.

For example, "Blowin' in the Wind," follows a rhyme scheme of ABCBDB. The first, third, and fifth lines are each given new letters because they don't rhyme with any other words. The second, fourth, and sixth lines all use the letter "B" to show that "man," "sand," and "banned" are rhymes.

*How many roads must a man walk **down***	A
*Before you call him a **man?***	B
*How many seas must a white dove **sail***	C
*Before she sleeps in the **sand?***	B
*Yes, and how many times must the cannonballs **fly***	D
*Before they're forever **banned?***	B

We then expect each equivalent musical stanza to have the same rhyme scheme. That's not to say that the words in the second stanza should rhyme with the final words in the first stanza, but internally the ABCBDB pattern should remain the same. Does the last stanza of "Blowin' in the Wind" have the same rhyme scheme as the first stanza?

*Yes, and how many times must a man look **up***

*Before he can see the **sky**?*

*And how many ears must one man **have***

*Before he can hear people **cry**?*

*Yes, and how many deaths will it take 'til he **knows***

*That too many people have **died**?*

Yes! Even though "died" is an assonant rhyme with "sky" and "cry" instead of a pure rhyme, the rhyme scheme is still ABCBDB.

There are no "correct" or "incorrect" rhyme schemes, but rhyme relates to style. Songs that are too rhyme-y can sound childish, like nursery rhymes, whereas songs that have few rhymes or long spaces between rhymes can sound very "art-y" and less accessible. Many young songwriters rhyme too quickly and too often for the styles in which they are writing. In reality, many lines can pass without rhyming and not every line needs to end with a rhyme.

The next few pages contain a list of short four- or five-line stanzas that demonstrate different rhyme schemes. Notice the immense variety of possible rhymes, even in short stanzas.

AAAA

Yesterday	A
All my troubles seemed so far away	A
Now it looks as though they're here to stay	A
Oh, I believe in yesterday	A

    — "Yesterday," The Beatles

AABB

But people are strangers, they change with the curve	A
From time zone to time zone as we can observe	A
They shut down their borders and think they're immune	B
They stand on their differences and shoot at the moon	B

    — "Cars are Cars," Paul Simon

ABAB

Then one night you found me in my army issue cot	A
And you told me of your flash of inspiration	B
You said fusion was the broken heart that's lonely's only thought	A
And all night long you drove me wild with your equations	B

> — "The Temptation of Adam," Josh Ritter

ABCB

Which will you go for?	A
Which will you love?	B
Which will you choose from?	C
From the stars above?	B

> — "Which Will," Nick Drake

AAABB

Stones taught me to fly	A
Love – it taught me to lie	A
Life – it taught me to die	A
So it's not hard to fall	B
When you float like a cannonball	B

> — "Cannonball," Damien Rice

AABBA (aka limerick form)

They tried to make me go to rehab but I said, 'No, no, no.'	A
Yes, I've been black but when I come back you'll know, know, know	A
I ain't got the time	B
And if my daddy thinks I'm fine	B
He's tried to make me go to rehab but I won't go, go, go	A

> — "Rehab," Amy Winehouse

AABBC

Once I thought my innocence was gone	A
Now I know that happiness goes on	A
That's where you found me,	B
When you put your arms around me	B
I haven't been there for the longest time	C

> — "The Longest Time," Billy Joel

AABBAA

She's out of my life	A
She's out of my life	A
And I don't know whether to laugh or cry	B
I don't know whether to live or die	B
And it cuts like a knife	A
She's out of my life	A

— "She's Out of My Life," Michael Jackson

AAAB / CCCB (Cross-Stanza Rhyme)

Going to see the river man	A
Going to tell him all I can	A
About the ban	A
On feeling free.	B

If he tells me all he knows	C
About the way his river flows	C
I don't suppose	C
It's meant for me	B

— "River Man," Nick Drake

Other Types of Rhyme

Pararhyme occurs when two rhyming words share *all* of their consonant sounds but have different vowels. While pararhyme does not necessarily obviously create a rhyming effect, it creates a poetic texture through repeated consonant sounds.

Examples of pararhyme include:

- *Monosyllabic:* dead/dad, dawn/down, park/pork, dumb/dam, killed/cold
- *Polysyllabic:* linger/longer, waiter/water, dapper/dipper

*There's a **jouster** and a **jester**
And a man who owns a store
There's a **drummer** and a **dreamer**
And you know there may be more*

— "Cactus Tree," Joni Mitchell

*I'm **depraved** on account
of I'm **deprived***

— "Gee, Officer Krupke,"
Leonard Bernstein/
Stephen Sondheim

Repetitive rhyme refers to creating the effect of a rhyme by using the same word twice. It can be used to add humor, shape a character, or provide a beating club rhythm.

> *It had to be **you***
> *Wonderful **you***
> *It had to be **you***
>
> — "It Had to Be You,"
> Isham Jones/Gus Kahn

> *I have my **faults***
> *She likes my **faults***
> *I'm not very **bright***
> *She's not very **bright***
>
> — "Nobody Else but Me,"
> Jerome Kern/
> Oscar Hammerstein II

> *Don't you dare look **back***
> *Just keep your eyes on **me***
> *She said, 'You're holding **back'***
> *She said, 'Shut up and dance with **me'***
>
> — "Shut Up and Dance,"
> Walk the Moon

Takeaways

1. Rhyme is a spectrum, not a yes/no binary. Songwriters should not feel limited to using pure rhymes and can expand their rhyming palette through assonant and consonant rhymes.

2. Rhymes match the sounds of the final stressed syllable and all subsequent syllables. Feminine rhymes require two or more syllables to rhyme because their final stressed syllable is followed by additional unstressed syllables that must also rhyme.

3. The amount and placement of rhyme is related to style. Experiment with rhyme schemes and remember that there's no need to rhyme the end of every line.

4. Once a rhyme scheme for a musical section is established, strive to maintain it in similar musical sections. Maintaining the same rhyme scheme helps listeners form expectations that keep them engaged and interested.

Practice

1. For each of the following words, identify 5 words that are pure, assonant, and consonant rhymes. The first chart is completed for you.

Fun

Vowel sound : "<u>uh</u>"

Final consonant sound: "<u>n</u>"

Pure	Assonant	Consonant
done	dug	dine
sun	pus	fine
gun	mutt	thine
none	love	thin
won	stuff	tune

Fire

Vowel sound: _____

Final consonant sound: ______

Pure	Assonant	Consonant

Know

Vowel sound: _____

Final consonant sound: ______

Pure	Assonant	Consonant

Hot

Vowel sound: _____
Final consonant sound: ______

Pure	Assonant	Consonant

Underneath

Vowel sound: _____
Final consonant sound: ______

Pure	Assonant	Consonant

About

Vowel sound: _____
Final consonant sound: ______

Pure	Assonant	Consonant

Kangaroo

Vowel sound: _____
Final consonant sound: ______

Pure	Assonant	Consonant

2. Identify whether the following words require masculine or feminine rhyme. Then invent 5 rhymes for each.

Example:

Alive   M/F: Masculine (accent is on live)

Rhymes: Thrive, five, dive, strive, hive

Sitting   M/F:

Rhymes:

Dully   M/F:

Rhymes:

Arrest   M/F:

Rhymes:

Understanding   M/F:

Rhymes:

Interfere   M/F:

Rhymes:

Trolley   M/F:

Rhymes:

Amount   M/F:

Rhymes:

3. Analyze the rhyme schemes of the following stanzas. (all stanzas taken from Sufjan Stevens'
    2005 album, *Illinoise*.

Thinking outrageously, I write in cursive
I hide in my bed with the lights on the floor
Wearing three layers of coats and leg warmers
I see my own breath on the face of the door

> — "The Predatory Wasp of the
>   Palisades is Out to Get Us!"
>   Sufjan Stevens

I drove to New York
In a van with my friend
We slept in parking lots
I don't mind, I don't mind

> — "Chicago,"
>   Sufjan Stevens

I'm not afraid of the black man running
He's got it right, he's got a better life coming
And I don't care what the captain said
I fold it right at the top of my head
I lost my sight and the state packs in
I follow my heart and it leads me right to Jackson

> — "Jacksonville," Sufjan Stevens

Cannot conversations
cull united nations?
If you got the patience
celebrate the ancients
Cannot all creation
call it celebration?
Or united nation
put it to your head

> — "Come On!
>   Feel the Illinoise,"
>   Sufjan Stevens

Our stepmom, we did everything to hate her
She took us down to the edge of Decatur
We saw the lion and the kangaroo take her
Down to the river where they caught a wild alligator

> — "Decatur," Sufjan Stevens

In the morning, through the window shade
When the light pressed up against your shoulder blade
I could see what you were reading
All the glory that the Lord has made
And the complications you could do without
When I kissed you on the mouth

> — "Casimir Pulaski Day," Sufjan Stevens

4. Write a stanza each about love at first sight at a dog park using the following rhyme schemes. For example, for an ABAB rhyme scheme:

She gasped when she saw his golden **retriever**	A
Prancing across the green **lawn**	B
And immediately felt like a new **true believer**	A
Like a switch inside of her turned **on**	B

____	A
____	A
____	A
____	A

____	A
____	A
____	B
____	B

____	A
____	B
____	A
____	B

____	A
____	B
____	C
____	B

_______________________________________ A

_______________________________________ B

_______________________________________ A

_______________________________________ C

_______________________________________ A

_______________________________________ A

_______________________________________ B   (short)

_______________________________________ B   (short)

_______________________________________ A

5. Write down the lyrics to a favorite song and determine the rhyme scheme. Does the songwriter use the same rhyme scheme each time the musical section returns?

____

____

____

____

____

4. Show, Don't Tell

Scan Here for
Chapter 4 Page

Although "I love you" is one of the most common sentiments expressed in songs, you'd probably be hard-pressed to name more than a couple of songs whose lyrics plainly say, "I love you." In fact, when Cole Porter released a song called "I Love You" in 1944, the *New York Times* reviewed it as having "a title almost startling in its forthrightness."

The directness of the title wasn't entirely Porter's idea; it was his effort to win a friendly bet. Porter's friend, actor Monty Woolley, believed that Porter was such a master of language that he could never write a song with plain or clichéd lyrics. He challenged Porter to include a song bearing the blunt title "I Love You" in a Broadway musical.

Porter met the challenge through a clever workaround. For his musical, *Mexican Hayride*, he invented a character named David Winthrop, who claims to be the amateur composer of "I Love You," his first attempt at a love song. In the verse that precedes the main melody of the song, Winthrop bemoans his song's lack of subtlety:

> *If a love song I could only write*
> *A song with words and music divine*
> *I would serenade you every night*
> *You would relent and consent to be mine*
>
> *But, alas, just an amateur am I*
> *So do not be surprised, my dear*
> *If you smile and politely pass it by*
> *When this, my first love song, you hear*

Musically, Porter mocks this character's amateurism by assigning the most romantic, heart-felt words, "I love you" to a major seventh leap in the melody. The major seventh interval is a notoriously awkward one to sing as it is one half step less than an octave, creating a rub against the more consonant octave interval. By pairing an overly direct lyric with a purposefully awkward melody, Winthrop's song acts as a meta-commentary on songwriting, with Porter virtuosically demonstrating what *not* to do when writing a song.

The episode with Porter reveals his distaste for obvious and direct language in favor of nuance, imagery, and detail. The contrast between an amateur like Winthrop and a master songwriter like Porter illustrates the importance of "show, don't tell."

A Golden Rule

"Show, don't tell" is a rule of writing that directs a writer to use scenes, details, and examples to bring emotions to life rather than simply stating a feeling or introducing a situation. Although "show, don't tell" is universally applicable, it is particularly relevant for songs that have characters and tell a story. A deep understanding of this rule will not only improve the quality and vividness of your lyric but also help you generate more material by moving from general statements to specific storytelling.

What is the difference between showing and telling? The chart below compares basic emotional statements to observable actions that bring the statements to life.

Telling	Showing
she is sad	<ul><li>her eyes start to water</li><li>she spends all day in bed</li><li>she can't bring herself to smile</li><li>her head hangs low</li></ul>
John is in love with Leah	<ul><li>John keeps peeking across the table at Leah</li><li>John secretly writes Leah's name in his journal over and over again</li><li>John feels butterflies in his stomach every time Leah talks to him</li><li>John thinks about Leah before going to sleep each night</li></ul>
Darlene is lonely	<ul><li>Darlene cooks a frozen dinner for one</li><li>Darlene sits quietly watching the snow fall</li><li>Darlene arrives at a dive bar and sits by herself</li><li>Darlene picks up the phone to call a friend, but then puts it back down without dialing</li></ul>

The "showing" phrases are not only more nuanced and interesting than the "telling" phrases, but they're also more dynamic. Whereas the "telling" phrases all use a form of the verb "to be" ("she is sad," "Darlene *is* lonely"), the "showing" phrases create a sense of motion by using action verbs: Darlene *cooks*, *sits*, *arrives*, *picks up* the phone, and *puts it* back down. The emotional meaning is not lost by omitting words like "sad" and "lonely." Listeners easily infer the emotions stated in the "telling" phrase from the "showing" examples while getting the satisfaction of forming their own connections and conclusions. Songs that focus on "showing" engage the listener by inviting them to see and feel the emotional world of the lyric.

Great writers know the power of a well-placed, "showing" detail to tell a larger story. In Joni Mitchell's song, "The Last Time I Saw Richard," the singer is debating with her ex, Richard, about whether a person can remain a Romantic into middle age. She gives these details about her ex:

> *Richard got married to a figure skater*
> *And he bought her a dishwasher and a coffee percolator*

The dishwasher and the coffee percolator evoke a domestic, routine-oriented life. They telegraph to the audience that Richard has "settled down" and that he's through with his life as a traveler and dreamer. The implication is that he's "conformed," that – to the singer's dismay – he wants to fit in rather than pursue higher causes like art, love, and adventure. The dishwasher and coffee percolator speak volumes!

Similarly, in her song, "All too Well," Taylor Swift presents a surprising scene and lets listeners infer the emotions:

> 'Cause there we are again in the middle of the night
> We're dancing 'round the kitchen in the refrigerator light

The kitchen setting and middle-of-the-night timing give this scene a sense of joyful abandon while the image of "refrigerator light" cues the listener's imagination to picture a specific place. Because the kitchen is not the usual place for a dance party, listeners infer that the protagonists are in a state of carefree celebration of youth, love, and endless possibility.

These master songwriters use "show, don't tell" to tell the listener volumes using only a few words. The next sections describe insights, strategies, and activities to help you express yourself through showing rather than telling:

Crafting Characters

People are at the center of most songs. Painting a detailed portrait of a character activates an audience's imagination and nudges them towards feeling a strong connection (or aversion) to the personalities populating a song. There are five important ways in which audiences become acquainted with a song's characters, each presented with an example from Dolly Parton's classic song, "Jolene":

Method 1: How They Are Described

Songwriters can directly describe characters. How a character is described discloses something about the character while simultaneously revealing the way that the narrator views the character.

Because physical descriptions are so revealing, songwriters should think expansively about the many facets of a person they can include. Beyond describing their outward appearance, a description might include how they stand, walk, and move. It might include choices they make like which outfit they've chosen, whether they wear jewelry and hats, and if they carry a purse or bag. Other sensory experiences like the sound of a character's voice, the strength of their handshake, and the smell of their perfume could spark the listener's imagination.

Example from Jolene:

> Your beauty is beyond compare
> With flaming locks of auburn hair
> With ivory skin and eyes of emerald green
> Your smile is like a breath of spring
> Your skin is soft like summer rain
> And I cannot compete with you, Jolene

The point of this section is clear: Jolene is incredibly beautiful, or at least the singer thinks that she is. Words like "compare" and "compete" underscore the singer's focus on her feelings of inferiority and the multiple mentions of spring and summer ("emerald green"/"breath of spring"/ "summer rain") imply that Jolene is perhaps younger as well.

Method 2: What They Do

Characters' actions are important because they reveal their mental and emotional state. If John is peeking at Leah, the audience can take educated guesses as to why.

Although a character's actions might seem more objective than descriptions, bear in mind that every writer makes choices regarding which of their characters' actions to include or exclude in order to shape their audiences' perception. For instance, if a songwriter just mentions that a character is singing in the shower, they are revealing the character's optimism or carefree state of mind. We might assume that they are newly in love or expecting a big promotion at the office. However, our feelings about the character would change radically if it was disclosed that they were showering to wash away the evidence of a violent crime.

Example from Jolene:

> *He talks about you in his sleep*

The fact that the singer's "man" talks about Jolene in his sleep reveals that she's constantly on his mind. The detail is particularly effective because the moment of dreaming is a moment of emotional honesty, whereas during the day, he can consciously hide his interest from his partner.

Method 3: What They Say

Characters can talk, even in songs. Many songs include **dialogue**, sections in which one character speaks or multiple characters banter back and forth. Screenwriter Aaron Sorkin observed, "What your character does reveals who they are. What they say reveals who they see themselves as." This reminds writers to note who a character is talking to and how they want to appear to their interlocutor.

Example from Jolene:

> *Jolene, Jolene, Jolene, Jolene*
> *Oh, I'm begging of you please don't take my man*
> *Jolene, Jolene, Jolene, Jolene*
> *Please don't take him even though you can*

Because the song is filled with personal details in line with an internal monologue, the listener assumes that the singer is talking to a "hypothetical" Jolene, not talking directly to her actual rival. Still, what she's saying and how she's saying it reveals something about her. The imploring nature of the words "begging" and "please" suggest that the singer is desperate and in a highly emotional state. One wonders if this is exactly what the singer says to a real Jolene or if she would modify and soften her phrasing if Jolene were in front of her.

Method 4: What They Think

Writers have the option to give audiences direct access into a character's brain. In prose, a perspective that encompasses a character's inner monologue is described as **third person omniscient** but because songs are frequently sung in the first person, narrators' thoughts are often simply laid bare as part of the song's lyric.

Example from Jolene:

> *My happiness depends on you*
> *And whatever you decide to do, Jolene*

Although in many ways, the entire song details the thoughts of the singer, this moment feels especially revealing. It shows the depth of the singer's desperation and the degree to which they've become obsessed about the future of their relationship.

Method 5: What Others Say About Them

A final way to learn about characters is to hear about them through other sources, like other characters introduced in the song. Any time that more than one character is involved, the way one character talks about another reveals something about both of them, the person doing the talking and the one being talked about.

Example from Jolene:

> *Your beauty is beyond compare*

This line also appears in the "how they are described" section. In this case, because the singer is both the narrator and a character in the love-triangle drama, a line like this falls under both categories. This particular line is especially relevant because the singer is clearly giving her *opinion* about Jolene's beauty.

Examining these five elements, the most revealing ways in which we learn about characters are often the least direct. Characters often show their true selves when they say something different than they think, choose descriptions that seem to exaggerate reality, or act differently in private than in public. Skilled writers craft complex characters by revealing the cracks between characters' self-perception and reality.

The following exercises can help a songwriter invent meaningful details to include in their songs:

Investigating the Setting

The setting is an incredibly relevant detail because it acts as a metaphor reflecting how characters are feeling or presaging what's in store for them. A sunny day usually bodes well for a character, whereas a rainy day usually signals heartbreak. Providing carefully chosen details about the time and place prepares a listener for the emotional journey of the song.

Because Taylor Swift's dance party in "All Too Well" takes place in a kitchen, the audience understands the characters' carefree youth. Joni Mitchell molds the mood of "The Last Time I Saw Richard" by including both universal and specific details on the setting. She provides context by marking the exact time and place in the song's first line, "The last time I saw Richard was Detroit in '68." The specificity of the year situates the song in the distant past and mentioning the city seems to indicate that the singer was away from home, on the road. As the song continues, Mitchell shares that her conversation is taking place around closing time in a bar where the waitress wears "fishnet stockings and a bowtie." These details give us the feeling of something faded, past its prime, and about to come to an end.

The following questions are intended to help you get specific and imaginative about the setting of your song:

A. When?

1. What time of day? What day of the week and month?

It's getting late have you seen my mates
Ma tell me when the boys get here
It's seven o'clock and I want to rock
Want to get a belly full of beer

> — "Saturday Night's Alright for Fighting,"
> Elton John

It's quarter to three
There's no one in this place 'cept
You and me

> — "One for My Baby (And One More
> for the Road)," Frank Sinatra

2. What season? What weather?

All the leaves are brown
And the sky is gray
I've been for a walk
On a winter's day
I'd be safe and warm
If I was in LA

> — "California Dreamin', "
> The Mamas and
> The Papas

Summertime and the livin' is easy
Fish are jumpin' and the cotton is high
Oh, your daddy's rich and your ma is good lookin'
So hush, little baby, don't you cry

> — "Summertime,"
> George Gershwin/DuBose Heyward

3.   **What year or historical moment?**

B. Where?

1.   **What city/country/continent?**

2.   **Outside or inside? What kind of building or space?**

I am sitting in the morning
At the diner on the corner
I am waiting at the counter
For the man to pour the coffee
And he fills it only halfway
And before I even argue
He is looking out the window
At somebody coming in

   — "Tom's Diner," Suzanne Vega

I took my love, I took it down
Climbed a mountain and I turned around
And I saw my reflection in the snow covered hills
'Til the landslide brought me down

   — "Landslide," Fleetwood Mac

3.   **What else is around? Objects? People?**

Dirty old river, must you keep rolling
Flowing into the night?
People so busy, make me feel dizzy
Taxi light shines so bright
But I don't need no friends
As long as I gaze on
Waterloo sunset
I am in Paradise

   — "Waterloo Sunset," The Kinks

And the piano, it sounds like a carnival
And the microphone smells like a beer
And they sit at the bar and put bread in my jar
And say, "Man, what are you doin' here?"

   — "Piano Man," Billy Joel

Of course, not every song answers all of these questions or provides a firm setting. But answering these questions helps hone your imagination to create unique and memorable images.

Lights, Camera, Action

Another way to get into a "showing" mindset is to imagine your song as a movie that dramatizes the emotion on screen, picturing how the world of your song would look and sound on a moment-to-moment basis. While picturing the movie, scan the scenery for revealing objects in the setting, watch the gestures and mannerisms of the actors, and notice the angles, zoom, and positioning of the camera.

Picturing an important moment from your song, try the following:

Pan the Camera

Move the camera to different parts of the scene to discover new visuals you have not considered.

For instance: imagine a depressed girl splayed out on a couch. First, start with the girl herself. Scan her body for detail from head to toe: How does her hair look? Is her forehead wrinkled? What color are her eyes? Are her cheeks red? Is she wearing makeup and has it streaked? Are her nails painted? Is she wearing rings or bracelets? Do her legs have goosebumps? Are her feet tucked into the blanket or wearing fuzzy socks?

Then, scan above her, below her, and to her left and right. For instance:

Above: a ceiling fan lazily whirs on its slowest setting

Below: decorative pillows have been tossed from the couch onto the carpeted floor

To the left: the wooden door with stained glass windows is locked

To the right: years' worth of Sears family portraits stare down from the walls, each with a picture-perfect smiling family wearing matching outfits

Zoom In/Zoom Out

The technique of zoom in/zoom out is very similar to panning the camera, except it focuses on perspective. Imagine taking the camera and zooming in to the closest and broadest possible shots. Some of the results will overlap with the first exercise, but others may be different.

Here is a framework to use as inspiration:

- Molecular/atomic level
- In the body
- In the room
- In the neighborhood
- In the news
- From the sky
- In the universe

For instance, to describe the sad girl on the couch, a writer could choose details like:

Molecular/atomic level: cells stop dividing by mitosis and just stand still

In the body: she fills her lungs with air, practicing deep-breathing exercises to keep herself calm and centered

In the room: the air feels stagnant and heavy despite the ceiling fan's soft whir

In the neighborhood: sirens scream as firefighters rush to help an elderly woman who started a housefire in her kitchen

In the news: a famous child actor has died unexpectedly

From the sky: one lonely cloud hovers over the sun, setting the city in shadow

In the universe: the moon softly, and silently turns around earth, showing its colorless face

Each detail accentuates the sad, listless state of the protagonist. While using more than one of the ideas in this exercise might be overkill, choosing just the right detail to surprise your listeners can make a song memorable instead of generic.

Inventing Unexpected Details

Senses

Senses are the way in which humans perceive the world. Because our senses filter and shape our observations, good writers intentionally include sensory details. To practice, put yourself in the mind of a character and imagine what they are seeing, hearing, smelling, tasting, and touching. For instance, if a character is lying on the couch, processing the end of a relationship, they might be experiencing the following:

Sight: the couch pillow smothering her face

Sound: the background noise of the unchanged television channel

Smell: the stale kitty litter that needs to be changed

Taste: the salty-sweet aftertaste of a good crying session

Touch: the scratchy, too-hot blanket wrapped around her

Taking the time to intentionally activate each of the senses will make you a more perceptive writer.

Chain of Details

Frequently, the most poignant details are not the most obvious ones. Any writer can tell you about the pretty dress or funky dress a woman is wearing, but when Leonard Cohen writes "Suzanne," he digs deeper, choosing evocative words and describing the source of the outfit:

> *Now Suzanne takes your hand*
> *And she leads you to the river*
> *She is wearing rags and feathers*
> *From Salvation Army counters*

As a brainstorming exercise, practice pushing past your first thought by forming a "chain of details." The exercise entails linking phrases through connecting words like "that," "because," "in," "where," etc. Although the chain of details can venture into the realm of the absurd, it can also lead to unexpectedly useful breakthroughs. Here's an example of a chain of details:

Original sentence: She covered herself with a blanket

<that>

felt too warm

<because>

it was the middle of summer

<in>

a beachside town in Florida

<where>

everyone's backyards were swampy

<because>

it had been a season of heavy rains

Original sentence: She covered herself with a blanket

<that>

had blue and white stripes

<that>

were fading into shades of beige

<because>

it kept having to go through the wash

<because>

when the dog was a puppy, it peed on the blanket constantly

Challenge yourself to create as long of a chain of details as you possibly can, at least five phrases long. As the examples demonstrate, creating a chain of details can lead to world-building ideation and unexpected back-stories that can make the song spring to life.

Takeaways

1. "Show, don't tell" is a golden rule for writers because it encourages imaginative storytelling that listeners can picture.

2. Characters are formed based on how they are described, what they say, what they think, what they do, and what others say about them. Consider how characters unintentionally reveal themselves.

3. Create a detailed vision of setting, the time and place, to become a meaningful metaphor for what the song is trying to express.

4. Imagine your song as a movie and ask yourself what would be shown on screen. Use panning and zooming exercises to imagine the complete scene.

5. Invent unexpected details for your song through activities like exploring senses and creating a chain of details.

Practice

1. For each "Telling" phrase on the left, write five ways to show it in action in the "Showing" column on the right. Avoid using any of the descriptive words from the "telling" phrase in your phrases.

Telling	Showing
We came to party	
Jeanine is a great dancer	
The dog loves her master	
The setting is a church	
Beatrice thinks she's in charge	
The relationship between Emma and Irene is tense	
They pulled an all-nighter last night	

2. For each famous character, invent details that complete all five categories. The details need not be factual to any film or book, they should come from your imagination. Strive to have the details you provide reveal the most important aspects of their persona.

A. Indiana Jones

physical description:

what they do:

what they say:

what they think:

what others say about them:

B. Willy Wonka

physical description:

what they do:

what they say:

what they think:

what others say about them:

C. Princess Leia

physical description:

what they do:

what they say:

what they think:

what others say about them:

D. James Bond

physical description:

what they do:

what they say:

what they think:

what others say about them:

E. Harry Potter

physical description:

what they do:

what they say:

what they think:

what others say about them:

3. Invent phrases for each sense that might capture the sensory experience of each scene:

   A. **Sitting in the teacher's lounge at lunch, Mr. Steadmeyer realizes he left his baby unattended**

   Sight:

   Sound:

   Smell:

   Taste:

   Touch:

   B. **At fifty years old, Paula takes her first swimming lesson**

   Sight:

   Sound:

   Smell:

   Taste:

   Touch:

   C. **She receives her first kiss in a movie theater**

   Sight:

   Sound:

   Smell:

   Taste:

   Touch:

D. The child is getting ready to open Christmas presents

Sight:

Sound:

Smell:

Taste:

Touch:

4. Given the scenario, invent a chain of details at least four details long. The first connecting word is provided for you. In each successive phrase, circle the connecting word that you wish to use.

A. A fly buzzed against the window

[that]

____

[that] [because] [where] [when] [in] [which]

____

[that] [because] [where] [when] [in] [which]

____

[that] [because] [where] [when] [in] [which]

____

B. Adrienne feels a pain in her stomach

[because]

____

[that] [because] [where] [when] [in] [which]

____

[that] [because] [where] [when] [in] [which]

____

[that] [because] [where] [when] [in] [which]

____

C. She feels satisfied petting the cat

[that]

____

[that] [because] [where] [when] [in] [which]

____

[that] [because] [where] [when] [in] [which]

____

[that] [because] [where] [when] [in] [which]

____

D. She stumbles into the café to use the wifi

[where]

____

[that] [because] [where] [when] [in] [which]

____

[that] [because] [where] [when] [in] [which]

____

[that] [because] [where] [when] [in] [which]

____

5. Invent answers to the questions to create very specific details about where a scene might be set.

A. A princess and prince share a passionate, but forbidden, kiss

When?

What time of day? What day of the week?

____

What season? What weather?

____

What year or historical moment?

____

Where?

What city/country/continent?

____

Inside or outside? What kind of building or space?

____

What else is around? Objects? People?

____

B. A war is about to break out between two inner-city gangs

When?

What time of day? What day of the week?

____

What season? What weather?

____

What year or historical moment?

____

Where?

What city/country/continent?

____

Inside or outside? What kind of building or space?

____

What else is around? Objects? People?

____

C. A mother is helping her daughter get dressed for her wedding day

When?

What time of day? What day of the week?

____

What season? What weather?

____

What year or historical moment?

____

Where?

What city/country/continent?

____

Inside or outside? What kind of building or space?

____

What else is around? Objects? People?

____

D. Unpopular Jody unexpectedly runs into the popular kids from high school

When?

What time of day? What day of the week?

____

What season? What weather?

____

What year or historical moment?

____

What city/country/continent?

____

Inside or outside? What kind of building or space?

____

What else is around? Objects? People?

____

6. For each situation, practice panning an imaginary camera to invent the indicated descriptions.

A. Joelle sees her prom date dressed up for the first time

Hair:

Eyes:

Mouth:

Arms:

Hands:

Legs:

Feet:

Above:

Below:

Right Side:

Left Side:

B. An uncooperative kid is having their photo taken at school photo day

Hair:

Eyes:

Mouth:

Arms:

Hands:

Legs:

Feet:

Above:

Below:

Right Side:

Left Side:

7. For each situation, practice zooming in and out the imaginary camera to invent details for each prompt that can enrich the level of detail of the description.

   A. They held hands for the first time on a park bench

   Molecular/atomic level:

   In the body:

   In the room:

   In the neighborhood:

   In the news:

   In the sky:

   In the universe:

B. When he looked into his bank account, all his money was gone

Molecular/atomic level:

In the body:

In the room:

In the neighborhood:

In the news:

In the sky:

In the universe:

5. Strophic Songs

Scan Here for
Chapter 5 Page

There's a famous family story that when I was four years old, I brought my mom a big pink valentine cut from construction paper. Her heart melted, assuming that the valentine was a loving gift for her. But instead of offering her the card, I asked, "Can you help me mail this to Raffi?"

That's right, Raffi. If you're not familiar with Raffi, he's a Canadian singer-songwriter who specializes in children's music with big hits like "Bananaphone," "Baby Beluga," "Apples and Bananas," and "Down by the Bay." As a kid, I couldn't get enough of his acoustic guitar, silly wordplay, and Dixieland-inspired arrangements.

At that age, I didn't realize that many of my favorite Raffi songs are strophic songs, songs with a single, repeated musical section. Strophic songs are ideal for children because kids don't tire of repetition and can easily latch onto the melody of a repeated verse. In addition to the repeated music, many children's songs repeat their lyrics almost exactly, changing only one or two words per verse. For instance, in "Old MacDonald had a Farm," only the animal name and the sound it makes change during each repetition.

Although strophic form is simple, it's not just for kids. It's central to many traditional song forms like spirituals, hymns, and folk songs and appears in the work of great modern songwriters like Bob Dylan, Bruce Springsteen, Johnny Cash, and Paul Simon. Learning to write within the limitations of strophic form will push you to write with more organization, discipline, and creativity.

Strophic Song Basics

A **strophic song** consists of a single, repeated musical section that is presented with different lyrics each time. The strophic song form is most widely used in the folk and singer-songwriter genres, where the lyrics and storytelling take precedence over musical variety. It also appears in classical music, Broadway, and hymns.

Each new set of lyrics is commonly referred to as a **stanza**, though the more technical term, drawn from poetry, is **strophe**, the word that gives the form its name. In songwriting, each set of lyrics is more commonly referred to as a **verse**. Although the length of the verse and the number of verses can vary greatly from song to song, a typical strophic song might have a 16-measure verse repeated four to six times. To add variety, songwriters sometimes include an **interlude**, an instrumental section that introduces contrasting musical material. A typical strophic song could have one or two interludes spaced throughout the song.

Strophic songs typically maintain a consistent rhyme scheme across their verses. The rhyme scheme established in the first verse should be replicated in each successive verse. For example, if the first verse follows an ABAB-

CC rhyme scheme, each successive verse should repeat the same ABABCC rhyme scheme with a new lyric.

Although the melody should be similar between one verse and the next, songwriters may subtly add, subtract, or adjust pitches in order to accommodate inevitable differences in syllable counts between verses. Although the number of accented syllables should remain the same, the number of unaccented syllables may vary to accommodate slight lyrical shifts from one verse to the next.

The Refrain

Many strophic songs tie stanzas together with a **refrain**, a lyric that recurs in every verse. Refrains are most commonly placed at the end of each stanza and often relate to the title of the song, describe a lesson learned, or summarize the song's message. Refrains need to be universal enough to remain relevant in each stanza even as the story or situation develops from one verse to the next.

A refrain doesn't need to be a complete sentence, but can be a phrase that transforms to match the text of each stanza. For instance, in Bob Dylan's "Simple Twist of Fate," although each stanza ends with "a simple twist of fate," the lead-in to that phrase changes based on the grammar and content of what came before:

> **Verse 1:** …and watched out for a simple twist of fate
>
> **Verse 2:** …moving with a simple twist of fate
>
> **Verse 3:** …and forgot about a simple twist of fate
>
> **Verse 4:** …brought on by a simple twist of fate
>
> **Verse 5:** …one more time for a simple twist of fate
>
> **Verse 6:** …blame it on a simple twist of fate

Structuring Strophic Songs

Because the repetitive music of strophic songs directs the listener's focus to the lyrics, strophic songs often tell stories. When writing a **story song**, each verse usually describes a new scene in the narrative, and offers a moral, lesson, or summary. In order to provide an appropriate denouement, the final verse often offers a concluding thought that reflects upon the events rather than furthering the narrative. For instance, a strophic song about a first love might have the following structure:

> **Verse 1:** locking eyes for the first time
>
> **Verse 2:** first date
>
> **Verse 3:** the good times
>
> **Verse 4:** starting to fall apart
>
> **Verse 5:** reflection on the experience
>
> **Refrain:** My heart starts beating like it's brand new

Alternatively, strophic songs can present a central theme or idea, then explore supporting examples in each verse. For instance, if the "thesis" of the song is that traveling expands one's horizons, each verse could be written about traveling to a different location, followed by a summary of lessons learned.

Verse 1: Spain

Verse 2: Japan

Verse 3: African safari

Verse 4: India

Verse 5: Middle East

Verse 6: Summary: travel is arduous, but worth it

Refrain: I thought I was seeing the world, but I was really seeing myself

If the song's subject is that love changes people, there are a few different ways it could be structured. Each verse could be about a different person who was changed by love, the different ways one person was changed by a single love affair, or about the ways a person has evolved throughout their life in response to their partners. For instance:

Verse 1: I notice natural beauty more

Verse 2: I think more about the future now

Verse 3: I get more sentimental when looking at old photos

Verse 4: Summary

Refrain: When I met you, I was changed for good

Scarborough Fair

Traditional English Folk Song

"Scarborough Fair" is a traditional folk song that regained relevance in 1968 when Simon and Garfunkel released a modern recording called "Scarborough Fair/Canticle," which presents the song in conversation with Simon's original song, "Canticle." The lyric presents a list of impossible tasks that a former lover must complete to win back the singer's love.

Basic Info

Verse Length: 16 measures, although some sources notate the song in 6/8, compressing the verse into 8 measures

Number of Verses: The version presented in this text has 6 verses. But, as a folk song, the form is not officially "fixed" and might vary based on the performer, region, or setting.

Rhyme Scheme: ABAB

Refrain: This song is unique for its **double refrain**. The second line of each stanza repeats "parsley, sage, rosemary, and thyme" and the fourth line always ends with "true love of mine."

Interlude: None in Simon & Garfunkel version

Lyrics

The six stanzas of "Scarborough Fair" are presented below. The breaks that separate the four-line groups differentiate between the verses.

Are you going to Scarborough Fair?
Parsley, sage, rosemary, and thyme
Remember me to one who lives there
He once was a true love of mine

Tell him to make me a cambric shirt
Parsley, sage, rosemary, and thyme
Without no seams nor needle work
Then he'll be a true love of mine

Have him wash it in yonder dry well
Parsley, sage, rosemary, and thyme
Where ne'er a drop of water e'er fell
And then he'll be a true love of mine

Tell him to find me an acre of land
Parsley, sage, rosemary, and thyme
Between salt water and the sea strands
Then he'll be a true love of mine

Tell him to reap it with a sickle of leather
Parsley, sage, rosemary, and thyme
And gather it all in a bunch of heather
Then he'll be a true love of mine

Are you going to Scarborough Fair?
Parsley, sage, rosemary, and thyme
Remember me to one who lives there
He once was a true love of mine

Analysis

Music: The melody of "Scarborough Fair" uses the dorian mode, which lends the song an old-fashioned, Renaissance-era feeling. The dorian mode's lowered seventh scale degree (the D natural in the key of E minor) precludes the use of traditional dominant chords. Chords based on B, the typical dominant (V) chord in this key, are conspicuously absent throughout. Without dominant chords, the responsibility for tension and release shifts away from the harmony and onto the lilting three-four meter, and the rise and fall of the melodic shape.

Lyrics: The signature moment in the lyric is the repeated list of herbs, which is never fully explained in the song. Historians believe that these herbs were thought to influence feelings, particularly to soothe bitterness, mirroring the singer's aspirations towards their ex-beloved. As a listener, the herbs signal harmony with nature along with witchcraft and magic, which match the sorts of supernatural challenges the singer proposes. Intentional or not, the word "thyme" has an obvious homophone, "time," and the lyric implicitly hints at the role of the passage of time in healing love's wounds.

Structure: "Scarborough Fair" establishes a theme in the opening stanza and presents variations on the theme in each successive stanza. The theme is that the singer has a rare chance to pass on a message to the lover who wronged them. In each successive stanza, they taunt their ex with a new, more impossible way to win them back.

The first and last stanzas bookend the song with identical lyrics. Ironically, the repeated request to "remember me to one who lives there" suggests that the singer actually longs to reconnect with the person who they are supposedly rejecting so forcefully. In fact, the very act of singing such a lengthy song proves that the singer has been ruminating about their "true love" and might not want them to stay away as badly as they are letting on.

Mack the Knife

Kurt Weill, music/Bertolt Brecht, lyrics/Marc Blitzstein, English lyric

Originally from the 1928 German musical *Threepenny Opera*, "The Ballad of Mack the Knife," commonly referred to as "Mack the Knife" has become a favorite song of jazz singers and crooners like Louis Armstrong and Bobby Darin. Presented as part of the play's prologue, "Mack the Knife" introduces gangster antihero Macheath, whose past involves a sordid history of murder.

The original lyric by Bertolt Brecht is written in German, but the English translation presented here is by Marc Blitzstein.

Basic Info

Verse Length: 16 measures

Number of Verses: 6

Rhyme Scheme: ABAB, although the rhymes for the A's are often somewhat weak ("disappeared dear" / "like a sailor")

Refrain: No true refrain, but "Now that Mackie's back in town" at the end of the fourth and sixth stanzas hints at a refrain

Interlude: Not generally included, but many versions include key changes between verses to create contrast

Full Lyrics

Oh, the shark has pretty teeth, dear
And he shows them pearly white
Just a jack knife has Macheath, dear
And he keeps it out of sight

his teeth, dear
Scarlet billows start to spread
Fancy gloves, though, wears Macheath, dear
So there's not a trace of red

On the sidewalk Sunday morning
Lies a body oozing life
Someone's sneaking 'round the corner
Is that someone Mack the Knife?

From a tugboat by the river
A cement bag's dropping down
The cement's just for the weight, dear
Bet you Mackie's back in town

Louie Miller disappeared, dear
After drawing out his cash
And Macheath spends like a sailor
Did our boy do something rash?

Sukey Tawdry, Jenny Diver,
Polly Peachum, Lucy Brown
Oh, the line forms on the right, dear
Now that Mackie's back in town

Analysis

Music: The predominantly major-key harmony and jazzy, syncopated dotted rhythms contrast with the grisly and sinister subject matter to create the feeling of "dark humor" for which Weill and Brecht are known. The melody manages to maintain interest despite utilizing nearly identical rhythms for each phrase. Each phrase starts with two quarter-note pickups, and six of the eight phrases have the exact same rhythm. Weill masterfully modifies the melodic shape of successive phrases to maintain melodic and harmonic interest despite the repetitive nature of the rhythm.

Structure: "Mack the Knife" presents the evidence needed to convince the listener of Macheath's (aka Mack's) misdeeds. With each stanza, the listener learns more about Mack's sinister methods: his weapon of choice, his approach to disposing bodies, and his financial motives. The journey of the song involves both a shift from broad images to specific details and a movement through time, from past to present.

Lyrics: Throughout the song, Blitzstein's lyric balances implicating Macheath while not directly accusing him. In the first two stanzas, he replaces the image of Macheath stabbing his victim with an analogy of a shark biting a swimmer to obfuscate the directness of the accusation. In other stanzas, Blitzstein describes only the circumstantial evidence of "a body oozing life" and "a cement bag dropping down" while asking rhetorical questions about Mack's involvement. The song's ambiguity creates a feeling of intrigue and avoids passing judgment, allowing Mack to become an antihero rather than a blatantly unlikeable criminal.

The final stanza connects Mack's background with the situation that catalyzes the musical: Mack and all of his "baggage" have arrived back on the scene. The women listed in the last stanza are not victims of Macheath's murders but his current romantic and business partners. With this context, the listener can't help but wonder what will become of these women now that Mack is back in their lives.

Simple Twist of Fate

Music and Lyrics by Bob Dylan

Bob Dylan's "Simple Twist of Fate," from the album *Blood on the Tracks,* is a modern folk song that tells the story of a missed romantic connection.

The full lyrics of the song won't be presented in this book as the song is not yet in the public domain. Feel free to listen to the full song and research the full lyrics using your resource of choice.

Basic Info

Verse Length: 16 measures

Number of Verses: 6

Rhyme Scheme: AAABBCC

Refrain: "...simple twist of fate" in the last line of each stanza

Interlude: Between the third and fourth verses, there's a harmonica solo over the chords of the verse.

Analysis

Music: Dylan's melody uses repeated notes to highlight the lyrics' conversational tone and spotlight the richly poetic language. The song's musical color derives more from the chromatically descending bassline than the melodic interest. However, the melody does have a memorable moment with its grand ascent in measures 11-12, in which it rises by an octave to reach its climactic peak, a high F. It is common in virtually all styles for musical sections to reach a **melodic climax**, the highest note, about three fourths of the way through the section, allowing time to descend back to a typical range.

Lyrics: Dylan creates a dreamlike atmosphere through vivid imagery and shifting perspective. The song's unexpected scenes and vibrant images appeal to the senses, including the yearning sound of "a saxophone someplace far off played," the tragedy of a "beat-up shade" on a lamp in a seedy hotel, the mythical weight of a "blind man at the gate," and the whimsical symbolism of "a parrot that talks."

Although the majority of the song is sung in the third person, the perspective shifts at important moments to present the story from various vantage points, like a Picasso painting that simultaneously captures its subject from multiple angles. After beginning the song with "They sat together in the park," the second stanza, includes the first-person phrase, "I remember [it] well," before returning to a third-person "he" later in the stanza:

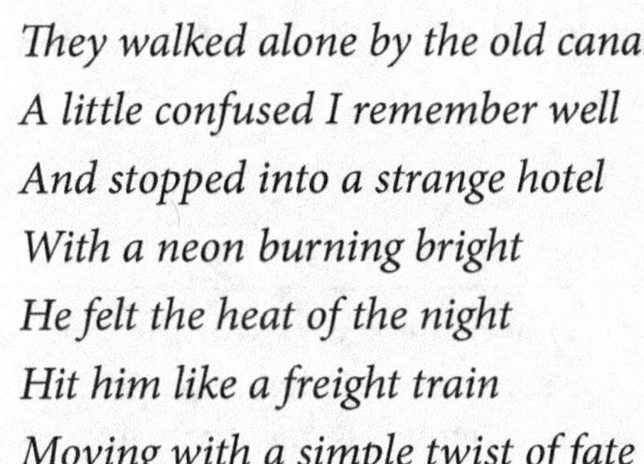

Structure: "Simple Twist of Fate" is a story song. Each verse conveys a new scene in which a couple has a short love affair and then separates, leaving the man feeling lonely, confused, and lost. Interestingly, most of the song, four out of the six stanzas, is about the aftermath of the love affair, rather than the romance itself. Instead of continuing the story, the final stanza switches to the past tense to reflect on the experience from a distance. The singer again seems to "forget" that the story is about someone else and reverts to the first person:

This last stanza is full of symbolism. While the language is essentially mysterious, one could hypothesize that "she was my twin" indicates the singer felt a deep, soulmate-like connection; "lost the ring" perhaps refers to lost romance or commitment (like a wedding ring); and "born in spring" indicates that his lover from the song is younger than him. Besides lending the whole situation a dreamlike quality, the change in perspective and symbolic language suggests that the singer is in denial about their experience and perhaps feels embarrassed to have "know[n] and [felt] too much within."

Takeaways

1. Strophic songs have a single repeated musical section, but different lyrics for each verse.

2. Some strophic songs have a refrain, a repeated line usually placed at the end of each verse. Refrains often share lessons learned or provide a summary.

3. The rhyme scheme established in the first verse is generally maintained throughout the subsequent verses.

4. Musical interludes provide contrast and refresh the listener's ears between repeated verses.

5. Strophic songs can tell a story or present an argument with each verse providing different "supporting evidence" for the argument.

Practice

1. Draw a line between the stanzas on the right (1-4) and the stanzas on the left (A-D) that would belong together in a strophic song. All of the songs are written about a similar subject matter, but differ in their syllable counts and rhyme schemes. Remember, stanzas from the same strophic song should share similar syllable counts and rhyme schemes between stanzas.

   1. *Sail away*
      Far beyond this friendly bay
      Seagulls soar and dolphins play
      We'll leave behind this quiet bay

   2. *Sail across the sea with me*
      To a moonlit isle
      When land appears we'll surely be
      Free to stay a while

   3. *Excitement spreads quick through the decks*
      The sailors are nearly aflame
      For adventures await those men for whom fate
      Has destined for fortune and fame.

   4. *Seasick dreams awake me*
      Gloomy skies await me
      Folks at home forsake me
      As we sail away

   A. *The men search each cavern for gold*
      For with fortune a man can be free
      But the dolphins and seals refuse to reveal
      The secrets that hide in the sea

   B. *Mermaid calls allure me*
      Lonely hours unmoor me
      Sailors must endure me
      As we sail away

   C. *Luck abounds*
      Up ahead are fortunes found
      Piled in gleaming, golden mounds
      You're the richest man around

   D. *Sail with me to treasure troves*
      Glist'ning in the sun
      They're just beyond the friendly cove
      Hidden one by one

2. Choose one of the three example songs from this unit and write two brand-new verses that fit the established music, continuing with the same story or subject matter. Be sure to maintain the same rhyme scheme for each stanza while roughly matching the number of syllables and accent pattern of the melody.

3. Choose one of the example songs from this chapter and write different music, both melody and chords, for the lyrics.

5A Writing a Strophic Song

This is the first of five special chapters that walk you through the process of writing a song. Please bear in mind that these chapters demonstrate only one of the countless ways to write. Feel free to follow the instructions in these chapters closely, reference them for brainstorming and ideation, or ignore them completely.

The following steps guide you through writing a strophic song. To demonstrate, I wrote my own strophic song, showing you each stage of my writing process as it unfolded. The method detailed in this chapter is **non-linear**, meaning that it doesn't start with the first phrase and proceed to the last. Instead, I'm showing you how to work from the outside inwards, using outlines, rhyming words, rhyme schemes, and syllabic stress to generate ideas and focus your writing.

Step One: Make a Plan

Deciding on the subject, structure, and refrain of your song first creates an outline of a strophic form that you can fill in with lyrical and musical details.

Subject

Because of their lack of repetition, strophic songs are great vehicles for telling a story. When writing a story song, you don't necessarily have to draw upon personal experience. Legends, novels, and myths provide ready-made plots for you to retell while inevitably adding your unique perspective. Songwriters can consciously choose to disguise a well-known story by modifying details like character names and settings to create a new, if derivative, narrative.

I've chosen the life of the biblical character Moses as my subject. When choosing a story, it is important that something in the story *changes* from the beginning to the end. Without a change, a songwriter often ends up painting a picture of a scene instead of creating a narrative arc with tension and release. I chose Moses' story in part because so many changes take place in his life.

Structure

To give yourself a sense of what the song will be about, brainstorm all of the possible "chapters" of your story, everything that you can think to write about your character. Remember to imagine each scene like a movie, asking yourself what would appear on screen.

Brainstorm at least ten different potential chapters for your story, going "overboard" to give yourself options later on. The following list presents fifteen scenes I can imagine writing about the life of Moses:

1. birth to Jewish mother
2. basket in the Nile
3. kills Egyptian guard
4. burning bush
5. "let my people go"
6. causes plagues in Egypt
7. death of the firstborn
8. golden calf incident
9. parting the Red Sea
10. celebration after escape from Egypt
11. bread did not rise
12. forty years of wandering
13. receives ten commandments
14. gets within sight of the promised land
15. dies without seeing the promised land

Out of these fifteen, choose four to six subjects for verses that provide enough inspiration to write a whole stanza, create good contrasts, and fully tell the story. You can modify your choices as you write if the structure doesn't fit the song as it develops. I came up with the following structure for my song, which I put in chronological order:

Verse 1: Basket in the Nile
Verse 2: The Burning Bush
Verse 3: Confronting Pharaoh
Verse 4: Wilderness Wandering
Verse 5: The Promised Land

Refrain

Lastly, invent a refrain, the line that repeats in each stanza. Although not every strophic song needs a refrain, I prefer to use them because refrains provide helpful organization and a starting place from which I can brainstorm other lyrics.

The refrain needs to be applicable to all five chapters. In other words, it needs to say something about Moses' life that is as true for him when he's a baby discovered in the Nile as when he searches for the promised land in his old age. After deciding on the general direction of the refrain, you can change the verb tense or the wording to make it fit in each different stage of the story. Brainstorm at least five possibilities for the refrain, even if some of them are bad or awkward. Here are my five brainstorms:

1. he was searching for the promised land
2. the journey was long, but he didn't turn back
3. his faith was the strength that led him on
4. this is the man who would part the seas
5. belief is stronger than any army

When deciding which refrain to use, keep in mind how easy or hard it is to rhyme with the last word of each option. In most cases, at least one line in each stanza rhymes with the refrain, meaning that you have to invent five convincing rhymes for the same word in a five-stanza song.

In my refrains, for instance, I think that it would be hard to rhyme with "army" using five different words. Ultimately, I chose the second option, "the journey was long, but he didn't turn back." I like the chant-like rhythm, the theme of perseverance, and how easy it is to rhyme with "back."

Step Two: Rhyme with the Refrain

Once the refrain is established, brainstorm rhymes with the final word of the refrain. For my chosen refrain, "the journey was long, but he didn't turn back," I've brainstormed words that rhyme with "back." Don't forget to consider both pure rhymes and near rhymes and to include multisyllabic words. Here are some words that rhyme with "back."

Pure Rhymes: *lack, stack, sack, rack, track, crack, pack, whack, black, aback, attack, shellack*

Near Rhymes: *act, pact, hatch, catch, patch, latch, match, pat, sat, fat, mat, mad, sad, fad, cad, rad, pan, ran, tan, attract, react, impact, contract, abstract, subtract, interact*

Then, write lines that complement the refrain using the rhyming words you brainstormed. Remember that you can write poetically, using different words than you would in conversational speech. For instance:

1. **About the burning bush:**

    While the fire burned, they forged their pact
    The journey was long, but he didn't turn back

2. **About advising Pharaoh:**

    So the Pharaoh knew he'd met his match
    The journey was long, but he didn't turn back

3. **About crossing the Red Sea:**

    The sand was red and the sky was black
    The journey was long, but they didn't turn back

Step Three: Complete the Lyrics for One Verse

Choose your favorite rhyming lines and complete the rest of the stanza. It's important to complete one full stanza first because this model will be used as the blueprint for writing the rest of the stanzas.

I chose to start with the third option, about crossing the Red Sea. I liked the parallel structure and the legend-like tone of "the sand was red and the sky was black." Because a typical strophic stanza only contains a few lines, you need to have a clear idea of what essential points you're trying to convey. Start by brainstorming what details should appear in the verse:

- Israelites are fleeing Egypt
- they are being chased
- they can't cross the sea
- Moses parts the waters using his staff

The last element seems to be the most essential, so let's decide we will rhyme with "staff." What rhymes with staff?

Pure Rhymes: *laugh, gaffe, half, carafe, graph, giraffe*

Near Rhymes: *math, wrath, bath, path, fast, last, past, aghast*

Of those words, three stand out to me:

1. **half** – the sea parts in half
2. **wrath** – they are fleeing the Egyptians' wrath
3. **fast** – to flee, they need to move fast

As a next step, I wrote three versions of the verse using each of the three rhymes:

1. Half

   With Pharaoh's men in hot pursuit
   He tapped the earth with his wooden staff
   Before them rose a brand-new route
   The waters of the Red Sea split in half
   The sand was red and the sky was black
   The journey was long, but they didn't turn back

2. Wrath

   His men ran far and they ran quick
   As they ran from Pharaoh's wrath
   The waves were deep and the foam was thick
   'Til he low'red his holy staff
   His people stared, amazed
   But he said, "no time for delays"
   The sand was red and the sky was black
   The journey was long, but they didn't turn back

3. Fast

> *Moses told the people they should get out fast*
> *Before Pharaoh changed his mind*
> *He tapped three times with his wooden staff*
> *To summon help divine*
> *The sea went left and the sea went right*
> *And his people hurried through*
> *The shepherd boy summoned the Almighty's might*
> *Then he disappeared from view*
> *The sand was red and the sky was black*
> *The journey was long, but they didn't turn back*

I chose #2, which uses *wrath* as the rhyming word. The stanza is not too long (like #3) and although I liked #1, I felt that the rhymes of *staff*/*half*/*black*/*back* were all a little close together and might sound like a jumble to the listener.

Before moving on, notice how *active* this process is. At no point am I simply staring at a page hoping for inspiration. Instead, I'm brainstorming rhymes, comparing stanzas, and writing options, even if they don't get chosen. As this process unfolds, not only is it getting the current stanza written, but I'm also brainstorming other material for other stanzas, or perhaps other songs.

Step Four: Set the Verse to Music

Now that the lyric is set, write music for the verse. Establishing the music now is essential because subsequent verses need to fit this musical scheme.

How do you create music for a lyric?

1. Speak the lyric with a metronome or a drum loop to find the natural rhythm of the accent patterns. Use pickups if the first word of a line doesn't naturally want to be stressed.

2. Using the rhythmic inspiration, sing the melody with a metronome. You can't think your way to a melody – you have to follow your musical instincts. However, if you need inspiration, play yourself a pentatonic scale in your intended key and stay close to the scale.

3. Decide what key you're in and write out the common diatonic chords in your key (I call this a "chord bank," like a "word bank" you sometimes see in word searches). If you're able, sing and experiment with chords on your instrument, finding your chord progression through call and response. If not, use chords from your chord bank that include prominent melody notes.

Since this song has the feeling of a legend or folk song, a minor key felt very appropriate. Each melodic phrase starts with pickups because the first syllable of each line is an unstressed syllable (*his* men, *the* waves, *his* people, *the* sand). Here's what I came up with:

Step Five: Write a Second Verse

Now that the musical form has been established, it's time to write lyrics for the other verses, designed to fit with the same melody and chords. Besides the rhythm of the melody, the rhyme scheme should also remain the same for each verse. In my song, the rhyme scheme is ABABCCDD. Remember that the actual phonetic sounds don't have to repeat from verse to verse, just this ABABCCDD form. Between matching rhythm of the melody and the repeating the rhyme scheme, writing the subsequent verses can feel like a crossword or sudoku puzzle in which both horizontal and vertical elements need to align.

When creating additional verses, write the new lyrics beneath the old lyrics line by line to test whether their rhythm matches. Revisit the rhymes and lines that you have already brainstormed, for instance, "While the fire burned, they forged their pact," which is used in the next stanza. The letters at the end of each line mark the rhyme scheme.

His men ran far and they ran quick	A1
A bush called out and spoke his name	A2
As they ran from Pharaoh's wrath	B1
Burning hot with holy light	B2
The waves were deep and the foam was thick	A1
The flames burned high but the bush stayed safe	A2
'Til he low'red his holy staff.	B1
And he knew a holy sight	B2
His people stared, amazed	C1
He promises to heed	C2
But he said, "no time for delays"	C1
And he's told, "it's time to lead"	C2
The sand was red and the sky was black	D1
The flames burned hot as they forged their pact	D2
The journey was long, but they didn't turn back	D1
The journey was long, but he didn't turn back	D2

The next musical example shows the second verse set to music.

The only part where the syllables don't match exactly is between these lines:

But he said, "no time for delays"	C1
And he's told, "it's time to lead"	C2

The top line, the original, has eight syllables whereas the new line has only seven. While a syllable could be added for the new line, the music sounded rushed, so having fewer syllables is a welcome change.

When two verses have different numbers of syllables, the extra note should be notated as a smaller note, sometimes called a **cue note**, to indicate that it should be used for some, but not all of the verses. The F is written as a cue note in measure 10 to accommodate the word *but*.

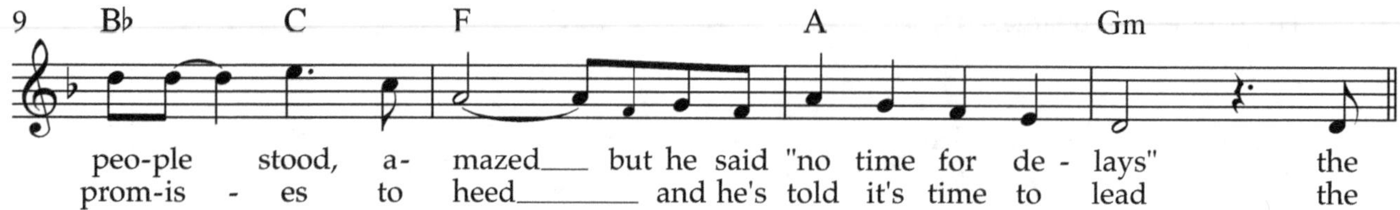

Step Six: Write the Other Verses

Now two verses are complete. The final three verses need to be written following the same pattern, remaining mindful of the syllable count and the rhyme scheme. This level of craft is the time-consuming part, which can take hours of work, especially if the writer is obsessive about getting the details right.

I completed the song about Moses following my original structure. Here are the five stanzas that I wrote:

Verse 1: Basket in the Nile

A basket brought him down the stream
Floating towards his destiny
The waves were fast and the reeds were green
For a moment he was free
A princess grabs his wrist
And the story breaks, then twists
His fate is fixed on its lonely track
The journey was long, but he didn't turn back

Verse 2: The Burning Bush

A bush called out and spoke his name
Burning hot with holy light
The flames burned high but the bush stayed safe
And he knew a holy sight
He promises to heed
And he's told, "it's time to lead"
The flames burned hot as they forged their pact
The journey was long, but he didn't turn back

Verse 3: Parting the Red Sea

His men ran far and they ran quick
As they ran from Pharaoh's wrath
The waves were deep and the foam was thick
'Til he low'red his holy staff
His people stared, amazed
But he said, "no time for delays"
The sand was red and the sky was black
The journey was long, but they didn't turn back

Verse 4: Wilderness Wandering

For forty springs and forty falls
Through the desert's heat, they roamed
Through rabbi's prayers and shepherd's calls
They dreamt of holy homes
When manna came, they ate
And they trusted in their fate
He helped them keep their beliefs intact
The journey was long, but they didn't turn back

Verse 5: The Promised Land

He peers out at the promised land
From atop an auburn hill
From Canaan's glory
He was banned by the
Strength of holy will
He came so close, so near
And his face was filled with tears
His fate was fixed on its lonely track
The journey was long, but he didn't turn back

Step Seven: Edit

A song is never truly done because good songwriters continuously edit their drafts. My favorite form of editing goes like this:

1. Choose the three weakest parts of the song. Even if you love everything about your song, choose the three parts that you love the least!

2. Write an alternate version for each of the three parts.

3. Decide whether the original version or alternate version is better and keep the one that you prefer.

4. Repeat the process, identifying the next three weakest parts of the song.

For instance, the three parts of this song I would choose are:

1. **Lines:** *He promises to heed*
   And he's told, 'it's time to lead' (Verse 2)

   Why: the connection between the lines isn't firm
   Alternate: *As sparks sizzle and spray*
   He swears he will obey

2. **Lines:** *When manna came, they ate*
   And they trusted in their fate (Verse 4)
   Why: second line feels generic
   Alternate: *When manna came, they ate*
   Holding steadfast in their faith

3. **Lines:** *He came so close, so near*
   And his face was filled with tears (Verse 5)

   Why: "so close" and "so near" are redundant

   Alternate: *Though his soul knew he was near*
   His destiny was clear

In each of these cases, I think that I like the rewrite better than the original and I will replace the lyrics in the final song. After these three sections are replaced, I should identify the *new* three weakest sections and write alternates for these until I am ready to move on to another song.

To see and hear the final version, visit the website for this chapter by scanning the QR code at the beginning.

Takeaways

1. Think of the subject, structure, and refrain for your song before writing. Although you can always make changes to these elements later, having a plan makes writing the song feel less overwhelming.

2. Songs can be built through rhymes. Once the refrain is set, brainstorm rhyming words and lines that to pair with the refrain.

3. Once the first stanza is completed, use it as a model to build the other stanzas. Be intentional about writing stanzas with similar syllable counts and emphasis patterns as the first. Writing each line underneath the equivalent line of the previous stanza is a good way to stay focused.

4. The syllable counts of each verse do not have to match the original exactly. Notes can be added or taken away from the original stanza as long as the melody remains recognizable.

5. Always edit a song after you have finished writing. Find the three weakest parts of the song and brainstorm alternatives. After the brainstorm, you don't have to select the alternative, but you might find you like it better.

Practice

1. Write three different samples of structures and refrains for potential strophic songs:

   A. Refrain:

   Verse 1:

   Verse 2:

   Verse 3:

   Verse 4:

   Verse 5:

B. Refrain:

Verse 1:

Verse 2:

Verse 3:

Verse 4:

Verse 5:

C. Refrain:

Verse 1:

Verse 2:

Verse 3:

Verse 4:

Verse 5:

2. Choose one refrain from your previous exercise. Brainstorm rhymes that fit with the last word and then write three different lines to pair with the refrain.

Pure Rhymes:

Near Rhymes:

Line 1:

Line 2:

Line 3:

3. Choose your favorite lines from the previous exercise and turn them into a whole stanza. Write 6-10 lines.

4. Take your stanza from the previous exercise and create a musical setting, with melody and chords.

5. Write a second verse keeping in mind that the rhyme scheme and syllable count should match the original verse.

6. Finish your strophic song! Complete your plan by writing the missing verses to match your original plan.

7. As part of the editing process, choose the three weakest sections of your song and write an alternate version. After you write your new lines, you can decide whether you prefer the original or alternate version.

1. **Lines:**

   Alternate:

2. **Lines:**

   Alternate:

3. **Lines:**

   Alternate:

6. Major and Minor Harmony

This story is about me, your author. The week that I began college at a music conservatory, there was a "mixer" event designed to help students connect. As a Jazz Performance major, I arrived with dreams of a career performing on big stages. I met other new students who played wind instruments, composed, and sang…and then I met a student who introduced themselves as a Music Theory major. I'm embarrassed to say it, but I think I laughed out loud. *How dull*, I thought! Isn't theory, with its rules and mathematics, kind of the enemy of creativity?

As my study of music deepened, however, my views shifted. After two years in college, I added a second major: Music Theory! I had come to appreciate that theory is actually not opposed to creativity, but a pathway to a more expansive creative palette. When I hear an amazing chord in someone else's song, I use theory to analyze the chord and determine how I can use a similar sound in my own song. When a melody surprises me, I take it apart like a watchmaker examining the inner workings of a watch, then use the same components to create a melody of my own. For me, music theory is a way to escape from the patterns in which I inevitably get stuck as a songwriter and pursue new paths forward.

I know that harmony tends to be an area that frightens many songwriters. Finding appropriate chords for your song requires both proficiency on a chordal instrument like piano or guitar and a basic understanding of music theory, which can feel more like math than art. So if some of the terms in the next section feel intimidating, remember: theory isn't here to box you in, it's here to expand your mind and invigorate your sound.

Major Diatonic Harmony

Understanding the importance of keys is the first step to understanding harmony. In any songwriting style, the vast majority of songs establish a harmonic home base, the **tonic**, and all of the other chords are heard in relation to it.

Diatonic Triads

When music is **diatonic**, it stays within a key without adding additional accidentals like sharps, flats, or naturals. Most rock and pop songs are completely diatonic. Knowing the **diatonic triads**, the three-note chords that occur within a key, gives songwriters a palette of harmonies to draw from, like the colors a painter chooses to create their canvas. The three-step process for finding diatonic triads is as follows:

1. Write a seven-note scale starting on the tonic note (G in G major), placing one note on each successive line and space.

2. Stack **thirds** above the notes of a scale to create three-note chords; the interval of a third stacks notes either all on lines or all in spaces.

3. Apply the accidentals from the key signature, adding flats or sharps to the appropriate notes.

For instance, to find the diatonic triads in G major:

1. Write a seven-note scale starting from G.

2. Stack thirds above each note of the scale to form triads, stacking notes vertically, either all on lines or all on spaces.

3. Apply the key signature of G major (one sharp), by adding sharps to all F's.

Or, to find the diatonic triads in E-flat major:

1. Write a seven-note scale starting from E-flat.

2. Stack thirds above each note of the scale, stacking notes vertically, either all on lines or all on spaces.

3. Apply the E-flat major key signature (three flats) by adding flats to all B's, E's and A's

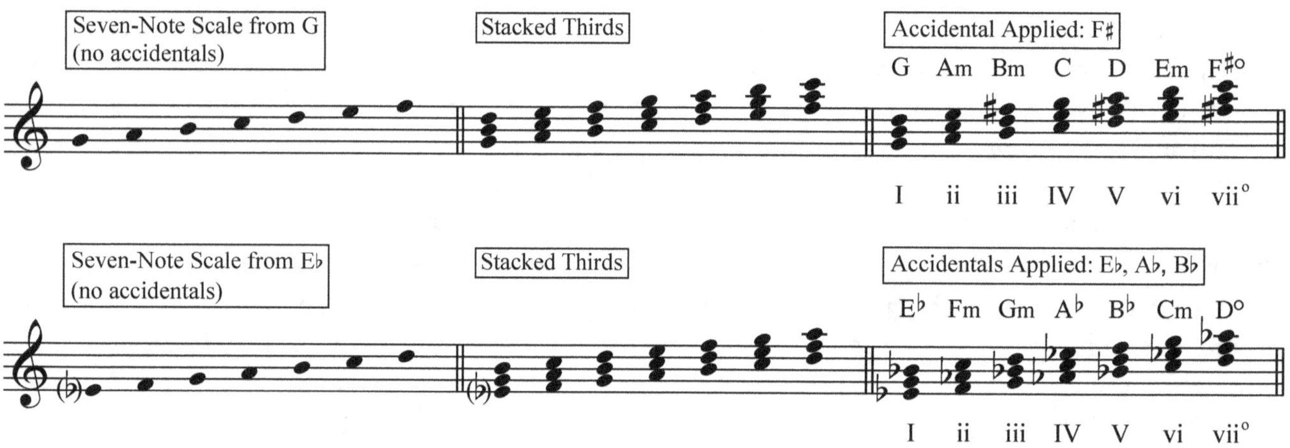

Chords within a key are identified using Roman numerals, beginning with I for the tonic chord. Capital letters identify **major triads** (I, IV, V) whereas lowercase letters identify **minor triads** (ii, iii, vi). The final chord (vii°) is a **diminished triad**, a chord which is avoided in most songwriting styles. It is indicated with a lowercase Roman numeral followed by a superscript "o".

Notes within triads are named based on their position within the scale, rather than their position in the chord. The lowest note of the triad gets a special name, the **root**, because it provides the foundation from which the entire harmonic system "grows." The middle note is called the **third** and the highest is called the **fifth**. For example, for a C major triad, C is the root, E is the third, and G is the fifth. For a D minor triad, D is the root, F is the third, and A is the fifth. These names don't change, even if the notes are organized differently, as shown in the example.

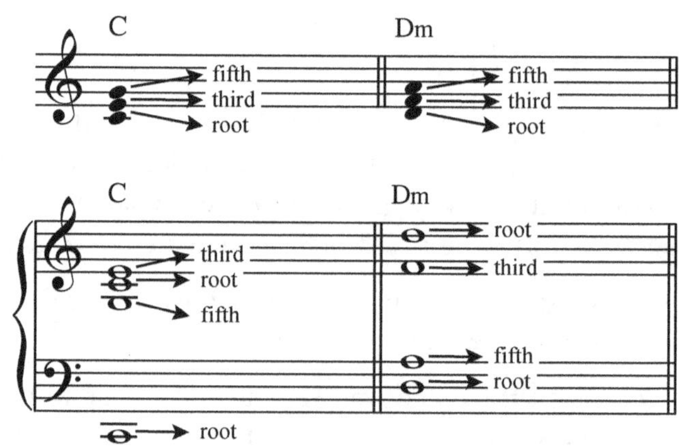

Understanding Diatonic Harmony

Diatonic harmony can be used in two principal ways, to create functional harmony and non-functional harmony. Whether a piece primarily employs functional or non-functional harmony is a key factor in defining its genre.

Functional Harmony

Functional harmony strategically targets the tonic chord using traditional methods of tension and release. Most functional progressions are based on the **diatonic circle of fifths**, a progression in which the roots of the chords descend by the interval of a fifth while staying within the key. For songwriters who want to improve their harmonic knowledge, memorizing and internalizing this progression is a foundational exercise.

The roman numeral formula that can be used to create the diatonic circle of fifths in any key is as follows:

$$\text{I - IV - vii}^{\circ}\text{ - iii - vi - ii - V - I}$$

The chord symbols for the diatonic circle of fifths in C and E-flat are given below:

$$\text{C - F - B}^{\circ}\text{ - Em - Am - Dm - G - C}$$
$$\text{E}\flat\text{ - A}\flat\text{ - D}^{\circ}\text{ - Gm - Cm - Fm - B}\flat\text{ - E}\flat$$

Notice how the root of each chord shifts downwards by a fifth, for instance, from C to F to B to E to A, etc. The small exception is the movement from F to B, which sounds funky because its interval is a **diminished fifth**, a half-step smaller than the others. The next example presents the diatonic circle of fifths in C and E-flat major as root position chords, in tight inversions, and using a more sophisticated pianistic approach that divides the chord between bass in the left hand and triad in the right. As you play these chords, listen for how the progression creates a predictable journey from the stable tonic chord to increasingly unstable territory before returning back to the tonic.

Although the diatonic circle of fifths is a crucial building block for nearly all harmonic styles, it is particularly important for Great American Songbook-style pieces, which combine fragments of the diatonic circle to create larger progressions. A quintessential progression of that era is the repeated vi-ii-V-I progression (or I-vi-ii-V progression, depending on where you start), which **vamps**, or repeats, the last four chords of the diatonic circle of fifths. The next example shows two famous songs, "Fly Me to the Moon" and "Heart and Soul," that include this progression.

Non-Functional Harmony

Whereas functional harmony is the bedrock of the Great American Songbook, non-functional harmony defines many pop and rock chord progressions. **Non-functional harmony** refers to moving freely between chords without considering the order of the circle of fifths or traditional conceptions of tension and release.

Songs that use non-functional harmony are usually still diatonic and rarely move outside of the seven triads found within a key. However, in these songs, the order of these triads is scrambled to create interesting colors rather than to lead logically to the tonic. Nevertheless, the tonic chord maintains a feeling of stability as the "home" chord in both functional and non-functional progressions. The next example shows how snippets of Adele's "Someone Like You" and The Beatles' "She Loves You" build their harmony using diatonic triads.

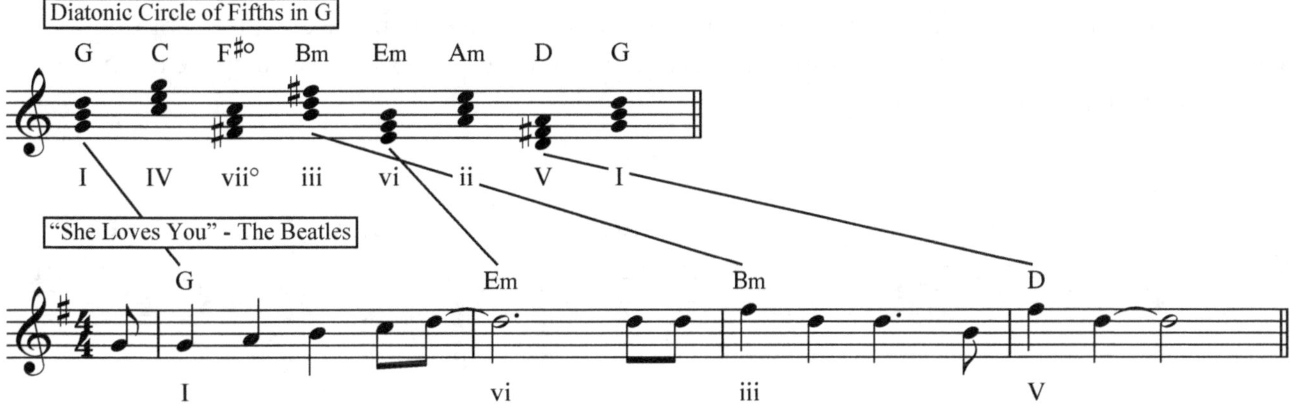

Minor Key Harmony

While major keys conform to a single scale and seven triads, minor keys hold significantly more possibilities. All these options make minor keys more complex, and potentially richer, settings for harmonic experimentation.

Whereas there is only one major scale, there's no such thing as "*the* minor scale." There are three minor scales that are essential for understanding the scope of minor-key harmony. Each of these scales is compared to the **parallel major scale**, the scale based on the same root, like C major and C minor.

1. **Natural Minor:** Starting from its parallel major scale, the **natural minor scale** lowers the third, sixth, and seventh scale degree. It shares its key signature with the minor key's **relative major**, the major scale based on its third scale degree (A minor is relative of C major).

2. **Harmonic Minor:** Starting from its parallel major scale, the **harmonic minor scale** lowers the third and sixth only. It maintains the key's **leading tone**, the seventh note of the scale that pulls upwards and makes listeners feel firmly settled in that key.

3. **Melodic Minor:** The **melodic minor scale** has different notes depending on whether the scale is ascending or descending. When ascending, it only lowers one note, the third, as compared to the major scale. When descending, it matches the natural minor scale with three notes distinguishing it from its parallel major scale.

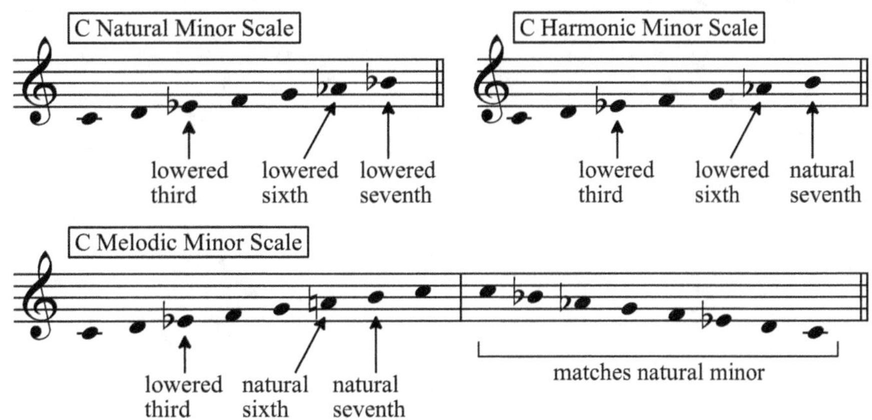

Because there are three different scales for each minor key, each key contains more than just seven possible triads. For now, let's focus on the triads based on the natural minor scale, with one exception: for the V chord, the **dominant chord** that leads strongly back to the tonic, use the triad created by the harmonic minor scale, which includes the leading tone.

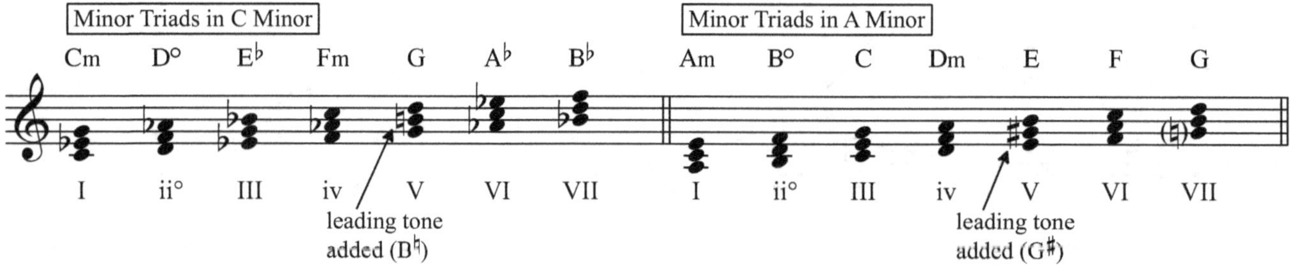

This group of chords represents one possibility, not the definitive set of triads in minor keys. Notice that the location of major and minor triads has changed. Now, the diminished triad to avoid is on the second scale degree, rather than the seventh.

Minor keys have their own version of the diatonic circle of fifths that guides how functional harmony can develop and resolve. Practice the triads in the pattern shown below, listening for the differences in color between the major and minor sonorities.

Both functional and non-functional harmony are possible in minor keys as well. Like in major keys, songs in minor keys often move through the diatonic circle of fifths. "I Will Survive" by Gloria Gaynor, is a well-known song that repeatedly loops all the way through the progression in A minor.

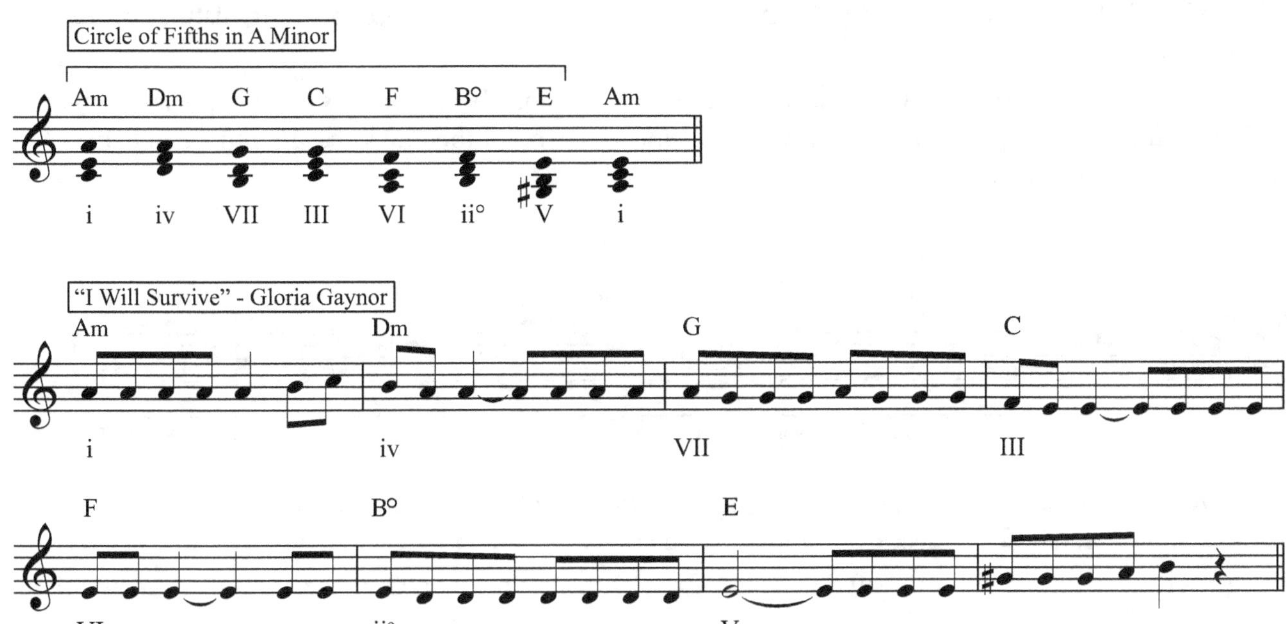

If you know Gaynor's song, you know that it creates an endless loop, one that repeats and gains momentum. The energy of the loop is largely generated by the harmony's journey through the circle of fifths, which slingshots the chords back to the tonic every eight measures.

Non-functional harmony is possible within minor keys as well. Although Nirvana mostly uses **power chords**, chords with only the root and fifth, rather than triads, the iconic chords of "Smells Like Teen Spirit" outline chords in the key of F minor in a non-functional progression.

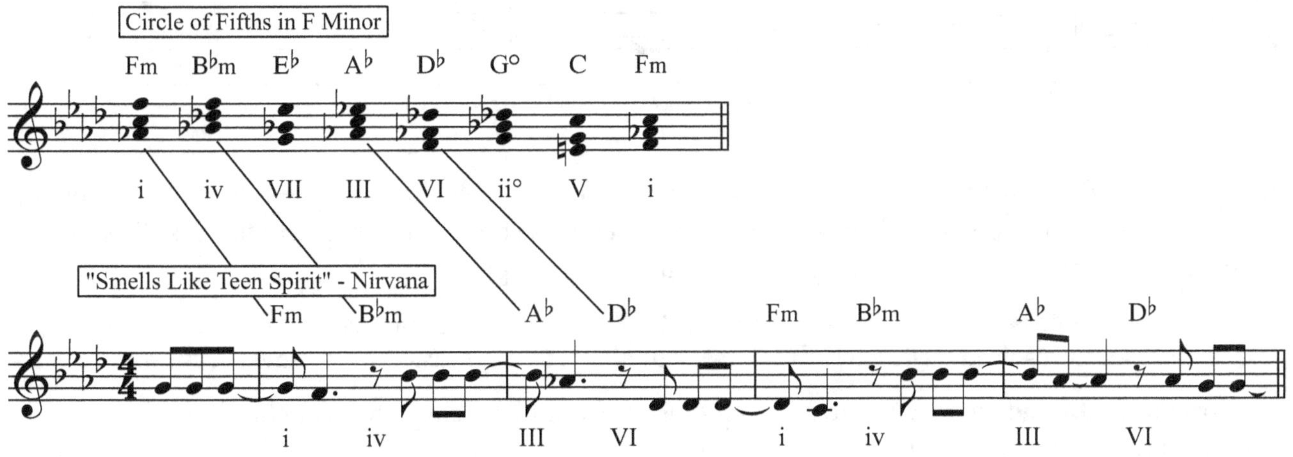

Harmonic Rhythm and Cadences

Harmonic rhythm refers to how quickly or slowly chords change. For instance, chords could change every four beats, every two beats, or on every single beat. The greatest songs typically include a variety of harmonic rhythm and skilled songwriters understand that changing harmonic rhythm is one way to distinguish between sections.

In the opening of Billy Joel's "Uptown Girl," some chords last for four beats whereas others only last for two beats. Notice that the change in harmonic rhythm occurs at the end of the four-measure phrase to help organize the phrase structure.

In Stevie Wonder's song, "If It's Magic," from the *Songs in the Key of Life* album, the harmonic rhythm helps to distinguish between different sections. At the opening, the chords consistently change every two beats. Then, in the bridge, the harmonic rhythm accelerates so that the chords change every beat, creating an unmistakable sense of forward momentum.

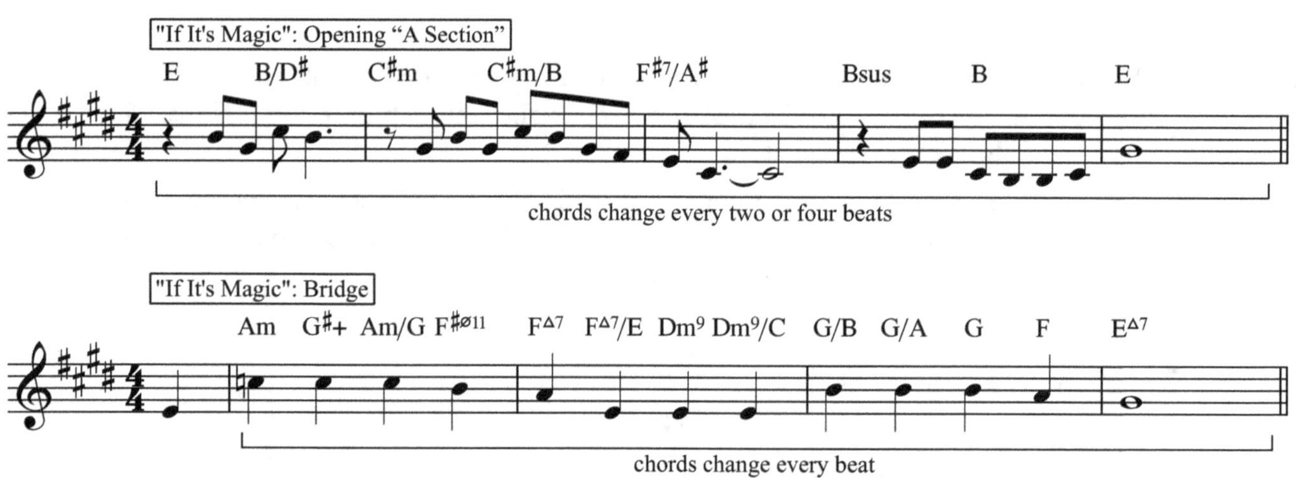

Cadences are chord progressions that give a sense of finality to a phrase. Think of cadences as musical punctuation, the harmonic periods and commas that allow a brief pause before continuing to the next thought. There are three types of cadences that are particularly useful for songwriters:

1. A **half cadence** is a progression that ends on the V chord. It functions as a "cliffhanger" that creates an unresolved feeling. Half cadences often launch the music into the next section.

2. An **authentic cadence** is a progression that moves from the V chord to the I chord, producing a traditional sense of finality.

3. A **plagal cadence** is a progression that moves from the IV chord to the I chord, establishing finality with a sound typical of a gospel or blues tradition. Plagal cadences are sometimes jokingly referred to as the "amen cadence" because the same chords are used for the congregation to sing "amen" after a hymn in church.

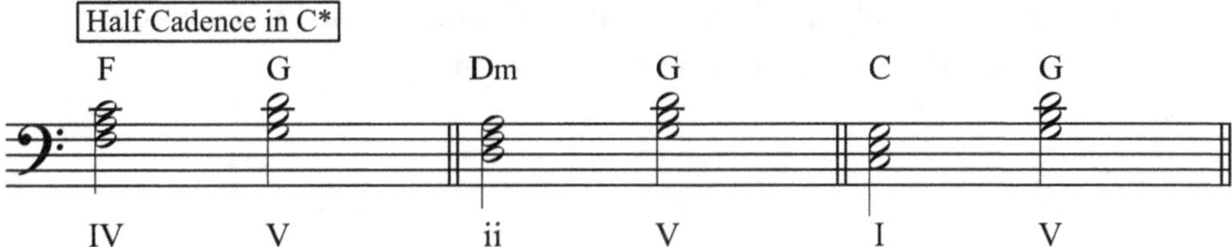

* Any progression ending in V qualifies as a half cadence.
The IV, ii, and I are chords that commonly precede the V.

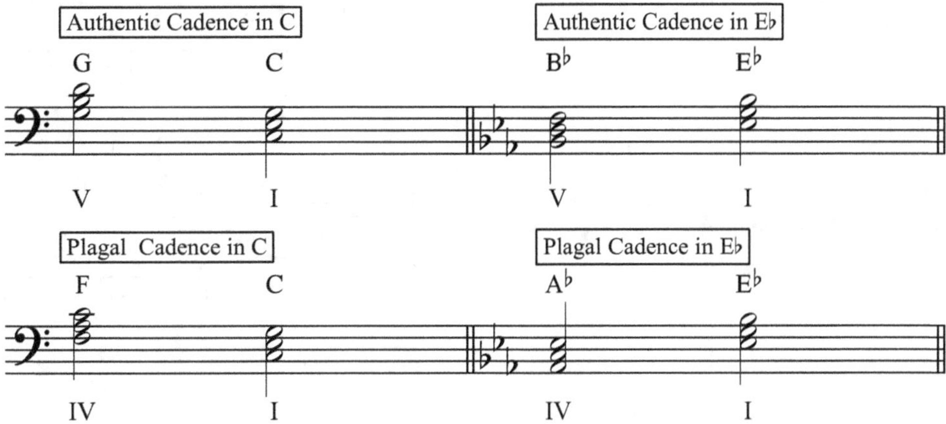

Harmonic rhythm frequently accelerates leading into cadences, building a bit of tension before settling into a resolution. In Willie Nelson's "Crazy," made famous by Patsy Cline, chords last for four beats each until the music begins preparing for a cadence. In the last four measures, to propel the music into the final authentic cadence, the chords change every two beats.

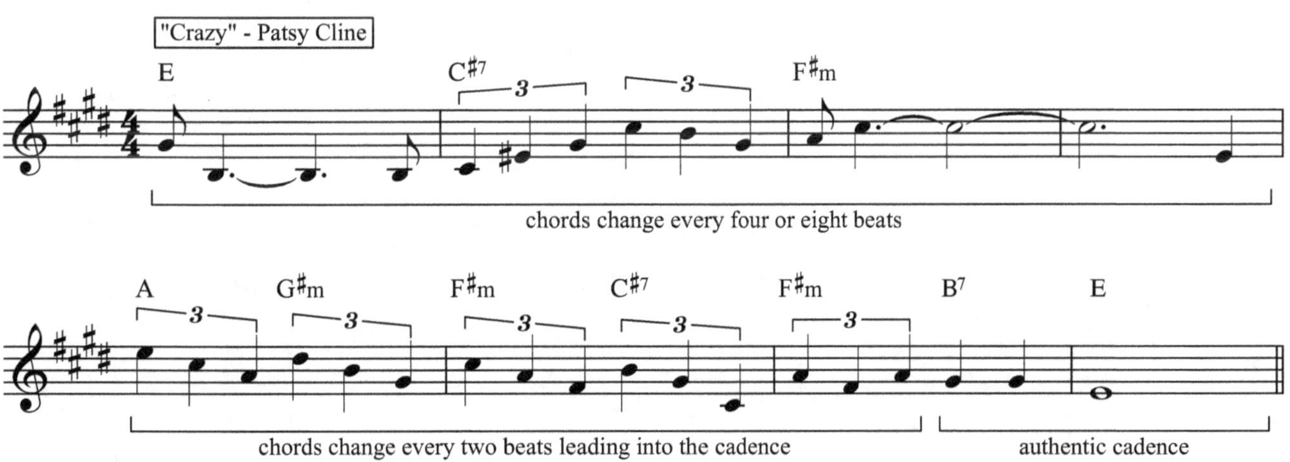

The plagal cadences in the chorus of the Beatles' anthem, "Let It Be," are an important element in creating the song's gospel, bluesy tone. The final plagal cadence includes harmonic embellishments that accelerate the harmonic rhythm and give the end of the chorus a sense of finality.

Takeaways

1. The diatonic triads in each key are the harmonic palette with which many songwriters paint.

2. Learning the diatonic circle of fifths is a great exercise to figure out how harmony tends to move, especially for any song with a Great American Songbook flavor.

3. Minor keys hold more possibilities than major keys because of the varied possibilities for the sixth and seventh scale degrees in the natural, harmonic, and melodic minor scales.

4. Harmonic rhythm refers to how fast or slow the chords change. Sophisticated songwriters vary the harmonic rhythm throughout a song to distinguish between sections and to emphasize cadences.

5. Cadences are musical resting places that separate musical phrases in the same way that punctuation organizes sentences. Songwriters should understand how to form and use authentic, half, and plagal cadences.

Practice

1. Write the diatonic triads for each key indicated.

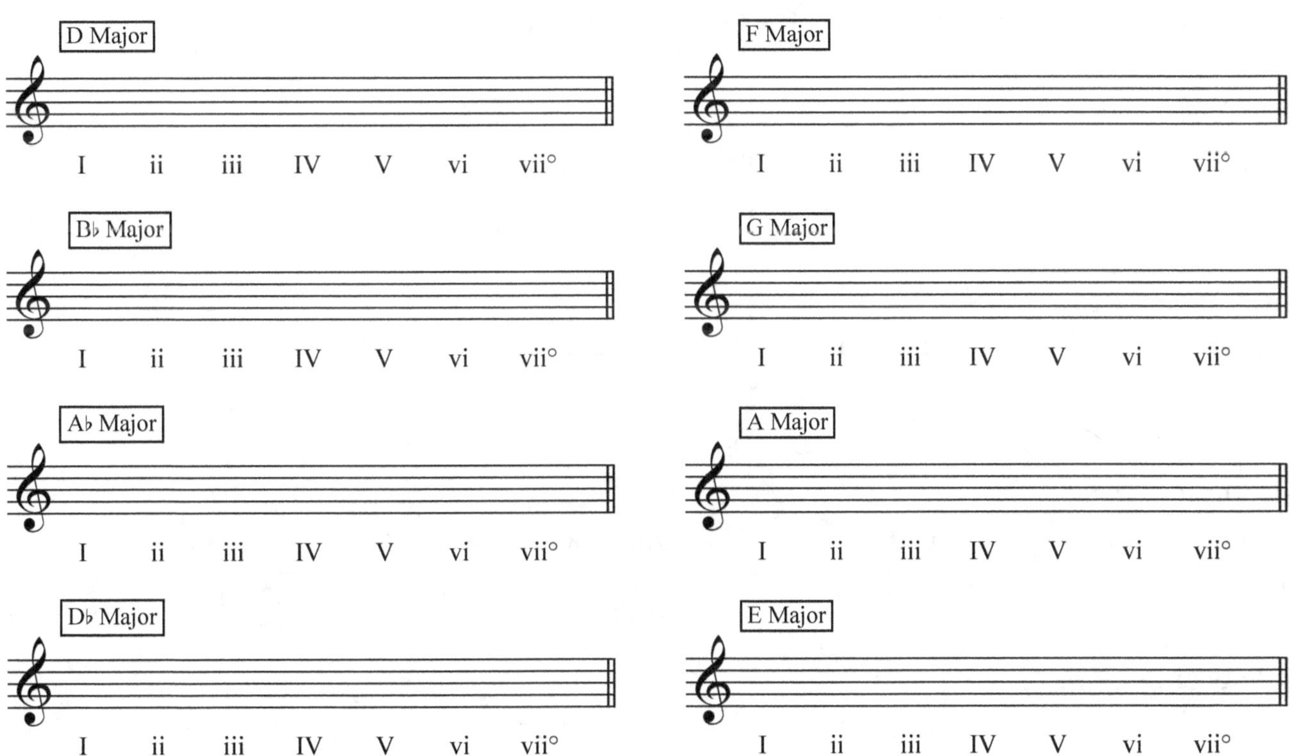

2. Write the diatonic circle of fifths for each key given. Write either triads in root position or triads in close inversions.

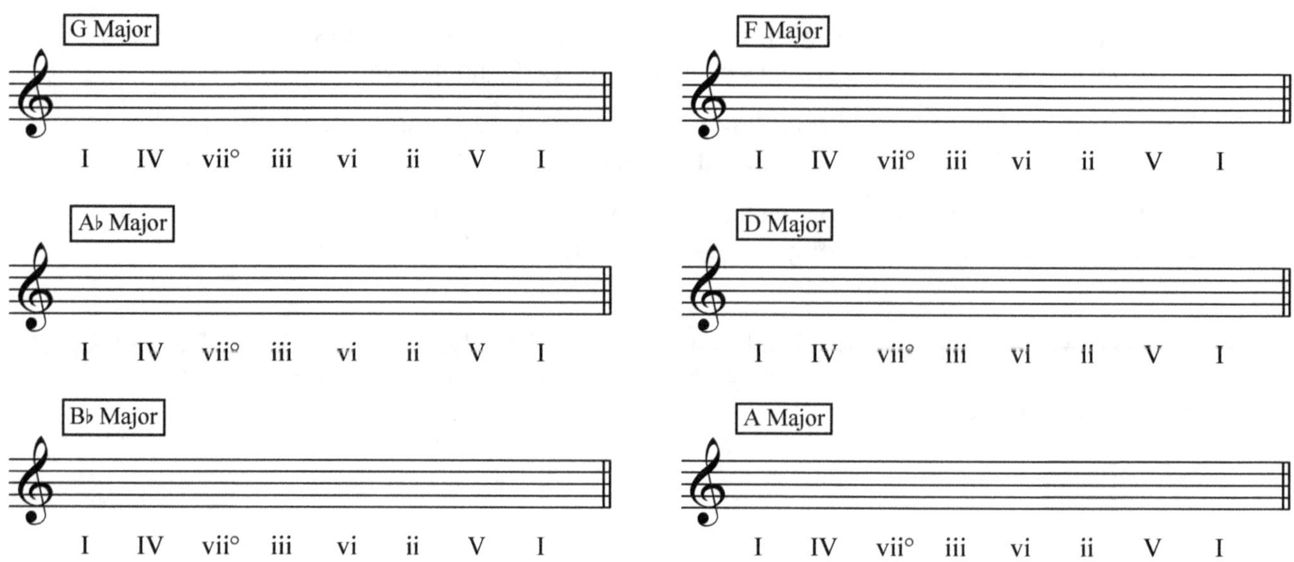

3. Analyze the Roman numerals of the following (simplified) chord progressions from Beatles songs. Remember to indicate major chords (I, IV, V) with capital letters and minor chords (ii, iii, iv) with lowercase letters. The first one is done for you.

Hey Jude (Key: F)

Chords:	F	C	C	F	B♭	F	C	F
Analysis:	I	V	V	I	IV	I	V	I

Let It Be (Key: C)

Chords:	C	G	Am	F	C	G	F	C
Analysis:								

Hello, Goodbye (Key: C)

Chords:	F	C	G	Am	G	Am	G	G	C
Analysis:									

Yellow Submarine (Key: G)

Chords:	D	G	Am	D	D	G	Am	D
Analysis:								

Here, There and Everywhere (Key: G)

Chords:	G	Am	Bm	C	G	Am	Bm	C
Analysis:								

Octopus' Garden (Key: E)

Chords: E   C#m   A   B   E   C#m   A   B

Analysis:

4. Write the triads in order for each minor key indicated in order.

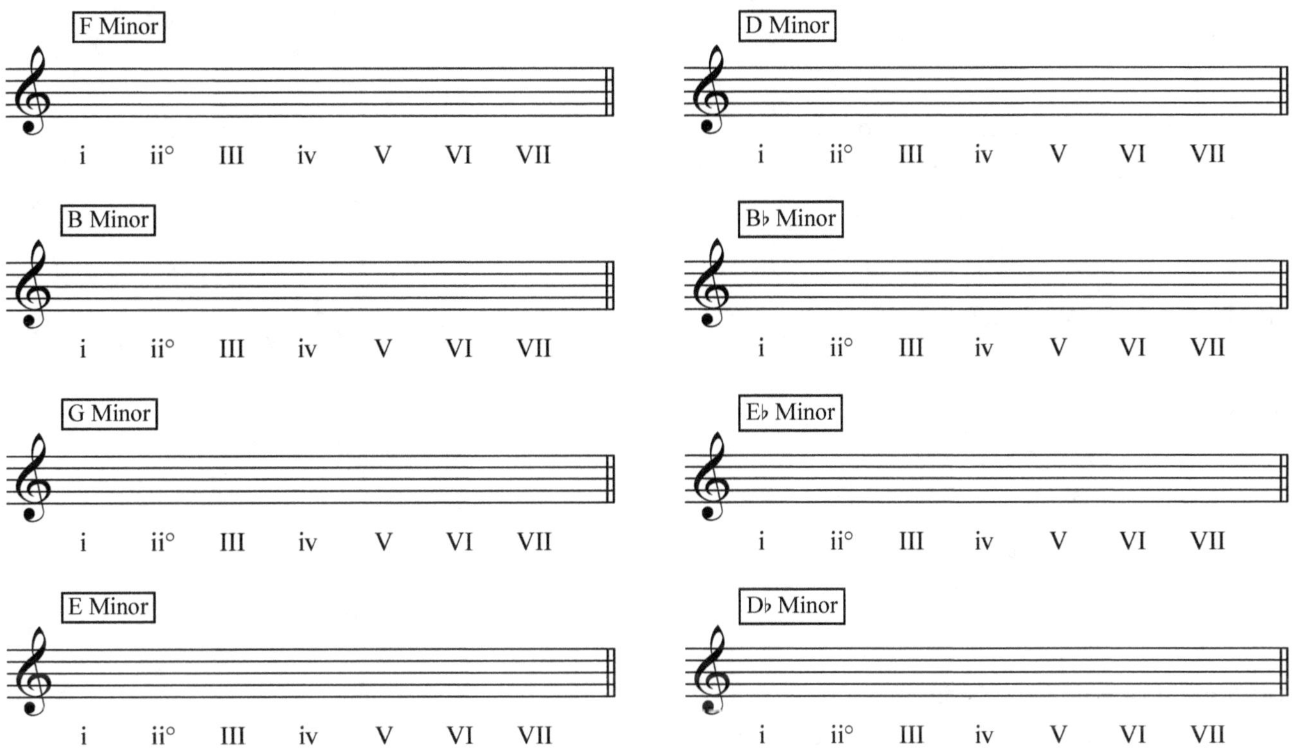

5. Write triads in the circle of fifths for each minor key given. Use triads in root position or triads in inversions as demonstrated.

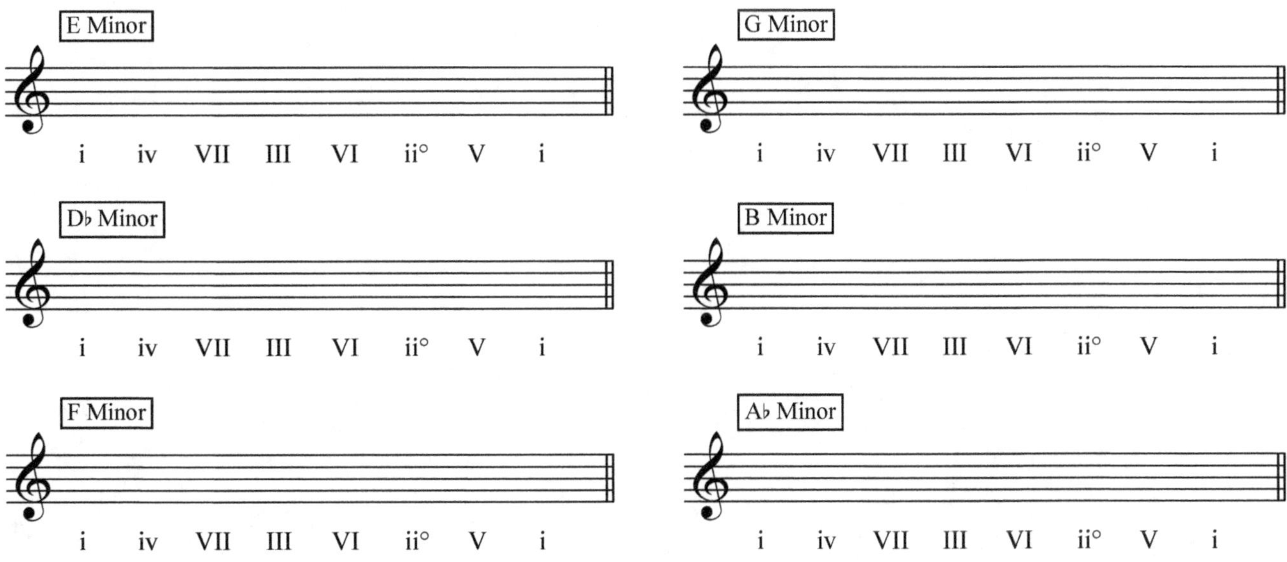

6. Analyze the Roman Numerals of the following (simplified) chord progressions from songs by Lady Gaga. Remember to indicate major chords (III, V, VI, VII) with capital letters and minor chords (i, iv) with lowercase letters. The first one is done for you.

Just Dance (verse) (Key: C minor)

Chords: Cm   E♭   B♭   Fm

Analysis:

Bad Romance (intro) (Key: A minor)

Chords: F   G   Am   C

Analysis:

Telephone (Key: A minor)

Chords: F   G   Am   C

Analysis:

Poker Face (chorus) (Key: G minor)

Chords: Gm   E♭   B♭   F

Analysis:

Applause (chorus) (key: G minor)

Chords: Gm   F   E♭   Cm   F   Gm

Analysis:

Paparazzi (chorus) (key: F minor/A♭ major – analyze in F minor)

Chords: A♭   E♭   Fm   D♭   A♭   E♭   Fm   D♭

Analysis:

7. Create your own four-measure progression using triads belonging to the suggested key. Write one chord symbol in each box and notice the changing harmonic rhythm. Finally, finish by executing the suggested cadence.

If you are comfortable with notation, write the notes for each chord on the staff.

7. Similes and Metaphors

Once you start studying similes and metaphors, it's easy to go a little bit crazy realizing that nearly *everything* people say can be interpreted through the lens of comparison. We call the bottoms of the table "legs" because we're comparing the table to an animal that "stands" on four legs. We say a situation is "fishy" when there's something hard to ignore about it, like the hard-to-ignore scent emanating from a fish. We say that someone kind has a "heart of gold," one that's pure, shining, and highly valued, like the precious metal. And it doesn't end there: we compare someone who stays up late to the nocturnal owl, describe round vegetables as having "heads" like humans, and insist that we can't "stand" someone as though their presence makes it hard to remain upright.

The new words people have invented to describe computer technology have relied heavily on the language of comparison. It's as though imagining new technology through the lens of familiar concepts helps people understand the concepts faster. Our hard drives become a new version of our offices, as we save "files" into "folders," and eventually move them into the "trash" or "recycling bin." We "scroll" across the screen, mimicking the unrolling of an ancient scroll, we "copy" and "paste" text from one document to another, and we save items to buy into a "shopping cart." When something goes wrong, a computer "crashes" like a vehicle, gets a "virus" like a human, or "freezes" like a lake in winter.

For songwriters, comparisons help keep language fresh, invent unexpected images, and engage the listener in deep imagination. The following chapters examine similes and metaphors in the songwriting tradition and suggest creative ways to use comparisons to enrich the language of your lyrics.

Simile and Metaphor Basics

Similes and metaphors are two methods of comparison that help a writer to create vivid, evocative images for their audience. **Similes** compare two unlike objects using the words "like" and "as," whereas **metaphors** compare two unlike objects without qualifying words. Comparing a face to a rose, a simile would say, "Your face is like a rose" whereas a metaphor would say, "Your face is a rose." Similes are, in a sense, true: your face might be *like* a rose, in that it is beautiful and round. On the other hand, strictly speaking, metaphors are false: no matter how beautiful your face is, it is not, in fact, a rose.

The word "unlike" is a surprisingly important detail in the definition. The statement "that shirt is like a sweater" is not a simile, or at least, it's not a very good one. To say, "that red is like a pink," similarly falls short. In fact, these statements seem to be correcting the identification – maybe that *is* a sweater rather than a shirt or that color *should actually* be called pink, not red – rather than evoking imaginative imagery.

Tenor and Vehicle

The rhetorician I.A. Richards suggests identifying the two parts of these comparisons, which he names a "tenor" and a "vehicle". The **tenor** is the thing being described whereas the **vehicle** is the external concept introduced to describe it. In the example, "Your face is like a rose," *face* is the tenor and *rose* is the vehicle.

Each of the famous metaphors from songs can be divided into a tenor and a vehicle:

Baby, you're a firework ("Firework" – Katy Perry)

> **Tenor:** you
> **Vehicle:** a firework

You are my fire ("I Want it That Way" – Backstreet Boys)

> **Tenor:** you
> **Vehicle:** fire

You ain't nothin' but a hound dog ("Hound Dog" – Elvis)

> **Tenor:** you
> **Vehicle:** hound dog

You are the sunshine of my life ("You Are the Sunshine of My Life" – Stevie Wonder)

> **Tenor:** you
> **Vehicle:** sunshine

With an understanding of the tenor and vehicle, you can consider how to maximize both parts of a comparison to achieve more exciting results.

Writing Effective Tenors

In each of the previous examples, the tenor is a person, specifically "you." The prevalence of "you" in these metaphors is somewhat unsurprising because songwriters often write about people, especially objects of their love or desire. However, songwriters can also consider other types of tenors, such as places, objects, or ideas. The song "Luck Be a Lady," from Guys and Dolls uses a concept, luck, as the tenor and a lady as the vehicle:

> *Luck, let a gentleman see*
> *Just how nice a dame you can be*
> *I know the way you've treated other guys you've been with*
> *Luck be a lady with me*

Tenor: luck
Vehicle: a lady

Tenors do not necessarily have to be nouns. Songwriters can use an adjective as the tenor to create an **adjectival simile** or choose a verb as a tenor to create an **adverbial simile**. These formulations are always similes because syntax requires the use of "like" or "as" to make these comparisons.

How does an adjectival simile work? The tenor is an adjective that describes a single aspect or quality of something. For instance, one could say, *Your hat is as red as a rose.* In the example, what's being compared is the *redness* of the hat, not the hat itself. Although the hat probably differs from a rose in nearly every conceivable way: it has no thorns, does not bloom, and does not symbolize romance, the simile isolates their shared redness.

Your hat is as red as a rose.

> **Tenor:** the redness of the hat
> **Vehicle:** the redness of the rose

In the song, "My Cherie Amour," Stevie Wonder creates an adjectival metaphor that evokes the freshness of summer.

My Cherie Amour, lovely as a summer's day

> **Tenor:** the loveliness of "my Cherie Amour"
> **Vehicle:** the loveliness of a summer's day

At first, listeners might think Wonder is comparing "my Cherie Amour" directly to "a summer's day," but in reality, only one aspect, her loveliness, is being compared. The importance of this distinction becomes clearer in the next line:

My cherie amour, distant as the Milky Way

> **Tenor:** distance of "my Cherie Amour"
> **Vehicle:** distance of the Milky Way

In this example, it does not feel exactly like saying "my Cherie Amour is like the Milky Way." If this were the lyric, listeners might wonder, "Is she really expansive? Does she have planets? Does she have stars?" It is crucial to see that only the *distance* is being compared.

An **adverbial simile** creates a comparison that helps listeners to imagine an action. For instance, when someone says, "You sing like a bird," they are comparing how you sing to how a bird sings. In Miley Cyrus' hit song, "Wrecking Ball," an adverbial simile creates the song's most iconic line:

You came in like a wrecking ball

> **Tenor:** how you came in
> **Vehicle:** how a wrecking ball swings

The way you entered was destructive, sudden, and flattened everything in your path! Because of the strength of the metaphor, Cyrus is able to tell the whole story of the song in just one line while conjuring a dynamic mental image.

An adverbial metaphor in "On Your Wings," by Sam Beam (Iron and Wine), summons poetic beauty through the detailed richness of both his tenor and vehicle.

How we rise when we're born like the ravens from the corn

> **Tenor:** how we come into the world ("rise") when we're born
> **Vehicle:** the way ravens rise from corn

Beam's simile conveys a feeling of peace, awe, and holiness. Just as the ravens rise from the cornfield simultaneously, in instinctive unity, souls enter the world with a sense of cosmic order.

Writing Vivid Vehicles

Vehicles and Tone

Vehicles are called "vehicles" because they move the lyric to a new place. When choosing a vehicle, the first consideration is **tone**, or how you want the song to feel. Should the song feel romantic, spooky, exciting, epic, melancholy, etc.? A vehicle, in addition to making a comparison, creates a mood. For instance, what is the difference between:

A. *Your shirt is red as a rose*
B. *Your shirt is red as blood*

Taken literally, although these metaphors both define a purple-red hue, they would play very differently in a song. Letter A would suggest romantic undertones whereas letter B might arouse suspicion.

What about these two?

A. *The clouds are ships floating above us*
B. *The clouds are leaky ships floating above us*

Again, the actual comparison is more or less the same, but whereas letter A generates a sense of peaceful slowness, letter B evokes the panic of an impending disaster.

The lyrics for the song "Midnight Sun" by Johnny Mercer and Johnny Burke masterfully introduce vehicles that create a very specific tone:

> *Your lips were like a red and ruby chalice*
> *warmer than the summer night*
> *The clouds were like an alabaster palace*
> *rising to a snowy height*
> *Each star its own aurora borealis*
> *Suddenly you held me tight*

The vehicles are "red and ruby chalice" (a chalice is a fancy drinking glass), "summer night," "alabaster palace" (alabaster is a white mineral often used for ornamentation), and "aurora borealis." Regardless of what they modify, the inclusion of these images generates a tone of luxury, expanse, and ease. They place the love story in a fantasyland of storybook love, deserving of epic descriptions.

Extended Vehicles

Vehicles can stretch beyond a single word or a short phrase. They can extend as long as the writer chooses. In fact, the poet John Milton famously wrote vehicles in *Paradise Lost* that go on for multiple pages and contained stories within them.

Consider Katy Perry's line, "Baby, you're a firework." If a lyricist wanted to expand the vehicle, the result could look something like this:

- Baby, you're a firework that exploded too soon
- Baby, you're a firework that burst in my ear
- Baby, you're the last firework of the grand finale
- Baby, you're a firework that left only smoke for me to choke on
- Baby, you're an illegal firework I smuggled over state lines on the night that my dog died, even though I didn't hear the news until the next morning

In fact, Katy Perry does expand on a vehicle in a different part of "Firework." She opens the song with a question that includes a simile with an extended vehicle:

Do you ever feel like a plastic bag
Drifting through the wind, wanting to start again?

> **Tenor:** *the way you feel*
> **Vehicle:** *a plastic bag*
> **Extension:** *drifting through the wind, wanting to start again*

By extending the vehicle, Perry conjures not just the inert apathy of a plastic bag, but also the lost, wandering feeling of drifting on the wind. Similarly, the lyric for "All the Things You Are," a Great American Songbook tune by Jerome Kern and Oscar Hammerstein II, consists almost entirely of metaphors with extended vehicles:

You are the promised kiss of springtime
That makes the lonely winter seem long

> **Tenor:** you
> **Vehicle:** the promised kiss of springtime
> **Extension:** that makes the lonely winter seem long

You are the breathless hush of evening
That trembles on the brink of a lovely song

> **Tenor:** you
> **Vehicle:** the breathless hush of evening
> **Extension:** that trembles on the brink of a lovely song

The extended vehicles give the lyricist an opportunity to infuse the song with poetry. The natural, delicate descriptions ("promised," "breathless," "trembles") express tenderness, hope, and the thrill of possibility.

Implied Vehicles

A vehicle does not have to be explicitly stated to create a comparison. By using words that are associated with a vehicle, a skilled writer can imply a comparison without stating it outright. Consider the following examples:

My soul is blooming with new, brightly colored flowers

Although a comparison is clearly being made here, because the vehicle is implied, it's not immediately clear to what the soul is being compared. We only know that the soul is likened to a place where flowers bloom. Since flowers bloom in meadows, we can guess that the implied vehicle is a meadow.

> **Tenor:** my soul
> **Vehicle:** a meadow (implied)

The tides of my mind ebb and flow relentlessly

Tides occur only in one place: an ocean. Even though the word "ocean" is never stated, it serves as the vehicle in this metaphor.

> **Tenor:** my mind
> **Vehicle:** an ocean (implied)

Types of Similes and Metaphors

Similes and metaphors do not always have to arrive in the form of simple declarations. To create different nuances in tones, songwriters can choose to present their comparisons in the form of questions, hypotheticals, analogies, and more.

Questions

Asking a simile or metaphor as a question softens the comparison, implying that the comparison may or may not be true. For instance, the previous section included an extended metaphor in which Katy Perry asks, "Do you ever feel like a plastic bag drifting through the wind?" Perry is not imposing the metaphor but rather asking the listener to consider it.

In the song, "Like a Rolling Stone," Bob Dylan creates a simile within a question:

> *How does it feel, how does it feel*
> *To be without a home*
> *Like a complete unknown*
> *Like a rolling stone?*

In this question, Dylan is not so much asking whether the "you" of the song feels like a rolling stone, but instead wonders what effect it has on them. Placing the simile in the context of a question lessens the feeling of direct attribution or accusation and heightens the sense of curiosity.

Hypotheticals

Songs frequently propose the possibility of a comparison instead of stating it emphatically, often starting with the word "if." For instance, in Pharrell's song "Happy," he directs the listeners:

> *Clap along if you feel*
> *Like a room without a roof*

The listeners are not told that they feel "like a room without a roof," but are given the option to decide for themselves. In the song "If I Were a Bell" from Frank Loesser's *Guys and Dolls*, an inebriated character, Sarah Brown, expresses her unbridled enthusiasm by imagining herself as ecstatic inanimate objects.

> *If I were a bell, I'd be ringing*
> *If I were a lamp, I'd light*
> *If I were a banner, I'd wave*
> *And if I were a watch, I'd start*
> *Popping my strings*

In the context of the musical, these hypotheticals are particularly effective because the conservative Brown prefers to stay in denial about her ecstatic feelings. Using both hypotheticals and metaphors gives her some plausible deniability.

Analogies

Analogies are two-part metaphors, often stated in the form "A is to B as C is to D." For instance, Fiona Apple's song "Hot Knife" presents an analogy in hypothetical form:

> *If I'm butter*
> *If I'm butter*
> *If I'm butter*
> *Then he's a hot knife*

Tenor: I
Vehicle: butter

Tenor: he
Vehicle: hot knife

In Apple's analogy, there are two metaphors: "I am butter" and "he is a hot knife." These metaphors are presented as an analogy because they are interdependent. She is only butter because she's so easily "cut through" by him, and he's a hot knife only to "cut" her.

Apple also uses a series of memorable analogies to dramatize a toxic relationship in her song "Werewolf":

> *I could liken you to a werewolf the way you left me for dead*
> *But I admit that I provided a full moon*
> *And I could liken you to a shark the way you bit off my head*
> *But then again, I was waving around a bleeding open wound*
>
> *And you are such a super guy 'til the second you get a whiff of me*
> *We're like a wishing well and a bolt of electricity*

This passage contains three analogies:

Analogy 1

Tenor: you   **Tenor:** I
Vehicle: werewolf   **Vehicle:** full moon

Analogy 2

Tenor: you   **Tenor:** I
Vehicle: shark   **Vehicle:** someone with a bloody wound

Analogy 3

Tenor: one partner   **Tenor:** other partner
Vehicle: wishing well   **Vehicle:** bolt of electricity

Using analogies, Apple is able to bemoan the combustibility of the relationship while balancing the two sides to imply equal culpability for the explosive situation.

In Gregory Alan Isakov's song, "Big Black Car," he starts his verses with analogies that describe complex relationships.

> *You were a phonograph, I was a kid*
> *I sat with an ear close, just listening*

Tenor: you   **Tenor:** I
Vehicle: phonograph   **Vehicle:** kid (listening)

> *You were a dancer and I was a rag*
> *The song in my head, it was all that I had*

Tenor: you   **Tenor:** I
Vehicle: dancer   **Vehicle:** rag

These nostalgic analogies convey a closely interconnected relationship between the two characters in which one provides the music and the other listens and dances.

Nouns as Adjectives

Metaphors aren't always presented as two balanced sides of an equal scale. Instead, nouns can be used in place of adjectives to modify other nouns, implying a metaphor. For instance, in the song "Do I Do," Stevie Wonder could have used adjectives like "sweet" or "tasty" to describe "kisses" to create phrases like "tasty kisses" or "sweet kisses." Instead, his lyric is:

> *Yes, I've got some candy kisses for your lips*

In the phrase, "candy kisses," "candy" is used in place of an adjective, even though the word is a noun. The result is an implied metaphor with "kisses" as the tenor and "candy" as the vehicle. Through the metaphor, listeners perceive all of the adjectives associated with candy, including sweet and tasty, through a vivid and concise phrase.

John Mayer uses similar imagery in his first big hit, "Your Body is a Wonderland." In this formulation, Mayer creates two metaphors that imply that a body is sensually delicious:

> *One pair of candy lips and*
> *Your bubblegum tongue*

Tenor: lips
Vehicle: candy

Tenor: tongue
Vehicle: bubblegum

In Oasis' famous anthem, "Champagne Supernova," the titular phrase has a noun in the adjective position.

> *Someday you will find me*
> *Caught beneath the landslide*
> *In a champagne supernova*
> *A champagne supernova in the sky*

Although the meaning of the phrase is poetic and open for interpretation, it evokes an explosion of stars resembling the bubbles in a glass of champagne or a huge event like a supernova being celebrated with champagne toasts.

Settings

Because writers are afforded so few words in songs and poems, any mention of the setting often serves as a metaphor for the singer's internal state. Seasons are a particularly common example. Spring signifies new love, summer represents growth and energy, autumn indicates decay and nostalgia, and winter means death. When the setting or season is used as the vehicle in a metaphor, the implied tenor is the speaker's state of mind.

For instance, in the English lyric of the jazz standard "Autumn Leaves" (the song is originally written in French), the singer doesn't clearly define their emotions but lets the listener infer the emotions from the seasonal changes.

> *The falling leaves*   *I see your lips*
> *Drift by my window*   *The summer kisses*
> *The autumn leaves*   *The sunburnt hands*
> *Of red and gold*   *I used to know*

Tenor: the speaker's state of mind
Vehicle: autumn/decay

Autumn's arrival serves as a metaphor for the nostalgia of the speaker who is remembering a lost love. The mood of autumn is contrasted with the joy of warmer seasons, indicated by "summer" kisses (notice the noun used as an adjective) and "sunburnt" hands.

The bleakness of winter perfectly matches the mood in the Counting Crows' song, "A Long December" in which the hopelessness of the lyric reflects the barrenness of the natural world.

> *The smell of hospitals in winter*
> *And the feeling that it's all a lot of oysters*
> *But no pearls*
> *All at once you look across a crowded room*
> *To see the way that light attaches to a girl*

Additionally, the obvious metaphor of the seasons can even help to draw a contrast between external and internal states. In "Spring is Here," by Richard Rodgers and Lorenz Hart, the singer wonders why they don't feel happy, despite the arrival of spring.

> *Spring is here*
> *Why doesn't my heart go dancing?*
> *Spring is here*

When choosing when and where to set your songs, consider making the setting a metaphor for the singer's internal mood. You might find that the listener intuits many of the important emotions without needing to hear them stated explicitly.

Extended Metaphors

Sometimes a metaphor extends for an entire stanza or even an entire song. If a metaphor lasts for more than just a couple of lines, it can be called an **extended metaphor**.

For instance, the 2011 song "Stereo Hearts" is based entirely on the metaphor comparing the tenor "heart" to the vehicle "stereo." Each section of the song expands upon the metaphor from a different angle.

> *If I was just another dusty record on the shelf*
> *Would you blow me off and play me like everybody else?*
> *If I asked you to scratch my back, could you manage that?*
> *Like yea [scratched], check it Travie, I can handle that*
> *Furthermore, I apologize for any skipping tracks*
> *It's just the last girl that played me left a couple cracks*
> *I used to used to, used to, now I'm over that*
> *'Cause holding grudges over love is ancient artifacts*

Britney Spears' 2008 hit, "Circus," compares a pop career to a circus using an extended metaphor in which Spears compares herself to different roles in a carnival show, including a ringleader and a lion tamer.

> *All eyes on me in the center of the ring just like a circus*
> *When I crack that whip everybody gon' trip just like a circus*
> *Don't stand there watching me, follow me, show me what you can do*
> *Everybody let go, we can make a dance floor just like a circus*

Special Comparisons

Personification

Personification is a comparison in which the tenor is something non-human and the vehicle is a person. Writers use personification to give human attributes to objects or emotions. For instance, in the lyric from George and Ira Gershwin's song, "Love Walked In," love is being given human attributes.

> *Love walked right in and drove the shadows away*
> *Love walked right in and brought my sunniest day*

Tenor: love
Vehicle: a person

Since love cannot literally walk, personifying the emotion sparks a memorable mental image for the listener.

Stevie Wonder's song, "Another Star," employs personification in the bridge to bring a new perspective to a familiar subject: falling in love.

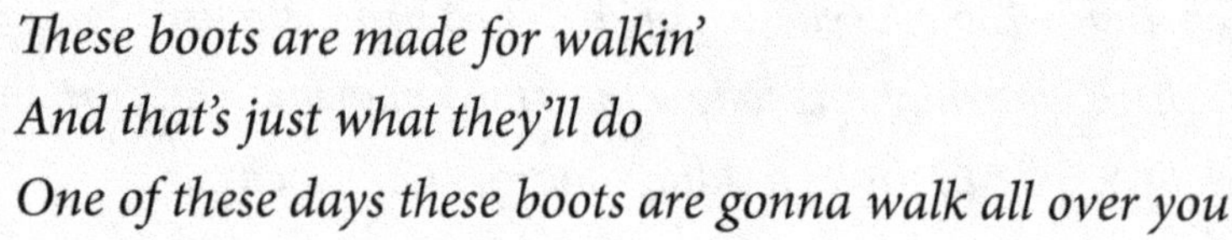

Wonder describes the feeling of falling in love while avoiding many of the most tired clichés. By personifying his emotions, Wonder can describe his emotions with more nuance, for instance, distinguishing between demanding and informing.

Synecdoche and Metonymy

Synecdoche and metonymy are two metaphorical ways of replacing a subject with something that represents the subject. **Synecdoche** is a device in which a part of something is used to represent the whole. Here are a few examples:

- "His feet followed me." (*he* followed me, but he is being represented by his feet)
- "The tires drove on, from Maine to Maryland." (*a whole car* drove, represented by the tires)
- "That wagging tail was his best friend." (a *dog* with a wagging tail was his best friend)

In the Nancy Sinatra song, "These Boots Are Made for Walkin'," the boots serve as a synecdoche representing a person.

> These boots are made for walkin'
> And that's just what they'll do
> One of these days these boots are gonna walk all over you

The focus on the boots makes the singer's march to triumph seem inevitable and encourages the audience to picture the song from a unique angle, the ground level.

While synecdoche uses a part to represent the whole, **metonymy** uses a representative symbol to replace a noun. Symbols used for metonymy are often commonly understood representations.

- "Since the cradle, he has been difficult." ("the cradle" is a symbol for infancy)
- "I can't wait to be in the limelight" ("the limelight" is a symbol for fame)
- "Someday, I will have your heart" ("heart" is a symbol for love or affection)

In the Stevie Wonder/Paul McCartney song, "Ebony and Ivory," ebony and ivory function as symbols for African Americans and Caucasians.

> *Ebony and ivory*
> *Live together in perfect harmony*
> *Side by side on my piano keyboard*
> *Oh lord, why don't we?*

Dolly Parton's song "9 to 5" expresses several clichés of professional life through representative symbols.

> *They let you dream just to watch 'em shatter*
> *You're just a step on the bossman's ladder*
> *But you've got dreams he'll never take away*
> *In the same boat with a lot of your friends*
> *Waitin' for the day your ship'll come in*
> *And the tide's gonna turn an' it's all gonna roll your way*

In Parton's song, the "ladder" stands in for professional advancement, the "boat" represents economic status, "your ship" symbolizes a financial windfall, and "the tide" signifies economic prospects.

Takeaways

1. Similes and metaphors are everywhere. They are essential tools for adding detail and color to a song.

2. Similes and metaphors compare unlike objects. The more unlike the objects are, the more interesting the comparison will be.

3. The word "tenor" denotes what is being compared whereas the word "vehicle" denotes what is being brought into the song to make a comparison.

4. Tenors don't have to be people – they can be things, places, or even ideas. Adjectival and adverbial metaphors use adjectives and verbs as tenors.

5. Vehicles can stretch for as long as the songwriter wants or be completely absent, implied through contextual language.

6. Similes and metaphors can take many forms including questions, conditional statements, analogies, and settings.

Practice

1. Identify the tenor and the vehicle for the following similes or metaphors. Vehicles may be implied.

   A. She is a firecracker.

   Tenor: Vehicle:

   B. Your face is like a lily.

   Tenor: Vehicle:

   C. After the party, her bed became a church for her to worship in.

   Tenor: Vehicle:

   D. He shines like a star.

   Tenor: Vehicle:

   E. Elizabeth is as sneaky as a fox.

   Tenor: Vehicle:

   F. Juan sails through life on easy seas.

   Tenor: Vehicle:

   G. Your sunset eyes are beautiful.

   Tenor: Vehicle:

   H. The accused slithers by the jury.

   Tenor: Vehicle:

   I. Joshua stared at the cowboy sky.

   Tenor: Vehicle:

   J. The car roared and prepared to chase its prey.

   Tenor: Vehicle:

2. Extend the vehicle of these similes or metaphors to create a more specific comparison. The first example is done for you.

   A. The breakup hurts like a papercut.

   Extended Vehicle: The breakup hurts like a papercut on the tip of her pinky finger.

   B. I think of you as much as my childhood dog.

   With Extended Vehicle:

   C. Her outfit was a work of art.

   With Extended Vehicle:

D. When she saw him, her heart started to sink.
With Extended Vehicle:

E. Could you be like a house to me?
With Extended Vehicle:

F. Maria bloomed like a flower.
With Extended Vehicle:

G. My body is like a sports car.
With Extended Vehicle:

3. Take the following statements and turn them into a metaphor or simile by adding a vehicle that is not included in the initial statement. The first comparison is written for you.

A. Statement: He is destructive.
Simile/Metaphor: He is a tornado, uprooting everything in his path.

B. Statement: Adele is beautiful.
Simile/Metaphor:

C. Statement: The night is full of stars.
Simile/Metaphor:

D. Statement: You're ignoring me.
Simile/Metaphor:

E. Statement: Dolores is a good friend.
Simile/Metaphor:

F. Statement: The city streets are empty tonight.
Simile/Metaphor:

G. Statement: The moon is very bright.
Simile/Metaphor:

H. Statement: Your story is very confusing.
Simile/Metaphor:

I. Statement: The music is very beautiful.
Simile/Metaphor:

4. Rewrite the metaphor provided as either an adjectival or adverbial metaphor by changing the tenor. This is a creative exercise, there is not a single correct answer. The first metaphor is rewritten for you.

    A. He is a cheetah.

       Rewrite: He runs as fast as a cheetah.

    B. You are a star.

       Rewrite:

    C. You are rock 'n' roll.

       Rewrite:

    D. My mind is a circus.

       Rewrite:

    E. Her thoughts are like an airport.

       Rewrite:

    F. My feet are like soldiers.

       Rewrite:

    G. Love is like a war.

       Rewrite:

    H. My parents are like butterflies.

       Rewrite:

8. The Lyricist's Toolbox

Scan Here for
Chapter 8 Page

Listeners often assume that a great song is an intentionally crafted window into a songwriter's soul. Of course, many songs aim to tell a story, express emotion, or make an argument. However, other songs can be the result of complex processes or randomized games that use language, not meaning, as their chief inspiration.

David Bowie describes creating lyrics through a "cut-up" method. He literally cuts paragraphs into small strips of paper using scissors, then forms a new narrative by placing the strips in a random order. According to Bowie, after randomizing the order, "You can use them as is or, if you have a craven need to not lose control, bounce off these ideas and write whole new sections." Bowie's use of the evocative word "craven" suggests that he relishes surrendering control of a song's precise meaning to the whims of language.

Bowie isn't alone. Kurt Cobain describes using a nearly identical process. He combines "lines from different poems I've written" to support a theme because he struggles to "come up with an idea of what a song is about." Ben Bridwell of Band of Horses seeks inspiration from the words that appear in crossword puzzles and friends' social media feeds. He describes finding inspiration in "anything else but my own thoughts" when brainstorming lyrical ideas. Justin Vernon of Bon Iver starts with open vowels that complement the melody, then finds words that match those vowel sounds. Vernon theorizes that this approach allows him to "surprise [himself] by what [he is] singing about" because he doesn't start with a fixed idea.

These **aleatoric methods** of songwriting demonstrate the beauty of unexpected combinations of words and unconventional relationships between ideas. Even when evading grammar rules or breaking logic, focusing on the raw power of language often produces evocative and poetic lyrics. To that end, this chapter dissects the smallest details of language: nouns, verbs, adjectives, adverbs, and more. Although you most likely know the textbook definitions of the core parts of speech, it's worth pausing to consider how to maximize the potential of each and every word in your song to craft more vivid and unpredictable lyrics.

Nouns

Nouns are the characters, settings, objects, and ideas that populate your song. From a grammatical perspective, nouns usually function as subjects or objects in a sentence. A **subject** performs the verb's action whereas an **object** receives it. To avoid excessively repeating the same nouns, writers often replace nouns with pronouns, words like "I," "you," "he," "she," "they," and "it" that act as placeholders for specific people, places, and things.

In the sentence, "The captain steers the boat," *captain* and *boat* are both nouns, with *captain* as the subject and *boat* as the object. The sentence could be modified to "He steers the boat," in which case *he* is a pronoun; or even "He steers it," which has two pronouns, *he* and *it*.

To place a song in a specific place, time, or cultural space, songwriters can use **proper nouns**, which name distinct, unique entities, including cities, states, or countries; books, albums, or works of art; celebrities or historical figures; and companies or brand names. Commercial genres like pop and rap often include proper nouns to make their songs current and signal an understanding of their intended audience. Knowing the same celebrities or brands signals in-group belonging, letting the audience know "this song is for *you*." For instance, when Ke$ha mentions "P. Diddy" and "a bottle of Jack" in her song, "TiK ToK," the audience infers that the 2009 song is directed towards young people who engage with pop culture and the club-scene night-life. The slang-y abbreviation "Jack" (for "Jack Daniels") conveys a casual, conversational tone and a comfort with giving brand names cultural meaning.

> *Wake up in the morning feeling like P Diddy*
> *Grab my glasses, I'm out the door, I'm gonna hit the city*
> *Before I leave, brush my teeth with a bottle of Jack*
> *'Cause when I leave for the night, I ain't coming back*

Taylor Swift creates a different effect by using a proper noun in her song, "Style":

> *You've got that James Dean daydream look in your eyes*

The reference to Dean, a star from a bygone era, creates an atmosphere of nostalgia and timelessness, and forms a memorable assonant rhyme with "daydream." Dean's specific reputation signals rebellious youth and a "style" that includes a clean-cut white t-shirt and a monochrome jacket. Finally, naming Dean, who famously died in a car crash, reinforces the danger indicated in the opening lines, which question whether the couple's long drive will "end in burning flames or paradise."

Perspective

Nouns introduce the question of **perspective**: who is narrating the song and to whom? Perspective is deeply related to a song's tone, and changing the perspective can make a song feel more or less personal, tender, or vulnerable. Consider the effects of using the three following types of perspective:

- In a **first-person perspective**, the narrator is the protagonist and uses the pronoun "I." In a **first-person plural perspective**, the narrator is a group of protagonists and uses the pronoun "we."

- In a **second-person perspective**, the story is presented from the listener's perspective and uses the pronoun "you."

- In a **third-person perspective**, a third party is the protagonist in the story and is named using "he," "she," or "they."

Songs most commonly use a first-person perspective. In the **confessional singer-songwriter tradition**, listeners assume that the singer is vulnerably telling their own story to a general audience. But songs don't have to be told from the perspective of the songwriter or sung without a particular listener in mind. Songs in Broadway musicals, for instance, are written to be sung by fictional characters, often to other fictional characters on stage. Songs in rock and pop can also play with the idea of perspective. Here are a few examples of famous songs that are notable for the perspective of the narrator and/or the specific audience being addressed

- "Space Oddity" by David Bowie: a series of conversations between Major Tom and "ground control"
- "Valerie" by Amy Winehouse: sung in the first person directed specifically to Valerie
- "Eleanor Rigby" by The Beatles: tells the stories of invented characters, mostly in the third person
- "Living for the City" by Stevie Wonder: a story narrated in the third person
- "Candle in the Wind" by Elton John: sung in the first person, directed towards Marilyn Monroe
- "Royals" by Lorde: the chorus primarily uses a first-person plural perspective
- "Try" by Colbie Caillat: sung in the second person
- "Put Your Records On" by Corinne Bailey Rae: sung in the first person, directed specifically to "you"

Using a second- or third-person perspective can be a practical tool for songwriters who feel uncomfortable sharing their feelings or telling their stories openly. Placing a song's stories or emotions in the mouth of a character often diminishes some of the anxiety that comes with frank self-expression.

Verbs

Verbs set your song's characters into motion. The verbs you choose determine how vibrant and alive your lyric feels. While the verb "to be" and its conjugations, including "am," "are," and "is," are the most common verbs, they passively describe a scene rather than putting anything into motion. **Action verbs**, verbs that express movement and change, make a lyric more dynamic and vigorous.

John Mayer's song, "The Heart of Life," uses action verbs to add drama and physicality to typically static feelings like "pain" and "love."

> *Pain throws your heart to the ground*
> *Love turns the whole thing around*
> *No it won't all go the way it should*
> *But I know the heart of life is good*

The action verbs, particularly "throws" and "turns," personify the song's emotions and give the listeners a memorable and dramatic visual.

Similarly, in the opening of Frank Ocean's song, "Thinkin Bout You," the lyric paints a picture of a messy room. Instead of simply describing that "my room is messy," Ocean invents a dramatic, active backstory of a storm that employs the action verbs "flew," "shed," and "pour."

> *A tornado flew around my room before you came*
> *Excuse the mess it made, it usually doesn't rain*
> *In Southern California, much like Arizona*
> *My eyes don't shed tears, but boy they pour*

Creating Action Verbs

Some lyrical ideas can initially seem resistant to the inclusion of action verbs. In these cases, you can change the verbs available to you by modifying the subject of the sentence.

Start by swapping the subject and object of the sentence. Taking the earlier example of, "The captain steers the boat," invert "captain" and "boat" so that "boat" becomes the subject of the sentence. Now, the sentence might read:

- The boat obeys the captain.
- The boat follows the lead of the captain.
- The boat hastens where the captain directs it.

If a sentence does not have an object, consider whether one might be implied. For instance, in the two-word sentence, "He ate," the implied object is *food*. In the sentence, "She thinks," the implied object is her *thoughts*. Songwriters can infer these unspoken objects and use them as the subject of their sentences.

- Instead of "He ate," you can say, "The food flew into his mouth" or "The food entered the dark cave of his mouth."
- Instead of saying, "She thinks," you can say, "The thoughts darted through her mind" or "The thought weighed on her mind without a chance of moving."

Many sentences also have a stated or implied **indirect object**, a noun that exists in relation to the object, such as "water" in the sentence "The captain steers the boat on the water." Using the indirect object as the subject can open up other opportunities for action verbs:

- The water flows beneath the boat.
- The water kisses the bottom of the boat.
- The water lifts the boat up as the captain steers.

Finally, the original subject could be replaced by a more (or, potentially less) specific noun. For instance, in the example from Frank Ocean, instead of saying "I don't cry," Ocean replaces the generic subject "I" with the more specific "my eyes" and says, "My eyes don't shed tears."

In the captain-boat example, instead of saying "The captain steers the boat," one could say:

- The captain's hands rotate the wheel. (new subject: hands)
- His fingertips turn the wheel. (new subject: fingertips)
- His mind calculates the next direction. (new subject: mind)
- His toes curl around the gas pedal. (new subject: toes)

Verb Tense

Verb tense refers to the way in which a verb indicates whether a song is unfolding at this moment, recalling a distant past, issuing urgent commands, or dreaming of future possibilities. The same song can take on different meanings and mood depending on *when* the listener is brought into the action. Consider how each of the following verb tenses communicates the passage of time:

1. A verb in **present tense** indicates that the action is happening now, suggests a recurring or reliable action, or states a fact.

   > *Pain **throws** your heart to the ground.*

2. A verb in **past tense** indicates a completed action.

   > *Pain **threw** your heart to the ground.*

3. A verb in **future tense** indicates a prediction or an action that is expected to happen in the future.

   > *Pain **will throw** your heart to the ground.*

4. A verb in **imperative tense** demands that something be done.

   > ***Throw** your heart to the ground.*

5. A verb in **conditional tense** indicates that something might happen in the future, usually using the words "would," "could," or "should."

   > *Pain **could throw** your heart to the ground.*

6. The **present continuous tense** uses a verb in **gerund form** (ending in -ing) to indicate an ongoing action.

   > *Pain **is throwing** your heart to the ground.*

More complex tenses can be formed by combining verb forms of "is" and "have," such as *pain was throwing, pain has thrown, pain had thrown, pain will be throwing,* pain *will have been throwing,* etc.

Most songs do not choose a single verb tense and stick with it, but move freely between tenses, mapping the complex relationship between fact, memory, and conjecture. Examine how Gloria Gaynor's legendary song, "I Will Survive," moves between different verb tenses and timeframes to tell a story of redemption.

It starts in the past tense, using verbs "was" and "kept thinking," then moves into the conjecture of conditional tense "could live":

> *At first I **was** afraid, I **was** petrified*
> ***Kept thinking** I **could live** without you by my side*

Next, the song moves into the present tense, indicated by the word "Now" and the verbs "are" (part of the contraction "you're") and "find."

> *Now **you're** back*
> *From outer space*
> *And I **find** you here*
> *With that sad look upon your face*

Gaynor then issues orders using the imperative tense ("go," "walk," "turn").

> **Go on, go, walk** out the door
> **Turn** around now
> You're not welcome anymore

And, of course, Gaynor ultimately predicts her ability to thrive without her ex using the future tense, using verbs "will survive" and "will stay."

> *No, not I, I **will survive***
> *Long as I know how to love, I know I'll **stay alive***

Changing verb tenses can alter the mood of a song and sharpen its narrative arc. Experiment with shifting the verb tense of your songs to find a fresh angle to present your story and feelings.

Adjectives & Adverbs

Adjectives force the listener to imagine the elements of a song more vividly. Interesting adjectives can unlock poetic expression and transform a song from bland to impactful. However, it is difficult to find adjectives that don't feel "obvious" or add meaningful context to the noun. For instance, how many adjectives can you think of to describe a sky? Calling the sky "blue" is somewhat redundant and using typical words like "sunny" or "cloudy" is effective but simple.

The following three ideas can help you invent more expressive and surprising adjectives:

1. **Inaccurate Descriptions:** The most fascinating adjectives are often the ones that don't accurately describe the noun. For instance, one of Nat "King" Cole's most famous songs describes an "orange-colored sky." In context, the orange-colored sky is describing the after-effects of the metaphorical "explosions" caused by the sudden emergence of romance. But the image of an orange-colored sky also gives the song a sense of an unreal or hyperreal landscape. Imagine describing a "scarlet" sky, a "purple" sky, a "polka-dotted sky" or a "tech-

nicolor" sky. The purposefully inaccurate descriptions grab a listener's attention and force them to scan the scene for poetic meaning.

> *We were married on a rainy day*
> *The sky was* **yellow**
> *And the grass was* **grey**
>
> – "I Do It for Your Love,"
> Paul Simon

> *I never meant to cause you any sorrow*
> *I never meant to cause you any pain*
> *I only wanted one time to see you laughing*
> *I only wanted to see you laughing in the* **purple** *rain*
>
> – "Purple Rain,"
> Prince

2. **Describe Something Different:** Adjectives that describe a general situation can be applied to a specific noun, creating an intriguing mismatch. For example, in a song in which the narrator is probably feeling "hopeless," "lonely," or "desperate," the songwriter could describe a "hopeless sky," a "lonely sky," or a "desperate sky." In this way, the lyric evokes the narrator's feeling without having to state their truth in an obvious or clunky way ("I feel lonely," "I feel hopeless").

> *And in the* **lonely** *cool before dawn*
> *You hear their engines roaring on*
>
> – "Thunder Road,"
> Bruce Springsteen

3. **Nouns as Adjectives:** Poets and songwriters often use nouns as adjectives to create unusual and evocative descriptions. For instance, one could describe a "cowboy sky," a "kangaroo sky," a "bumblebee sky," or a "popcorn sky." These words, "cowboy," "kangaroo," "bumble," and "popcorn," are nouns, not adjectives, but they are placed in the adjectival position. Using nouns as adjectives conjures all the rich associations that the listener has with the noun and incites them to form their own image of what the songwriter intends. You can read more about this strategy in the "Similes and Metaphors" chapter.

> *Picture yourself in a boat on a river*
> *With **tangerine** trees and **marmalade** skies*
> *Somebody calls you, you answer quite slowly*
> *A girl with **kaleidoscope** eyes*
>
> – "Lucy in the Sky with Diamonds,"
> The Beatles

> ***Blue jean** baby, L.A. Lady*
> *Seamstress for the band*
> *Pretty-eyed, **pirate** smile*
> *You'll marry a music man*
>
> - "Tiny Dancer,"
> Elton John

Adverbs are another way to add color to your song. Whereas adjectives describe a noun, adverbs, which often end in "-ly," modify verbs, adjectives, or other adverbs. Observe how the adverb "slightly" can modify each of these different parts of speech:

Verb: "He moved **slightly** in his sleep." (modifies "moved")
Adjective: "The picture is **slightly** crooked." (modifies "crooked")
Adverb: "He's **slightly** overly stimulated." (modifies "overly")

Unlike most other parts of speech, adverbs can often be moved to at least two places in a sentence, making them useful tools for shaping rhythm and syllable count. Notice how the word "naturally" fits in different places within the sentence "He wants to spend time with her."

"**Naturally**, he wants to spend time with her."
"He **naturally** wants to spend time with her."
"He wants to spend time with her, **naturally**."

A single well-placed adjective or adverb can tilt a lyric from cliché to poetry. Strive to find novel descriptions that vividly paint the world of your song.

Coining Words

Can't think of the word you need? Songwriters often **coin**, or invent, new words to serve the music, add humor, be clever, or create a lyrical "signature."

It isn't as easy to invent a new word as you might think. Three proven methods that help songwriters invent words are:

Nonsense words

Nonsense words are sounds that do not carry a meaning. The concept of nonsense words overlaps with **"scat" syllables**, sounds that jazz singers traditionally use to imitate an instrument like a saxophone, trumpet, or drum.

> *Ob-La-Di, Ob-La-Da, life goes on*
> *La, la, la, la life goes on*
>
> – "Ob-La-Di, Ob-La-Da,"
> The Beatles

Nonexistent forms of real words

Songwriters can take a common word and invent a new form, for instance making an adjective out of a verb, even when that form doesn't exist. These new forms are particularly useful to create unexpected and delightful rhymes.

> *Don't be fancy, just get **dance-y***
>
> – "Raise Your Glass,"
> P!nk

> *Don't ever fix your lips like collagen*
> *To say something when you gon' end up **apologin'***
>
> – "Can't Tell Me Nothing,"
> Kanye West

Combine two words

A **portmanteau** is a word that combines two existing words into a single word. Common English portmanteaus include "smog" ("smoke + fog") and "brunch" ("breakfast" + "lunch"). Portmanteaus often feel playful and slangy, and understanding the same portmanteaus can make listeners feel like they're in the "inside group" as the artists.

> *Psychic spies from China*
> *Try to steal your mind's elation*
> *Little girls from Sweden*
> *Dream of silver screen quotations*
> *And if you want these kind of dreams*
> *It's **Californication***
>
> - "Californication," Red Hot Chili Peppers

"Californication" is the portmanteau combining "California" and "fornication"

> *I don't think you're ready for this jelly*
> *I don't think you're ready for this jelly*
> *I don't think you're ready for this*
> *'Cause my body too **bootylicious** for ya, babe*
>
> - "Bootylicious," Destiny's Child

"bootylicious" is the portmanteau combining "booty" and "delicious"

Takeaways

1. Consider the perspective of the song and experiment with second- and third-person narration.

2. Proper nouns, including celebrities, places, and brand names, create specificity and cultural identity in your songs.

3. Include action verbs to make a song dynamic. Alter the subject of the sentence to expand verb possibilities.

4. Verb tense affects the tone of the song. Experiment with writing in the past, imperative, conditional, and future verb tenses to change the tone of the lyric.

5. Writing adjectives that contribute meaningfully to the imagery of a song requires creativity. Some tricks to invent useful adjectives include using adjectives that are purposefully inaccurate, describing something other than the noun the adjective is modifying, and employing nouns to serve as descriptors.

6. Lyricists often coin new words by including nonsense "scat" syllables, inventing nonexistent forms of existing words, and combining two words into a portmanteau.

Practice

1. Underline the nouns and circle the proper nouns in the following passages:

   A.   *Wolves in the middle of town*
   And the chapel bell ringing through the wind-blown trees
   To wave to the butcher's boy
   With the parking lot music everybody believes
   And then out like a dying bird
   In the corner of the penny arcade

   - "Song of the Shepherd's Dog" – Iron and Wine

   B.   *Some folks like to get away*
   Take a holiday from the neighborhood
   Hop a flight to Miami Beach
   Or to Hollywood
   But I'm taking a Greyhound
   On the Hudson River Line
   I'm in a New York state of mind

   - "New York State of Mind" – Billy Joel

C.	*While home in New York was champagne and disco*
Tapes from L.A. slash San Francisco
But actually Oakland and not Alameda
Your girl was in Berkeley with her Communist reader
Mine was entombed within boombox and Walkman
I was a hoarder but girl that was back then

- "Step" – Vampire Weekend

2.	Change the verbs in the following sentences by modifying the subject. First, move the object (either direct or indirect) into the subject position. Second, use a more specific subject than the original subject given. The first example is done for you.

A.	I sent you a valentine.

Object as Subject: A valentine is soaring towards you in the mail.

More Specific Subject: My fingers sealed the envelope of your valentine.

B.	He scrubbed the kitchen floors with a mop.

Object as Subject: ____

More Specific Subject: ____

C.	She was laughing at the goat.

Object as Subject: ____

More Specific Subject: ____

D.	Polly can't stop staring at the girl at the bar.

Object as Subject: ____

More Specific Subject: ____

E.	The sun shines on the wheat fields.

Object as Subject: ____

More Specific Subject: ____

F.	They kissed for the first time.

Object as Subject: ____

More Specific Subject: ____

3. Invent three adjectives for each of the given nouns other than the "obvious" ones listed in parentheses. The first example is done for you.

A. **Noun:** dress (pretty/frilly/long/formal/casual/short/cotton/flowing)
    Adjectives: midnight, commanding, lipstick

B. **Noun:** face (happy/sad/angry/pouty/mad/smiling/frowning)
    Adjectives:____

C. **Noun:** bed (soft/hard/wide/narrow/comfortable)
    Adjectives:____

D. **Noun:** ocean (blue/big/deep/wavy/salty)
    Adjectives:____

E. **Noun:** cloud (puffy/white/gray/stormy/friendly)
    Adjectives:____

F. **Noun:** sadness (tragic/overwhelming/deep/profound)
    Adjectives:____

G. **Noun:** forest (dark/bright/peaceful/natural/gloomy/magical)
    Adjectives:____

4. Rewrite each of the following lines from the Beach Boys' song "Kokomo" using the verb tenses indicated:

A. There is a place called Kokomo.
    Past: ____
    Conditional: ____
    Future: ____

B. We'll get there fast.
    Present: ____
    Imperative: ____
    Present Continuous: _______________________________________

C. That's where we want to go.
    Conditional: ____
    Future: ____
    Past: ____

D. Why don't we go?

Present Continuous: _______________________________________

Past: _______________________________________

Conditional: _______________________________________

5. For each sentence, add two different adverbs to create vivid images. Experiment with placing the adverbs in different locations in the sentence. The first example is done for you.

A. I don't know why I didn't come.
New sentence 1: I don't know why I stubbornly didn't come.
New sentence 2: Mystifyingly, I don't know why I didn't come.

B. I may not always love you.
New sentence 1: _______________________________________
New sentence 2: _______________________________________

C. Thunder only happens when it's raining.
New sentence 1: _______________________________________
New sentence 2: _______________________________________

D. Mother, mother, there's too many of you crying.
New sentence 1: _______________________________________
New sentence 2: _______________________________________

E. Just like the river, I've been running ever since.
New sentence 1: _______________________________________
New sentence 2: _______________________________________

F. I'm about to give you all my money.
New sentence 1: _______________________________________
New sentence 2: _______________________________________

9. Verse-Chorus Form

Have you ever had a euphoric experience at a concert? Audience members often report experiencing ecstatic, spiritually vibrant feelings during those special moments in which everybody is singing together, swaying in rhythm, and maybe even waving their cellphone lights side-to-side in the air. During these magical moments, it can feel like all the petty voices in our heads – the anxieties, fears, and insecurities – go silent. Hunger, thirst, and pain fade to the background, replaced by a magical feeling of connectivity, as though the performers and the audience have merged into a single perfect organism. Some people describe this feeling as "euphoria," others term it "collective effervescence," and still others explain it as akin to a religious epiphany or transcendent awakening.

The euphoric concert experience has a scientific basis. When you hear music you love, your brain emits pleasing chemicals such as oxytocin and dopamine, producing a natural "high." Oxytocin, in particular, brings feelings of recognition, trust, and attachment. With these pleasant chemicals surging in their brains, concertgoers report feeling unusually liberated with reduced perception of pain and discomfort. In some circumstances, audience members become somewhat "addicted" to the ecstatic concert feeling. Consider the culture of Deadheads, who abandon their lives to travel across the country attending Grateful Dead concerts.

That collective "high" most often occurs when everyone can sing along together. In other words, that moment requires a **chorus**, the catchy, repetitive, singable part of a pop song. To create those magical moments for your fans, songwriters need to understand not just how to write a great chorus but also how to build an energetic structure using verses, bridges, and pre-choruses that gives the chorus the appropriate "pay-off."

The term **verse-chorus form** describes a category of songs in which a series of verses lead into and provide contrast with the emotional "pay-off" of the chorus. Beyond verses and choruses, these songs often include other sections like pre-choruses, post-choruses, and bridges to shape the song's energy. While this form is common in almost every song tradition from folk to musical theater, the verse-chorus form is especially common in commercial genres like pop music, rock music, modern country, singer-songwriter styles, and R&B. It suits these genres well because the repetition of the chorus makes a song catchy and memorable, encouraging repeated listening. When you think of verse-chorus form, think of Michael Jackson, the Beatles, Adele, Prince, The Rolling Stones, Madonna, Whitney Houston, and virtually any popular artist from the '50s and beyond.

Verses and Choruses

A **verse** is a musical section whose lyrics change each time it repeats whereas a **chorus** is a musical section that maintains the same music and lyrics with each repetition. Verses and choruses can be viewed as an extension of the strophic song form. The chorus represents an expanded version of the "refrain," the lyrical "pay-off" that repeats in every stanza. The verse embodies the story-telling part of the stanza that changes with each repetition.

Verses and choruses are designed to create musical contrasts. When the two sections are well-crafted, listeners experience the journey of a song as a roller coaster of highs and lows. The steady simmer of a verse builds to the elevated energetic "release" of a chorus. Verses and choruses guide the listener by juxtaposing crucial musical elements: starting on different chords, using different phrase lengths, altering the vocal range, adding and subtracting elements of arrangement or production, and changing chords at different rates.

Each section has a function: the chorus is designed, above all, to be *memorable,* while the verse gives the song depth and meaning. Songwriters often use the word **"hook"** to describe a part of the chorus that gets caught in the listener's head. To effectively hook the listener, a chorus usually features melody and lyrics simple enough to encourage a sing-along, even after just one listen. In contrast, an effective verse digs deeper into the song's emotional universe. Verses are the place where writers explore their poetic voice, tell their story, support their ideas with evidence, and reveal the nuances of their emotions.

The following charts elucidate common points of contrast between verses and choruses:

Lyrics

	Verse	Chorus
Content	detail, storytelling	express emotion, offer a conclusion or summary
Style	more words, stream-of-consciousness	fewer words, repeated phrases and grammatical structures

Music

	Verse	Chorus
Pitch Level	lower	higher
Melodic Style	speech-like melodies with repeated pitches	longer, held notes; more expressive leaps
Production/ Arrangement	sparser, focus on lyric and story	more layers, new instruments or background vocals added

Examples

"Firework" – Katy Perry

"Firework" is a dance-pop hit from Katy Perry's 2010 album, *Teenage Dream.* Perry describes writing the work after reading a passage from Jack Kerouac's book, *On the Road,* in which Kerouac writes about friends' brilliance burning brightly and beautifully but only for a short time. In fact, the three-time repetition in the chorus resembles Kerouac's repetition in the line, "burn, burn, burn, like fabulous yellow roman candles exploding like spiders across the stars." The song is repeatedly used as an example throughout this chapter.

Verse

Lyrics: The verse asks a series of questions, using similes to describe a feeling of loneliness and struggle. The anaphora of "do you ever feel" introduces the first three lines and the lines that follow add layer upon layer of detail to each simile. Because of both the detailed similes and the three different descriptions of the feeling (plastic bag, paper thin, buried deep), the listener achieves a specific sense of the emotion being described.

Music: Melodic and harmonic repetition drive and organize this section. The four-chord harmonic progression is repeated exactly four times, and the repetitive melody only changes in the third system, measures 9-12. The melodic rhythm repeats both within every phrase and between all four lines of music. Using notes exclusively from the A-flat major pentatonic scale gives the melody a typical bubblegum pop sound and using relatively few melodic leaps keeps the emphasis on the lyric.

Chorus

Changes: Note the basic elements that change between the chorus and the verse:

- Phrasing: whereas the verse has one-measure phrases, the chorus has two-measure phrases
- Rhyme Frequency: the verse rhymes every four measures with an AAA rhyme scheme; the chorus rhymes every two measures with an AABB rhyme scheme

Lyrics: The song moves from a questioning mode to a declarative mode ("Baby, you *[are]* a firework"). Imperative verbs incite the listener to take action ("come on," "make 'em"). The onomatopoeic repetition of "ah, ah, ah" and "awe, awe, awe" is so simple and repetitive that a listener can easily remember and sing along. Although both the verse and chorus include comparisons, notice that the extended similes in the verses have a poetic sense whereas the metaphor in the chorus is simple and direct: "Baby, you're a firework."

Music: Although the harmony remains exactly the same as in the verse, the melody offers the necessary contrast. The pitch level ascends significantly, hovering around an octave above the low C's, B-flats, and A-flats of the verse. The long notes in nearly every measure are typical of a chorus as is the more wide-ranging, leap-heavy melody. In contrast to the verse, the only repeated consecutive pitches in the chorus are in the repeated "ahs"/ "awes" whereas every other note is ascending or descending.

Notice the rhythm of the "ahs"/ "awes." Each of these notes lasts for the equivalent of three eighth notes. Using groupings of three within a four-beat meter is called a **hemiola** and is a common and effective way to create pleasing rhythmic tension in songs. In "Firework," the rhythm of the hemiola takes center stage because it sets a repeated melody note and repeated lyric.

"Fire and Rain" – James Taylor

Released in 1970, "Fire and Rain" is James Taylor's most famous song and an iconic song representing the singer-songwriter movement. It is full of autobiographical details from Taylor's life, like the suicide of Taylor's childhood friend, Suzanne Schnerr, the collapse of his band Flying Machine, and his struggles with drug addiction in rehab. Taylor couches all of these events in poetic language so that the story being told is not immediately evident.

Verse

Lyrics: The verse of "Fire and Rain" is the beginning of a story. There are characters ("me," "they," "Suzanne," "you") and a particular time ("yesterday morning"). Like in good stories, something's changed, and here the change is that the speaker is informed of Suzanne's death and writes a song. The lyrics are in past tense and are poetic in the sense that they favor sound and rhythm over clear communication. For instance, it's up to the listener to guess at who "they" are and what destructive "plans" they made for Suzanne. Taylor also brings the listener into the story by telling it in a personal, informal manner, frequently leaving out the subject "I" and starting thoughts with verbs, as in "[I] walked out this morning" and "[I] just can't remember."

Music: The melody is rhythmically active, with four or five notes in each measure. With the exception of one leap (from measure three to four on the lyric "me know"), the melody is mostly static, either moving stepwise or skipping by just a third. The harmony centers around C with each four-measure phrase beginning on C, but it adds color through modal interchange with chords like G minor and B-flat major borrowed from the key of C minor. Notice the four-measure phrasing indicated by the holds and rests in the fourth measure of each system.

Chorus

Changes: Note the basic elements that change between the chorus and the verse:

- Rhyme Scheme: whereas the verse is ABAB, the chorus is either AAAA or ABBA depending on which words you think rhyme
- Starting Chords: every line of the verse starts on C, the lines of the chorus mainly start on F
- Verb Tense: the verbs change from simple past ("walked out") to present perfect (use of "I have seen")

Lyrics: The lyrics shift from a specific day to general statements about experience. Taylor uses antithesis to create a satisfying sense of symmetry ("fire"/ "rain," "sunny days"/ "lonely times") and anaphora to establish a pleasing parallelism between lyrical phrases, three times saying, "I've seen."

The final line introduces a lyrical twist using the word "but," which introduces a contrast between all of the dramatic things the speaker saw and the "you," probably Suzanne, who they will never see again.

Music: Notice that the melody is generally higher than the melody of the verse, reaching a C compared to the verse's highest A. The rhythmic repetition, especially in the second and third phrases (starting at measures 5 and 9), accentuates the parallel structure of the lyrics. The chord progression is highly repetitive, with the first three phrases sharing identical chords. Its stepwise bassline creates connection between the chords and helps to smooth the faster harmonic motion.

When the lyric takes on a more reflective tone in the final line, the music moves to a lower register to complement the more thoughtful and introspective mood of the speaker.

Pre-Chorus

A **pre-chorus** provides an energetic buildup to the emotional high of the chorus. If the verse and chorus create a roller coaster of ups and downs, the pre-chorus is the suspenseful moment in which the track is climbing to the peak before a dramatic drop. Additionally, if the verse and chorus are harmonically similar, the pre-chorus creates contrast to break the harmonic monotony and prepare the listeners' ears for the chorus.

The pre-chorus is usually the shortest section in a song, sometimes as short as two or four measures, compared to a typical sixteen-measure verse or chorus. The lyrics of a pre-chorus are usually, but not always, the same every time the section recurs.

How does the pre-chorus create energy?

- **Rising motion** – The melody and/or the bassline often ascend, especially in the final measures before the chorus.
- **Unstable harmony** – The pre-chorus begins away from the tonic and ends with the V chord.
- **Faster harmonic rhythm** – Chords usually move faster in the pre-chorus and accelerate further in the final measures before the chorus.
- **Faster repetition** – Melodic phrases and rhymes come faster, building the energy level through rapid-fire repetition.

How does the pre-chorus create contrast?

- **Change in verb tense** – The pre-chorus is a good time to "take a step back" from the main story and delve into the past or into universal truths.
- **Change in subject or perspective** – In order to offer another perspective, the subject of the sentence could change, for instance, from "I" to "we" or "they."
- **Harmonic contrast** – The first chord is often different from the other sections, and the harmonic rhythm often changes (as referenced previously).
- **Different arrangement/production** – New instruments enter to help build the volume, often including **pads** – long, held sounds – which are especially common in the pre-chorus.

Examples

"Firework" – Katy Perry

Music: "Firework" perfectly demonstrates an ascending melody. Looking at the first (tied over) note of each measure, the melody ascends by a step in the A-flat major scale. In this case, the rising melody both reflects the typical pre-chorus build and represents a firework launching into the sky. Notice the fast rate of repetition in which the two-note melodic rhythm (beat four and the "and of four") recurs every measure, even as other notes surround and embellish it towards the end of the pre-chorus.

Lyrics: The pre-chorus switches from questioning to instructing. In the pre-chorus, the listener is being told how to change their mindset using verbs like "ignite," "shine," and "own." The rate of rhymes increases with the "i" vowel recurring frequently, though unevenly. The combination of the rhymes and the melodic ascent create a sense of momentum and urgency leading into the chorus.

"Billie Jean" – Michael Jackson

In the top 50 of Rolling Stone's "Greatest Songs of All Time," "Billie Jean" was a breakout hit for Michael Jackson as the second single from the album, *Thriller*. The song tells the story of a woman who claims that the singer is the father of her son. The verse features an insistent, driving bassline alongside synthesized chords, with Jackson's signature percussive vocals on top.

Music: This pre-chorus needs to create contrast because the verse and chorus for "Billie Jean" use the same fairly static progression, alternating between F-sharp and B minor chords. Using the song's first major chord, D major, to begin the pre-chorus, freshens the listener's ear, preparing them to re-enter the world of F-sharp minor in the chorus.

Whereas the melody for the verses hangs around low C-sharps and B's, the melody for the pre-chorus centers a repeated F-sharp, ascending or descending to accentuate important syllables. When the last two measures complete a half cadence, ending on the V chord, the melody leaves the F-sharp minor pentatonic scale to use notes from the chord, notably E-sharp. The V chord, C-sharp major, creates the tension and suspense to satisfyingly launch the listener into the chorus. In the original production, the build is accentuated by the introduction of synthesized pads, leads, and background vocals.

Lyrics: Whereas the verse tells a story in the past tense and first person ("She told me her name was Billie Jean / as she caused a scene"), the pre-chorus solicits other opinions, from "people" in general and from "mother." The advice received is shared as like a maxim, a universally held truth, rather than a one-time consultation ("people *always* told me"). The lyrics create their own crescendo by repeating words and phrases more quickly, "be careful who you love / be careful what you do," using antithesis ("lie"/"truth"), and increasing the rate of rhyme ("do"/"truth"). The quick succession of rhymes, repetitions, and antitheses accelerates the listener into the release of the chorus.

The Bridge

The **bridge** is a palate-cleansing section that disrupts the alternation between verses and choruses. The typical bridge appears only once in a song, three-fourths of the way through, before the final statement or statements of the chorus. If a song is like a roller coaster, the bridge might be a scenic part without too much motion, but a great view of the amusement park below.

The bridge grows out of the interlude section of the strophic form. Historically, this section features an instrumental solo, as in the saxophone solo on Aretha Franklin's "Respect," or the digitally sped-up piano solo on The Beatles' "In My Life." In modern times, the bridge has often become an opportunity to feature a rapper collaborating with a pop artist, like Jay-Z on Rihanna's "Umbrella" or Ludacris on Usher's "Yeah!"

What are some of the typical aspects of the bridge?

- **Harmonic surprises** – The bridge is a songwriter's best opportunity to do something really surprising with the harmony. It typically starts in a very different place harmonically from the verse and chorus. For instance, the bridge of "Respect," which starts in C major, starts on an F-sharp minor chord.
- **Lower energy** - Many bridges start with a dip in energy caused by slower harmonic rhythm and a sparser melody. The length of the repetitive grooves created by the bass and drums often increase, for instance from two-measure loops to four-measure loops.
- **Lyrical Shift** – In a well-crafted bridge, the lyrics share a different perspective that enriches or changes the audience's perspective on the verse and chorus. The bridge is an opportunity for the lyricist to offer vulnerability or introduce doubt to contrast with the bravado of the chorus.
- **Climactic Ending** – Because the bridge is often followed by the last statement of the chorus, it should end with a sense of climax and anticipation. In pop songs, the last two measures of the bridge are frequently a place for the singer to show off their highest notes, often as part of a **vocal break** in which the accompaniment drops out.

Examples

"Firework" – Katy Perry

Lyrics: The repeated "boom, boom, boom," "moon, moon, moon" and "you, you, you" recall the repeated "aw(e)s" of the chorus but with a very different vowel sound. Words like "even," "always," and "now" intensify the emotion and urgency of the moment.

Music: Because the chorus, verse, and pre-chorus all have the same chord progression, the bridge represents an opportunity to finally change the progression. The harmonic rhythm slows from one chord per measure to one chord every two measures and at the end, the piece achieves its only half cadence and its only use of the V chord.

The melody cleverly expands upon the hemiola theme of the chorus before trailing off at the end. Although the descent at the end is a bit unusual, it occurs for a good reason. The bridge leads to two final statements of the chorus, known as a **double chorus**, the first with a stripped-down, drum-less arrangement, and the second at a higher energy.

"Forget You" – CeeLo Green (released in an uncensored version as "F* You")

"Forget You," a 2010 hit by CeeLo Green, written in collaboration with Bruno Mars and others. The song is about someone who was romantically rejected because they didn't have as much money as their rival. Instead of being sad, they are choosing to be dismissive, saying things like "Yeah, I'm sorry I can't afford a Ferrari / But that don't mean I can't get you there." Harmonically, "Forget You" is written in the key of C and uses exclusively major chords in both the verse and chorus: C, D, and F major.

Lyrics: After being dismissive in the verse and chorus, the singer starts playing the part of a lovesick child, asking their parents for advice. They vulnerably and melodramatically admit to being hurt, repeatedly yell out "Why?" Instead of swearing at the object of their affections, they confess that they really have feelings for her, repeating "I really love you." The singer is revealing that the "tough guy persona" is actually just an act to cover up their deep hurt. With Green's over-the-top performance on the original track, it's not crystal clear how seriously the listener is supposed to take this confession, or whether it's all an ironic, theatrical play.

Music: After exclusively using major chords in the verse and chorus, the bridge surprises the listeners by featuring minor chords, starting on the iii chord with stripped-back production. The smooth, long melodic phrases contrast with the more percussive, rhythmic singing in the verse and chorus. The rising melody and the half cadence at the end of the section launch the music into a climactic final statement of the chorus.

Post-Chorus

The **post-chorus** is a relatively rarely used section that allows the energy of the chorus to dissipate and transition smoothly back to the verse. Most common in modern pop, the post-chorus usually maintains the same chord progression and production from the chorus and often loops the end of the chorus or a simple melody on a neutral syllable like "ah" or "oh."

Because "Firework" doesn't have a proper post-chorus, Carly Rae Jepsen's "Call Me Maybe" is used as an example instead.

"Call Me Maybe" – Carly Rae Jepsen

The ultimate "song of the summer" from 2012, "Call Me Maybe" tells a story about coy, playful desire. Written in G major, the chorus ("Hey, I just met you / and this is crazy") is sung over a looped chord progression played by synthesized strings. In "Call Me Maybe," the post-chorus is only introduced after two verses and choruses are complete.

Chorus

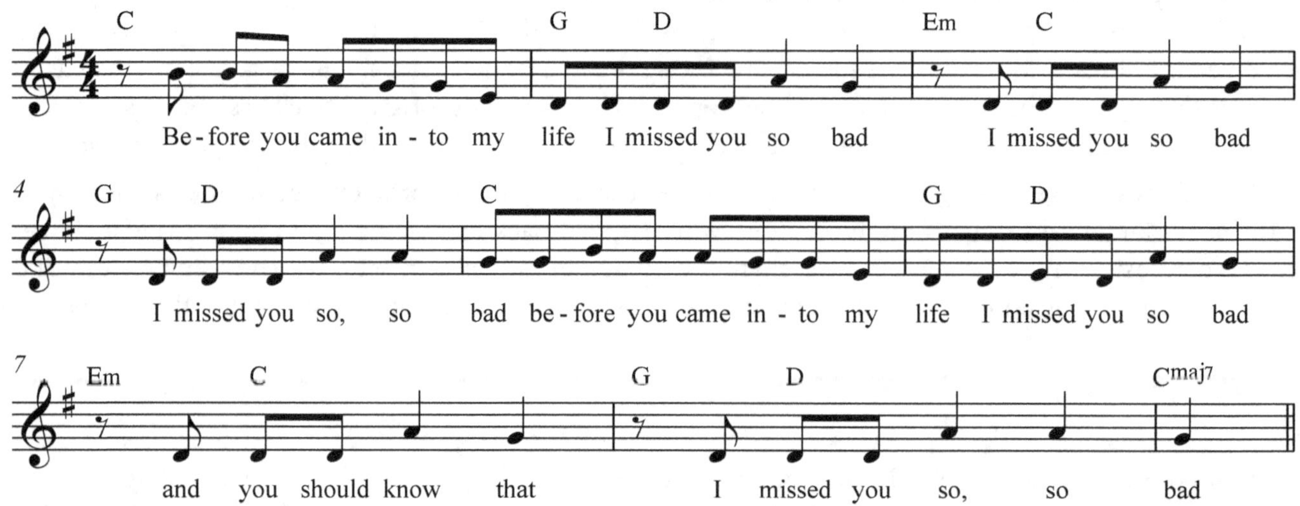

Music: The four-measure harmonic progression is identical to that of the chorus and the melody remains roughly at the same pitch level as the chorus, rather than returning to the lower pitch level of the verse. The melody, which is built from the G major pentatonic scale, is highly repetitive, especially while repeating "I missed you so bad." The post-chorus maintains the same production as the chorus while adding other layers, most notably a brass countermelody.

Lyrics: Whereas the majority of the song takes place in the present tense, this section reverts to the past tense and talks about the time before the two protagonists met. The lyrics pose a logical impossibility: how can you "miss someone" so bad before you even met them?

Putting the Sections Together

While each section has a specific musical and lyrical role, they can be combined in many different orders depending on the songwriter's intent. Here are a few examples, arranged from simpler to more complex forms:

"Fire and Rain" – James Taylor

"Fire and Rain" does not include a pre-chorus or a bridge. It simply alternates between verses and choruses.

Verse 1	*"Just yesterday mornin', they let me know you were gone"*
Chorus	*"I've seen fire and I've seen rain"*
Verse 2	*"Won't you look down upon me, Jesus"*
Chorus	*"I've seen fire and I've seen rain"*
Verse 3	*"Been walking my mind to an easy time"*
Chorus	*"I've seen fire and I've seen rain"*
Outro	*"Thought I'd see you one more time again"*

"Imagine" – John Lennon

Like "Fire and Rain," "Imagine" also only includes verses and choruses. It differs by "front-loading" two verses before arriving at the first statement of the chorus.

Verse 1	*"Imagine there's no heaven"*
Verse 2	*"Imagine there's no countries"*
Chorus	*"You may say that I'm a dreamer"*
Verse 3	*"Imagine no possessions"*
Chorus	*"You may say that I'm a dreamer"*

"Dreams" – Fleetwood Mac

Although the form of "Dreams" is very concise, each section is expansive, especially the pre-chorus, which is unusually extended. Before the outro, "Dreams" repeats the chorus twice.

Verse 1	*"Now here you go again"*
Pre-Chorus	*"Like a heartbeat drives you mad"*
Chorus	*"Thunder only happens when it's rainin'"*
Verse 2	*"Now, here I go again"*
Pre-Chorus	*"Like a heartbeat drives you mad"*
Double Chorus	*"Thunder only happens when it's rainin'"*
Outro	*"You'll know"*

"Firework" – Katy Perry

"Firework" functions like a typical pop song, with the slight wrinkle of two double choruses, made possible by the short (eight-measure) length of the chorus. The outro repeats melodic and lyrical material from the bridge juxtaposed with the chord progression of the verse.

Verse 1	*"Do you ever feel like a plastic bag"*
Pre-Chorus	*"You've just gotta ignite the light"*
Chorus	*"Baby you're a firework"*
Verse 2	*"You don't have to feel like a waste of space"*
Pre-Chorus	*"You've just gotta ignite the light"*
Double Chorus	*"Baby you're a firework"*
Bridge	*"Boom, boom, boom"*
Double Chorus	*"Baby you're a firework"* (once stripped down, once full volume)
Outro	*"Boom, boom, boom"*

"Billie Jean" – Michael Jackson

The form of "Billie Jean" reflects a relatively standard use of verses, pre-choruses, and choruses, but it replaces the bridge with a musical interlude. The material from the musical interlude returns in the outro.

Verse 1	*"She was more like a beauty queen"*
Pre-Chorus	*"People always told me"*
Chorus	*"Billie Jean is not my lover"*
Verse 2	*"For forty days and for forty nights"*
Pre-Chorus	*"People always told me"*
Chorus	*"Billie Jean is not my lover"*
Musical Interlude	
Chorus	*"Billie Jean is not my lover"*
Outro	*"She says I am the one"*

"Call Me Maybe" – Carly Rae Jepsen

The form of Jepsen's hit is most notable for the addition of the pre-chorus. Each chorus in "Call Me Maybe" feels like a double chorus because the same material is repeated twice.

Verse 1	*"I threw a wish in a well"*
Pre-Chorus	*"Your stare was holdin'"*
Chorus	*"Hey, I just met you"*
Verse 2	*"You took the time with the call"*
Pre-Chorus	*"Your stare was holdin'"*
Chorus	*"Hey, I just met you"*
Post-Chorus	*"Before you came into my life"*
Chorus	*"Hey, I just met you"*
Post-Chorus	*"Before you came into my life"*

"Rehab" – Amy Winehouse

From Winehouse's iconic album, *Back to Black*, "Rehab" is notable both for beginning with the chorus and for changing lyrics in each pre-chorus.

Chorus	*"They tried to make me go to rehab"*
Verse 1	*"I'd rather be at home with Ray"*
Pre-Chorus	*"I didn't get a lot in class"*
Chorus	*"They tried to make me go to rehab"*
Verse 2	*"The man said, 'Why do you think you here?'"*
Pre-Chorus	*"He said, 'I just think you're depressed'"*
Chorus	*"They tried to make me go to rehab"*
Verse 3	*"I don't ever wanna drink again"*
Pre-Chorus	*"It's not just my pride"*
Chorus	*"They tried to make me go to rehab"*

Takeaways

The verse-chorus song is a particularly effective form for pop music because the excitement and stickiness of the chorus make the song attractive for a wide range of listeners.

1. A verse usually has denser content whereas a chorus is simpler and more repetitive, providing an energetic release.

2. The pre-chorus is often the shortest section of a song. Its function is to create momentum leading into the chorus.

3. A bridge cleanses the palate and provides harmonic contrast, often at a lower energy level than the verse and chorus.

4. These sections can be organized in a variety of ways, with different numbers of verses, choruses, pre-choruses and bridges.

Practice

1. Determine whether each of the following lyrical snippets would better fit in a chorus or a verse:

   A. *Every day, I've got the blues*
      'Cause I can't get you out of my mind

      Verse or Chorus?_____________ Reason____

   B. *You're the one, you're my sun*
      You're my moon and my stars

      Verse or Chorus?_____________ Reason____

   C. *I stepped out on the street, and I saw your face*
      Staring at me from your parking space

      Verse or Chorus?_____________ Reason____

   D. *Hold me, hold me, hold me in your arms*
      Love me, love me, love me again

      Verse or Chorus?_____________ Reason____

   E. *The red of the lips and the blue of your eyes*
      Stopped me in my tracks, standing mesmerized

      Verse or Chorus?_____________ Reason____

   F. *Innocence is the word that I've heard people use*
      When you're too afraid to play 'cause you're too afraid to lose

      Verse or Chorus?_____________ Reason____

   G. *Undeniable, this love is*
      Undeniable

      Verse or Chorus?_____________ Reason____

2. Write a possible chorus that would fit with each of the following verses. Remember, that choruses should be general, they should zoom out, have fewer words, and could share a lesson.

   A. *Tight jeans, jawline, perfect skin*
      You're too hot for me to play it cool
      Look at me, and my head spins
      Smile at me, and watch me drool

   B. *While I wake up, my heart keeps sleeping*
      With pillows fluffed and ironed sheets
      My heart's too tired to start its beating
      Ever since your heart left me

   C. *He cooks me pigs in a blanket*
      On rainy, lazy Sundays at home
      When they crackle and pop on the griddle
      Life seems to rhyme like a poem

3. Write a possible verse that would fit with each of the following choruses. Remember, that verses should be more specific, tell the story, and use less repetition.

   A. *Oh, babe I feel like I'm falling for you*
      But I don't want to feel like a fool

   B. *When the sun sets on Sunset*
      And the circle meets the sea
      This place that everyone says feels fake
      Feels so real to me

   C. *I'm so full of life yet so full of fear*
      I'm gonna save each moment like a souvenir
      And savor each day until it disappears
      'Cause I'm only gonna live for 35 more years

4. Given the chorus, write either a pre-chorus or a bridge:

A.

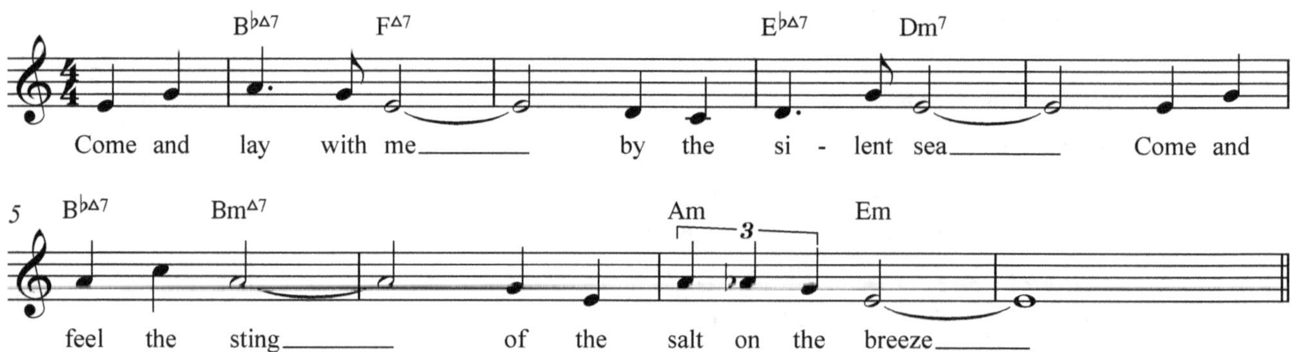

B.

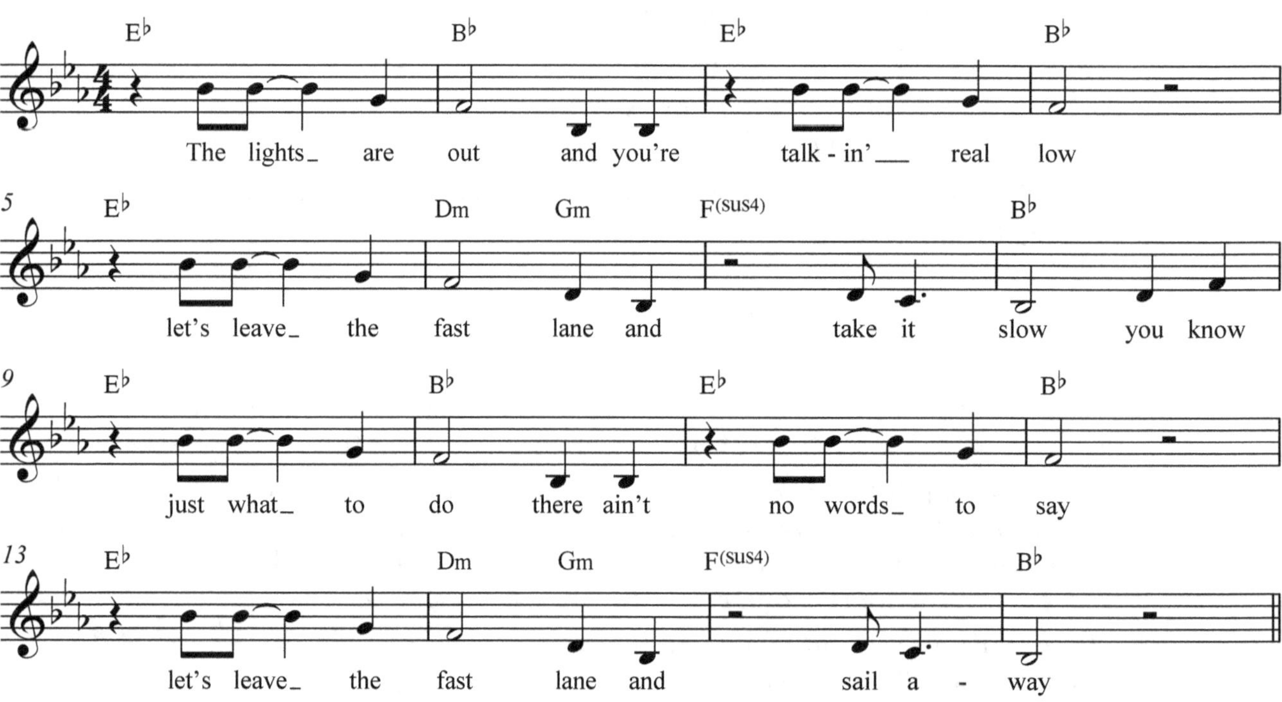

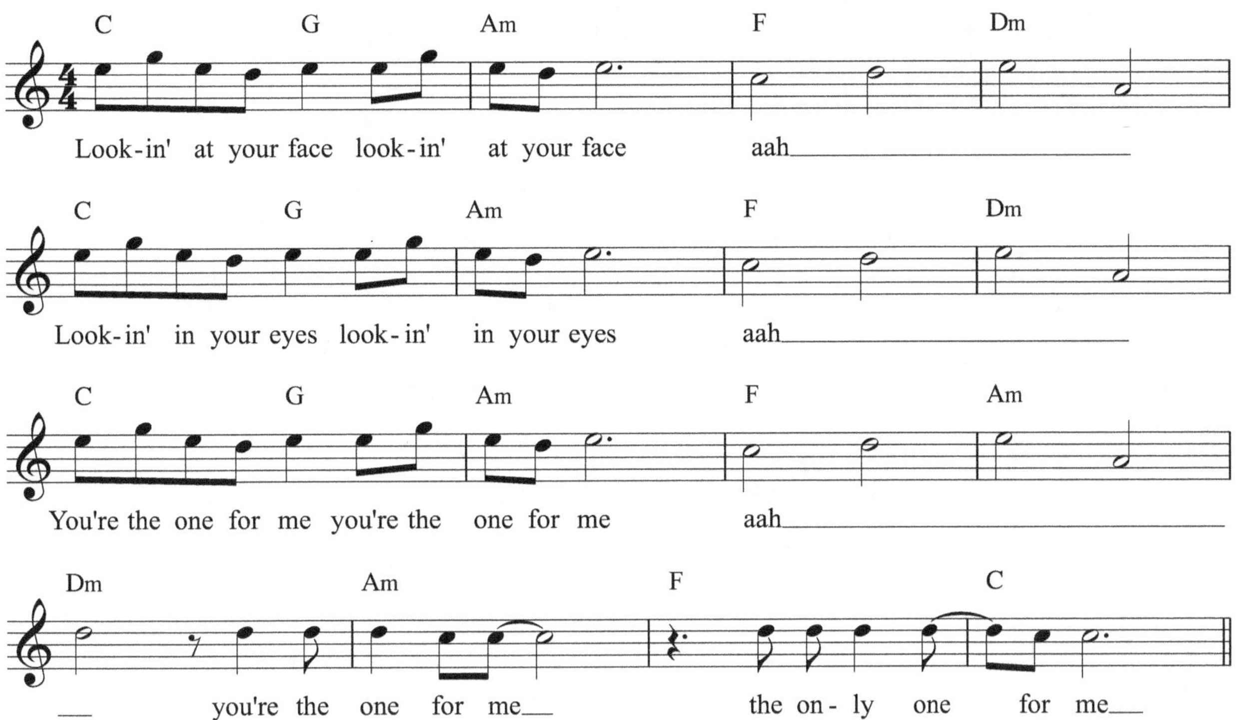
C   G   Am   F   Dm
Look-in' at your face look-in'   at your face   aah
C   G   Am   F   Dm
Look-in' in your eyes look-in'   in your eyes   aah
C   G   Am   F   Am
You're the one for me you're the   one for me   aah
Dm   Am   F   C
__   you're the   one   for me__   the on-ly   one   for me__

9A Writing a Verse-Chorus Song

Step One: Brainstorm a Subject

One effective way to start a song is to restate a profound idea in your own words. The idea could be something personal, like an important lesson you recently learned; or it could be more general, like a quote from a great thinker.

Here are several well-known quotes that I could imagine sparking lyrical ideas:

1. "The arc of the moral universe is long, but it bends towards justice." – Martin Luther King Jr.

2. "The weak can never forgive. Forgiveness is the attribute of the strong." – Mahatma Gandhi

3. "The roots of education are bitter, but the fruit is sweet." – Aristotle

4. "Morality is simply the attitude we adopt towards people we personally dislike." – Oscar Wilde

5. "Too much sanity may be madness." – Miguel de Cervantes

6. "To fall in love is to create a religion that has a fallible god." – Jorge Luis Borges

7. "We all know that Art is not truth. Art is a lie that makes us realize the truth." – Pablo Picasso

8. "Death and love are the two wings that bear the good man to heaven." – Michelangelo

Once you've chosen a subject, write at least five lyrics inspired by the quote, using your own voice to convey the message. Start with just a few lines, adding rhymes where they feel appropriate.

I wrote five passages based on the fourth quote, by Oscar Wilde:

"Morality is simply the attitude we adopt towards people we personally dislike."

1. *My Mama taught me to be honest*
   She taught me to be true
   But if I'm being honest
   I simply don't like you

2. *You can talk about being brave*
   You can talk about being free
   But what I want to hear you say
   Is that, deep down, you really like me

3. *Do you like me?*
   That's all that matters
   Would you save me
   If my life was left in tatters?

4. *Philosophy, psychology*
   That stuff don't mean too much to me
   We're two small people in one small room
   Staring at the same small moon.

5.   *You can take it personally*

   If you don't hear from me

   I don't make time for people I don't like

Notice that the words "morality," "personally," "attitude," and "adopt" don't appear in any of my lyrics. For me, these words sound awkward in a song, especially because so many of them are multisyllabic mouthfuls. Other words, like "honest," "true," "brave," "free," etc. can replace Wilde's original language to make the lyric more conversational.

The examples take a much more grounded approach to Wilde's concept, showing the principle in action, rather than explicating it. In other words, the lyrics dramatize the idea, showing rather than telling.

Step Two: Write a Chorus

Lyrics derived from the quote likely express the song's core idea, which makes them perfect for a chorus. Remember that the chorus expresses the main theme of the song whereas the verse shares details and lists examples.

For my chorus, I selected lyric #4, because of the internal repetition (*small people/small room/small moon*) and because I like the ambiguity of the relationship of the "two small people." Although the lyrics are wordy, I can imagine this section working for a piano-based ballad in the style of Elton John or Father John Misty. First, I set the existing lyric to music, creating this snippet of music, whose repetition is typical of a chorus:

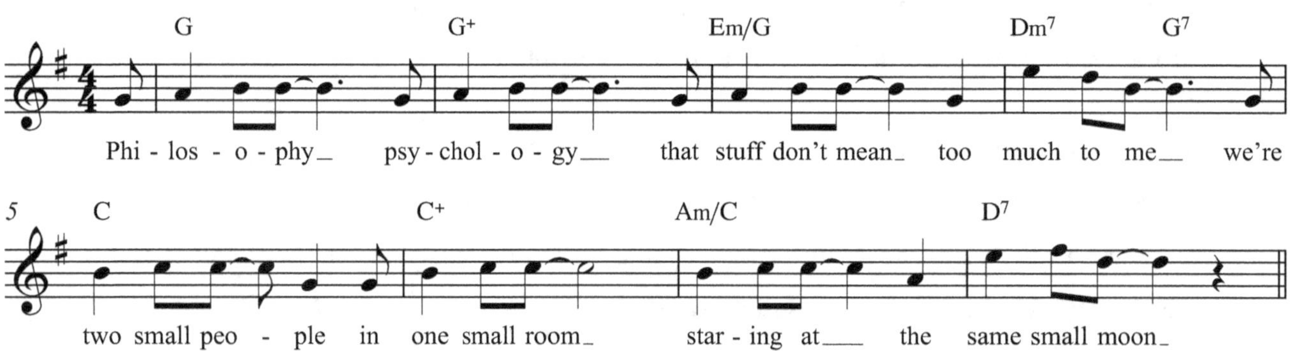

After I set this lyric to music, I stopped thinking about the original Oscar Wilde quote, which, after all, is just a brainstorming tool to help start the song. Instead, I played and sang the beginning of the chorus repeatedly, asking myself where the music wants to go. I felt that the repetitive melody wanted to break free and hit a long, high note. Lyrically, I felt that the next few lines should be less intellectual and more emotional. After a few false starts, I came up with this full chorus:

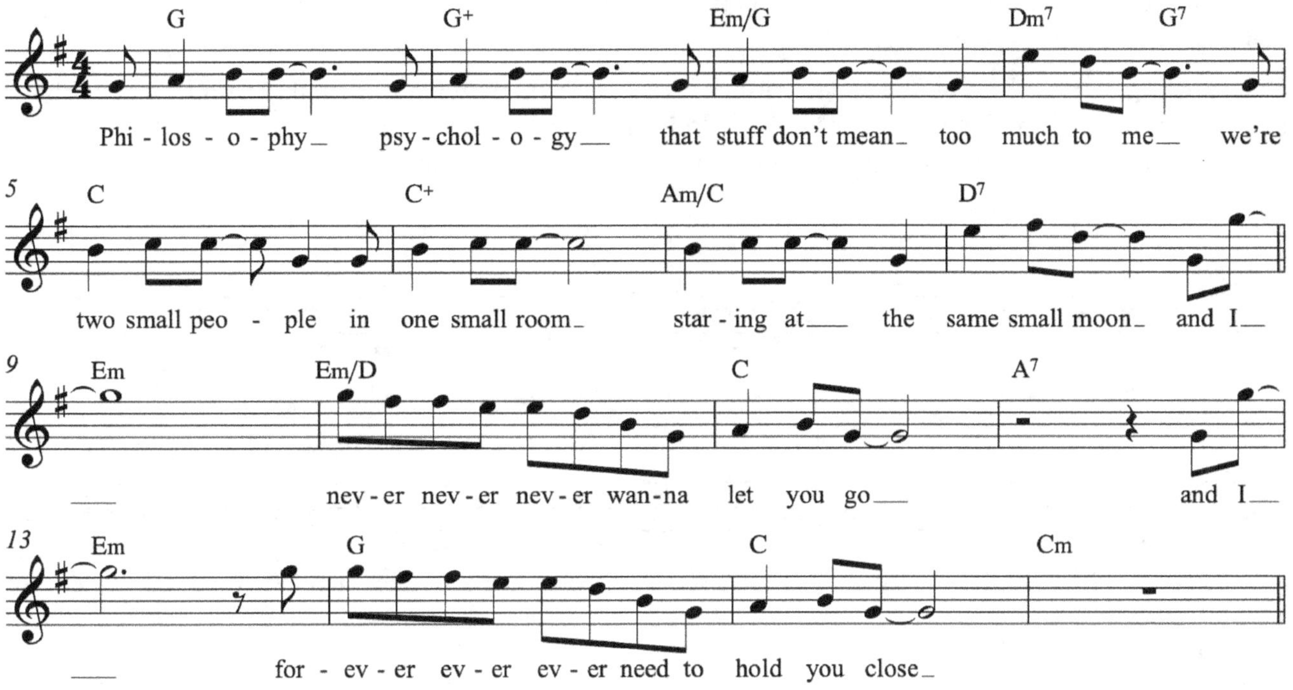

Step Three: Write a Verse

Now that the chorus is established, the next step is to write verses that vividly bring the song's themes to life. It's important to precisely establish the structure for one verse because subsequent verses should be based on the model provided by the first.

Start by writing at least five ideas for a verse that dramatizes the statements of the chorus. It is important to generate multiple ideas when brainstorming because (1) the first idea is not always the best idea; (2) it removes pressure to make anything "good" during a brainstorm.

Examining the chorus, I see a tension between brain and heart, intellect and feeling. The narrator also appears insecure in their relationship: even though the two people are in the same room, their strongest connection is not with each other, but with the distant moon. I want the verses to engage in that tension and get more specific about the battle between feeling and thinking. Here are five possibilities I brainstormed:

1. *You keep reading me poetry*
   But I just want to look in your eyes

2. *I can see the worry*
   Written on your face
   You're wondering about the future
   Rehashing the past

3. *You said, "I've gotta think it through*
   I just don't know what to do"

4. *Your nose is always buried in a book*
   You're lost in your thoughts
   far from the here and now

5. *"What's it all mean?"*
   You keep asking me
   Like you really think
   I might have an idea

I chose to work with #5 because the dismissiveness of the narrator matches their attitude in the chorus. From this opening, I wrote a full verse, alternating between writing music and lyrics while constantly revisiting the context and revising previous phrases.

When writing music, I kept in mind that wordier passages are often melodically flat in order to help listeners understand the lyric and help the singer sing it. Notice that the two quotations ("What's it all mean?" and "What's it all for?") sit on a repeated B to highlight the conversational tone.

Step Four: Write a Second Verse

The second verse should maintain the same musical landmarks as the first verse. It should use the same chord progression, repeat the same rhyme scheme, and maintain the general outline melody. However, as a songwriter, you have leeway to alter the melody to reflect the developing lyric, especially to add or subtract repeated notes to match each verse's natural speech pattern. Writing the new verse below the original helps you craft structural similarities, including the rhyme scheme, which is listed on the right-hand side:

"What's it all mean?" you keep asking me	A1
Modern anxiety can swallow you whole	A2
Like you really think I might have an idea	A1
You're invited to the auction where they're selling your soul	A2
You're always searching, probing, seeking, trying to find	B1
But you're reading, thinking, meditating, doing your best	B2
A hint of beauty and truth	C1
To stand apart from the crowd	C2
"What's it all for?" you ask me at dinner	D1
What to believe and where to express it	D2
"Are we all saved, or are we all sinners?"	D1
How to find joy and where to find respite	D2
And when my answer's a smile, you stare back confused	C1
You ask me if I'm lost, I say I'm found	C2

For my song, I prioritized keeping the memorable melodies in measures 5 and 13, but the rest of the melody is negotiable. At measure 5, I preserved the grammatical structure, presenting a list of -ing verbs like in the first verse. However, other elements change: the second verse does not include any quotes, and sixteenth notes are added to accommodate the extra syllables.

Step Five: Write a Pre-Chorus

Examining my two sections, I think that a pre-chorus could help the listeners connect between the ideas of the verse and those of the chorus. Because the pre-chorus is designed to join the verse and chorus, it is useful to summarize the lyrical content of each section before brainstorming pre-chorus ideas. I summarized my song's dramatic tension like this:

Verse: "You" is overthinking, stressed, pondering

Chorus: "You" and "me" are together, and that's the important thing

Next, I wrote five lyrics to connect between these ideas. Here are my bridge concepts:

1. *When we're together*
   I never wonder whether I'm where I'm supposed to be

2. *I love your wandering mind*
   But I wish sometimes you'd be still with me

3. *I love to watch you think*
   But I wish you'd think a little less

4. *Some questions don't have answers*
   And that's okay with me

5. *The world outside our window*
   Can tear itself to pieces

I liked option #3, because it balances tenderness with reproach, and unlike many of the other options, it doesn't end with "be" or "me," words that rhymes with the words in the chorus (*philosophy, psychology*). After choosing your favorite concept, brainstorm lines that complete your thought, starting with potential rhymes. Possible rhymes for my pre-chorus include *mess, test, regrets, possess, success, acquiesce, impress, digest, decompress, obsess, complex,* and *express*.

Starting from my lines, "*I love to watch you think /But I wish you'd think a little less,*" I brainstormed these five options:

1. *If you let me try, baby*
   I can help you decompress

2. *When you're in my arms, babe*
   Nothing has to be complex

3. *You don't have to study*
   You will always pass my chemistry test

4. *Every moment that we spend*
   Is a moment I will not regret

5. *Love ain't an equation*
   It's a feeling that you've gotta express

I chose option #2, because there was a tenderness about it that felt true to the song's characters. Now, it's time to set the pre-chorus to music. My most important musical goals for this section are:

1. create harmonic contrast at the beginning by starting somewhere other than the tonic (in this piece, the tonic is G major)

2. ascend in the bass at the end of the section

3. end with a half cadence to build suspense and tension leading into the arrival in the chorus

I wrote the following music for my pre-chorus, tightening up the lyrics to accommodate the music:

Step Six: Write a Bridge

Lyrically, the bridge allows for the most freedom and exploration. It often expresses vulnerability or suggests an alternate perspective to the viewpoint presented in the verse and chorus. It can also summarize the meaning of the song in a succinct or direct way.

Two good sources for bridge ideas are: (1) the original source material, in this case the Oscar Wilde quote; (2) the brainstorms for the pre-chorus, whose role often overlaps with that of the bridge.

Start by brainstorming five ideas for the direction of the bridge:

1. the world around us might be falling apart

2. I will be here with you through ups and downs

3. you're my guiding light

4. there's no right or wrong, there's just you and me

5. don't think about the future, don't worry about the past

I liked idea #4 because it reframes the Oscar Wilde quote in an interesting way, plus its rhythm already has the cadence of a song lyric. The antithesis suggests a whole section built on contrasts and paradoxes (*right/ wrong, me/you* and maybe *good/bad*).

Musically, the bridge should provide contrast. Given the wordiness of both the verse and chorus, I created a bridge with more held melody notes and fewer total syllables. Harmonically, since my chorus ends on a C minor chord, a key with three flats, I decided to create further contrast by visiting flat keys that contrast with my overall key of G major.

My bridge starts with a G in the melody (the original tonic), but puts an unexpected chord, E-flat major, beneath it. The G acts as a "pivot" note, creating a **common tone modulation** in which a common note (in this case, G), connects two mostly unrelated keys (here, G major and E-flat major). Notice that the music works its way back to a half cadence targeting the original key of G at the end of the bridge.

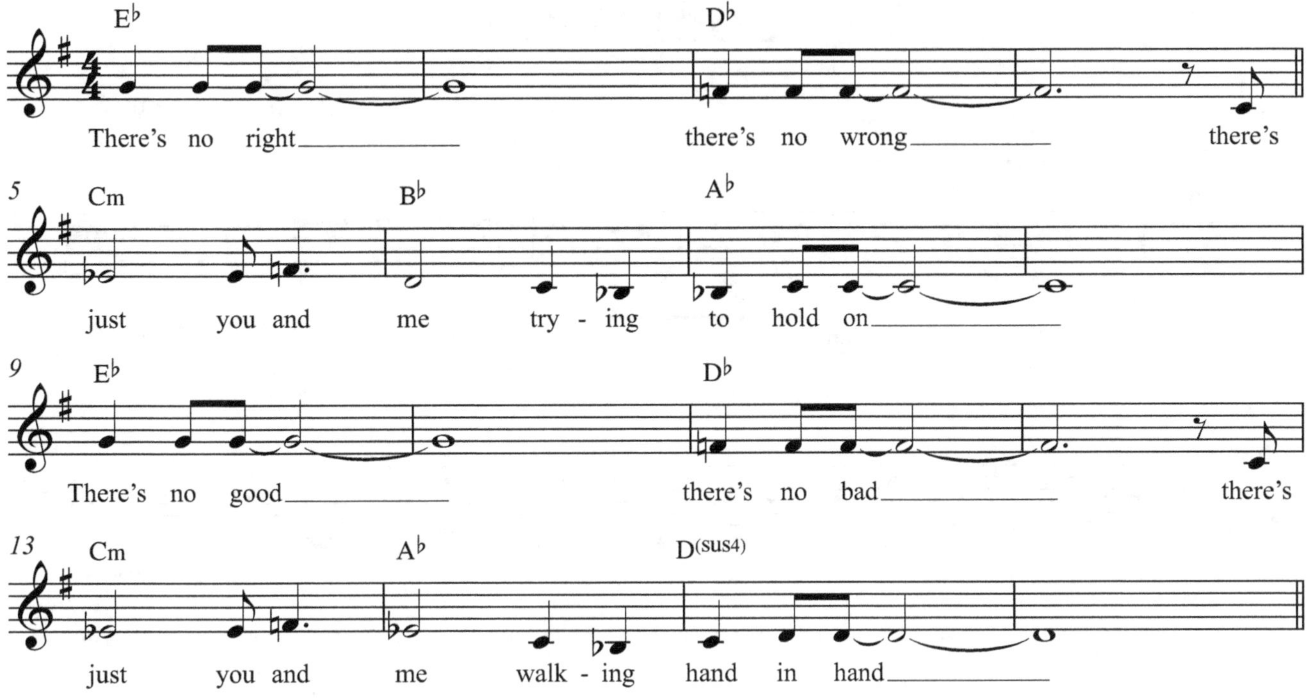

Step Seven: Organize and Connect Sections

With all of the sections completed, the next step is to arrange them into a complete song. I chose the following form for my song, which I named "Complex":

> *Verse 1*
>
> *Pre-chorus*
>
> *Chorus*
>
> *Verse 2*
>
> *Pre-chorus*
>
> *Chorus*
>
> *Bridge*
>
> *Chorus*

When putting the sections together, songwriters need to examine and modify connections between sections to achieve a natural flow. For "Complex," I added transitional chords to smooth harmonic shifts between sections.

The entire piece is presented in the following pages. The lyrics for verse 1 and 2 are written in the same measures, with the verse 2 lyrics appearing below the lyrics for verse 1. When notes appear with multiple stems, the notes with upwards stems represent verse 1 whereas the notes with downwards stems represent verse 2.

Complex

Jeremy Siskind

16
D(sus4)   D7   Prechorus   C   Gm/B♭   Am   G
I love to watch_ you think but I wish that you'd_ think less_

19
C   C#o7   D(sus4)   Chorus   G
when you're in__ my arms the world don't feel com - plex_ Phi - los - o - phy_ psy -

22
G+   Em/G   Dm7   G7
chol - o - gy___ that stuff don't mean_ too much to me___ we're

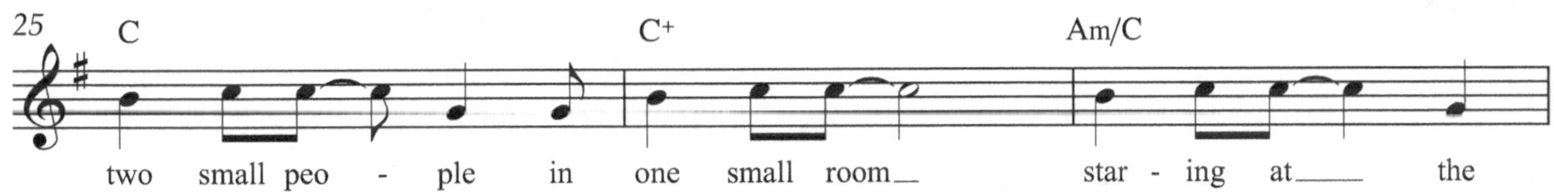
25
C   C+   Am/C
two small peo - ple in one small room_ star - ing at___ the

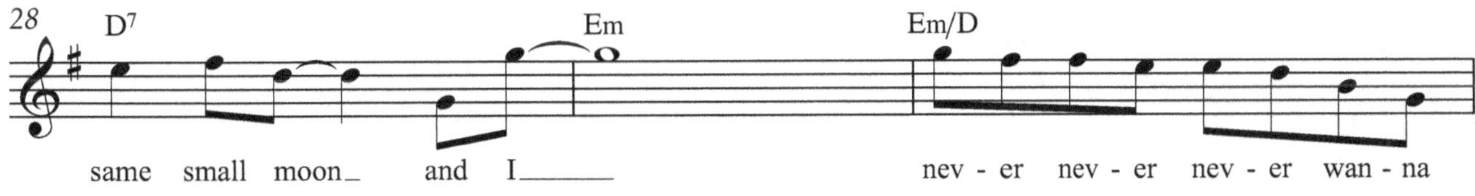
28
D7   Em   Em/D
same small moon_ and I___ nev - er nev - er nev - er wan - na

31
C   A7   Em
let you go___ and I___ for -

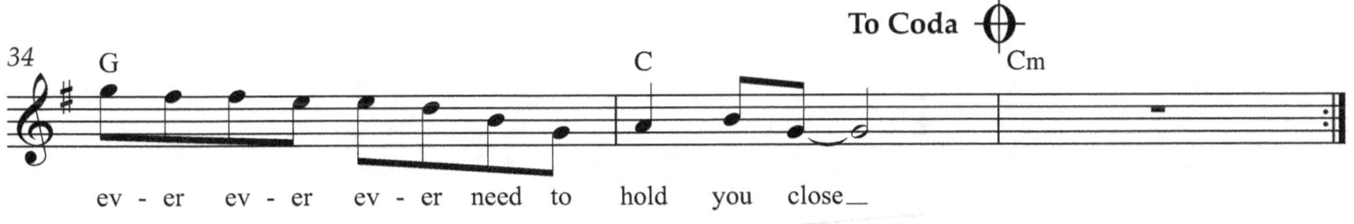
To Coda
34
G   C   Cm
ev - er ev - er ev - er need to hold you close_

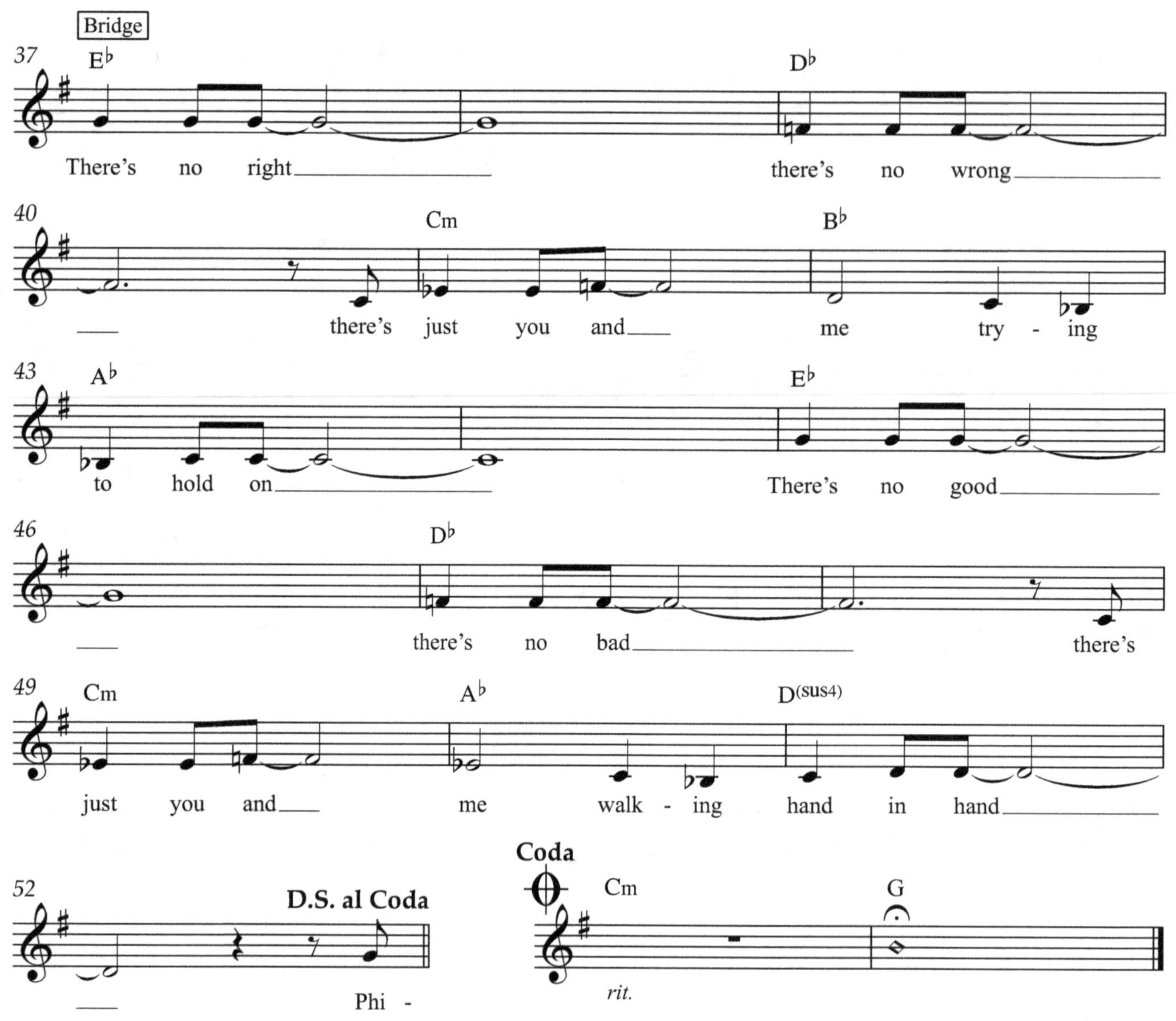

Bridge
37
Eb
Db
There's no right there's no wrong
40
Cm
Bb
there's just you and me try - ing
43
Ab
Eb
to hold on There's no good
46
Db
there's no bad there's
49
Cm
Ab
D(sus4)
just you and me walk - ing hand in hand
52
D.S. al Coda
Phi -
Coda
Cm
G
rit.

Step Eight: Edit

With all the sections assembled, I've now finished the first draft of my song. The next step, editing the song, requires discipline and patience. My preferred editing strategy is to identify the three weakest parts of the song and write alternate versions. After writing an alternate version, you can decide whether you prefer the original version or the alternate.

For me, the three weakest moments in the song are:

1. **Lines:**   I love to watch you think (pre-chorus)
   But I wish you'd think less

   Reason: "I wish you'd think less" feels borderline misogynistic

   Alternate: *I love that you're so thoughtful*
   But ya don't have to stress

2. **Lines:**   *You're always searching, probing, seeking,*
   Trying to find
   A hint of beauty and truth (Verse 1)

   Reason: "Trying" feels bland and I'm not sure what "a hint of" means in this case

   Alternate: *You're always searching, probing, seeking,*
   Striving to see
   A glimpse of beauty and truth

3. **Lines:**   *There's no right*
   There's no wrong
   There's just me and you trying to hold on (Bridge)

   Reason: the last line, in particular, is very cliché ("hold on")

   Alternate: *There's no right*
   There's no wrong
   After darkest night comes the brightest dawn

By and large, I think that these rewrites are stronger than the original versions. Visit the webpage for this unit by scanning the QR code to see the final full score and hear a performance of "Complex."

Takeaways

1. One way to brainstorm for a song is to start with something profound and put it in your own words. Philosophical quotes by famous thinkers can inspire extremely personal songs.

2. Brainstorm multiple ideas for each section. Generating five or more ideas for each section keeps you actively writing and reduces your self-criticism and fear of failure.

3. Keep the function of each section in mind to help guide the writing process. For instance, remember that a pre-chorus should connect between the ideas of the verse and chorus whereas the bridge provides musical contrast while offering an alternate perspective.

4. After each section is done, use connecting chords to help the song achieve a musical flow.

5. Always edit your song after finishing your first draft. Find the weakest moments in your song and brainstorm alternatives.

Practice

1. Make a list of eight quotes that interest you. These could be from philosophers, politicians, artists, and musicians, or from family and friends.

   1)

   2)

   3)

   4)

   5)

   6)

   7)

   8)

2. Write five brief lyrical ideas (roughly two lines each) based on your favorite quote.

    1)

    2)

    3)

    4)

    5)

3. Write a chorus (lyrics and music) based on your favorite of the five fragments you brain-
    stormed.

4. Brainstorm five lyrical ideas for a verse based on your chorus lyrics:

    1)

    2)

    3)

    4)

    5)

5. Create a full verse (lyrics and music) based on your favorite idea.

6. Write one (or two) lyrics for more verses based on the format that you've established. To maintain the structure of the first verse, write each line of your new verse(s) beneath the corresponding line of the first verse.

7. Summarize the themes of your verses and chorus:

Verses:

Chorus:

Then, brainstorm five possible opening lines for a pre-chorus. The lines should connect between the main ideas of the verse and chorus.

1)

2)

3)

4)

5)

8. Pick your favorite opening line and generate more lyrics to complete your pre-chorus. Add music, remember to end on a V chord and build momentum going into the chorus.

9. Brainstorm five possible opening lines for a bridge. Recall that a bridge is often a moment of vulnerability or summary.

1)

2)

3)

4)

5)

10. Pick your favorite idea and write a complete bridge (music and lyrics), providing a harmonic contrast to the verse and chorus sections.

11. Put the sections of your song together to create your first draft, adding transitions to connect between sections.

12. Choose your three least favorite moments of your song and write alternate versions. After you write the alternate versions, you can decide whether you want to keep the original or replace it with your new version.

1. **Lines:**

   Alternate:

2. **Lines:**

   Alternate:

3. **Lines:**

   Alternate:

10. Harmony Beyond Major and Minor

Few songwriters have achieved the staggering success of Harlan Howard, who wrote more than 100 Country Top 10 hit songs. His most famous songs include "I Fall to Pieces," "Busted," and "Heartaches by the Number," sung by legends like Patsy Cline, Johnny Cash, and Ray Charles. His songs are so good, his legacy so towering, that Willie Nelson, himself a legendary songwriter, recorded a tribute album dedicated completely to Howard's songs in 2023, decades after his biggest hits.

Howard famously described a good country song as needing just "three chords and the truth." He has a point. If a song tells a compelling story, captures a recognizable feeling, or simply makes us dance, it doesn't need to be harmonically complex. Indeed, many songwriters, both inside and outside of country music, who have taken Howard's dictum to heart, have written brilliant songs utilizing very few chords.

While many songs thrive on simplicity, others utilize a wider harmonic palette. Whether due to genre, the type of story being told, or the songwriter's personal preference, songs commonly expand not only beyond Howard's I, IV, and V chords, but also outside of the home key altogether.

"Three chords and the truth" is an unquestionable part of songwriting lore. But while "the truth" is sometimes hard to find, the perfect chord doesn't have to be. Expanding your harmonic choices expands the scope of the stories that you can tell. Armed with knowledge about seventh chords, modal interchange, secondary dominants, and slash chords, you can find that chord that gives your audience goosebumps, time after time. This chapter will help you create harmony that accompanies your truth with colorful, dramatic, poignant, surprising, or timeless chords.

Diatonic Seventh Chords

Seventh chords, four-note chords that include the seventh scale degree, add a jazzy character to a song's harmony. Whereas diatonic triads stack two intervals of a third above a scale, **diatonic seventh chords** stack *three* notes above a scale, creating four-note chords with no added accidentals within the home key. The set of diatonic seventh chords within a major key includes two major seventh chords (I, IV), three minor seventh chords (ii, iii, vi), a dominant seventh chord (V), and a half-diminished seventh chord (vii⁰7, a minor seventh chord with a lowered fifth), which is usually avoided.

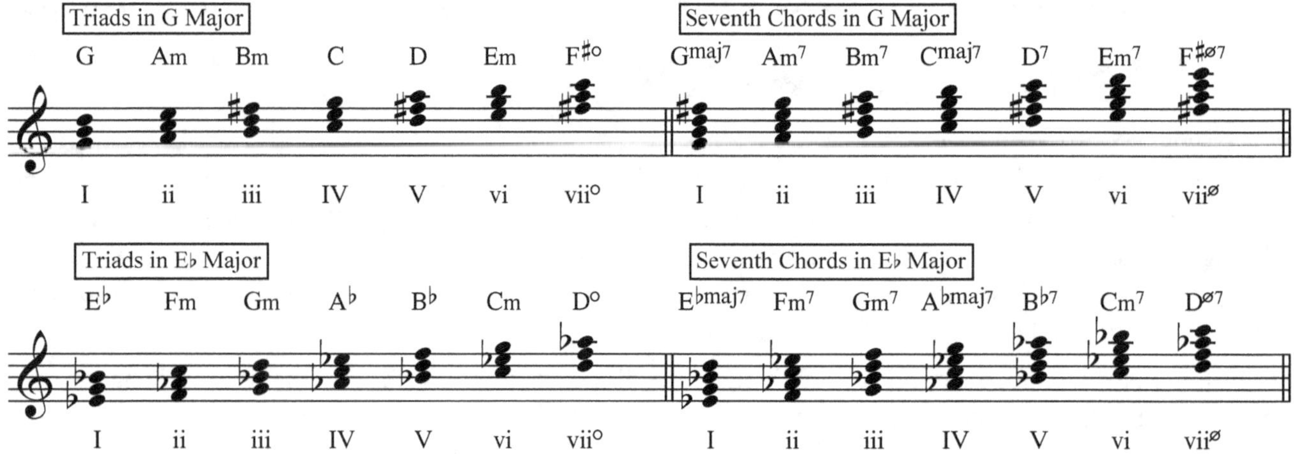

Seventh chords sound inherently lush. Adding a fourth note to the triad creates a thicker, warmer, more complex chord that is associated with jazz, R&B, and neo-soul. With the seventh on top, major chords reveal a tinge of bittersweet nostalgia within their characteristic joy, while minor chords aren't simply sad, they're ambivalent, cool, or calm.

In Great American Songbook tunes like "Fly Me to the Moon," the style dictates that nearly every chord is a seventh chord. Without the addition of the seventh, these chords don't quite fit into the idiom, which uses simple chord progressions but decorates the chords with **upper extensions**, notes stacked above the triad.

Jazz-influenced artists ranging from Stevie Wonder to Bruno Mars also utilize seventh chords in their writing. The next example shows "Espresso" by Sabrina Carpenter and "Ordinary People" by John Legend, which both use seventh chords as their primary color.

In addition to the seventh chords, both of these songs take the jazz influence a step further, adding the **ninth**, yet another note stacked in thirds above the seventh. The ninth, which is equivalent to the second scale degree, adds even more lush richness, either as an additional note in the chord or as a surprising color in the melody. Musicians sometimes refer to the ninth as a "butter" note, a note in the cracks of the harmony that sounds smooth, melty, and rich.

By adding sevenths and ninths, a songwriter can change the color of the song to more sophisticated, rich, soulful sounds without making big edits to their chord progression.

Inversions and Slash Chords

Inversions

All of the chords presented so far have been in **root position**, with the root on the bottom. **Inversions** are chords that are rearranged so that a note other than the root is on bottom. Inversions create different colors without straying too far from traditional harmonic progressions.

Inversions are notated by writing the original chord, then a slash, then the lowest note, such as "C/E" for a C major triad with E in the bass or "Fm/C" for an F minor chord with C in the bass. The names of the inversions can be unintuitive. Examine how the names identify each different chord type:

- **Root Position:** a chord with the root on bottom (C)
- **First Inversion:** a chord with the third on bottom (C/E)
- **Second Inversion:** a chord with the fifth on bottom (C/G)
- **Third Inversion:** a chord with the seventh on bottom; only seventh chords have a third inversion (Cmaj7/B)

The next example presents inversions for a C triad and a C dominant seventh chord in two ways: as simple triads and arranged as for the piano. In the second version, changing only the lowest note, played in the left hand, alters the inversion even while the right-hand chord remains the same.

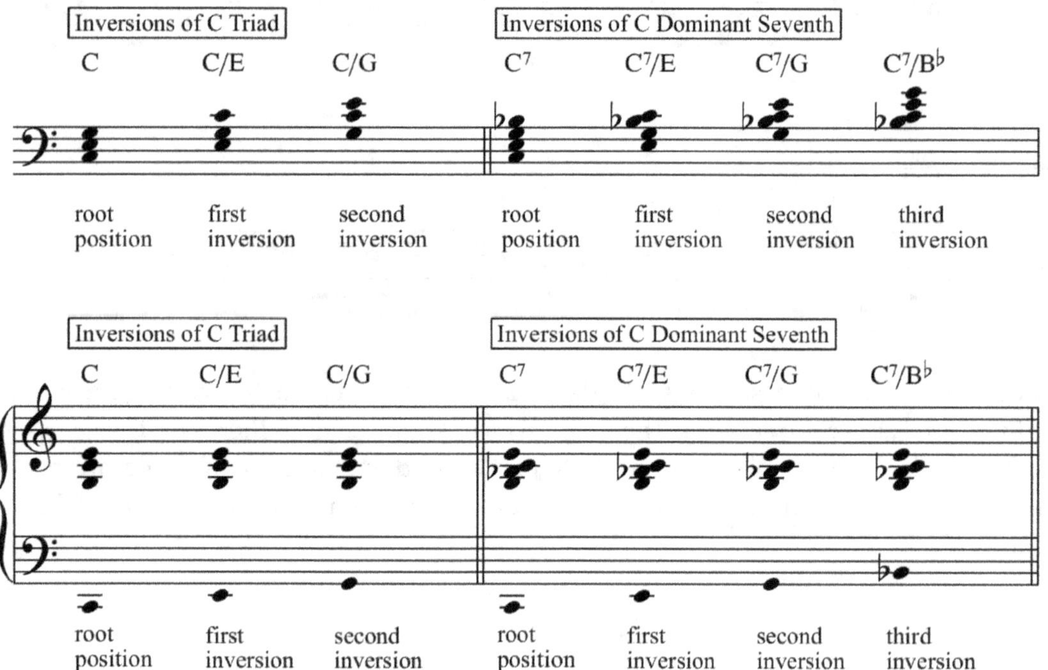

Slash Chords

Although slash chords look like inversions, they function slightly differently. **Slash chords** pair a chord with a bass note that is *not* part of the chord. For instance, the chord symbol "C/D" indicates a C triad above the bass note D. C/D is considered a slash chord rather than an inversion because D is not a member of the C triad. Songwriters use slash chords to create fresh, jazzy harmonies without needing a deep knowledge of jazz theory and seventh chords. The sound of slash chords is particularly associated with singer-songwriters from '60s and '70s like Joni Mitchell, Laura Nyro, Carole King, and James Taylor.

The next example shows possible slash chords pairing different bass notes with C major and C minor triads followed by a brief example of slash chords in a piano accompaniment from Joni Mitchell's "Blue."

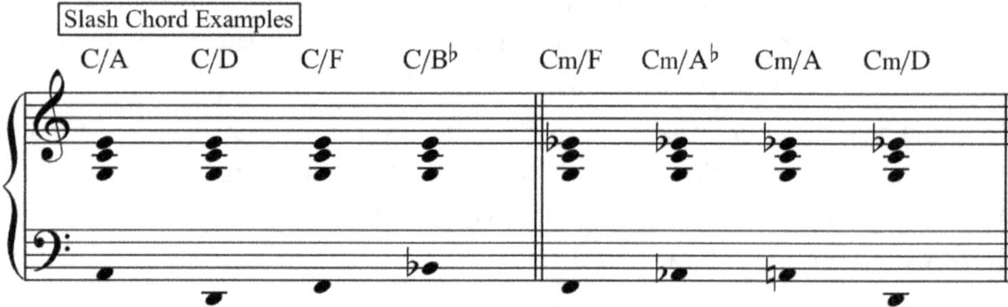

Basslines

Inversions and slash chords are both used to create **stepwise basslines**, scalar bass melodies that move by half or whole step. Stepwise basslines can knit together complex harmonic progressions with a sense of cohesion and direction. In the next examples, the bass moves down by a step for every new chord, which unifies these iconic chord progressions.

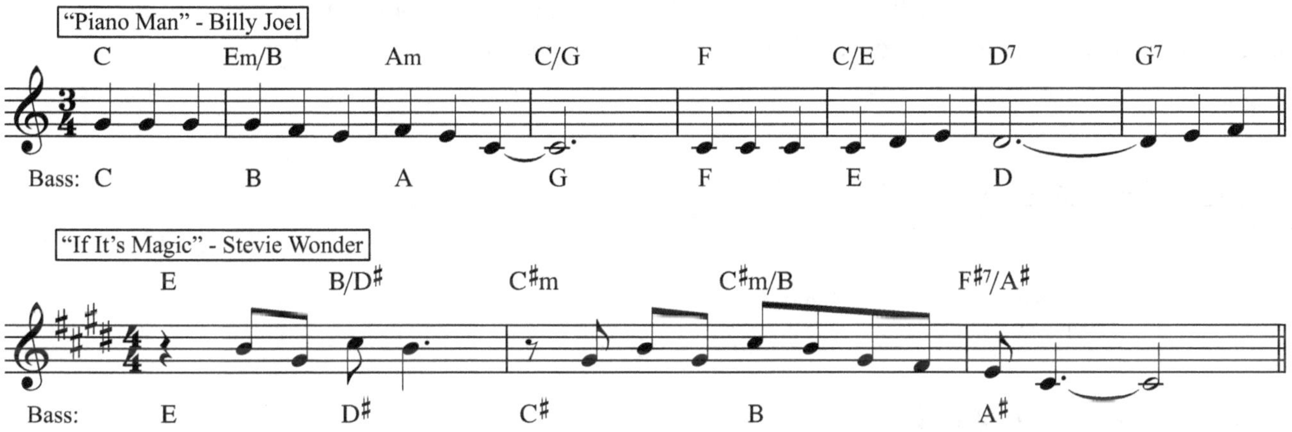

A **pedal point** is a technique in which the bass remains the same for an extended period while chords change above the bass note, creating inversions and slash chords. The term "pedal point" derives from organ music, in which an organist can leave their foot on a single pedal to sustain a bass note, while changing chords on the keyboard. Pedal points can build tension and accommodate dissonances that might sound overly harsh in other settings.

The next example shows the chord progression for the famous introduction to Elton John's "Your Song," in which the chords change (E-flat, A-flat, B-flat, A-flat) over a static bass note (a pedal point of E-flat). Without the pedal point, the progression is a straightforward I-IV-V-IV, but the constant bass note adds magic, tension, and originality.

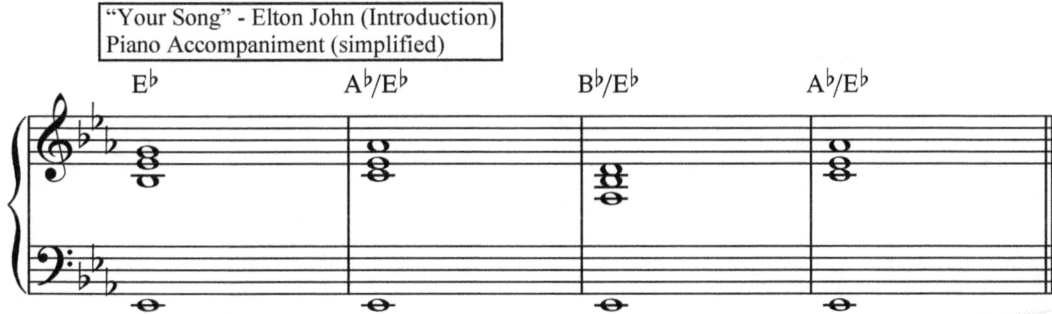

Changing the bass note beneath a chord to create inversions, slash chords, or pedal points can freshen the harmonic landscape, create unexpected connections, and build harmonic momentum without requiring expert harmonic knowledge.

Secondary Dominants

Secondary dominants are dominant seventh chords that target a diatonic triad other than the tonic. The added dominant chord, which is always a fifth above the target chord, momentarily shifts the tonal center toward the target chord. Secondary dominant chords are not diatonic chords.

The next two examples detail how to create secondary dominant chords in two keys.

Secondary Dominant in the Key of C

Potential Targets: Any major or minor diatonic chord in the key of C (Dm, Em, F, G, or Am) could be targeted with a secondary dominant.

For Example: Target D minor. Since Dm is the ii chord, the secondary dominant targeting D minor chord will be named "V/ii" ("the five of two").

How to: Add a dominant seventh chord a fifth above D, an A dominant seventh (A^7). This chord includes a C-sharp, a non-diatonic note in the overall key of C major. Resolve to the D minor triad.

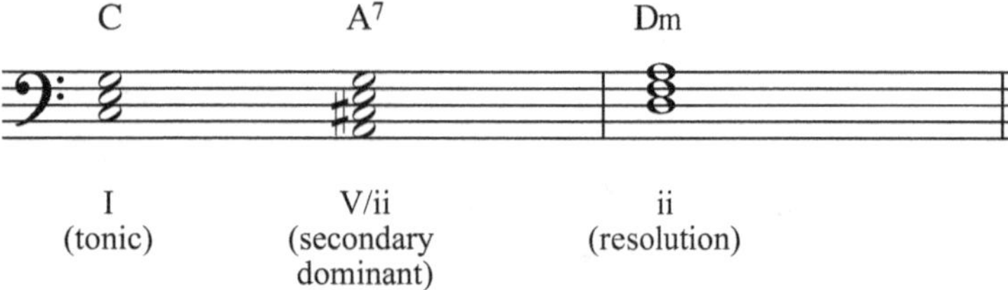

Secondary Dominant Key of F

Potential Targets: Any major or minor diatonic chord in the key of F (Gm, Am, B♭, C, or Dm) could be targeted with a secondary dominant.

For Example: Target C major. Since C is the V chord, the secondary dominant targeting C major will be named "V/V" ("the five of five").

How to: Add a dominant seventh chord a fifth above C, a G dominant seventh (G^7). This chord includes a B natural, a non-diatonic note in the overall key of F major. Resolve to the C major triad.

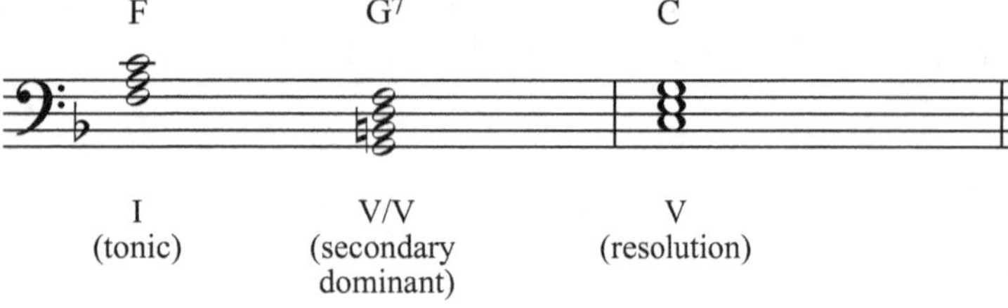

Beyond the two examples given, each of these keys has a total of five potential secondary dominant chords available to target the diatonic triads ii, iii, IV, V, and vi. The next example shows the full range of potential secondary dominant chords resolving to their targets.

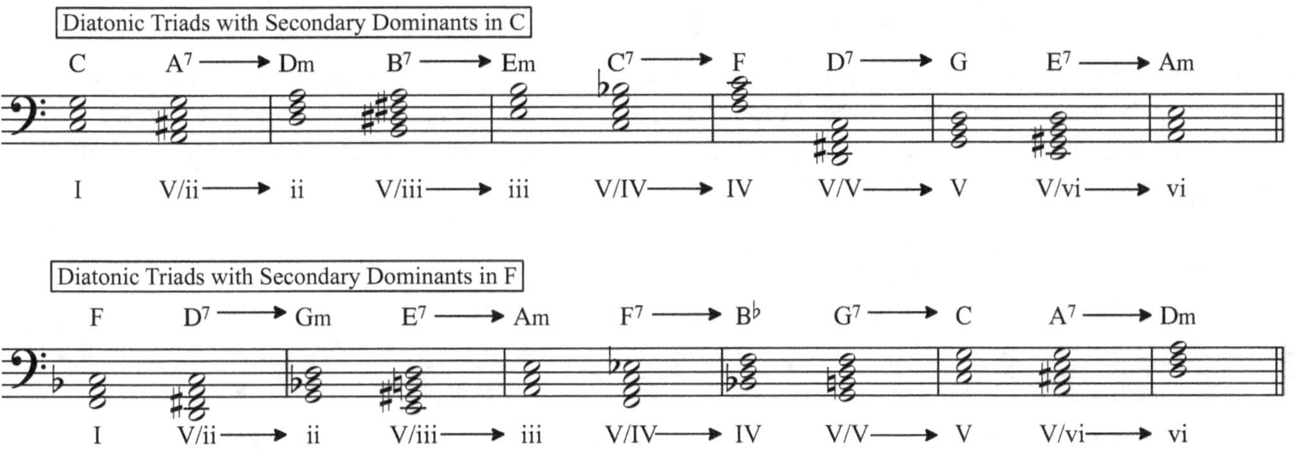

Secondary dominants are common in many musical styles ranging from jazz to rock to pop, by songwriters ranging from George Gershwin to Paul McCartney. They tend to make a piece sound more "sophisticated" and "classic" and less "poppy." The next example shows four songs from various styles that use secondary dominants in their opening measures.

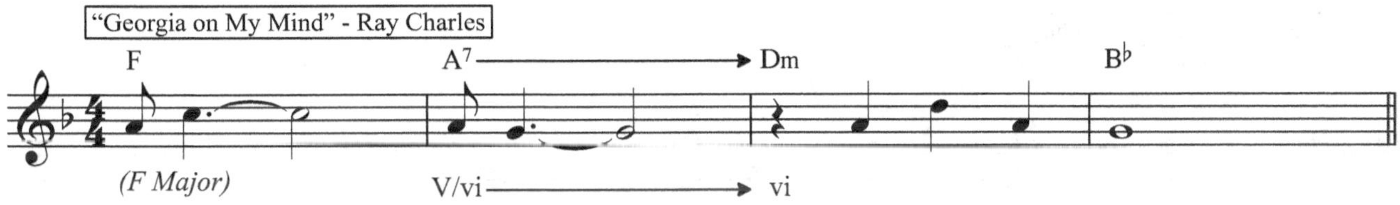

Modal Interchange

Modal interchange or **modal borrowing** refers to intermingling chords from **parallel keys**, major and minor keys based on the same tonic, like C major and C minor. For instance, when writing a piece in C major, a songwriter can insert a chord "borrowed" from the key of C minor, and vice versa.

For songs in major keys, the most commonly borrowed chords are the ii°⁷, the iv, the (♭)VI and the (♭)VII. Because of their minor-key flavors, these chords sound dramatic and poignant when added to a song in a major key. Songwriters use these chords at moments of heightened vulnerability to create the kind of haunting progressions that put a lump in listeners' throats.

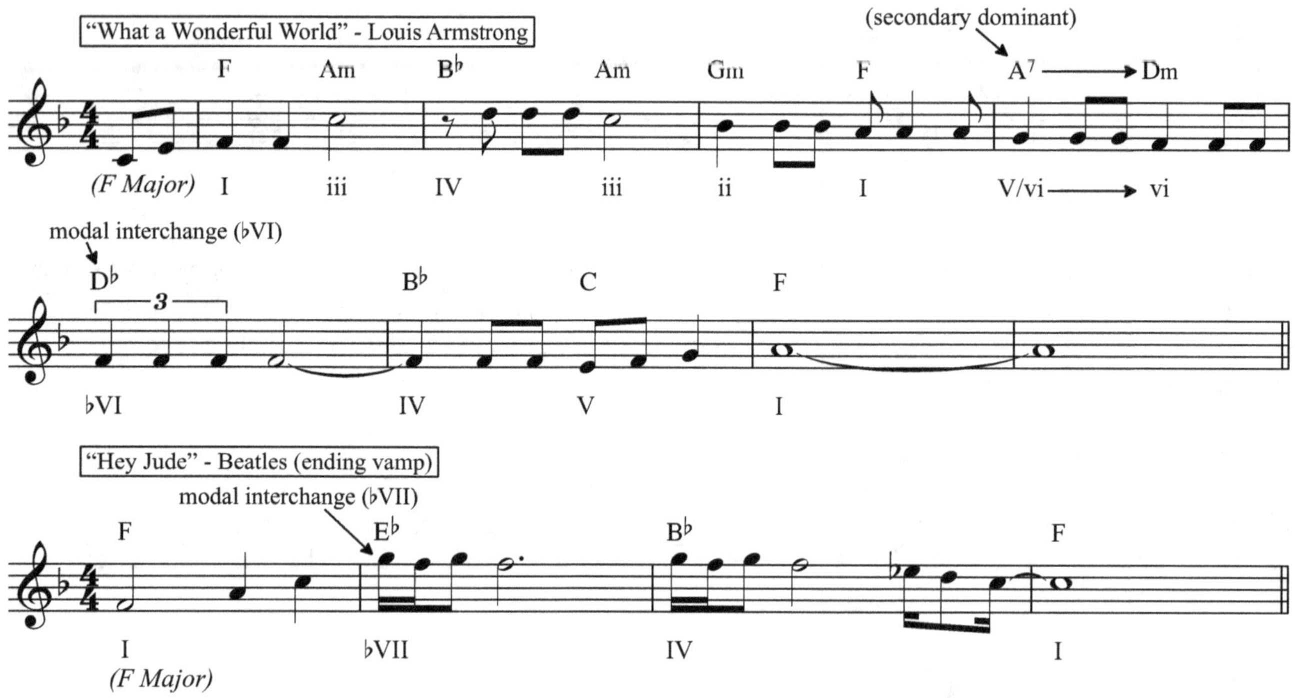

The minor v is a special chord imported into a major key from the parallel minor. Unlike the other chords commonly used in modal interchange, the minor v is formed by stacking notes from the natural minor scale *without* raising the leading tone. The sound of the minor v could be associated with the band Coldplay, who used it prominently in hit songs like "Clocks" and "Speed of Sound."

When a song is in a minor key, the options are not as rich. The most common chord borrowed from the parallel major key is the IV chord, which brings a bright, bluesy color to the minor key. Other chords, like the ii and vi, are not as common, but can be borrowed for a touch of brightness.

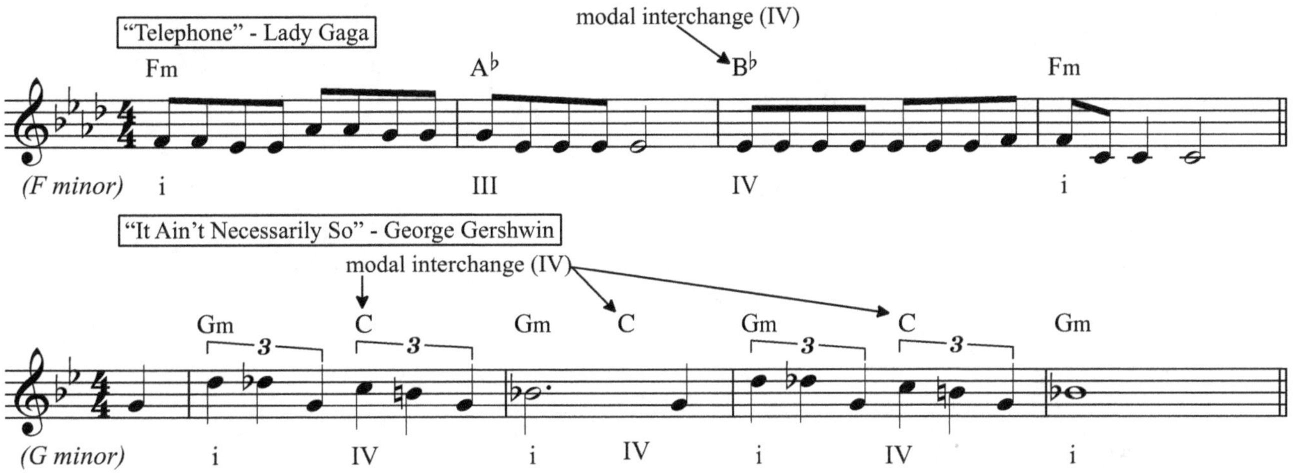

Takeaways

1. Seventh chords add a hint of the rich color of jazz harmony. Use seventh chords for writing in the Great American Songbook, R&B, and neo-soul styles.

2. Not all chords have the root on the bottom. Use inversions to create a stepwise bassline and slash chords to find unexpected sounds.

3. Secondary dominants target diatonic triads while stepping outside of the diatonic key. Although they use notes from outside of the key center, they maintain a clear musical direction and relation to the home key.

4. Include modal interchange in your songs to build emotional intensity and add heightened drama.

Practice

1. Create a stepwise bassline by putting these chords in inversion or creating slash chords. There are many possibilities, and some chords can be left in root position. The first example is done for you.

Original:	C	G	F	C
With Inversions:	C	G/B	F/A	C/G

1.	B♭	Dm	Gm	Dm
2.	Fm	E♭	A♭	B♭m
3.	Cm	B♭	E♭	F
4.	Am^7	Am^7	Dm	C
5.	D	D^7	G	D^7
6.	C	G	Am	G^7
7.	C^7	F	C^7	F
8.	D	Dmaj^7	Bm	D
9.	Gm	D^7	B♭	Cm^7
10.	E♭m	A♭m	G♭	B♭

2. Write the appropriate dominant chord to lead to each of the chords indicated. The first example is completed for you.

1. Example: Cm   Dominant: G^7

2. Chord: D   Dominant:

3. Chord: B♭   Dominant:

4. Chord: Gm   Dominant:

5. Chord: F   Dominant:

6. Chord: B   Dominant:

7. Chord: E♭⁷   Dominant:

8. Chord: A♭   Dominant:

9. Chord: C♯m   Dominant:

10. Chord: Am   Dominant:

11. Chord: Em   Dominant:

3. Name the secondary dominant chord with the indicated function. The first example is completed for you.

1. Example: V/V in D   Secondary Dominant: E^7

2. V/ii in C   Secondary Dominant:

3. V/IV in F   Secondary Dominant:

4. V/vi in G   Secondary Dominant:

5. V/V in B♭   Secondary Dominant:

6. V/iv in Cm   Secondary Dominant:

7. V/III in Dm   Secondary Dominant:

8. V/VII in Fm   Secondary Dominant:

9. V/iii in A   Secondary Dominant:

10. V/V in Fm   Secondary Dominant:

11. V/vi in E♭   Secondary Dominant:

4. Replace the underlined chord with a chord from the parallel key to create modal interchange. In minor keys, primarily change the iv to a IV. Remember, in major keys, change the following:

iii → ♭III | IV → iv | V → v | vi → ♭VI

<u>Example</u>: (key of C)	C	F	G	<u>F</u>
<u>Change to:</u>	C	F	G	Fm

1. Progression (key of D)   A   G   <u>G</u>   D

   Change to:

2. Progression (key of G)   G   C   <u>Em</u>   G

   Change to:

3. Progression (key of Fm)   Fm   <u>B♭m</u>   Fm   C

   Change to:

4. Progression (key of C)   C   <u>Em</u>   <u>Am</u>   G

   Change to:

5. Progression (key of Dm)   <u>Gm</u>   Dm   C   Dm

   Change to:

6. Progression (key of E♭)   <u>B♭</u>   E♭   <u>A♭</u>   <u>E♭</u>

   Change to:

11. Repeated Sounds and Structures

In the third season of the 2020s television show, *Only Murders in the* Building, Steve Martin's character is tasked with performing an impossible **patter song**, a song with rapid-fire, mostly-spoken lyrics focusing on rhythm and wordplay. The song, "Which of the Pickwick Triplets Did It?" written for the show by song-writing duo Benj Pasek and Justin Paul in collaboration with Marc Shaiman and Scott Wittman, plays into Martin's genius for comedic silliness. The subject of the song – deciding which of three infant triplets is the mastermind at the heart of a murder mystery – is funny enough. But it's the obsessive play with sounds that puts this song over the top.

Look more closely at the title, "Which of the Pickwick Triplets Did It?" Besides the de-emphasized syllables "of the," a single short "i" vowel sound repeats seven times. Other lines also repeat vowel sounds. Notice the repeated "ee" and "ah" vowel sounds in the following passages:

> *It's time to give these teething, seething three*
> *The third degree*
>
> *But could that rotten tot be behind this evil plot?*

Other lines focus on repeating consonant sounds, especially the repeated "p" drawn from "Pickwick":

> *Preening Patrick is pernicious with an appetite so vicious*
> *Proving he's a perp amidst this Pickwick triptych*
> *Could Paco's passion prove apocalyptic?*

The dazzling volley of repeated sounds, internal rhymes, and tongue-twisting wordplay calls for a virtuosic performance from Martin's character. Predictably, he struggles to master the song until the season finale, when he finally pulls it off to great acclaim.

Although this example demonstrates pushing sonic wordplay to the point of absurdity, repeated sounds can be much more than a gimmick. They can make a song more poetically melodious, add exuberant humor, help a performer enunciate, and tie together seemingly unrelated ideas. Repeated sounds make songs memorable and inspire songwriters to explore new directions.

Basics of Repeated Sounds

This book has already spent time discussing one important type of repeated sound: rhyme. Recall that words rhyme when the *final stressed syllables* of two words share a vowel and/or final consonant sound. However, when sounds are repeated in other parts of words, the repetitions fall into other categories: alliteration, assonance, and consonance. These three devices track repeated **phonemes** – individual sounds within a word. The next section distinguishes between the three types of repetitions, each using the word "pal" as an example.

Three Types of Phonemes

⇨ **Assonance** refers to the repetition of a vowel sound anywhere within nearby words, including at the beginning.

For the word pal:

Gap, *sag*, and *happy* form assonance with *pal* because they share the "a" vowel sound.

⇨ **Consonance** refers to the repetition of a consonant sound anywhere within nearby words.

For the word pal:

Doll and *chill* form consonance with *pal* because they share the "l" sound.

Mop and *coop* form consonance with *pal* because they share the "p" sound, but not at the beginning of the word.

Loop and *lap* form consonance with *pal* because they share both the "p" and "l" sounds.

⇨ **Alliteration** refers to the repetition of consonant sounds at the beginning of nearby words.

For the word pal:

Pig, *palpitate*, *perambulate*, and *poor* form alliteration with *pal* because they share the "p" consonant sound at the beginning of the word.

The next chart shows possible assonance, consonance, and alliteration for the four example words: *sue*, *dog*, *tail*, and *monster*. Notice that the heard sound rather than the written letter matters when considering sonic repetition:

Example Word	Assonance	Consonance	Alliteration
sue	gr<u>ue</u>l, d<u>o</u>, tr<u>oo</u>p	hi<u>ss</u>, la<u>ss</u>o, po<u>sses</u>s	<u>s</u>oggy, <u>s</u>upper, <u>s</u>ummary
dog	b<u>o</u>p, c<u>o</u>t, s<u>a</u>lt	ba<u>g</u>, ro<u>d</u>, <u>g</u>oo<u>d</u>	<u>d</u>ill, <u>d</u>ig, <u>d</u>ark
tail	p<u>ai</u>n, m<u>a</u>le, h<u>a</u>re	mi<u>ll</u>, fa<u>t</u>, <u>l</u>a<u>t</u>e	<u>t</u>ough, <u>t</u>alk, <u>t</u>ip
monster	l<u>o</u>ss, fl<u>au</u>nt, t<u>a</u>ll	lo<u>st</u>, pri<u>m</u>, <u>st</u>ep	<u>m</u>ythic, <u>m</u>alt, <u>m</u>ute

It can be confusing to determine how to properly identify which device best describes the relationship between two words. The next section addresses some common questions.

Q: **If two words share the same first vowel sound, should the result be called alliteration or assonance? For instance, how about the words *apple, alligator,* and *avarice*?**

A: There is no special name for repeated vowel sounds at the beginning of words. Any repeated vowel sound, even at the beginning of a word, is referred to as assonance.

Q: **What should I call it if there are two repeated consonant sounds – one at the beginning of a word and one at the middle or end of a word?**

A: It should be referred to as consonance. For example, looking at "f" sounds: *fall* and *gaffe* create consonance, even though *fall* begins with an "f." Taken as a three-word group, *fall, fact,* and *gaffe* form consonance, even though two of the three words are alliterative.

Q: **What about combined consonant sounds, like the "sk" in *sky*? Does another word have to have the exact "sk" sound to be alliterative, or can it match a part of the sound, for instance, just the "s" sound?**

A: To be true alliteration, the combined sound should match exactly. For instance, *sky* is alliterative with *scale* and *skimp*. However, most ears will still pick up on a weaker sonic match if only part of the sound is shared. For instance, if *sky* is placed in the same sentence as *sea*, the two words together might create pleasing sonic interplay even if the outcome is not precisely alliteration. In these cases, it is useful to categorize alliteration as "exact" (*sky/scale*) or "inexact" (*sky/sun*).

Q: **Can a pair of words activate more than one device at a time, for instance, alliteration and assonance?**

A: Absolutely – words can reflect multiple devices in one. For instance, *left* and *level* create alliteration with their shared initial "l"s, assonance with the repeated "eh" vowel sounds, and consonance between the initial "l" of *left* and the final "l" of *level*. Because of the multiplicity of relationships, these two words sound very musical when placed next to one another.

Using Repeated Sounds Purposefully

Songwriters repeat sounds to create poetic beauty, heighten rhythmic momentum, imprint lyrics and titles into listeners' memories, and introduce humor through overuse. Besides their appeal to listeners, focusing on sonic repetitions can help songwriters brainstorm unconventional word choices.

Poetic Beauty

In poetry, the musical sound of words is carefully crafted to complement their literal meanings. Good lyricists, like good poets, know that intentional sonic choices can alter a lyric's tone, and that repeating a certain phoneme can sharpen the writer's intent. For instance, softer consonant sounds usually create a feeling of tranquility and wonder whereas harsh consonant sounds might indicate precision and severity.

Amy Winehouse elevates her poetic language through alliteration in the song, "Love is a Losing Game." Besides the repeated "l"s in the title, Winehouse includes the alliterative phrases "five-story fire," "battle blind," "final frame," and "memories mar my mind," which stands out because of the unusual word, "mar." Despite the intense and depressing subject matter, the repeated consonants mesmerize the listener, softening the song's dark subject matter to match Winehouse's calm, cool delivery.

In the song, "Amelia," Joni Mitchell uses phrases that combine alliteration, consonance, and assonance, like "hexagram of the heavens," "false alarm," "picture postcard charms," and "this is how I hide the hurt." In each of these phrases, there's a play of sounds that enchants the listener, using soft consonants and open, resonant vowels to animate the flowing nature of the song, which achieves a sense of wide-open spaces and nostalgic wondering.

Memorable Titles and Phrases

Repeated sounds, especially alliteration, imprint a song title or refrain into the memory of a listener. For instance, the title/refrain, "Walking in a Winter Wonderland" which prominently repeats a "w" sound is fun to sing, joyful to hear, and makes the title and lyric more memorable. Other examples of song titles that use repeated sounds include "Mean Mr. Mustard" (Beatles), "Lay Lady Lay" (Dylan), "Pastime Paradise" (Wonder), "Back to Black" (Winehouse), "All Too Well" (Swift), and "Paper Planes" (M.I.A.).

Rhythmic Momentum

Repeated sounds can make lines more pleasing to speak and emphasize a song's rhythmic momentum.

"My Favorite Things," by Rodgers and Hammerstein, is all about delights, and it delights the listener with repeated sounds like "warm woolen mittens" and "blue satin sashes." Many of the repeated sounds also highlight the song's waltz rhythm, with lines like "raindrops on roses" using alliteration to emphasize three-beat patterns and others like "whiskers on kittens," "silver-white winters," and "wild geese that fly" using assonance to mark the beat.

Stephen Sondheim uses a "t" sound purposefully in the first line of "The Ballad of Sweeney Todd." In the line, "attend the tale of Sweeney Todd," the sharpness and precision of the "t" lends an ominous harshness to the song's rhythmic opening. Elsewhere in the song, Sondheim uses similarly sharp sounds, like the "kw" in "quick and quiet and clean, he was," and the repeated "p" in "an apron, a towel, a pail and a mop." These popping consonants give the song rhythmic urgency and usher the audience into a world where everything is bleak and severe.

"Love Me or Leave Me" a Great American Songbook tune from 1928, creates rhythm in its first phrase, "love me or leave me or let me be lonely," repeating an initial "l" sound on beats 1 and 3 of the first two measures. In addition to forming alliteration, the titular words "love" and "leave" are examples of a special class of words that form **pararhyme**. These are words with identical consonant sounds but different vowel sounds, like "lighter" and "later," and "fate" and "foot."

Humor

If repeated sonic devices are overused, they can call attention to themselves and create a humorous effect. Children's songs often overuse repeated sounds for humor, like in Raffi's song "Shake My Sillies Out." In each verse, Raffi chooses a different consonant and then sings that he will "clap my crazies out," "jump my jiggles out," and "wiggle my waggles away."

Cole Porter was a master of making audiences laugh through linguistic backflips. In his humorous list song, "Let's Do It," Porter references "cold cape cod clams" and then challenges the singer to a virtuosic tongue-twister with the phrase "in shallow shoals, English soles do it." In a verse about zoo animals, Porter chooses his adjectives to create alliteration, describing "courageous kangaroos" and "heavy hippopotami."

Inspiring Unusual Choices

Ira Gershwin was almost certainly thinking of alliteration when he wrote this lyric in the song "I've Got a Crush on You":

> *Could you coo, could you care*
> *For a cunning cottage we could share?*

Focusing on the repeated "k" sound, Gershwin chooses highly unexpected words, especially "coo" and "cunning." Although "cunning" has a rare regional definition of "pretty or pleasing" that fits in this verse, it is not the first word that most would think of in that situation, unless you're searching for an adjective with a "k" sound.

Notice all of the alliteration in the first stanza of Elton John's "Tiny Dancer":

> *Blue-jean baby, L.A. lady*
> *Seamstress for the band*
> *Pretty-eyed, pirate smile*
> *You'll marry a music man*

Creative descriptors like "*pirate* smile" and "*blue-jean* baby" might have come to lyricist Bernie Taupin spontaneously, but they were likely the result of searching for words that share sounds with the more pedestrian words in the song, "baby," "lady," "pretty," and "smile."

When used strategically, assonance, consonance, and alliteration can produce poetic turns of phrase, generate memorable hooks, build rhythmic momentum, make your audience laugh, and inspire unusual word choices.

Repeating Larger Structures

In addition to repeating phonemes, lyricists can repeat larger structures, such as syllables or entire words, to achieve many of the same purposes outlined in the previous section.

Fair warning: In the next section, you'll find several long, likely unfamiliar words derived from the tradition of rhetorical debate. It's not essential to memorize the words. The words are included because having a name for something can help you remember what that something is. Even if the names feel archaic or overly technical, the strategies they refer to are very much worth learning.

Repeating Syllables

Songwriters often repeat the same syllable or syllables in two different words, with the repetition acting as a pivot between two ideas or a link between different words. For instance, in the verse to the previously mentioned song, "Let's Do It," Cole Porter writes:

The repetition of the syllable *blue* in "bluebird" and "bluebell" links two concepts that are not obviously related, a bird and a flower, while reinforcing the parallel structure of the verse. Later in the same song, Porter describes "sentimental centipedes," which repeats the syllable group "senti." This description pivots between the two words, delighting the audience while making Porter's description convincing, even though centipedes are not generally thought of as particularly emotional or mawkish.

In "Empire State of Mind," Jay-Z repeats the syllable *blind* in two different contexts, saying "Lights is blinding, girls need blinders." A few lines later, he says, "Lined with casualties who sip the life casually," repeating the syllable group "casual" as part of two very different words. In a hip-hop context, these repetitions primarily create a natural internal rhythm which separates the great emcees from the more novice rappers.

Polyptoton is a specific kind of syllabic repetition in which the repeated words share the same root word. For example, because "believer," "disbelief," and "believable," all share the same root word ("believe"), they form a polyptoton when placed in the same line or stanza. Besides the sonic repetition, polyptoton emphasizes a theme by presenting the root word from multiple perspectives.

For instance, the first line of Gershwin's "Embraceable You" is "Embrace me, my sweet embraceable you." "Embrace" and "embraceable" form a polyptoton because they're both derived from the root word, "embrace." They produce a rhythmic cadence and hammer home the longing for physical affection.

The last stanza of the song "Isn't it Romantic?" also contains a polyptoton:

The words "romantic" in the first line and "romance" in the last line are both derived from the same root word, "romance." The transformed repetition from "romantic" to "romance" gives the song a conclusive ending by bookending the stanza, without merely reiterating the word.

Repeating Words

Beyond phonemes and syllables, songs frequently repeat whole words in different contexts or settings. Repeating words creates rhythm, builds connection, creates clever wordplay, and raises questions about relationships.

Repetitions are paramount for creating rhythm and flow in the hip-hop tradition. Besides the syllabic repetitions covered in the last section, Jay-Z also repeats the words "Yankee" and "cab" in the following lines from "Empire State of Mind":

> *Catch me at the X with OG at a Yankee game*
> *I made the Yankee hat more famous than a Yankee can*
>
> *Yellow cab, gypsy cab, dollar cab, holla back*

Notice that each of these repetitions is put in the same pattern of stress. Each repetition of "Yankee" is followed with a monosyllabic word ("game," "hat," "can") whereas each repetition of "cab" is preceded by a two-syllable descriptor ("yellow," "gypsy," "dollar"). These repeated clusters give the rap an intentional rhythm that creates a compelling groove.

Antanaclasis is a device in which songwriters repeat the same word within a line or stanza, but each repetition carries a different meaning. Words that carry multiple meanings, like "bat" (flying animal or baseball stick) and "fire" (hot flames or job dismissal) are called **homonyms**. In songs, homonyms tend to be more subtle than "bat" or "fire," with their shifting meanings usually owing to common expressions, changes in parts of speech, or nuanced distinctions.

For instance, in "Since U Been Gone," Kelly Clarkson sings:

> *How can I put it*
> *You put me on*

The repeated use of the word *put* is an example of antanaclasis. In the first line, "put" means to "say" or "express" whereas in the second part of the phrase, "put me on" is an idiom meaning "tricked" or "pretended." The wordplay makes a somewhat commonplace situation much more attention-grabbing.

In Vampire Weekend's song, "Obvious Bicycle," antanaclasis helps to connect two complementary ideas:

> *You ought to spare your face the razor*
> *Because no one's gonna spare the time for you*

In the first line, "spare" means to "save from" or to "refrain from" whereas in the second line, "spare" means to "save for" or to "make available." The lines pivot on this word, connecting two ideas – the details of a morning routine and an overall disillusionment about life.

In Bruno Mars' song, "Treasure," the titular word appears as both a noun and a verb in the chorus:

> *Treasure, that is what you are*
> *Honey, you're my golden star*
> *You know you can make my wish come true*
> *If you let me treasure you*

Notice the unusual syntax that Mars uses in the first line to include "treasure" as a noun. Instead of saying "You are a treasure," as a person would say in everyday conversation, he puts the sentence's object at the beginning of the line to create a more awkward, poetic construction, saying "Treasure, that is what you are." The syntactic trick allows him to bookend the stanza using antanaclasis.

Special Types of Word Repetition

Songwriters can manipulate repetitions for maximum impact using anadiplosis, chiasmus, and antanaclasis.

Anadiplosis: Linking

Anadiplosis is a special kind of repetition in which the last word or phrase of one line becomes the first word or phrase of the next line. In anadiplosis, the meaning of the linking word can remain the same, but clever songwriters often combine anadiplosis with antanaclasis, connecting lines using homonyms.

Anadiplosis is clearly the driving factor of the chorus of the 2010s boy band The Wanted's song, "Glad you Came."

> *Turn the lights out now*
> *Now I'll take you by the hand*
> *Hand you another drink*
> *Drink it if you can*
> *Can you spend a little time?*
> *Time is slipping away*
> *Away from us, so stay*
> *Stay with me, I can make*
> *Make you glad you came*

Each line connects to the next line through a single word, like a linked chain. In the most artful connections, the words slightly change meaning. For example, both "hand" and "drink" change functions from a noun to a verb between their first usage and their second usage.

In the John Mayer song, "Daughters," the words "daughters" and "mothers" are repeated to reinforce the steps of Mayer's thought process.

> *Fathers be good to your daughters*
> *Daughters will love like you do*
> *Girls become lovers who turn into mothers*
> *So mothers be good to your daughters too*

The anadiplosis makes the stanza feel almost like a math equation (where if a=b and b=c, then by the transitive property, a=c). Using linking words helps the audience follow Mayer's argument to his conclusion.

In the Bruno Mars song, "When I Was Your Man," the refrain turns on the repetition of the word "dancing." The repetition pivots between a positive sentiment and a negative sentiment by adding the word "but."

> *Now my baby's dancing*
> *But she's dancing with another man*

Because audiences experience songs in real time, listeners get their hopes up in the first line only to have them dashed in the second line, with anadiplosis providing the crucial pivot. Notice that the connecting effect is still powerful even though the word "dancing" is not the *very* first word of the second line.

Chiasmus: Swapping

Chiasmus is a rhetorical device in which two words or phrases are repeated but in the reverse order of the original presentation. When using chiasmus, whichever element comes first in the original statement should come second in the repetition. For instance, the song "White Christmas" by Irving Berlin includes the phrase "white Christmas" in the first line, but concludes with a line that places "Christmas" before "white."

> *I'm dreaming of a white Christmas*
> *Just like the ones I used to know*
>
> *...*
>
> *May your days be merry and bright*
> *And may all your Christmases be white*

Chiasmus helps to conclude the song in a satisfying way while delightfully surprising the audience with the ingenuity of the reversal. Plus, "white" is a much easier word to rhyme than "Christmas"!

Carole King uses chiasmus to bookend a stanza in her song "Where You Lead":

> *Where you lead, I will follow*
> *Anywhere that you tell me to*
> *If you need, you need me to be with you*
> *I will follow where you lead*

By reversing the placement of the words "follow" and "lead" in the initial and final lines, King grammatically demonstrates the idea of following and leading, flipping the leader and follower.

In the bridge of his song "Cars are Cars," Paul Simon uses chiasmus to try a thought experiment. Whereas in the first line, "car" precedes "home," in the third line, "home" precedes "car":

> *I once had a car that was more like a home*
> *I lived in it, loved in it, polished its chrome*
> *If some of my homes had been more like my car*
> *I probably wouldn't have traveled this far*

Simon's "if" statement proposes a hypothetical that's the reverse of the situation in the first line. In this way, he gently guides the audience into a conjecture (*what if my homes had been more like my car?*) that otherwise might seem a bit fanciful or random.

Epanalepsis: Bookending

Finally, **epanalepsis** is a repetition of a word or phrase at the beginning and end of a stanza or song. Epanalepsis gives listeners the satisfaction of a symmetrical bookend to a song or stanza. It is most effective when the material is somehow transformed from its first use to its final use.

In each of the A sections of "Yesterday," Paul McCartney repeats an important word at the beginning and end of the stanza.

> *Yesterday*
> *All my troubles seemed so far away*
> *Now it looks as though they're here to stay*
> *Oh, I believe in yesterday*
>
> *Suddenly*
> *I'm not half the man I used to be*
> *There's a shadow hanging over me*
> *Oh, yesterday came suddenly*

For someone hearing this iconic song for the first time, the first word of each stanza is a mystery hanging in the air, waiting for additional context. By the time it returns at the end of the stanza, the intervening lines have made its return feel almost inevitable, both expected and satisfying.

Similarly, the Great American Songbook standard, "You Don't Know What Love Is" repeats the title phrase in both the opening and closing lines of the first stanza.

> *You don't know what love is*
> *Until you've learned the meaning of the blues*
> *Until you've loved a love you've had to lose*
> *You don't know what love is*

Grammatically, the clause functions as the beginning and then the end of a sentence, both opening a thought and then completing it. The stanza's third line also includes vivid, overlapping examples of alliteration ("loved"/"love"/"lose") and polyptoton ("loved"/"love") that generate a hypnotic rhythm.

Many entire songs start and end with the same phrases, particularly in the Great American Songbook tradition. Sammy Fain's "I'll Be Seeing You," which is highly associated with singer Billie Holiday, opens and closes the song with the title phrase. The quoted lines represent the first and final sections:

> *I'll be seeing you*
> *In all the old familiar places*
> *That this heart of mine embraces*
> *All day and through*
>
> …
>
> *I'll find you in the morning sun*
> *And when the night is new*
> *I'll be looking at the moon*
> *But I'll be seeing you*

The final flourish of the song is to distinguish between "looking" and "seeing." It becomes clear that the singer is not "looking" at this person, who is not present to be looked at, but is rather being "seen" in her mind's eye, in a more spiritual way.

You don't need to remember the long, Latin-sounding words *anadiplosis*, *chiasmus*, and *epanalepsis* for these devices. But including these elements makes a song feel "tight," well-constructed, and clever. By playing with words in these ways, your songs can make unexpected connections seem commonplace and help conclusions feel satisfying.

Takeaways

1. Assonance, consonance, and alliteration are devices that refer to repeating consonant and vowel sounds. They can be used to create poetic beauty, generate rhythmic momentum, make a memorable hook, and add humor.

2. Repeating syllables in different words creates rhythmic groove, acts as a logical pivot, and builds unexpected connections.

3. Repeating whole words in new contexts is common in songs, especially using antanaclasis, a device in which the word is presented in a new context or with a different meaning.

4. Repeated words can be swapped, used to create links between lines, or repeated to bookend a stanza or song. Manipulating repeated words in these ways combines familiarity with delightful surprise.

Practice

1. Provide an adjective for the given noun using each suggested device. Strive to think outside the box and brainstorm unexpected words. The first example is completed for you.

   A. Noun: moon

   Assonance: looming moon
   Consonance: green moon
   Alliteration: menacing moon

   B. Noun: parrot

   Assonance: _____________ parrot
   Consonance: _____________ parrot
   Alliteration: _____________ parrot

   C. Noun: sadness

   Assonance: _____________ sadness
   Consonance: _____________ sadness
   Alliteration: _____________ sadness

   D. Noun: house

   Assonance: _____________ house
   Consonance: _____________ house
   Alliteration: _____________ house

   E. Noun: road

   Assonance: _____________ road
   Consonance: _____________ road
   Alliteration: _____________ road

   F. Noun: lover

   Assonance: _____________ lover
   Consonance: _____________ lover
   Alliteration: _____________ lover

   G. Noun: promise

   Assonance: _____________ promise
   Consonance: _____________ promise
   Alliteration: _____________ promise

2. Now, choose a verb for each noun using the suggested device. The first one is done for you:

   A. The house <u>growls</u> (assonance)

   B. The cheetah __________________ (consonance)

   C. The pattern _________________ (alliteration)

   D. The air ___________________ (assonance)

   E. The sea __________________ (alliteration)

   F. The clouds ________________ (consonance)

   G. The darkness _______________ (alliteration)

   H. The spiral _________________ (consonance)

   I. The web _________________ (assonance)

   J. The chef _________________ (consonance)

   K. The puppy _______________ (consonance)

   L. The afterglow _______________ (assonance)

   M. The habits ________________ (alliteration)

   N. The wallpaper _______________ (consonance)

3. Write 8 words or phrases that include the given syllable, then write a sentence using at least three of the words. It's okay if the sentence is a little silly sounding! The first example is done for you.

   A. **Like**
      Words: likelihood, alike, likeness, likeable, dislike, childlike, ladylike, lookalike, like-minded
      Sentence: The likelihood that I'll be likeminded with my lookalike seems low.

   B. **For (four)**
      Words:

      Sentence:

   C. **Just**
      Words:

      Sentence:

D. **Tire**

   Words:

   Sentence:

E. **In**

   Words:

   Sentence:

F. **Opt**

   Words:

   Sentence:

4. Complete these lines using anadiplosis, that is, starting with the word or phrase that ended the previous line. Try to change the meaning or the repeated word or pivot the direction of the story. The first example is done for you.

   A. You told me that I should believe you
   <u>Well, I believe that I can't trust you anymore</u>

   B. Why don't you ever say that you love me

   ____

   C. I just don't know if I can love you, sometimes

   ____

   D. I love it when you tell me that I'm beautiful

   ____

   E. When you're near me, I feel like I'm going crazy

   ____

   F. I imagine fields of flowers and skies filled with sun

   ____

   G. Baby, I don't want you to see me crying

   ____

5. Complete the following stanzas using chiasmus. The first three provide the chiasmus for you, but the final few rely on you to create it. Aim to include at least one rhyme:

A. I had the scariest dream last night

____

____

Last night I had the scariest dream

B. He loves the most beautiful girl

____

____

The most beautiful girl loves him

C. Some days the world moves so slow

____

____

The world moves so slow some days

D. Ida was laughing at the architect

____

____

____

E. How does the moon shine so clear above the mountains?

____

____

____

6. Given the first lines, complete the following stanzas using either chiasmus or epanalepsis. Aim to include at least one rhyme:

A. I can't stop thinking about the boy at the coffee shop

____

____

____

B. Powerful is as powerful does

____

____

____

C. Every time I see her face I see a sunny sky

____

____

____

D. Deidre called me yesterday to share the news

____

____

____

12. Melody

There's a legend about David Raksin, a film composer, who was writing the score for a film noir movie, *Laura*, in which the main character falls in love with the portrait of a woman who appears to be dead. When the director told Raksin that he wanted to use a pre-existing song as the film's love theme, Raksin asked for the opportunity to write a custom theme that would better fit the mood. He was given one week to create the perfect song.

With no ideas and the clock ticking, Raksin arrived home to find a letter from his wife in which she explained that she was leaving him. In the liner notes to one of his recordings, Raksin explains what happened next:

> *I took the letter out of my pocket, put it up on the piano and began to play. Suddenly the meaning of the words on the page became clear to me: she was saying "hail, farewell," "better luck next life" and "get lost!" Knowing that, I felt the last of my strength go, and then – without willing it – I was playing the first phrase of what you now know as Laura.*

The songwriter is explaining that "Laura," a beloved song that has been recorded more than 400 times by artists like Frank Sinatra and Nat "King" Cole, simply arrived as though sent to him by a higher power, inspired by a moment of emotional clarity.

But Raksin says something else key – he only claims that the "first phrase" came without effort. Writing the rest of the song, we might assume, required him to draw on his vast experience as a composer. After the initial flash of inspiration, Raksin used craft and knowledge to develop, edit, and finalize the theme.

Fortunately, writing a good melody doesn't require a devastating breakup. However, the story demonstrates that creating a memorable melody is a combination of inspiration and training. Although there are aspects to melody writing that can't be taught, this chapter introduces practical tools that can help you to transform your moment of heightened emotion into an unforgettable melody. Working through this chapter will help you to brainstorm new ideas, break free from your habitual tendencies, and build a logical melody from an initial idea.

Melody Basics

There is no better way to create a melody than to sing. Whether you are a trained singer or can't carry a tune, a melody should start with the voice. Start by singing melodies that you love. Internalizing and memorizing the melodies of others using the voice is invaluable training that will sharpen your melodic instincts. When it comes time to create your own melody, keep singing! Even if you can't immediately determine which pitches you're choosing, your musical instincts will create an underlying structure for your melody through the rhythm and contour. Recording a few versions of yourself singing the lyrics is an ideal first step for creating a melody from a set of lyrics.

Because songs are meant to be sung, a songwriter needs to consider the physical limitations of the voice. The **range**, the distance between the highest and lowest note, must be achievable for the singer. Although vocal ranges vary widely from singer to singer, a good rule of thumb is not to exceed the interval of a twelfth, an octave and a half, between a melody's lowest and highest notes.

Great songwriters also tailor a melody's range to the vocal character that they want the singer to convey. Every vocalist has a **tessitura,** a portion of their overall range in which they can comfortably execute a passage. Beyond the tessitura, different parts of the vocal range can feel more natural for different singers, styles, and tonal choices. For instance, whereas climactic held notes are often placed in a higher register so that they can be belted powerfully, more conversational singing is usually executed in a lower register of the voice, closer to where the singer would naturally speak. In modern R&B, many singers favor their "head voice," a high part of the voice, to achieve an intimate tone in the upper register.

Singers also need to breathe, and for this reason, melodies should include rests. Good melodies are organized in **phrases**, complete musical statements that have a beginning and ending. Phrases usually match the lyric's sentence structure, and breaks between phrases are usually aligned with punctuation marks like periods and commas. Coordinating phrasing with sentence structure guides the listener through the story of the song and gives singers a place to breathe without disrupting the flow of the lyric.

Essential Scales

Scales exist to tell us which notes fit well together to form a melody. Understanding scales gives songwriters the confidence to turn their abstract melodic instincts into concrete melodies that beautifully match with the underlying chord progressions.

The Major Scale

The **major scale** is the foundational building block of most melodies. Major scales are built using a combination of **half steps**, adjacent notes like C and D-flat, and **whole steps**, non-adjacent notes like C and D, that skip over just one note. In any key, the major scale is built of all whole steps, with two exceptions:

1. a half step between the third and fourth notes

2. a half step between the seventh note and the repetition of the root

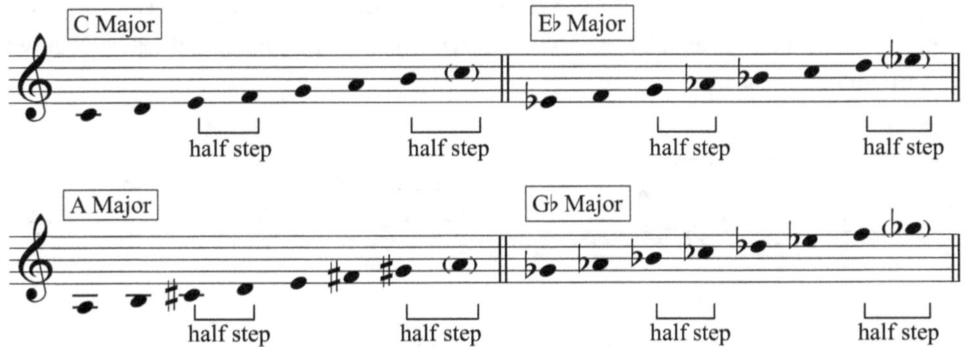

Many melodies are created from the major scale of the underlying key and don't usually change scales to reflect the underlying chords. Like harmony, melodies that stay completely within the major scale without adding extra sharps or flats, are said to be *diatonic*. **Diatonic melodies** are usually singable, memorable, and have a "classic" sound. "Somewhere Over the Rainbow" is one of the many iconic diatonic melodies that stays completely within the major scale. Notice how no additional accidentals are needed beyond the four flats of the A-flat major key signature.

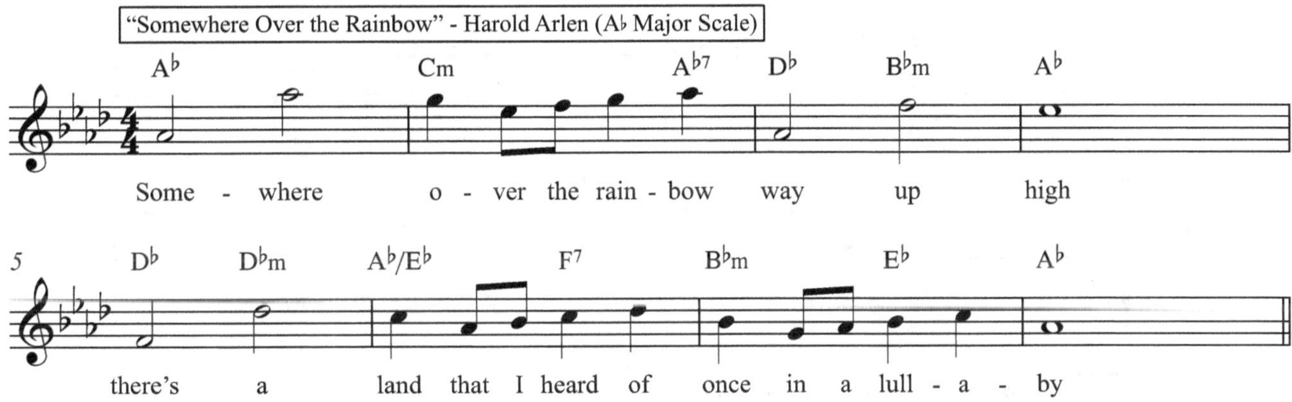

The Pentatonic Scales

Although the major scale is at the core of melodic invention, songwriters frequently select a smaller subset of the scale to further hone their melodic sound. The **major pentatonic scale** is a five-note scale commonly used in pop and folk music that consists of the scale degrees 1, 2, 3, 5, and 6 of the major scale. The pentatonic scale is particularly tuneful because it removes the tensest notes, the fourth and seventh scale degrees, from the major scale.

Although the pentatonic scale is named "pentatonic" because it has five notes, the number five plays another crucial role with regards to the scale. The pentatonic scale is formed by stacking perfect fifths, arguably the most "open sounding," neutral interval. The underlying structure of the perfect fifths is largely what gives the pentatonic scale its magical cohesion.

Because perfect fifths are the most acoustically pure interval in a scale, the pentatonic scale, which consists of notes stacked in fifths, resonates with both a pure consonance and, for many, a deep spirituality. Perhaps for this reason, the pentatonic scale is the primary melodic source for many folk and popular music traditions, ranging from Europe to Asia to Africa. Folk songs and children's songs like "Oh! Susanna" and "Old MacDonald Had a Farm" primarily or exclusively use the pentatonic scale, as demonstrated in the following excerpts, which both use the C major pentatonic scale.

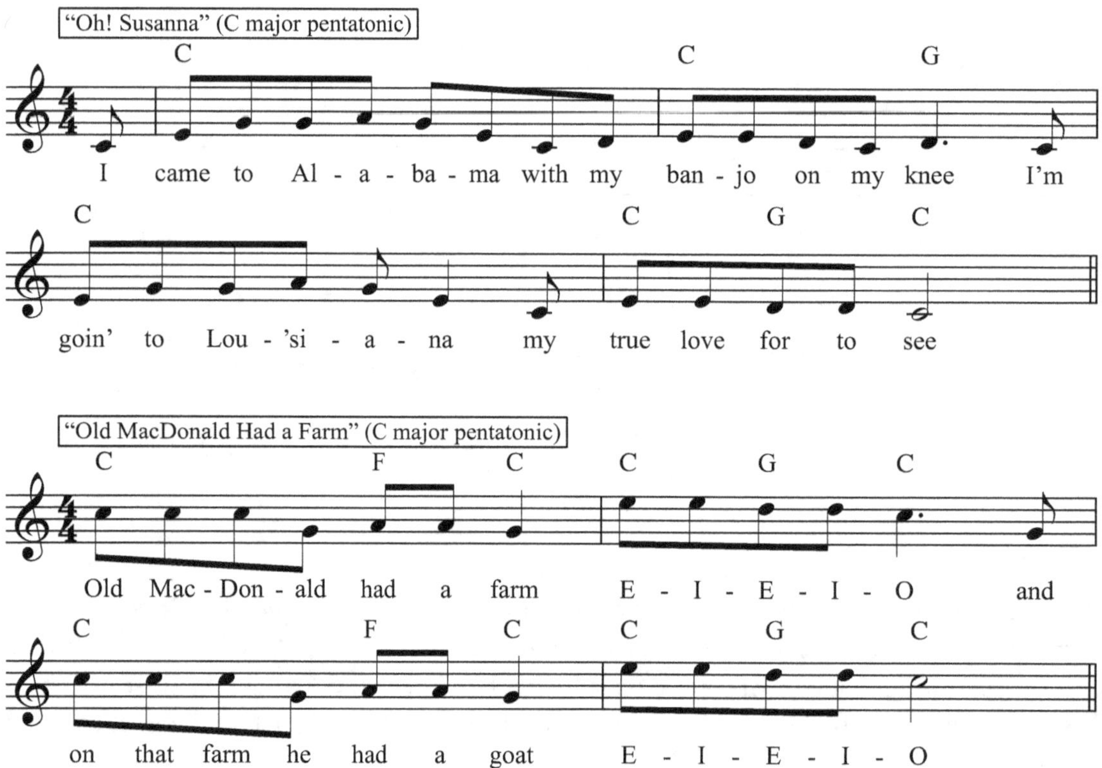

The pentatonic scale is a common feature for the "bubblegum pop" sound of typical radio hits. Because of the scale's acoustical properties, melodies that use the pentatonic scale are easy to sing, highly memorable, and feel familiar to most listeners. In addition, without the conflicts caused by the fourth and seventh, the major pentatonic scale fits well with any diatonic triad from the home key. The next example shows two excerpts from pop songs that stay completely within the pentatonic scale.

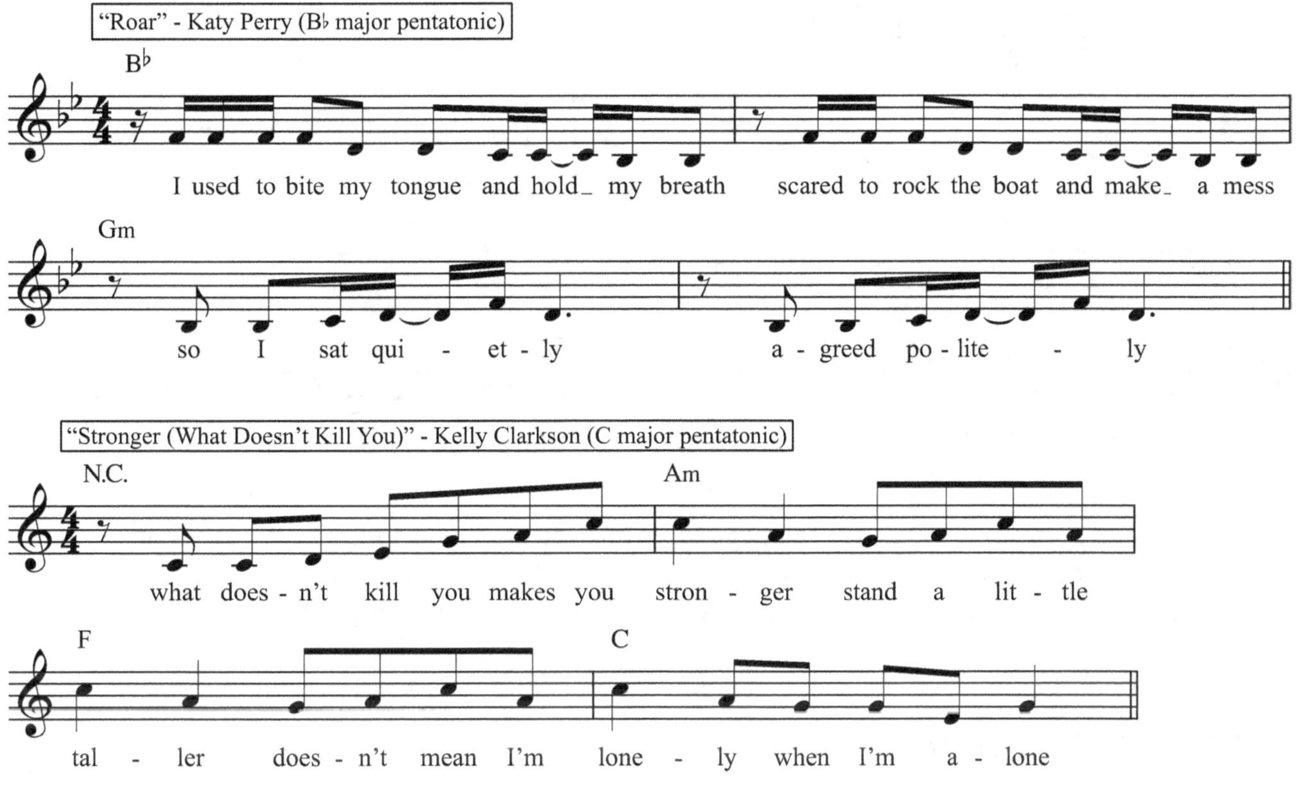

The **minor pentatonic scale** is a five-note scale with the same pitches as the major pentatonic scale of the relative major key. **Relative keys** are those with the same key signature, like C major and A minor, which share a key signature of no sharps or flats. So, the C major and A minor pentatonic scales have the same pitches, as do the pentatonic scales of F major and D minor.

Compared to the major scale based on the same root, the minor pentatonic scale consists of the 1, ♭3, 4, 5, and ♭7. The pentatonic scales of relative keys are placed on the same system in the next example for easy comparison.

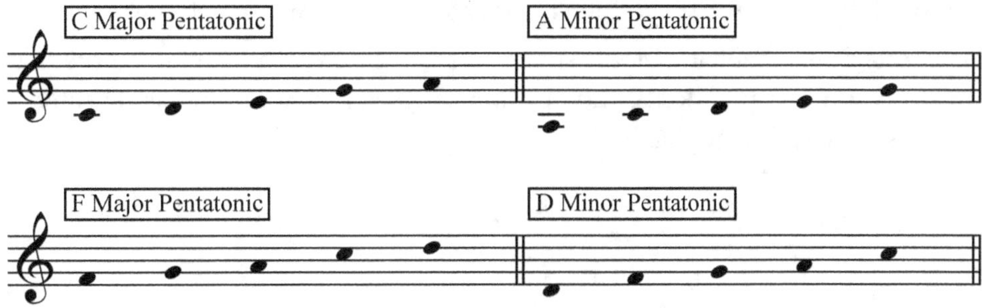

The minor pentatonic scale is used both in minor keys and in bluesy contexts, as demonstrated in the next two examples in which the minor third of the scale rubs up against the major third of the dominant chord. The dominant seventh, sharp ninth, chords in the next examples, are common in blues and blues-adjacent styles like funk and R&B, because they include both the major third and minor third, which is notated as a sharp ninth.

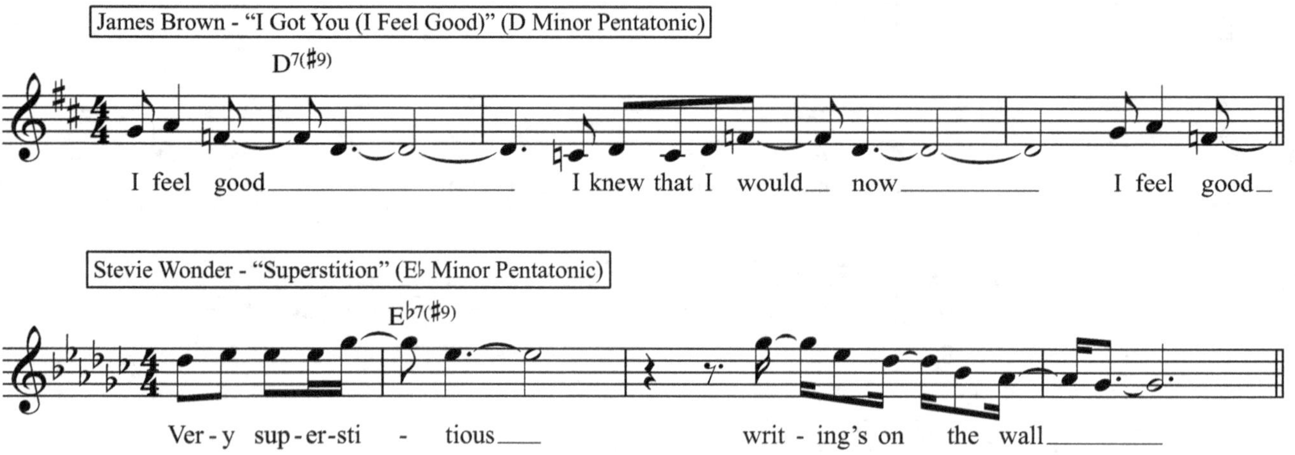

The pentatonic scales are crucial melodic building blocks that can inspire melodies for a wide range of styles including children songs, folk songs, bubble gum pop, and funk. Becoming familiar with the pentatonic scales gives you a useful toolkit for choosing melody notes that will naturally fit together.

Crafting a Melody

Although scales give us the notes with which to form a melody, melody writing is about more than just notes. Great melodies have logic, variety, surprise, and narrative arcs that they use to both comfort and delight listeners.

Melodic Shape

The contour of a melody is one of the defining elements. A melody's character is defined by where it ascends and descends and where it leaps versus steps. Shape is closely related to the character of a song's lyric. In general, songs with a lot of words utilize a flatter melody shape to make the lyric more comprehensible and help the singer perform the song more conversationally. On the other hand, songs with fewer words often use melodic shapes with more leaps and fewer repetitions to create more dramatic melodies.

The term **recitation tone** refers to a flat melodic shape consisting of a single melodic note that is repeated for multiple words. In many modern pop, R&B, and hip-hop songs, a recitation tone is repeated for the majority of the lyrics, with stressed syllables emphasized by a leap up or down.

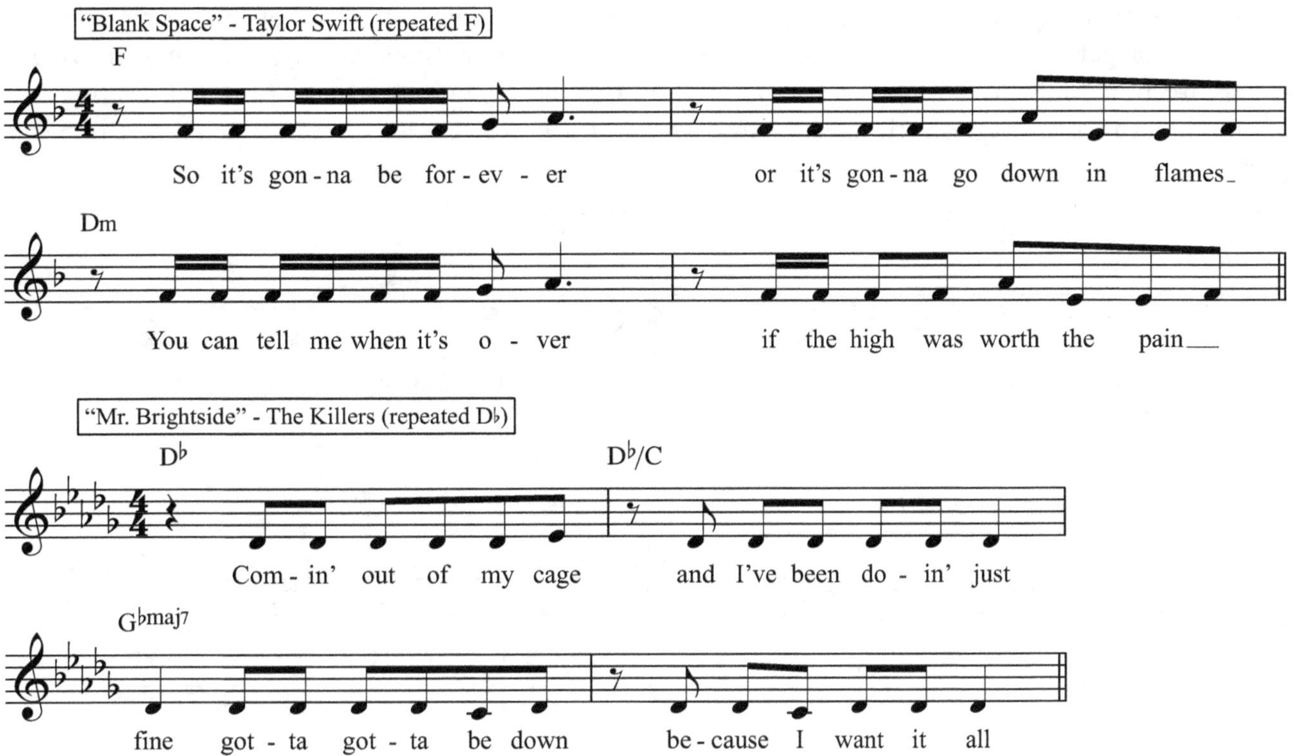

Besides moving up and down using notes of scales, a melody can **arpeggiate** chords, leaping between the root, third, fifth, and (if applicable) seventh of the underlying harmony. Arpeggio-based melodies fit naturally with the underlying harmony because they restate the very notes that form the chords. Due to the harmonic precision implied, arpeggiated melodies are most common in genres with tonal harmony like musical theater and Great American Songbook-style pieces.

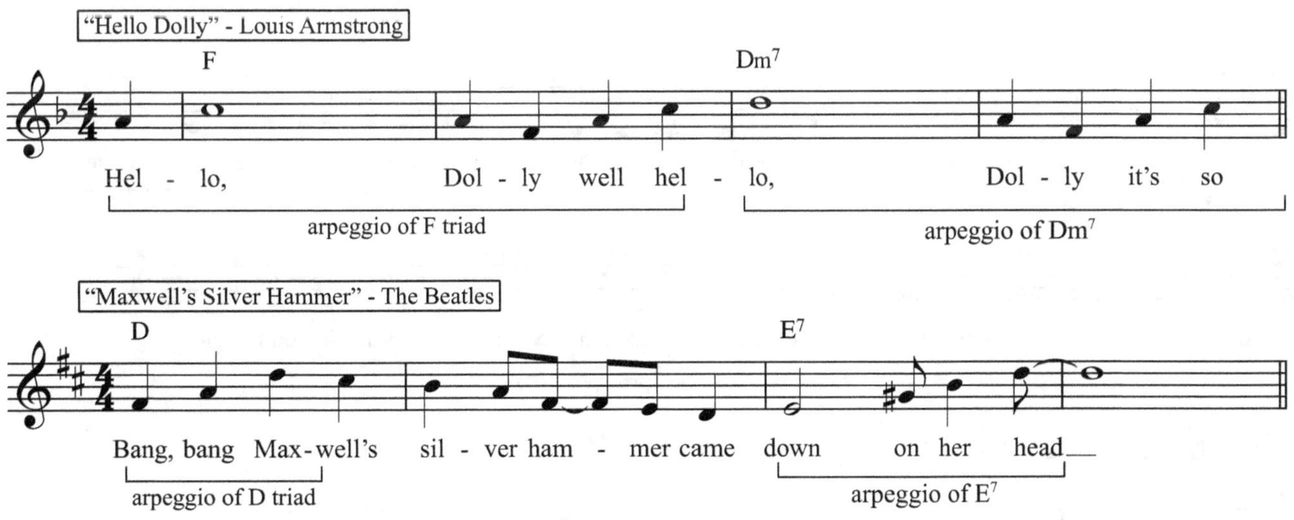

Including some **expressive leaps** makes melodies memorable and interesting. In particular, ascending leaps of a fifth or more are inherently emotive because singing higher is simply more physically demanding than singing lower. The perceived "reaching" of the vocalist is usually interpreted as the singer's intense yearning. Many of the most iconic melodies from the Great American Songbook start with an ascending leap.

Melody writers typically don't use multiple large leaps in a row. According to the ancient rules of melody writing, leaps bigger than a third are followed by stepwise motion, seconds (either major or minor) moving in either direction. In the next examples, you can see how this rule is followed, even in twentieth-century music. Each of the songs begins with an expressive ascending leap which is followed by a step down in the opposite direction.

Rhythm

Even though a measure begins on beat one, melodies frequently start on beats other than one. Many melodies start with either a **pickup**, a note or notes that precedes beat one, or a **delay**, a rest on beat one that can give a melody a "cool," "casual" feeling. Using pickups and delays is particularly essential when the lyric begins with an unstressed syllable, which will feel awkward if placed on the downbeat.

Syncopation, emphasizing offbeats, is a hallmark of melodies in jazz, rock, R&B, and pop because it reinforces the underlying groove and mimics the rhythms of speech. Syncopated melodies frequently **anticipate** notes, making them enter earlier than they would if they were placed squarely on the beat.

Shape and rhythm are crucial elements for creating a melody that expresses the lyrics and embodies the style. Take note of whether your melodies tend to leap or step, whether they start on or off of beat one, and whether they are on the beat or syncopated. A little bit of analysis might inspire different melodic directions.

Repetition and Sequencing

The best melodies generally follow an internal logic in which each phrase relates to the one that came before. Repetition gives melodies organization, makes them more memorable for audiences and singers, and forms expectations in listeners' minds that songwriters can either choose to meet or delightfully subvert.

The following list presents some of the most common methods that songwriters use to organize melodic phrases:

1. **Exact or Near Repetition** – Sometimes, songs simply repeat a melodic phrase two or more times. A repeated melodic phrase can repeat the same lyric or present a different set of words that matches the melody. For a slight variation, songwriters sometimes repeat an entire phrase but change the final note.

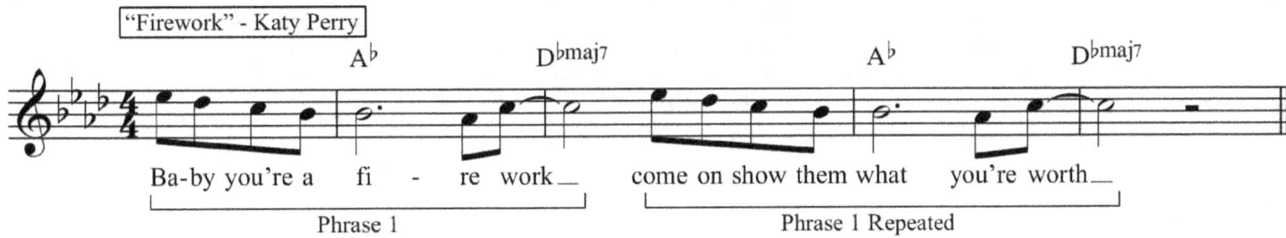

2. **Repetition Plus Addition** – Songwriters often replay a phrase but extend the beginning or ending to create a small variation. In "Isn't She Lovely," the added notes at the end of the second and fourth phrases accommodate the third syllable in the word "wonderful," which has one more syllable than "lovely," the corresponding word from the original phrase.

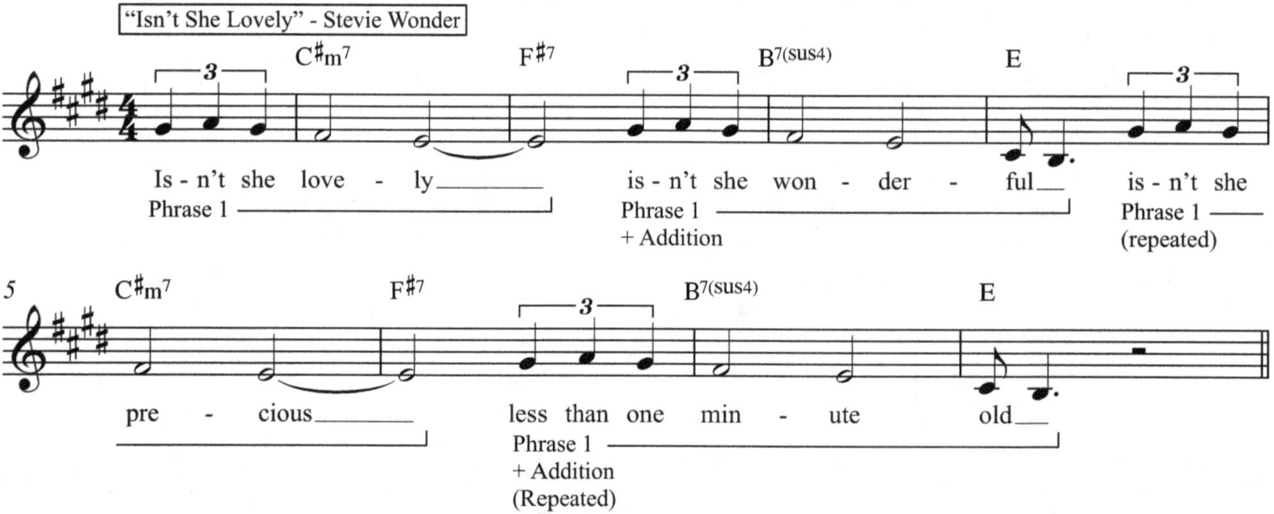

3. **Same Rhythm, Different Notes** – Melodies can repeat the rhythmic content of a melodic theme but change the melodic shape. The rhythmic repetition gives the listeners a sense of continuity while the different melody notes creates contrast. In "Yesterday," the melodic fragment called "Rhythm 2" is first presented with an ascending scale, then repeated with a descending scale.

4. **Sequence** – A **sequence** repeats the same melodic shape starting at different points in the scale. Sequences, which can repeat the shape up or down by any interval, are different from transposition because sequenced ideas stay inside the key diatonically, whereas transposition repeats the exact interval pattern regardless of the overall key.

   In the next example, the first line remains in the key of C even as the short melody is moved up and down and in the second line, just as the second line remains diatonic in F major.

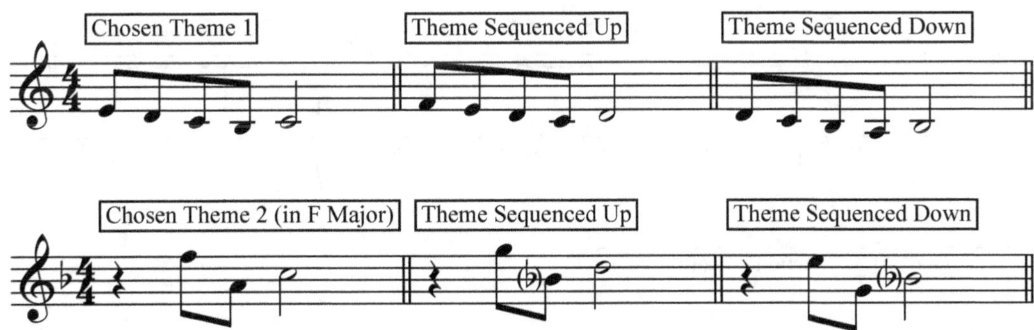

The chorus of "Smells Like Teen Spirit" uses a two-note melodic sighing gesture sequenced at three different places in the scale. A **sighing gesture** is a melodic figure that descends by step, like the melody of "Yesterday" in the previous example.

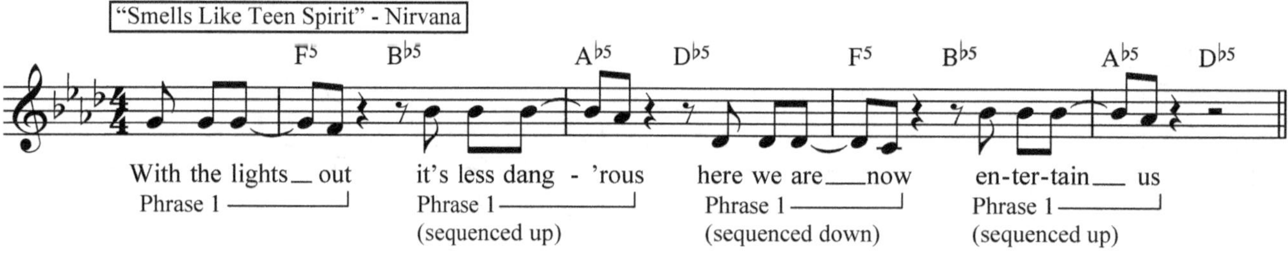

Combining Ideas

Great melodies intuitively combine and mix various devices to form a richly narrative experience for the listener. In the Rolling Stones' anthemic melodies, analysis can reveal the combination of a variety of repetition and sequencing devices.

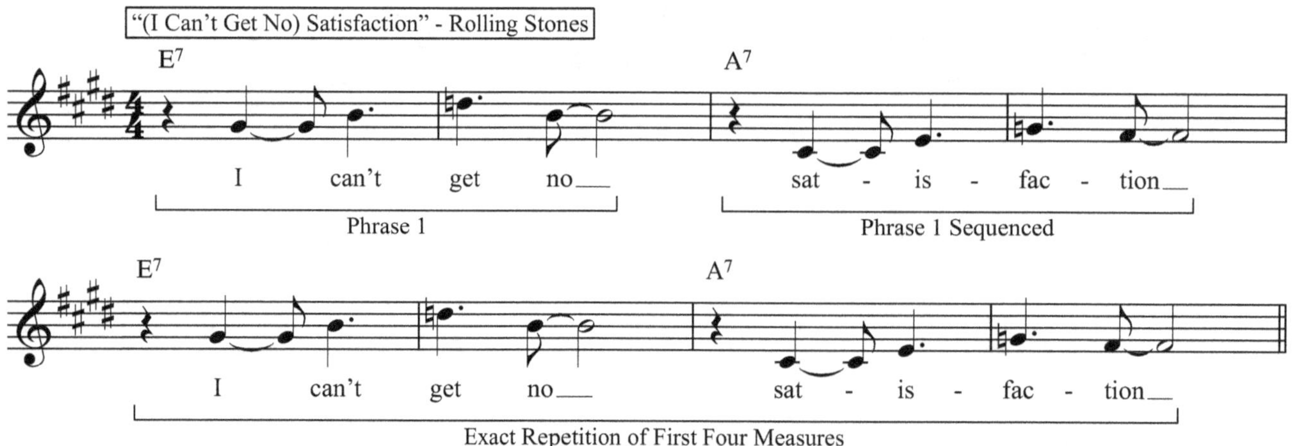

Melodies Beyond Major and Minor

Although most songs stay within a major scale, songwriters can consider notes that do not fit cleanly within scales. Adding notes outside the scale gives a song a jazzy or exotic sound when used intentionally.

Non-Chord Tones

Chromatic passing tones connect whole steps within a scale by filling in the "missing" in-between note. For instance, for the C major scale, a C-sharp could be used as a chromatic passing tone to connect C and D. Because the distance between the third and fourth and the seventh and root in the scale is already a half step, no passing tone is possible between these notes.

The next example presents the possible chromatic passing tones filling in notes of the C major scale. The passing tones are notated as regular eighth notes while the scale notes are presented as open circles. The example is a good reminder that chromatic notes that ascend are written as sharps whereas ones that descend are notated as flats.

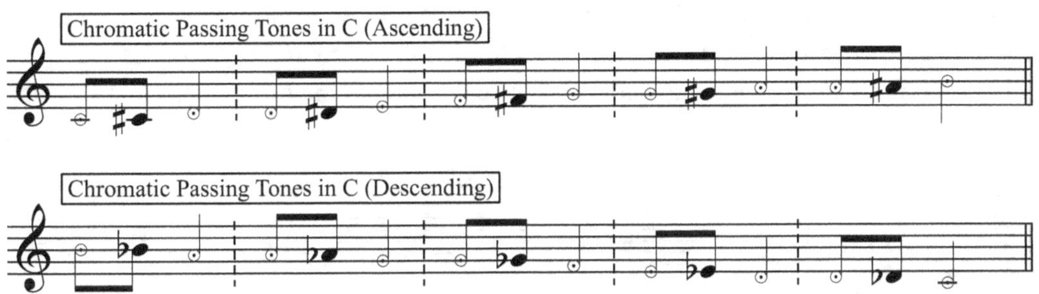

Chromatic neighbors are notes a half-step away from a scale note that decorate the target scale note. Chromatic neighbors typically give songs a jazzy sound and are most appropriate for Great American Songbook-style songs. **Lower chromatic neighbors**, notes a half-step below their target, reliably achieve the desired sound whereas **upper chromatic neighbors** may or may not be pleasing depending on their position within a scale. Neighbor tones are typically placed in weaker rhythmic positions relative to the notes from the scale or key.

The musical example shows chromatic lower neighbors in the keys of C and E-flat written as eighth notes, with the target notes presented as open circles. Note that the third and seventh scale degrees can be used as chromatic neighbors even though they are already notes of the scale.

The Beatles' jazzy "When I'm Sixty-Four" generously uses both kinds of non-chord tones to move outside of the key of D-flat major, creating a musical theater-adjacent sound that emphasizes the piece's humor.

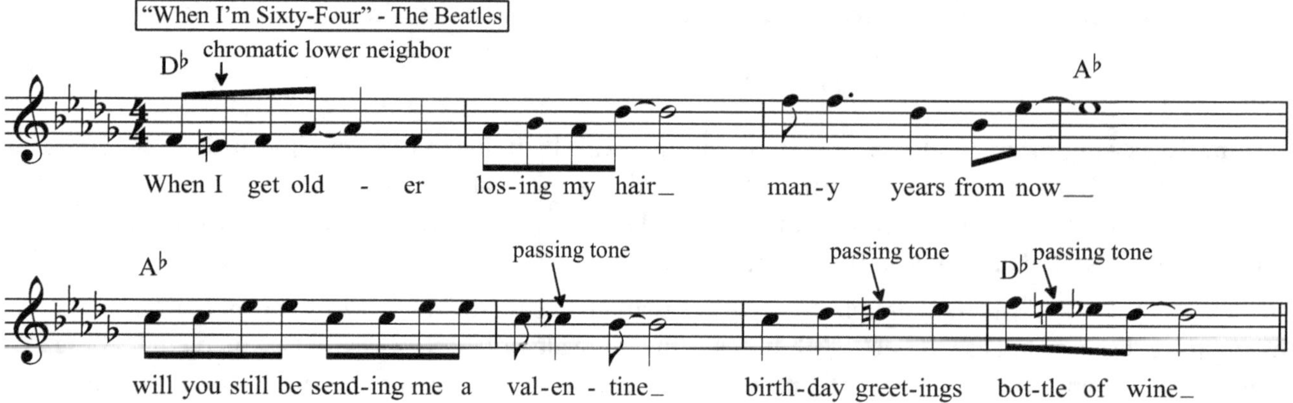

Other Scales and Modes

While most popular songs written in a minor key focus primarily on the minor pentatonic scale, some use other minor scales. The **dorian mode** is like a major scale with the third and seventh scale degrees lowered by a half step. It is particularly useful for songwriting because it contains the minor pentatonic scale within it.

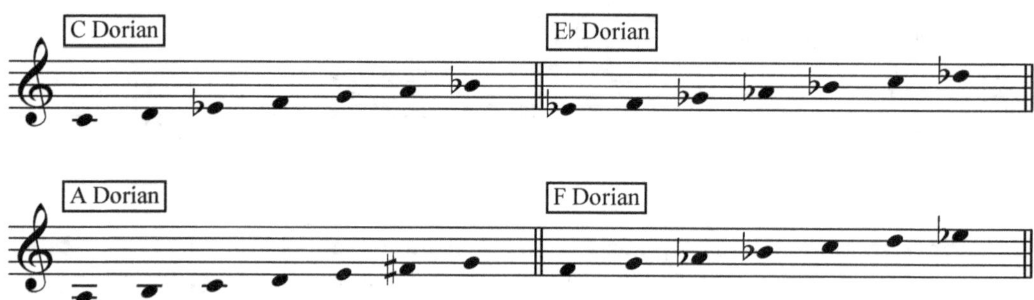

The raised sixth scale degree is the definitive marker of the dorian mode, which is not included in most other minor scales. Examine how the following songs use the dorian mode, defined by the sixth scale degree, C-sharp for E dorian:

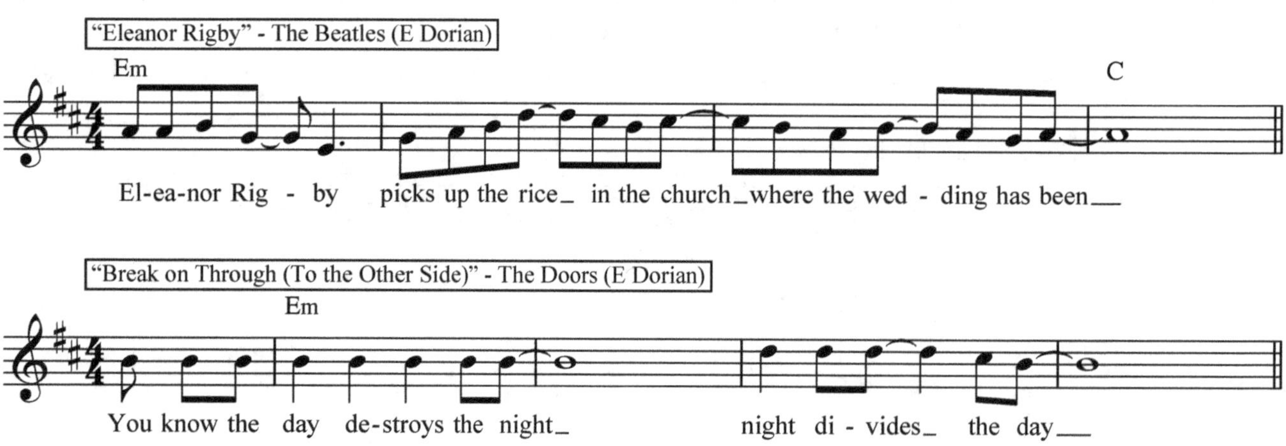

Dorian is an example of a "mode," a term that refers to the **modes of the major scale**, seven-note patterns that are built from starting the major scale from different scale degrees. For instance, one might start the C major scale on D, E, F, G, A, or B to find its different modes. When the major scale starts from different scale degrees, the patterns of half-steps and whole steps change.

Modes are always named after the starting note. The previous examples are identified as E dorian rather than D major (or D dorian) because the bass note indicated in the chord symbol is E. Other than dorian, the most important modes to know for songwriters are:

Mode Name	Compared to Major Scale	Character
Lydian	Raised fourth	Bright and pointy
Mixolydian	Lowered seventh	Major but dark and uncertain
Aeolian	Lowered third, sixth, and seventh	A darker, more wintery, velvety minor

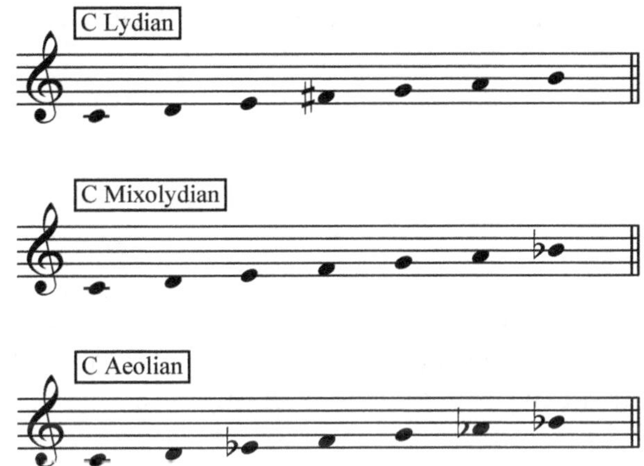

The next example shows songs written in each of the three modes described above. Each song has a slightly unusual sound based on its modal melody.

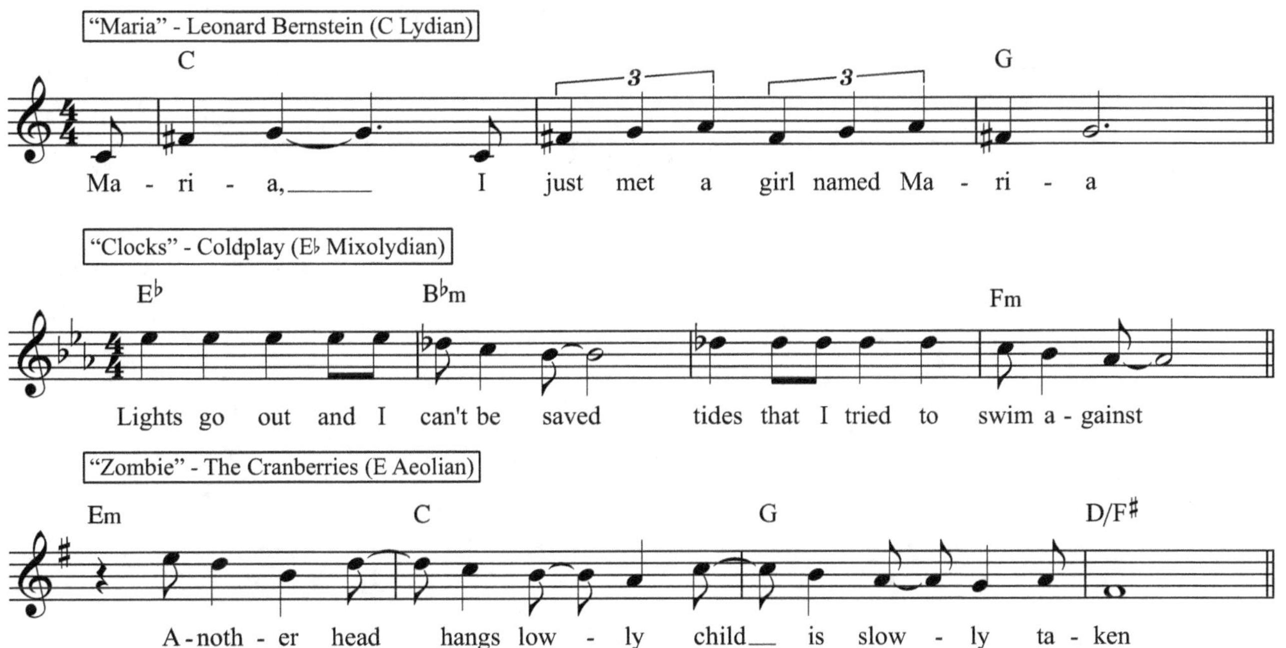

Takeaways

1. Learn to sing melodies of others and always sing your melodies as the first step. Make melodies singable by keeping them in a manageable range and organizing them into phrases with places to breathe.

2. Scales are building blocks of melodies, and the pentatonic scales (major and minor) are particularly important tools for songwriters writing in styles ranging from folk to pop.

3. The more words, the flatter a melody should be and the fewer words, the more curvaceous it should be. Expressive leaps give character to melodies without too many words.

4. Melodies are organized with repetition and variation, not written in a stream-of-consciousness fashion. Build a melody from the first phrase while listening for a balance between predictability and variety.

5. For a more exotic sound, venture outside of traditional scales using non-chord tones like chromatic neighbors and passing tones and modes like dorian, lydian, mixolydian, and aeolian.

Practice

1. Memorize the melodies for five songs that you love and be able to sing them accurately with no accompaniment. Write the five songs you're choosing here:

    1. ____

    2. ____

    3. ____

    4. ____

    5. ____

2. Write the scales indicated on the staff below:

A. Major Scales

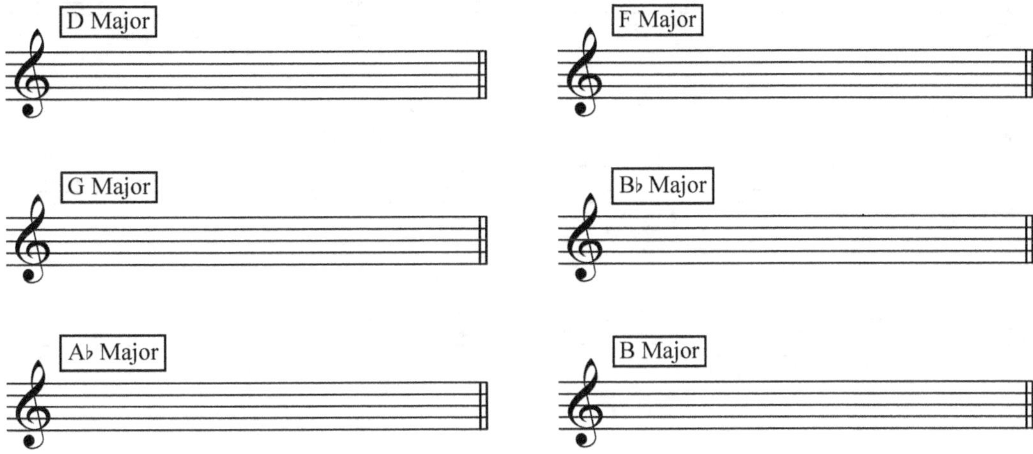

B. Pentatonic Scales

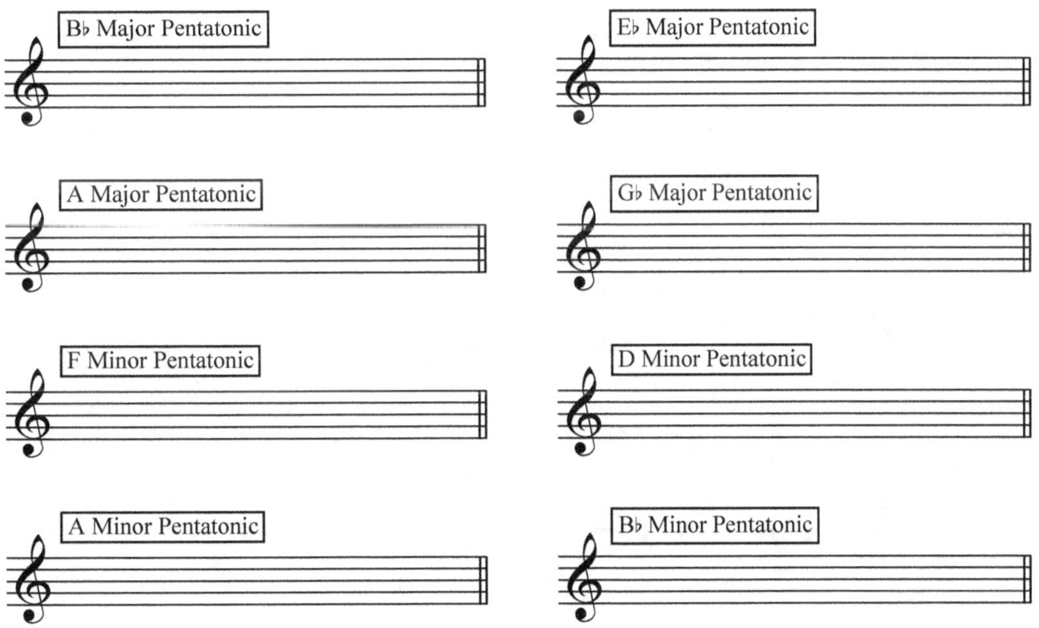

C. Modes

G Mixolydian
A Dorian
E Aeolian
D Aeolian
F Dorian
A♭ Mixolydian
B Aeolian
B♭ Dorian
Key of F Major
Sequence Up (by step)
Sequence Up Again (by step)
Sequence Up Again (by step)
Key of D Major
Sequence Down (by step)
Sequence Down Again (by step)
Sequence Down Again (by step)
Key of E♭ Major
Sequence Down (leap)
Mode of A Dorian
Sequence Up (leap)
(start here)

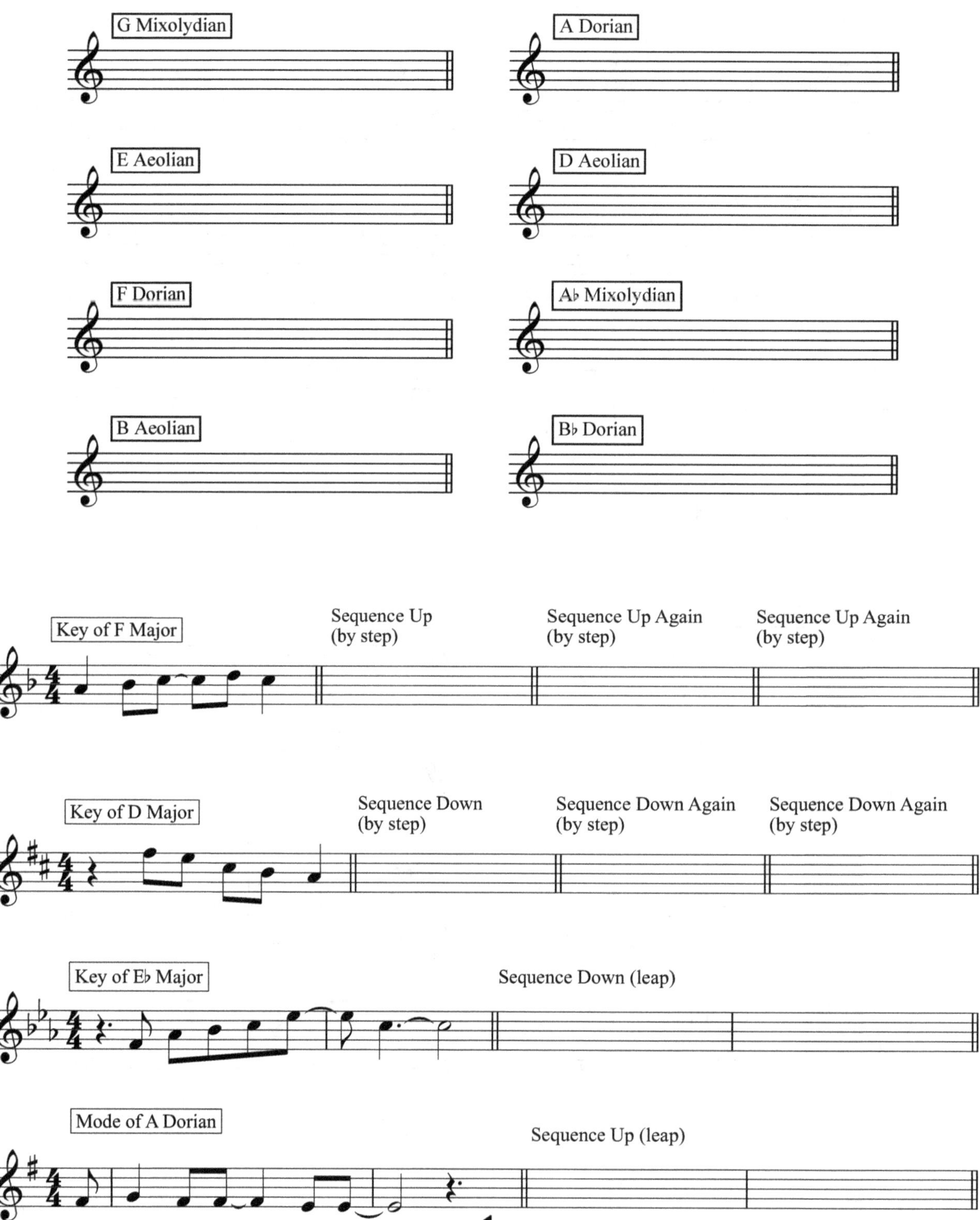

4. Syncopate the following "straight" rhythms to create a melody more appropriate for a popular style. There is not one "correct" answer, but many possible solutions. The first example is done for you.

5. Write a phrase with the same rhythm but different notes from the given phrase. The first example is completed for you.

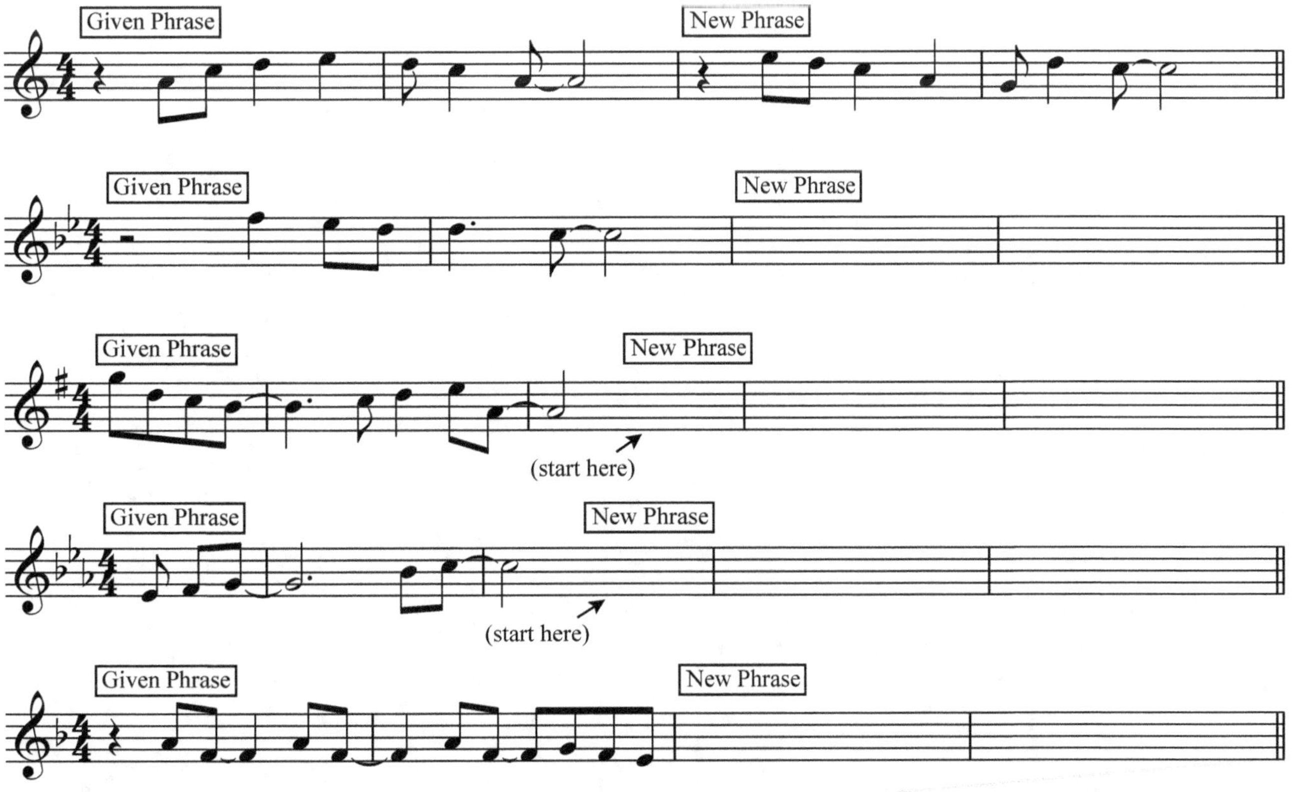

6. Add a chromatic note as indicated in the following melodies. Choose flats or sharps to indicate whether the note is going up or down.

13. Poetic Language

Song lyrics, read apart from the music, don't always make perfect sense. If the lyrics seem puzzling on the page, it's probably because they resemble poetry more than prose. So, what is poetry? The American poet Emily Dickinson included a lovely description of her artform in an 1870 letter:

If I read a book [and] it makes my whole body so cold no fire can ever warm me I know that is poetry. If I feel physically as if the top of my head were taken off, I know that is poetry.

Song lyrics are often described as **poetic**, as opposed to literal. Whereas literal language strives to express a thought in the clearest manner possible, poetic language targets an emotional impact, which often evades clear meanings. Poetry communicates through the logic of dreams, in which settings shift without warning, logic proves elusive and temporary, and the sounds that words make are as important as their meanings.

Take The Killers' pulsing radio hit, "Somebody Told Me":

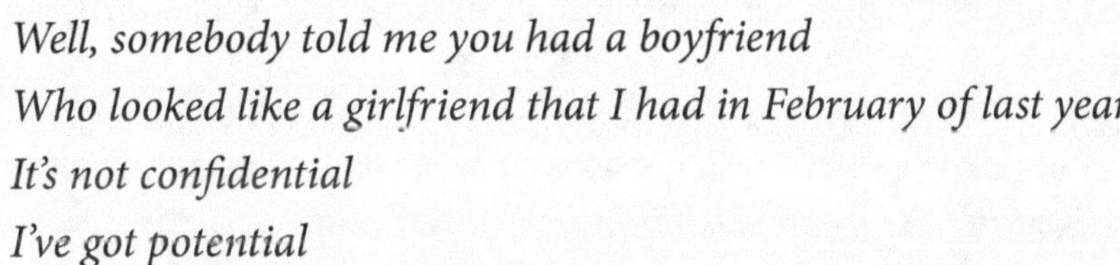

Well, somebody told me you had a boyfriend
Who looked like a girlfriend that I had in February of last year
It's not confidential
I've got potential

Although these lyrics aren't obviously what Emily Dickinson was referring to as poetry, millions of wedding guests and club-goers can attest that it induces a kind of ecstatic frenzy not so different from feeling "as if the top of [one's] head were taken off." However, the exact meaning of these lyrics is all but impossible to pin down. In fact, if you search the internet for theories about the meaning of this chorus, you'll discover a wide array of ideas, ranging from gender-bending romances to commentary on the way rumors spread through friend groups. One Reddit commenter simply says, "The only correct answer is that no one really knows." The song's power originates not from any deep meaning but from the hypnotic rhythm that this set of syllables creates when chanted over an irresistible dance beat.

The next section suggests tools for shaping your writing into poetry by focusing on sounds, playing with word order, repeating linguistic structures, and pairing words from similar categories.

Musical Language

One important aspect of poetry is its focus on the musical nature of language. Word painting and onomatopoeia are two ways to deliberately link the musical and verbal facets of a song.

Word painting is a technique in which a song musically dramatizes what the lyric is describing. For instance, if the lyrics include the word "stop," the instruments might stop playing for a couple of measures, as in Frank Sinatra's iconic version of "I've Got You Under My Skin." If the music includes the word "high," the melody might rise higher. Musical terms are ideal cues for word painting. Words like *soft, loud, low, high, rise, fall, slow, fast, long, short, major,* and *minor* commonly cue musical responses.

For instance, in Cole Porter's song, "Ev'ry Time We Say Goodbye," the last few lines describe the feeling of leave-taking in musical terms:

> *There's no love song finer*
> *But how strange the change*
> *From major to minor*
> *Every time we say goodbye*

To match the lyrical cues, Porter changes the harmony from a major chord to a minor chord, simulating the change from joy to sadness, as the lyric describes "the change from major to minor."

The first stanza of Leonard Cohen's "Hallelujah" contains a virtuosic example of word-painting, in which the lyric describes a chord progression while the music enacts it:

> *It goes like this, the fourth, the fifth*
> *The minor fall and the major lift*

When the lyrics discuss the "fourth" and the "fifth," the harmony moves to the IV (four chord) and V (five chord) chords. The chord progression also enacts the "*minor* fall" and "*major* lift" by accompanying those lyrics with minor and major chords, respectively.

The verses of "Stereo Hearts" by Gym Class Heroes compare a lover's heart to every imaginable aspect of a boombox. When the lyric describes "skipping tracks" left by careless lovers, the song repeats "used to, used to, used to" four times in imitation of a scratched CD or broken record stuck on a loop:

> *Furthermore, I apologize for any skipping tracks*
> *It's just the last girl that played me left a couple cracks*
> *I used to, used to, used to, used to, now I'm over that*
> *'Cause holding grudges over love is ancient artifacts*

Whereas word painting uses music to mirror lyrics, **onomatopoeia** uses words to mimic sounds. Onomatopoeic words simulate real-world sounds through the sonority of their consonants and vowels. For instance, the words "ding" and "dong" are often used to mimic the ringing of a bell in the song, "Ding! Dong! The Witch is Dead" from *The Wizard of Oz*. And various songs, including Cole Porter's "Night and Day" include the words "tick" and "tock" in imitation of a clock.

In the song "Orange-Colored Sky," made famous by Nat "King" Cole, a series of onomatopoetic words simulate an explosion:

> *I was humming a tune, drinking in sunshine*
> *When out of that orange-colored view*
> *Flash, bam, alakazam*
> *I got a look at you*

The onomatopoetic words "flash," "bam," and "alakazam" are highlighted by "explosive" instrumental responses to make the singer's sudden epiphany feel even more real.

In "The Trolley Song," made famous by Judy Garland, the words "clang," "ding," and "zing" reproduce the typical sounds of a city streetcar and the imagined sound of "heartstrings":

> *Clang, clang, clang went the trolley*
> *Ding, ding, ding went the bell*
> *Zing, zing, zing went my heartstrings*
> *From the moment I saw him I fell*

In both songs, the sound effects bring the lyric to life, creating a soundscape rather than merely describing one. Both onomatopoeia and word painting bring the musical and lyrical aspects closer together so that the listener has an immersive listening experience.

Poetic Phrases

Poetic lines do not have to follow the same grammatical rules of common speech. The next section describes a few ways in which grammatical structures can be loosened to animate a poetic voice.

Modifying Syntax

Syntax refers to sentence structure, the order of words within a sentence. Whereas literal speech follows conventional syntax for clarity, poetic lyrics often alter word order to emphasize rhythm, rhyme, and humor. For instance, in literal speech, adjectives almost always precede the noun that they are describing. We might describe a "bright star," but rarely refer to a "star bright" unless we're writing a poem.

In lyrics, as in poetry, adjectives sometimes follow nouns. Cole Porter starts the song, "You're the Top," with the lyric, "At words poetic, I'm so pathetic." Normally, the phrase would be "poetic words," but Porter flips the noun and adjective for the sake of rhythm and rhyme. Porter's lyric has an extra layer of richness – because the line itself refers to poetic speech, the unusual syntax reflects the song's meaning.

Similarly, in George and Ira Gershwin's "Someone to Watch Over Me," the song's verse begins:

There's a saying old
Says that love is blind

The phrase "saying old" represents an inversion of the usual adjective-noun syntax, "old saying." It's interesting that Gershwin's lyric, like Porter's, employs inverted syntax at a moment when the song is discussing an alternate way of speaking, in this case, an antiquated aphorism, a "saying old."

In the song, "And I Love Her," the Beatles place their adjectives in a very unusual place – at the beginnings of their sentences.

Bright are the stars that shine
Dark is the sky
I know this love of mine
Will never die

The reversal of word order turns cliché observations ("The stars are bright," "The sky is dark") into a lyric with a heightened, poetic sense of drama. Just by changing the syntax, the lyric goes from banal to philosophical.

Omitting Words

Song lyrics often omit or imply words to fit the rhythm of the music and incite rhythmic momentum. Omitting words imitates casual conversation or slang in which speakers habitually shorten words and sentences.

In the chorus of "Crazy in Love," Beyoncé omits the subject from the beginning of the first and third lines, only to backfill the subject in the line's repetition. The chorus repeats the line "Got me looking so crazy right now," later filling the sentences' subjects, "your love" and "your touch." Beyond this obvious omission, the last line of the next example omits the word "has" in order to keep the syllable count consistent from line to line.

Got me looking so crazy right now
Your love's got me looking so crazy right now
Got me looking so crazy right now
Your touch got me looking so crazy right now

Words are also omitted during the verse of Stevie Wonder's "Superstition," leaving the lyric full of related fragments rather than complete sentences.

Because the lyric exists in the realm of poetry, these fragments don't need to be made into complete sentences. The lyric gives us ample opportunity to enter the world of the song, even if traditional subject-verb structures and connecting words are largely absent.

Along with the title, many of the lines of Otis Redding's "Sittin' on the Dock of the Bay" achieve a casual, lazy feeling by omitting the subject of the sentence. The first and third lines omit the first word ("I'm") but the subject "I" is clarified in lines two and four:

In addition to omitting words, songwriters often shorten words or use colloquial forms to lighten syllable counts and sharpen rhythm. For example, the Rolling Stones say, "I can't get *no* satisfaction" instead of "I can't get *any* satisfaction" and Sam Cooke says, "A change is gonna come" instead of "A change is going to come." Using these slangy modifications makes the singers sound "hip" and gives them counter-culture credibility that they could not achieve through traditional grammar.

In the chorus of her hit song, "Royals," Lorde's propulsive rhythm is partially generated by substituting shorter words for longer ones. She replaces "doesn't" with "don't," uses the slangy "ain't" instead of "isn't," and substitutes the abbreviation "luxe" for the full word "luxury."

To be clear, this section is not criticizing songwriters for poor grammatical structure – quite the opposite! These songwriters are writing in poetic language, not obeying traditional syntax. By leaving out and altering words, they each created lyrics that matched the music and struck the appropriate tone for their hit songs.

Parallel Structure

Parallel structure is a lyrical device in which grammatical sequences are repeated with new words. Using parallel structure helps to organize ideas, achieve symmetrical flow, and inspire new, unconventional ways of presenting an idea.

For example, take the brief phrase "Jenny loves candy." The grammatical pattern here is "proper noun (subject)-verb-noun (object)." To create parallel structure, a writer replaces the original words with substitutes that follow the same pattern, as follows:

Original: Jenny loves candy.

Structure: *Proper noun-verb-noun.*

New: Arturo enjoys cars.

New: Dennis hates buildings.

New: John creates problems.

Although these sentences have the same structure, they feel random because all of the words are changed. To create phrases that feel more closely related, retain one or more of the words in the original sentence. For instance, "Jenny loves [noun]."

Original: Jenny loves candy.

Structure: *Jenny loves [noun].*

New: Jenny loves skateboards.

New: Jenny loves parties.

New: Jenny loves state fairs.

Building phrases using parallel structure can resemble a game of *Mad Libs*, in which the player swaps nouns, adjectives, and verbs into a set structure. Songwriters can further emphasize linguistic symmetry by choosing words with identical syllable counts and stress patterns. These structures are often matched with melodic repetitions or sequences to create a strong relationship between melody and lyric.

There are two primary ways that songwriters use parallel structure:

1. To connect phrases immediately

2. To connect between verses

The next sections unpack these two possibilities.

Connecting Phrases Immediately

Songwriters can repeat short structures to give the listener a pleasing sense of organization.

Within a line, parallel structure can make repeated two- or three-word phrases feel purposeful and rhythmic. In an example referenced earlier in this chapter, Leonard Cohen sings about "the minor fall" and "the major lift" in his song, "Hallelujah," following the pattern *the-adjective-noun*. Besides sharing parts of speech, the parallel words are strongly associated in the same category – "major" and "minor" are chord types whereas "fall" and "lift" are opposites.

The lyric for Elton John's song "Tiny Dancer" starts with the iconic line "Blue-jean baby, L.A. lady." This line offers two descriptions in parallel structure: a noun-serving-as-adjective (blue-jean, L.A.) followed by a noun (baby, lady). Because each phrase includes repeated sounds ("b"s in the first part, "l"s in the second) and the two nouns rhyme, this lyric is sonically satisfying.

Many songs use parallel structure in two consecutive lines. In this construction, it is very common for the lyrics to also include **anaphora**, a repetition of the beginnings of consecutive lines.

Prince's song, "Kiss," uses parallel structure and anaphora to tie together two lines in the chorus:

> *You don't have to be rich to be my girl*
> *You don't have to be cool to rule my world*

Structure: *You don't have to be [adjective] to [verb] my [noun]*

The first three lines of the verse of Alicia Keys' song, "If I Ain't Got You," are almost identical, with the last word representing the only significant change. These lines also use anaphora.

> *Some people live for the fortune*
> *Some people live just for the fame*
> *Some people live for the power*

Structure: *Some people live (just) for the [noun]*

Billy Joel's song, "Only the Good Die Young," uses parallel structure multiple times, including:

> *We ain't too pretty, we ain't too proud*

Structure: *we ain't too [adjective]*

> *(I'd rather) laugh with the sinners than cry with the saints*

Structure: *[verb] with the [noun]*

The next example demonstrates a more complex structure in which more words change between lines. The parallel structure is repeated exactly until the final two syllables, which break the pattern.

> *They showed you a statue and told you to pray*
> *They built you a temple and locked you away*

Structure: *They [verb]ed you a [noun] and [verb]ed you [two syllables]*

In many of these examples, the songwriters make the parallel structure even more satisfying by choosing parallel words that either repeat sounds through alliteration or assonance or belong to the same category like "laugh" and "cry" or "sinners" and "saints" (more on this later).

Connecting Between Stanzas

Parallel structure is a useful tool for generating additional verses after the first one is written. Starting with a suggested grammatical framework gives songwriters a jumping-off point for brainstorming new material.

Children's songs often use strict parallel structure, changing very little content, perhaps just one word or one line, from one stanza to the next. Maintaining consistent structure helps children track the song's form and memorize the lyrics. For example, in the Raffi song, "Down by the Bay," the entire lyric is repeated for each verse with only one exception: the penultimate line, whose silly rhyme provides the "punchline" for each stanza, changes. Even the variable penultimate line uses anaphora, always starting with "Did you ever see a…"

> *Down by the bay*
> *Where the watermelons grow*
> *Back to my home*
> *I dare not go*
> *For if I do*
> *My mother will say*
> *"Did you ever see a goose*
> *Kissing a moose?"*
> *Down by the bay*
>
> *Down by the bay*
> *Where the watermelons grow*
> *Back to my home*
> *I dare not go*
> *For if I do*
> *My mother will say*
> *"Did you ever see a whale*
> *With a polka dot tail?"*
> *Down by the bay*

In the Frank Sinatra song, "It Was a Very Good Year," the first and last lines of each stanza use exact parallel structure, where the singer's age is the only change between stanzas. Although the second line begins with parallel structure ("It was a very good year for [descriptor] girls"), the ends are not parallel:

> *When I was seventeen it was a very good year*
> *It was a very good year for small town girls and soft summer nights*
> *We'd hide from the lights*
> *On the village green*
> *When I was seventeen*
>
> *When I was twenty-one it was a very good year*
> *It was a very good year for city girls who lived up the stair*
> *With all that perfumed hair*
> *And it came undone*
> *When I was twenty-one*
>
> *When I was thirty-five it was a very good year*
> *It was a very good year for blue-blooded girls of independent means*
> *We'd ride in limousines*
> *Their chauffeurs would drive*
> *When I was thirty-five*

In his song, "If It's Magic," Stevie Wonder repeats grammatical structures for the first three lines of each verse and continues with anaphora for the following lines, occasionally swapping opposites like "never" and "ever" while maintaining the overall form.

> *If it's magic*
> *Then why can't it be everlasting*
> *Like the sun that always shines*
> *Like the poets in this rhyme*
> *Like the galaxies in time*
>
> *If it's pleasing*
> *Then why can't it be never leaving*
> *Like the day that never fails*
> *Like on seashores there are shells*
> *Like the time that always tells*

Structure:
If it's [adjective]
Then why can't it be [adjective]
Like the [noun] that [adverb] [verb]s

Using parallel structure gives the lyric a sheen of organization and intentionality. It allows the listener to enjoy predictable repetition without risking becoming overly monotonous or redundant.

Antithesis and Categories

The pleasing satisfaction created by symmetry isn't limited to grammatical structures. Words can achieve their own type of symmetrical balance using the devices antithesis and categories.

Antithesis

Antithesis refers to using two opposite words in close proximity of one another. Opposite words form a sort of a "logical rhyme" — once a listener hears one word, they feel satisfaction upon hearing its opposite.

Antithesis adds character to a generic idea, making it more descriptive and poetic. Look at how opposites make these phrases more vivid:

> Original: I'll love you no matter what
> With Antithesis: I'm going to love you come *rain* or come *shine*
> (from "Come Rain or Come Shine" – Harold Arlen)

> Original: You can't make up your mind
> With Antithesis: You're *hot* then you're *cold*.
> (from "Hot N Cold" – Katy Perry)

> Original: I'm not sure what to do
> With Antithesis: Should I *stay* or should I *go*?
> (from "Should I Stay or Should I Go?" – The Clash)

The versions with antithesis create vivid, specific images that color the song and encourage imagination.

Michael Jackson manages to rhyme two sets of opposites: "wrong/right" and "black/white" in the chorus to "Black or White."

> *And I told about equality*
> *And it's true, either you're wrong or you're right*
> *But if you're thinkin' about my baby*
> *It don't matter if you're black or white*

Many songs from the Great American Songbook use antithesis in the last few measures of a song to help create the feeling of a satisfying conclusion. Can you find the antitheses in the following examples?

You took the part that once was my heart
So why not take all of me
(from "All of Me" – Gerald Marks/Seymour Simons)

How deep is the ocean
How high is the sky
(from "How Deep is the Ocean" – Irving Berlin)

Lord above me
Make him love me
The way he should
I got it bad and that ain't good
(from "I Got it Bad and that Ain't Good" – Duke Ellington)

The opposites do not necessarily have to have the exact same grammatical form. In Sam Cooke's "A Change is Gonna Come," one can perceive the "logical rhyme" in the antithesis of "living" and "die."

It's been too hard living
But I'm afraid to die
'Cause I don't know what's up there
Beyond the sky

Similarly, Nirvana's "Smells Like Teen Spirit" contrasts the words "worse" and "best," a slight variation of the opposite pairs, "worst" and "best."

I'm worse at what I do best
And for this gift, I feel blessed

Categories

Sometimes, groups of words fit together logically, but are not exactly opposites. This text will refer to these related words as **categories**. For instance, the category of colors might include *red*, *green*, *blue*, and *yellow* and the category of fruit might include *apple*, *orange*, *banana*, and *strawberry*. Songwriters use categories in much the same way as they use antithesis – to create vivid examples and a satisfying sense of symmetry.

In her song, "You've Got a Friend," instead of saying simply "call anytime," Carole King uses the category of seasons to make her invitation more vivid:

> *Winter, spring, summer, or fall*
> *All you've got to do is call*

Listing all four seasons makes the listener pause to consider the seriousness of the offer and imagine the singer waiting by their phone all through the year.

The Marvin Gaye/Tammi Terrell duet "Ain't No Mountain High Enough" uses the category of geographical features to add images to the chorus. The elements *mountain*, *valley*, and *river* are inserted into three lines that use parallel structure, sung to a repeated melody.

> *Ain't no mountain high enough*
> *Ain't no valley low enough*
> *Ain't no river wide enough*
> *To keep me from gettin' to you, babe*

Structure: *Ain't no [noun] [adjective] enough*

In the buildup to the climax of the Irving Berlin song "Always," units of time, increasing in duration, are used for emphasis, while employing parallel structure:

> *Not for just an hour*
> *Not for just a day*
> *Not for just a year*
> *But always*

Structure: *Not for just a [unit of time]*

With each new line, the intensity of the promise grows and elongates, building to the payoff: the infinite promise of "always."

Antithesis and categories help a boring lyric spring to life, make it easier for singers and listeners to remember your song, and lead to more vivid imagery and emphasis.

Takeaways

1. Lyrics are typically more like poetry than conventional language. Instead of easily discernible meanings, lyrics prioritize sound and emotion.

2. Word painting and onomatopoeia are two ways to bring music and words closer together, knitting the elements of the song into a single fabric.

3. Songs don't need to follow traditional rules of sentence structure and songwriters can flip syntactical shapes or omit words to emphasize rhythm, create rhyme, or introduce humor.

4. Parallel structure helps to organize a song, either within a stanza or between stanzas.

5. Antithesis and categories add vivid imagery, create satisfying symmetry, and help transform ordinary lyrics into memorable poetry.

Practice

1. For each of the following phrases, choose at least two grammatical elements to swap and identify their grammatical function (noun, verb, adjective, etc.). Then, write two phrases that create parallel structure with the given phrase. There is not a single "correct" answer for this exercise, so you can choose which words you want to substitute. The model phrases are borrowed from Johnny Cash's song, "I Walk the Line."

   The first example is done for you.

   A.   As sure as night is dark

   Elements: As sure as [noun] is [adjective]

   Phrases: As sure as a year is long; as sure as thunder is deafening

   B.   I keep a close watch on this heart of mine

   Elements:

   Phrases:

   C.   I find it very, very easy to be true

   Elements:

   Phrases:

   D.   Yes, I'll admit that I'm a fool for you

   Elements:

   Phrases:

E.   Because you're mine, I walk the line

Elements:

Phrases:

F.   For you, I know I'd even try to turn the tide

Elements:

Phrases:

2. List an opposite for the following items. Then, use the two words in a sentence. The first example is done for you.

A.   **Unsure**

Opposite: Confident

Sentence: I was confident until I saw you, but now I'm unsure.

B.   **Depressed**

Opposite:

Sentence:

C.   **Colorful**

Opposite:

Sentence:

D.   **Exotic**

Opposite:

Sentence:

E.   **Nervous**

Opposite:

Sentence:

F.   **Furry**

Opposite:

Sentence:

G.   **Gentle**

Opposite:

Sentence:

H.   **Dilapidated**

Opposite:

Sentence:

I.   **Floating**

Opposite:

Sentence:

3. List 5 items in each category. Feel free to be creative:

A.   **Unusual colors**

____

____

____

____

B.   **Unusual fruits**

____

____

____

____

C.   **Types of homes**

____

____

____

____

D.   **Car types**

____

____

____

____

E.   **Pieces of Furniture**

____

____

____

____

F.   **Font Styles**

____

____

____

____

4. Rewrite the following sentences using antithesis or categories. The first one is done for you.

A. **Statement:** I love you no matter where you are.
    Rewrite: I love you whether we're in Timbuktu or Kathmandu.

B. **Statement:** My friend is a little unstable.
    Rewrite:

C. **Statement:** Your body is beautiful.
    Rewrite:

D. **Statement:** Freddie is indecisive.
    Rewrite:

E. **Statement:** I love all kinds of food!
    Rewrite:

F. **Statement:** This city is so big!
    Rewrite:

G. **Statement:** I am going to work very hard to make you like me.
    Rewrite:

14. AABA Form ("Song Form")

It's staggering how many songs are well known precisely because Frank Sinatra sang them: "Fly Me to the Moon"; "The Way You Look Tonight"; "Come Rain or Come Shine"; "My Way"; "New York, New York"; and so many more.

Although much of Sinatra's success can be credited to his warm voice, brilliant arrangements, and cooler-than-cool persona, some of his popularity stems from the songs he chose to sing. In fact, Sinatra cared deeply about songs and their writers and counted many of them among his friends.

Most importantly, he formed a powerful songwriting machine by introducing two of his lifelong friends, composer Jimmy Van Heusen and lyricist Sammy Cahn, who – perhaps in gratitude – offered Sinatra "right of first refusal" for their new songs. Sinatra ultimately recorded 89 songs by Van Heusen and Cahn including hits like "Come Fly with Me" (Van Heusen was a test pilot during World War II); "The Second Time Around"; "The Tender Trap"; "Love and Marriage"; and "All the Way." These weren't just business relationships – Sinatra was real-life friends with both men. Cahn met his first wife at a dinner party at Sinatra's home, and Van Heusen gifted Sinatra's family with their living room piano, a 9-foot-long behemoth of a Bösendorfer.

One reason so many of Sinatra's songs sparkle is because of the musical form underlying the snappy lyrics and hip melodies. Many of his hit songs, including many by Van Heusen and Cahn, are written in AABA form, one of two standard forms in the Great American Songbook tradition. The AABA form repeats the main themes enough to get the music caught in the listener's head, while allowing for enough contrast to complete a satisfying musical story. As you'll learn, the rigor required to write successfully in AABA form is valuable training for any songwriter striving to improve their craft.

AABA Basics

AABA form, also known as **song form**, is a musical structure consisting of three musically identical sections (marked "A") separated by a contrasting section (marked "B"), often referred to as the **bridge**. In its most common version, an AABA song is thirty-two measures long, comprising four eight-measure sections.

The AABA form is most closely associated with songs from the **Great American Songbook**, a term that refers to songs from musicals and movies written roughly between 1920 and 1960. Great American Songbook songs in AABA form include "The Way You Look Tonight"; "As Time Goes By"; "Somewhere Over the Rainbow"; "What a Wonderful World"; and "When You Wish Upon a Star." AABA form is also used in pop and rock music, especially for **ballads**, slow songs that express a deep emotion. These songs include "Yesterday" (Beatles); "She's Out of My Life" (Michael Jackson); "If It's Magic" (Stevie Wonder); "Make You Feel My Love" (Bob Dylan); "Crazy" (Willie Nelson/Patsy Cline); "At Last" (Etta James); and "She's Got a Way" (Billy Joel).

Because many Christmas songs were created by Great American Songbook composers and musicians, many are written in AABA form. Examples include "The Christmas Song (Chestnuts Roasting on an Open Fire)"; "Have Yourself a Merry Little Christmas"; "Frosty the Snowman"; "Rudolph the Red-Nosed Reindeer"; "Let It Snow! Let It Snow! Let It Snow!"; "Winter Wonderland"; and "Santa Baby," among many others.

Understanding how AABA form works might give you a new perspective when listening to these classic works.

How AABA Form Works

Although an AABA song typically has only thirty-two measures of music, performances are often expanded through repetition. When sections are repeated, arrangers frequently create contrast by replacing the vocal melody with an instrumental melody or an instrumental solo. Although the sections of the song are almost always performed in order, it is common to skip to the bridge of the song upon repetition, creating a total form of AABA | BA. Repetitions of the form usually simply restate the same lyrics that were sung for the first statement, although occasionally alternate lyrics are provided to reveal new layers of the story.

For instance, Ray Charles' iconic recording of "Georgia on My Mind" includes a full AABA performance of the tune, then repeats the final bridge and A section, restating the original lyrics. On the original Beatles' version of "Yesterday," Paul McCartney follows the same form. He sings the full AABA form before repeating the bridge and last A. Patsy Cline's version of "Crazy" goes through the entire AABA form, then repeats only the last A section, transposed a half-step up from the rest of the song.

Although the AABA form has a standard thirty-two-measure length, additional sections can be added to form a compelling arrangement. Besides repeating material, musicians often augment the AABA form using introductions, interludes, and codas, especially with tag endings. A **tag ending** is an ending that helps the tune wind down by repeating the last few measures.

Songs from musical theater frequently add a **verse**, a speech-like introduction that supplies crucial narrative background. When the verse is added, the main part of the song – the part with an AABA form – is usually referred to as the **chorus** or **refrain**. The verse is not included in any repetitions and is often omitted if the song is performed outside of a musical theater context. It's no coincidence that the terms used here – *verse, chorus,* and *refrain* – carry different meanings in different songwriting traditions. The craft of musical theater songs shaped later songwriting styles and the terminology evolved to meet the needs of each style.

Constructing an AABA Tune

Although the greatest AABA songs shine with the magic of creative genius, many of the fundamental rules governing AABA form can be explained, practiced, and mastered by anyone. To write an AABA form, songwriters need to understand the architecture underlying each eight-measure section.

First Two A Sections

The first two A sections establish the theme and mood of the song. Because the A sections are generally the most repeated parts of the song, it is important that the A sections include signature lyrics and memorable melodies.

Rhyme Scheme

Because the music repeats exactly or almost-exactly for each A section, the rhyme scheme should also be duplicated. Notice the repeated rhyme scheme in the A sections of "If I Had You," a Great American Songbook standard written by Jimmy Campbell, Roger Connelly, and Ted Shapiro:

A1:	*I could show the world how to smile*	**A**
	I could be glad all of the while	**A**
	I could change the gray skies to blue	**B**
	If I had you	**B**
A2:	*I could leave the old days behind*	**A**
	Leave all my pals, I wouldn't mind	**A**
	I could start my life anew	**B**
	If I had you	**B**
A3:	*I could be a king dear, uncrowned*	**A**
	Humble or poor, rich or renowned	**A**
	There is nothing I couldn't do	**B**
	If I had you	**B**

Cole Porter's classic standard, "Let's Do It," also repeats the rhyme scheme identically each A section. Note that the third-to-last syllable rhymes between the first two lines of each stanza (*bees/fleas, sets/Letts, means/beans*).

A1: *And that's why birds do it, bees do it* **A**

     Even educated fleas do it **A**

     Let's do it, let's fall in love **B**

A2: *In Spain, the best upper sets do it* **A**

     Lithuanians and Letts do it **A**

     Let's do it, let's fall in love **B**

A3: *Some Argentines, without means, do it* **A**

     People say in Boston even beans do it **A**

     Let's do it, let's fall in love **B**

Refrain

Many AABA songs create a refrain by restating the same lyrics, often the title phrase, in measures 5-7 of each A section. The lyrical repetition at the end of a stanza is similar to the refrain of a strophic song. For instance, the lyrics of "If I Had You," above, repeat the phrase "if I had you" at the end of each A section, in measure 6-7, 14-15, and 30-31 while "Let's Do It" features a longer refrain that lasts an entire line. The full score for Porter's piece can be found in the "List Songs" chapter.

Musically, the refrains vary in length. While the repetition of "If I Had You" enters at the very end of the A section, Cole Porter's refrain lasts four measures, occupying half of each A section.

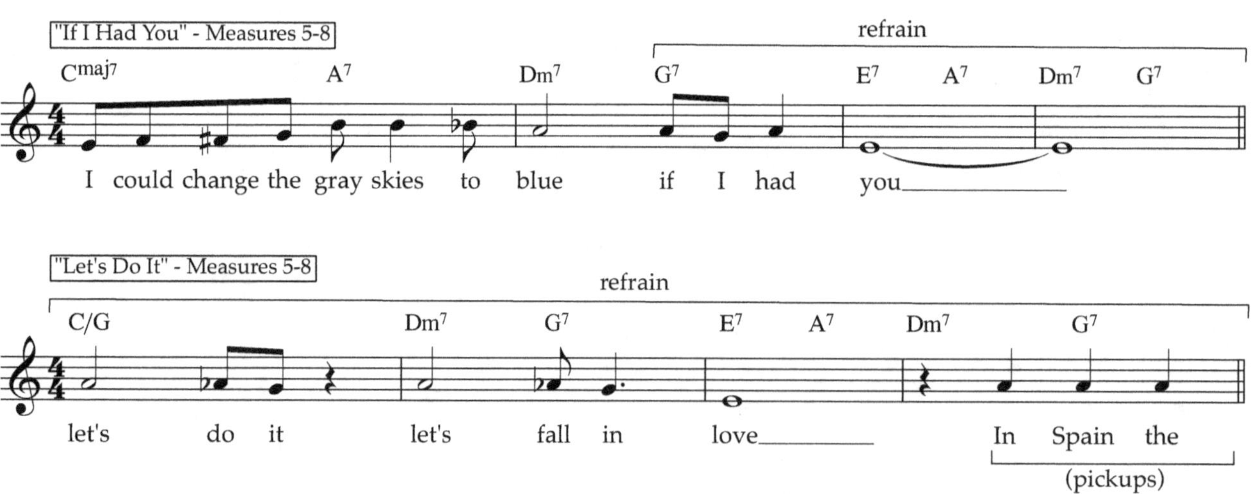

Phrase Endings

In addition to the lyrical conclusion provided by the refrain, songwriters need to understand the musical structure of phrase endings. Here are the keys to a successful phrase ending:

- Phrases typically end in the penultimate (seventh) measure, rather than the final (eighth) measure.
- The melody signals the end of a phrase with a rest or hold in the seventh measure of each section.
- Harmonically, the phrase ending is accompanied by a cadence that concludes with the melodic arrival, landing on the penultimate measure of each phrase.
- The final measure of each phrase typically includes a **turnaround**, a chord progression that leads into the harmony of the upcoming section, usually with a dominant chord targeting the first chord of the next section.

The next diagram shows the last four measures of a typical eight-measure section.

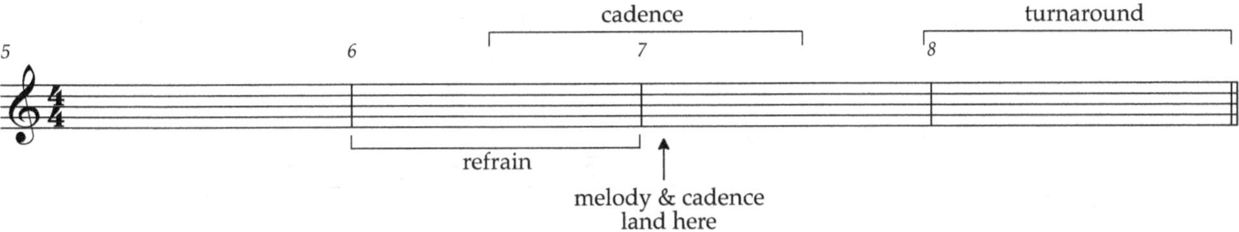

First A Section

The phrase ending for the first A section should give a weak sense of finality. Here's how:

- The melody should not end on the tonic note – instead, it should target the third or fifth of the home key.
- The harmony should use a deceptive cadence, one that creates tension with the V chord but resolves inconclusively to a chord other than the tonic. The iii and vi chords are commonly used to replace the I in a deceptive cadence because they share two notes with the tonic.

The next example shows the first A section of "If I Had You," which is in C major. Notice that the melody resolves to E (not C) and the cadence resolves from the V chord, a G dominant seventh, to E dominant seventh to create a deceptive cadence. The turnaround, which uses the ii and V of the key, is designed to "reset" the music back to the I chord in anticipation of the second A section.

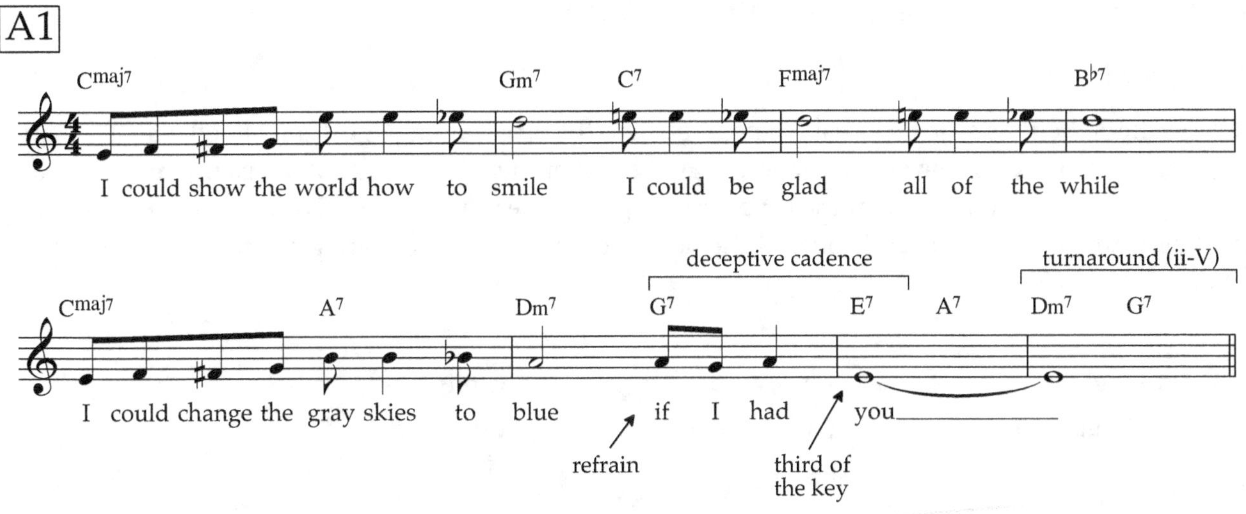

Second A Section

The second A section should arrive at a more final ending. Here's how:

- The melody usually resolves to the root
- An authentic (V-I) cadence firmly establishes the tonic key.
- Because the music will move to the B section next, the turnaround should target the first chord of the bridge.

The music for the second A section of "If I Had You" exactly repeats the music from the first A. The lyrics are different with the exception of the refrain, which repeats exactly. Notice the authentic cadence that lands on the tonic chord before the turnaround targets the beginning of the bridge, which starts on E minor.

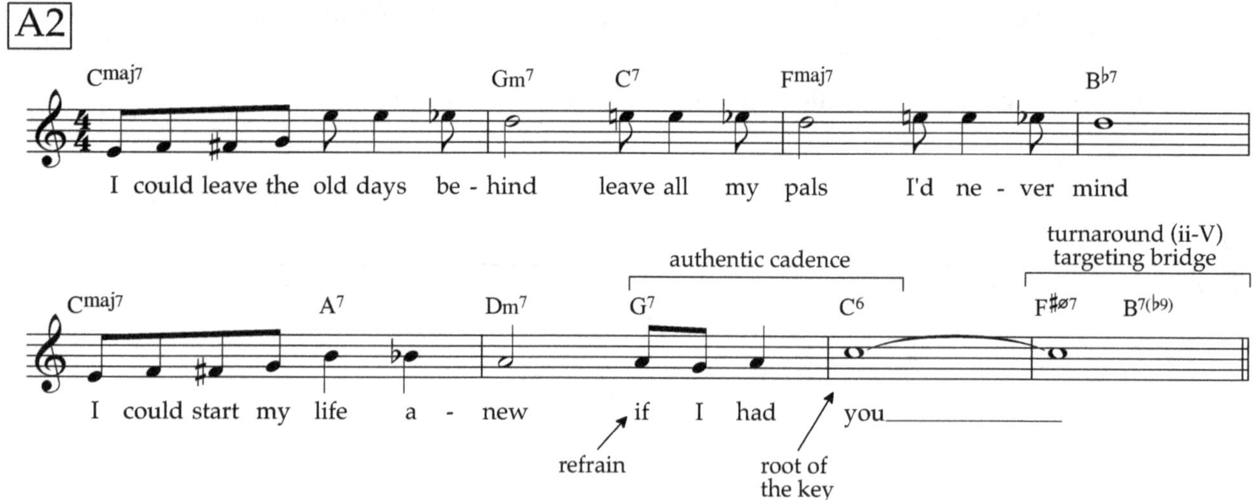

The Bridge

The bridge (the B section) offers the listener a musical respite from the repetitions of the A sections. To refresh the listeners' ears, it is essential that the bridge creates meaningful musical and lyrical contrast to the A sections. The bridge is usually indicated in sheet music by double barlines at the beginning and end.

Lyrical Contrasts

The lyrics for the B section often offer a different perspective to match the changes in music. The B section almost never repeats the refrain that repeats in the A section.

Pivot Words

Whereas the A sections state the speaker's point of view, the bridge is an opportunity to offer an alternative perspective. At the beginning of the bridge, songwriters often signal a lyrical shift by using a **pivot word**, a word or phrase that indicates that the lyric is moving in a different direction. The next list shows several pivot words that guide a listener through the logic of the piece by demonstrating connections between sections.

- but
- though
- although
- so
- for
- and
- then
- while
- yet

Some songs with bridges that use pivot words include:

- "The Girl from Ipanema" (Jobim) – ***But*** *I watch her so sadly...*
- "Skylark" (Carmichael) – ***And*** *in your lovely flight...*
- "Prelude to a Kiss" (Ellington) – *'**Though** it's just a simple melody...*
- "Have You Met Ms. Jones" (Rodgers/Hart) – ***And*** *all at once I lost my breath...*
- "Angel Eyes" (Dennis) – ***So*** *drink up, all you people....*
- "Rudolph, the Red-Nosed Reindeer" (May/Marks) – ***Then*** *one foggy Christmas Eve...*

Even when songs don't use a pivot word, it can be useful to imagine a pivot word to inspire the bridge. How would your lyric proceed if the first word were "although" or "but"?

Rhyme Scheme

To distinguish between the sections, the rhyme scheme typically changes between the A sections and the bridge of an AABA song. In "If I Had You" the rhyme scheme for the AABB A-section rhyme scheme changes to ABCB in the bridge.

A1:	*I could show the world how to smile*	**A**
	I could be glad all of the while	**A**
	I could change the gray skies to blue	**B**
	If I had you	**B**

B	*I could climb a snow-capped mountain*	**A**
	Sail the mighty ocean wide	**B**
	I could cross the burning desert	**C**
	If I had you by my side	**B**

For "Let's Do it," the rhyme scheme changes from AAB to ABAB and the bridge omits the refrain.

A1:	*And that's why birds do it, bees do it*	**A**
	Even educated fleas do it	**A**
	Let's do it, let's fall in love	**B**

B:	*The Dutch in old Amsterdam do it*	**A**
	Not to mention the Finns	**B**
	Folks in Siam do it	**A**
	Think of Siamese twins	**B**

The change in rhyme scheme usually coincides with changes in musical phrasing that will be discussed later in this section.

Verb Tense

Songs often change verb tense in the bridge, flashing back to an earlier perspective, suggesting guesses for the future, or speculating about what could be. AABA songs that change verb tenses between the A sections and the bridge include:

On the Sunny Side of the Street (McHugh/Fields)

A1: Imperative: *Grab your coat, and grab your hat …*

B: Past: *I used to walk in the rain…*

Bewitched, Bothered, and Bewildered (Rodgers/Hart)

A1: Present: *I'm wild again, beguiled again…*

B: Past: *Lost my heart, but what of it…*

Over the Rainbow (Arlen/Harburg)

A1: Present: *Somewhere over the rainbow way up high, there's a land…*

B: Future: *Someday I'll wish upon a star…*

What is This Thing Called Love (Porter)

A1: Present: *What is this thing called love?*

B: Past: *I saw you there one wonderful day…*

Musical Contrasts

First Chord

While most A sections start on the I chord, some AABA tunes use different harmonies for the beginning of their A section. For instance, Cole Porter's "What is This Thing Called Love," in the key of C major, starts on a chord quite distant from the key center, G half diminished. "All the Things You Are," by Jerome Kern, traditionally played in the key of A-flat major, starts on the vi chord, F minor.

Regardless of the first chord of the A section, the bridge almost always starts on a different chord, often visiting a different key center.

- If the song is written in a major key, the most common key centers for a bridge are iii, IV, and VI.
- If the song is written in a minor key center, the most common key centers for the bridge are III, iv, and VI.

The next chart shows different starting chords of the A and B sections of well-known AABA songs. The first few are in major keys while the last few are in minor.

Song	First Chord of A Section	First Chord of Bridge
"Georgia on My Mind"	I (C in C Major)	vi (Am in C major)
"Crazy"	I (C in C Major)	IV (F in C major)
"As Time Goes By"	ii (Dm in C Major)	IV (F in C major)
"Girl from Ipanema"	I (C in C Major)	♭II (D♭ in C major)
"She's Always a Woman"	I (C in C major)	vi (Am in C major)
"My Funny Valentine"	i (Cm in C minor)	III (E♭ in C minor)
"Angel Eyes"	i (Cm in C minor)	iv (Fm in C minor)
"All or Nothing at All"	i (Cm in C minor)	VII (B♭ in C minor)
"Blue Skies"	i (Cm in C minor)	III (E♭ in C minor)

Harmonic Rhythm

Changes in harmonic rhythm also help to create a contrast between sections by creating momentum or bringing the music to a stand-still. For instance, in Stevie Wonder's AABA song, "If It's Magic," the chords change every two or four beats in the A section but accelerate to change every single beat in the bridge.

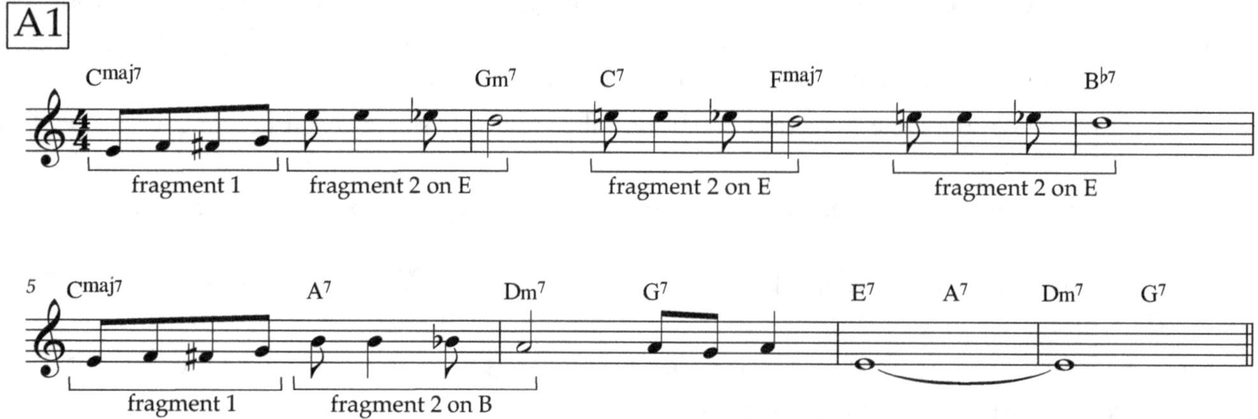

The increase in harmonic rhythm highlights the shift from shorter to longer phrases and creates a free-falling cascade with the descending bassline.

Phrase Structure

Although the AABA form is already highly repetitive, the melodies within each section are commonly constructed through internal repetition, both exact repetition and sequences. Repetition gives melodies a sense of coherence and predictability, making them easy for an audience to follow and remember.

The length and rhythm of repeated phrases distinguish the melodic character of the A and B sections. For instance, contrast the repetitions in the A and B sections of "If I Had You."

A Section: The short descending theme repeats three times starting on the same note. The phrase starts in the middle of the measure and leads to the downbeat.

B Section: A single two-measure fragment is repeated, starting from two different notes, E and B.

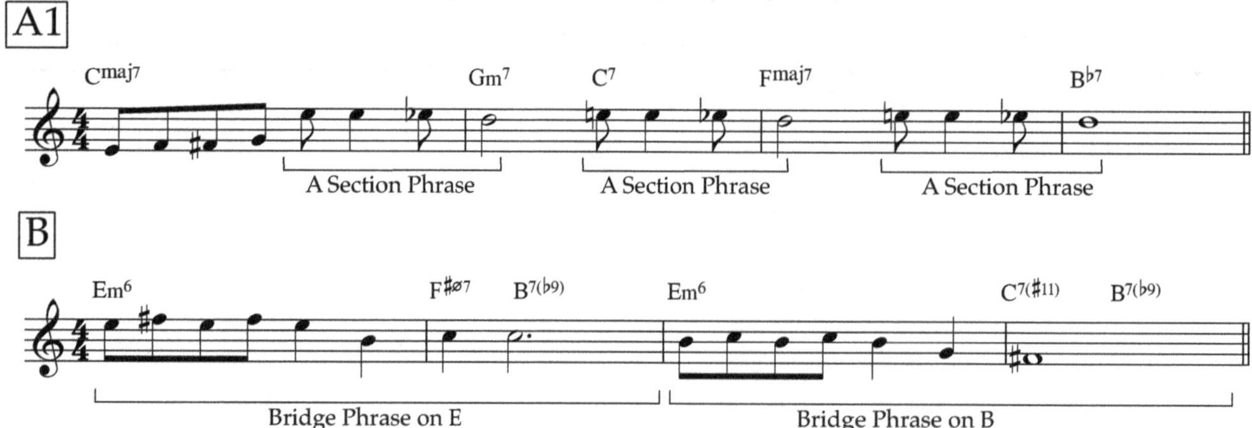

Whereas pickups in the A sections create a feeling of hope and striving, the downbeat-laden, repetitive phrases of the B section feel more stable and resigned.

Melodic Shape

Besides the phrasing, the shape of the melody often changes between the A section to the bridge. If a melody spans a wide register in the A section, it's likely to stay in a smaller register in the bridge. If it ascends quickly in one section, it might descend in the other.

In both sections of "If I Had You," the shape of the melody musically dramatizes hope and disappointment:

- In the A section, the melody starts with a grand hopeful ascent, quickly ascending by an octave. Though the phrases descend, the melody remains near its highest pitch, reflecting the speakers' longing.
- In the bridge, the melody starts on roughly its highest point and descends in each successive measure. Combined with the minor key, the shape of the melody leaves the bridge feeling less hopeful than the opening.

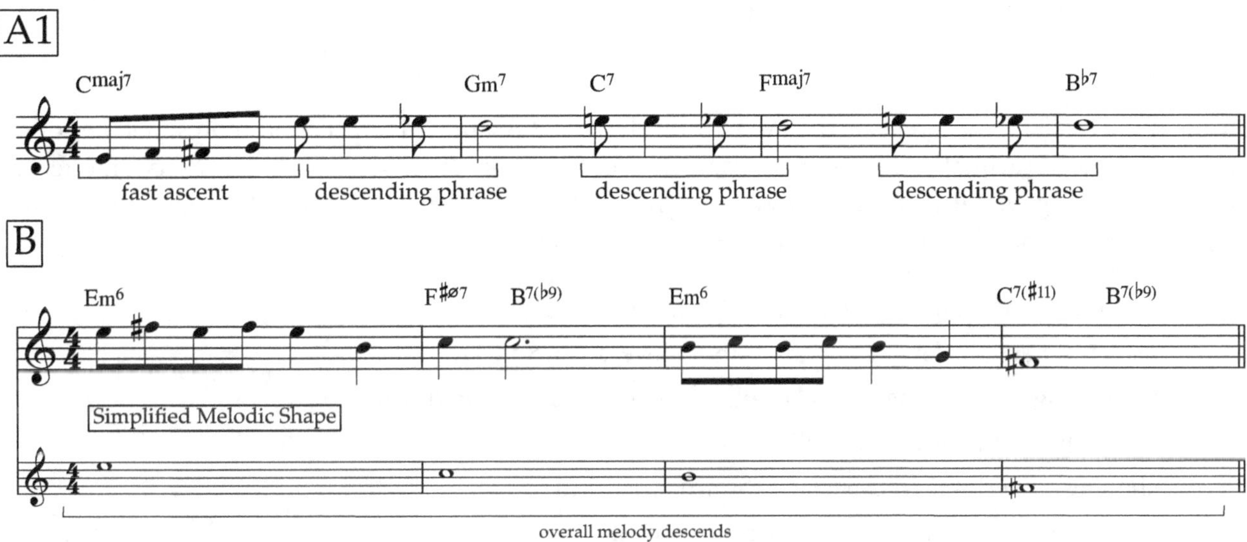

Phrase Ending

The bridge should end inconclusively, sending the music back to the beginning of the A section with renewed energy.

- The melody ends on a note away from the tonic, often a note from the V chord.
- Harmonically, the bridge should conclude with a half cadence, an open-ended sounding cadence finishing on a V chord.

Although "If I Had You" ends with a half cadence, the harmony abnormally ends on the final measure of the section rather than the penultimate measure. The F in the melody represents the seventh of the G dominant seventh chord.

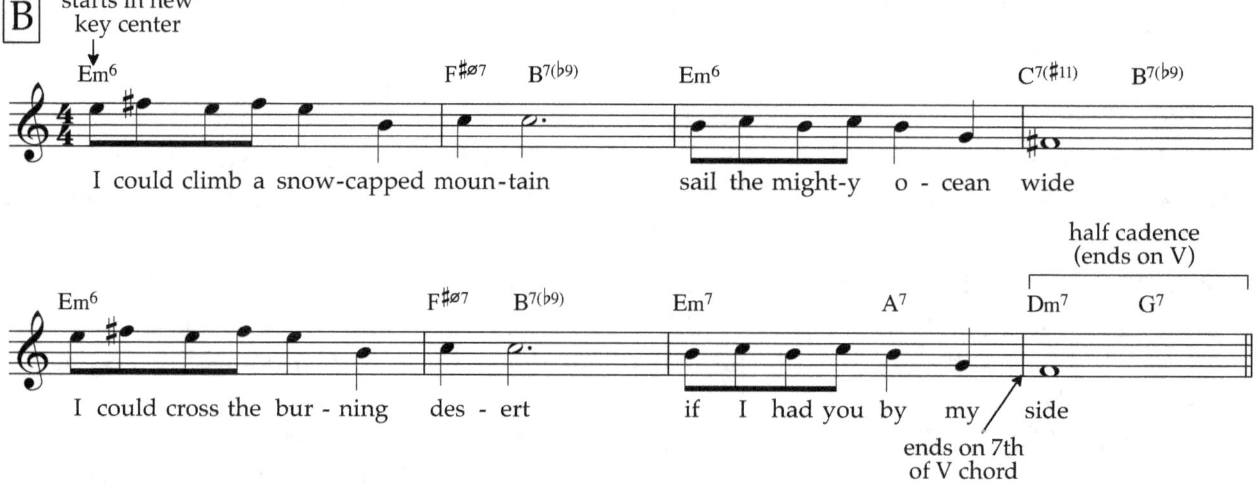

The Last A

Although the last A section repeats the music from the first 2 A's, the final A section represents the song's conclusion. After hearing the competing perspectives of the A and B sections, the final A section offers a chance for a strong lyrical synthesis. Songwriters frequently make changes to the last A section to intensify the song before it comes to an end. These changes might include:

- introduction of another character ("you," "he," etc.)
- use of hyperbolic language ("anything," "ever," "most," etc.)
- use of linguistic intensifiers like "oh," "please," and repeated words
- direct questions or calls to action
- changes of verb tense, especially towards the future
- return to an element from the beginning of the song
- inclusion of a pivot word similar to those introduced for the bridge; the last A might use more conclusive pivot words ("so," "then," "and," or even "therefore")

"All the Things You Are," a Great American Songbook standard by Jerome Kern and Oscar Hammerstein II, provides an example of many of the elements listed here.

The first two A's and B section present a series of ornate metaphors about the speaker's beloved. For instance:

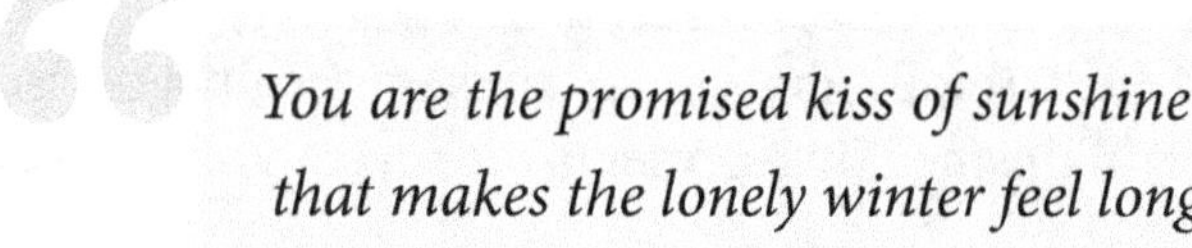

You are the promised kiss of sunshine
that makes the lonely winter feel long

In the last A section, the verbs shift to the future tense with a transitional word, "someday." The lyric concludes by returning to an element from the beginning of the song, the list of metaphors that each start with "you are." The lyric uses anadiplosis to pivot on the word "are," connecting the litany of "you are" metaphors to the speakers' pledge to win the affection of their beloved.

> *Someday, my happy arms will hold you*
> *And someday, I'll know that moment divine*
> *When all the things you are, are mine*

Other songs that include intensifications in the last A section include:

"My Funny Valentine" (Rodgers/Hart)

Lyric: *So, don't change a hair for me*
Analysis: "So" is a pivot word; imperative verb tense; call to action

"The Way You Look Tonight" (Kern/Fields)

Lyric: *Lovely, never, never change*
Analysis: hyperbolic language with "never, never"; imperative verb tense

"Over the Rainbow" (Arlen/Harburg)

Lyric: *Why, then, oh, why can't I?*
Analysis: intensification with "oh" and repetition of "why"; mode changes to questioning

"Make You Feel My Love" (Dylan)

Lyric: *No, there's nothing that I wouldn't do*
Analysis: intensification with repetition of "no" and "nothing"; hyperbolic language with "nothing"

Using intensifiers lets the audience know that this A section is different and signals that the song has reached its peak. The last A frequently reaches a satisfying conclusion when the refrain is repeated to give the lyric a sense of finality.

Phrase Ending

The phrase ending in the last A section should signal the end of the song. The end of the song is made clear through:

- Concluding with a perfect authentic cadence, that is, a V-I cadence where the melody ends on the root.
- At the end of AABA tunes, the turnaround is written in parentheses because it is omitted during the final repetition. Although the turnaround is needed in each initial repetition to cycle back to the beginning of the piece, during the final repetition, the song should end on the final stable chord, usually found in the penultimate measure.

"If I Had You" ends with a perfect authentic cadence in C. Despite the turnaround, the C major sixth chord in the penultimate measure is the appropriate final chord to create a satisfying conclusion.

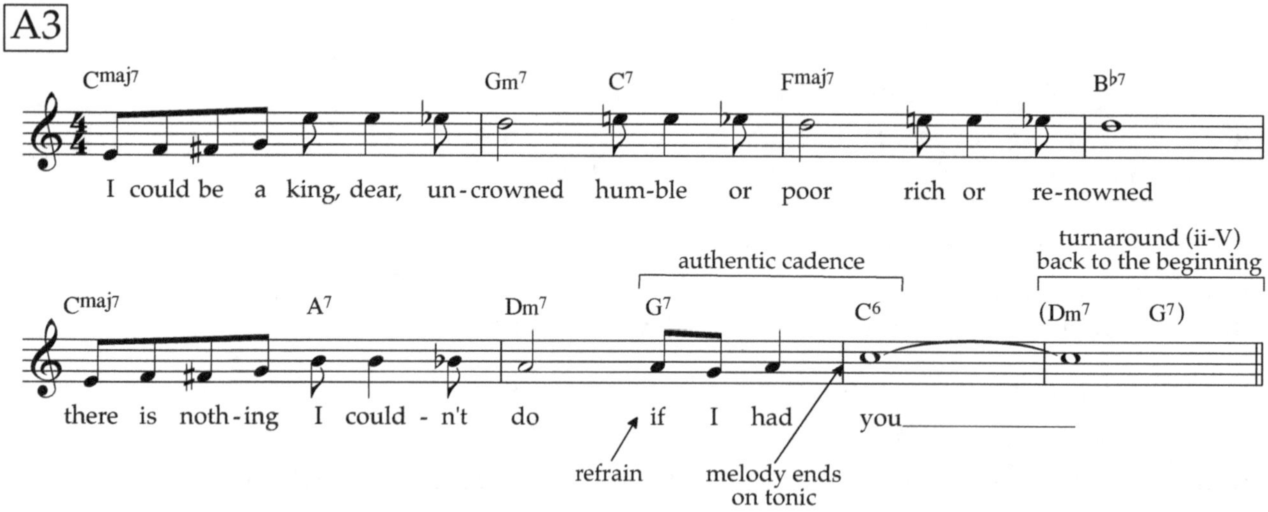

The next chart reviews the appropriate melody notes and cadences that most commonly end of each section in a typical AABA form.

AABA Phrase Endings

	Melody	Harmony
Measure 7 (first A)	holds the third or fifth of the key	deceptive cadence (V chord resolves to a chord other than I)
Measure 15 (second A)	tonic (root)	authentic cadence (V-I)
Measure 23 (bridge)	away from the tonic	half cadence (ends on V)
Measure 31 (last A)	tonic (root)	authentic cadence (V-I)

If I Had You

Ted Shapiro/Jimmy Campbell/Reg Connelly

Before viewing other AABA song examples, take a moment to examine the full leadsheet for "If I Had You," noticing the cadences, the contrasts, and the melodic structure.

Someone to Watch Over Me

George Gershwin/Ira Gershwin

"Someone to Watch Over Me" is one of the most iconic songs from the Great American Songbook. Surprisingly, the song was nearly cut from the musical *Oh, Kay* but was ultimately saved by the idea that the young actress should sing the song to her rag doll, changing the dramatic function. Although only the main "chorus" of the song is provided in the leadsheet below, the song has a famous verse which is frequently performed as an introduction.

Let's look at the way "Someone to Watch Over Me" is constructed and focus on how it matches our expectations for an AABA song.

Phrase Endings

Refrain: Lyrically, each A section ends with a four-measure refrain, some version of the song's title "someone to watch over me." The refrain changes slightly in the second A section based on the lyrical context, becoming "to one who'll watch over me."

Cadences: Note that each melody arrives at a long-note hold at the seventh measure of the phrase. The cadences perfectly match the expectations for an AABA form.

Bridge Contrast

The bridge starts with a melodic pickup in measure 16. Notice how the double barlines show the starting and ending points of the B section. Although both the A section and bridge start with a dramatic melodic ascent, the characters of the two sections are quite different.

Lyrics

Pivot word: The bridge lyric begins with "although" (*Although he may not be...*).

Rhyme scheme: Whereas the A sections include many rhymes in rapid-fire succession ("see"/"he"/"be," "woods"/"could"/"good"), the bridge has only one rhyme, an internal rhyme at the midpoint of each line ("man some" and "handsome"). The end of the bridge ("key") rhymes with the refrain in all three A sections ("me").

Perspective: The A section is focused on the longing of the speaker, using a first-person perspective, "I." The bridge changes the subject to the hypothetical person the speaker is longing for, "he."

Music

Starting Chord: The song is written in E-flat major. Although the A sections start on the I chord, the bridge starts on the IV chord, a very typical place to start.

Harmonic Rhythm: The harmonic rate of change slows down drastically in the bridge, with the first chord remaining static for eight beats, compared to a harmonic rhythm of two or four beats in the A sections.

Melodic shape: The A section melody covers a wide range, more than an octave in just the first two measures. In contrast, the bridge melody remains very stationary, spanning a very small interval. Whereas the rise of A-section melody simulates hope, the melodic shape in the bridge indicates uncertainty (especially when paired with the word "may" in "*Although he **may** not be the man...*").

Phrasing: The A section includes a succession of short phrases in measures 2-4. In contrast, the bridge is comprised of a single, long melodic phrase that stretches all the way from measure 17 to measure 23.

The Last A Section

The last section repeats the music exactly but includes three devices that increase the urgency leading to the final barline. The final A section:

- introduces "you," imploring the listener directly (*Won't **you** tell him please...*)
- includes intensifying words like "please" and "oh"
- changes to the imperative verb tense, directly spurring the listener to action; imperative verbs include "put" and "follow"

Softly, as in a Morning Sunrise

Sigmund Romberg/Oscar Hammerstein II

"Softly, as in a Morning Sunrise" (referred to in the rest of this chapter as "Softly") is a dramatic AABA song written in a minor key. Originally written for the 1928 operetta *The New Moon*, it has become a staple of the Great American Songbook and the jazz repertoire, with recordings by legends like John Coltrane, Bobby Darin, and George Benson, among others.

Phrase Endings

Refrain: Although "Softly" does not have a refrain, each of the phrase endings is connected through rhyme. The words at the arrival points for each A section ("day," "betray," and "away") all rhyme with one another.

Cadences: Each phrase ends with a long note in the seventh measure. Still, there are two surprises in the phrase endings:

- The first A section ends with a perfect authentic cadence instead of the expected deceptive cadence.
- Although the bridge melody ends in the seventh measure as expected, there's an added melodic "afterthought" or echo in the final measure of the bridge on the line "so goes the story."

Bridge Contrast

The bridge starts with an ascending scale in the sixteenth measure, melodic pickups that signal a gathering energy. Although the rhythm of the melody remains the same as the A section, it still creates meaningful contrast.

Lyrics

Pivot word: The bridge lyric begins with "for" during the pickup melody. (*For the passions that thrill love…*)

Rhyme scheme: The A sections only have between-section rhymes on "stealing" and "sealing," plus "day" and "betray". In contrast, the bridge has a prominent rhyme with "thrill love" and "kill love." The overall lack of rhymes makes the song sound poetic and artistic.

Perspective: Whereas the A sections mostly paint with vivid imagery, the bridge becomes more philosophical, speaking of generalized truths and giving advice.

Music

Starting Chord: The bridge starts on the III chord, E-flat major, the relative major of the tonic chord, C minor. This is the most common place for a bridge to start in a minor key.

Harmonic Rhythm: The harmonic rate of change slows down drastically in the bridge, with chords lasting eight beats, in contrast to the two- or four-beat harmonic rhythm of the A sections.

Melodic shape: The melodic shape for the first four measures of the bridge is largely similar to the melodic shape in the A section, with the exception of the ascending scales. The rising action in the last four measures leads the melody to its dramatic peak in contrast to the descending motion of the A sections.

Phrasing: Both sections employ a consistent two-measure phrasing pattern. However, the bridge phrasing feels a little bit more galvanized due to the addition of the scalar pickups in measures 16 and 20.

The Last A Section

The last A section creates a satisfying conclusion using a few important devices. Some of the ways the section concludes are:

- It repeats themes from earlier in the song. The theme of sunrise returns, but with a twist – the morning sunrise with an evening sunset. The "light of love" that was introduced in the first A section is now "the light that gave you glory."
- The verb changes to future tense, making an ominous prediction that "the light that gave you glory **will** take it all away."

Variations of AABA Form

Great songwriters love to innovate within established forms. Throughout its history, the AABA form has been stretched, adapted, and modified to meet the needs of each song. The next section examines two common ways to vary AABA form.

Changes Between A Sections

Although A sections are traditionally identical except for their cadences, some AABA songs modify A sections to create contrast.

The first two A sections of "Bye Bye Blackbird," a classic song from the Great American Songbook, have identical melodies in different key centers. While the first A section starts in the tonic chord of F major, the second starts on the ii chord, G minor. The melody is similarly sequenced up a step and the chords are adjusted to fit the new melody.

The beloved standard "My Funny Valentine" varies the first two A sections in a different way. While the chords repeat identically, the melody is sequenced to a higher pitch, starting a third higher than in the original statement.

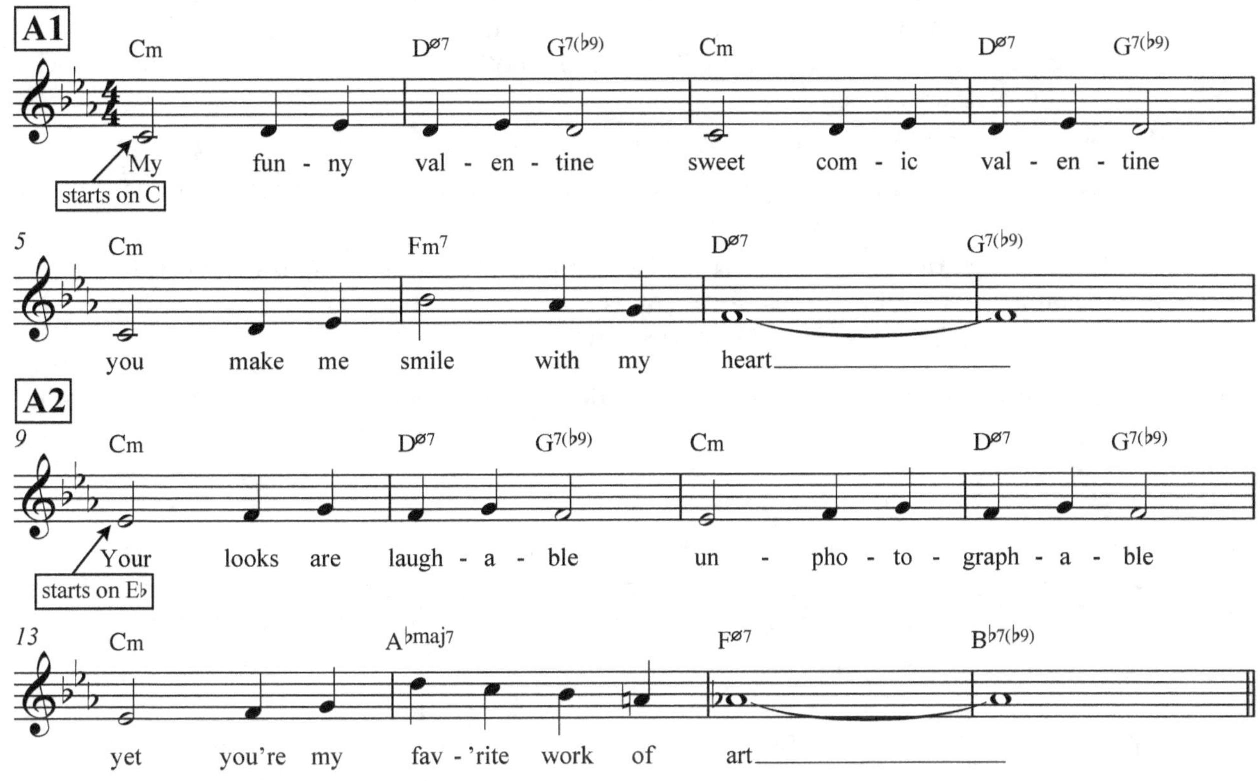

"Spring Can Really Hang You Up the Most," a 1955 song by Tommy Wolf and Fran Landesman, includes a unique twist in the last A section. Whereas each of the first two A sections starts in C major, the last A section starts in G major. Instead of repeating the entire section down a fourth, the melody twists back to the original key after just one measure, creating a musical burst of color.

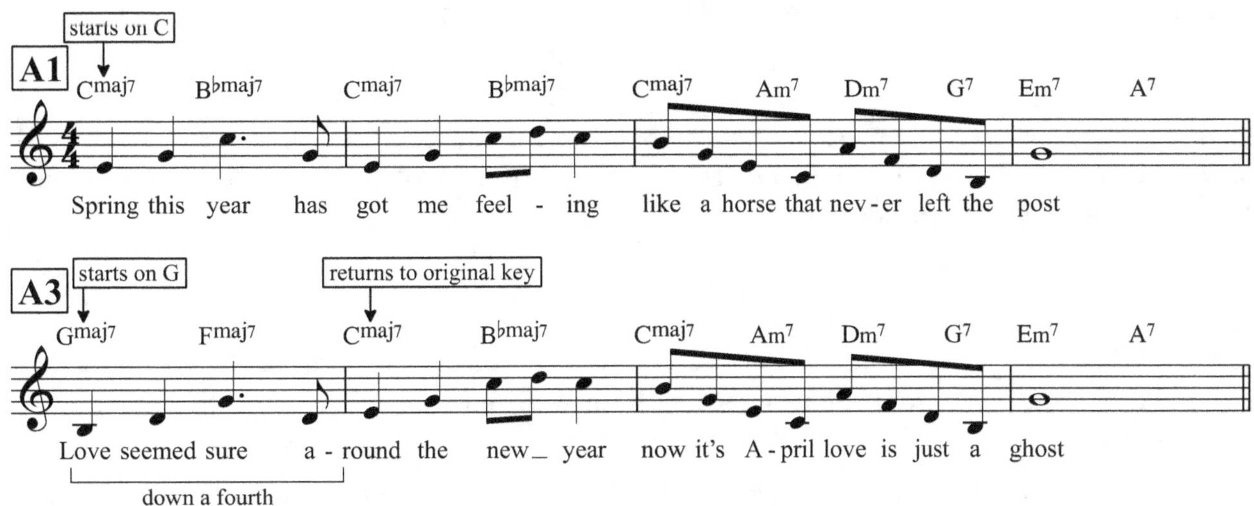

Other Section Lengths

Not all AABA songs are exactly thirty-two measures long. Some songs extend sections, most commonly doubling the length of one or all sections. Here are a few examples of AABA songs with extended sections:

- **"The Way You Look Tonight"** doubles the expected length of each section. With four sixteen-measure sections, the song is a total of sixty-four measures long instead of thirty-two. "Just the Way You Are," by Billy Joel, is another example of an AABA song with sixteen-measure sections.

- **"Yesterday"** has only seven-measure A sections, but has an eight-measure bridge.

- **"The Girl from Ipanema"** has eight-measure A sections but a sixteen-measure bridge, making it a total of forty measures.

- **"My Funny Valentine"** extends the last A section to twelve measures in order to create a melodic climax. Extending the last A section is somewhat common and can also be heard in "All the Things You Are" and "I Got Rhythm."

The next example shows the final, twelve-measure A section for "My Funny Valentine" with the melodic climax indicated:

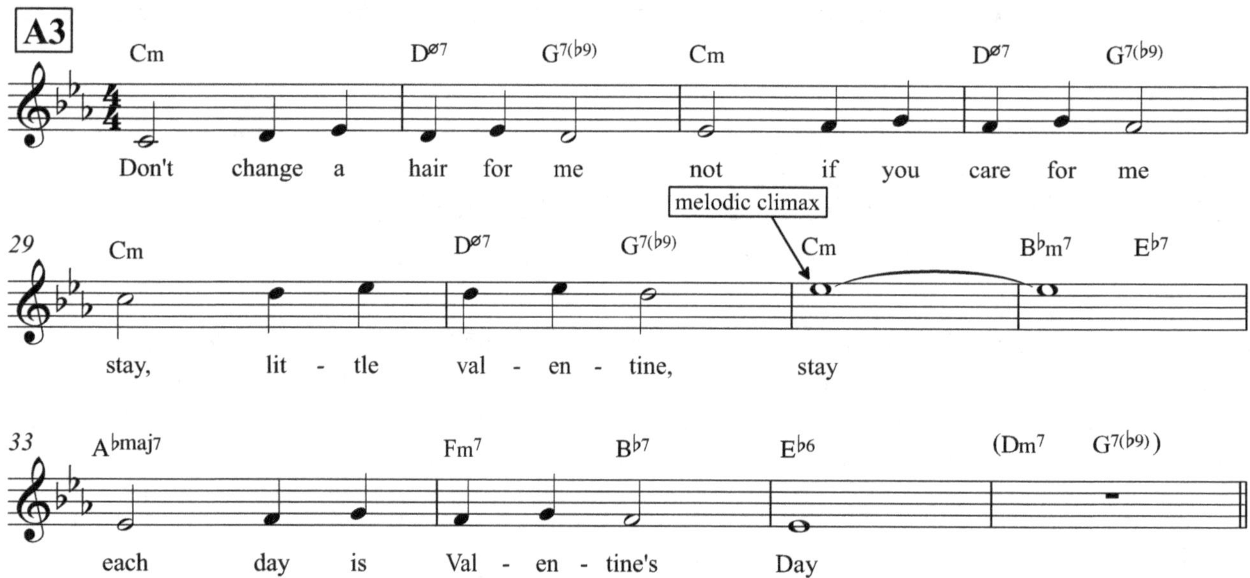

Each of these songwriters is able to play with the form because they have already mastered the traditional song form. Once you've mastered the traditional thirty-two measure AABA form, you too can experiment with varied A sections and expanded sections.

Takeaways

1. AABA form is a thirty-two-measure song form with four eight-measure sections that is primarily associated with the Great American Songbook.

2. Phrase endings and cadences are key to achieving the ideal pacing and flow in AABA form. Phrases usually end in the seventh measure in each section, leaving the eighth measure open for a turnaround.

3. The bridge is designed to create musical contrast through musical changes in harmony, melodic character, and phrasing, plus lyrical contrast through pivot words, changes in rhyme scheme, and changes in verb tense.

4. The last A section often creates a heightened emotion by introducing a new character, asking a direct question, changing verb tense, and/or reintroducing an element from the beginning of the song.

5. Not every AABA song follows the "script" exactly. Some songs create variations between the first two A's or extend the sections beyond the typical thirty-two measures.

Practice

A. The next example gives three A sections from AABA songs by Irving Berlin. Without listening to the original songs, treat these sections as the first A of your song and write the final three sections to complete the AABA form. Then, listen to the originals to see how your songs compare.

B. The next three examples show the bridge to famous AABA songs by Cole Porter.
Without listening to the originals, write the three A sections needed to complete each
song. Then, listen to the originals to see how your songs compare.

14A Writing an AABA Song

Scan Here for
Chapter 14A Page

With so much to accomplish in just thirty-two measures, writing a song in AABA form requires a high level of structure and craft. This chapter walks you through how to write an AABA form by starting with the crucial structural landmarks and working backward to fill in the song's details.

Step One: Invent a Refrain

The refrain of an AABA song, repeated at the end of each A section, is usually closely related to the song's title. One way to evoke the Great American Songbook tradition is to build a refrain around an **idiom**, a common but colorful bit of conversational language. Songs like "You Turned the Tables on Me," "I Get a Kick Out of You," "Just One of Those Things," "Nice Work if You Can Get It," and "Puttin' on the Ritz" all use idioms prominently. Here are several idioms that could inspire a refrain:

- once in a blue moon
- through thick and thin
- the ball is in your court
- bite the bullet
- speak of the devil
- go the extra mile
- butterflies in your stomach

- see eye to eye
- turn a blind eye
- be on solid ground
- hit below the belt
- throw in the towel
- spice things up
- throw caution to the wind

For my song, I chose the last idiom listed, "throw caution to the wind," as the focal point. To expand the idiom into a full refrain, I imagined how it would be used in the context of a romantic relationship. A more enthusiastic partner might be encouraging their shier companion to do something bold – go on a trip with them, move in with them, or even elope. I envisioned the partner saying, "Let's throw caution to the wind," which became my refrain.

To start the song, I placed that refrain at the end of each A section with the final word falling on or near the downbeat of the seventh measure of each section. Finishing each phrase in the seventh measure reserves the eighth measure for an important function: preparing the harmony for the next section.

The following score shows the full AABA form in C major with only the refrain and appropriate cadences placed at the end of each A section.

Caution to the Wind

Jeremy Siskind

Analysis

Melody: Inspired by the word "throwing" in the lyric, I decided to make the melody fling itself upward after the word "throw." The leap also simulates recklessness, reflecting the carefree perspective of the speaker.

Harmony: AABA songs typically employ the following cadences:

> **First A section:** half cadence, melody avoids root
> **Second A section:** authentic cadence, melody ends on root
> **Last A section:** authentic cadence, melody ends on root

With these cadences established, I created the preceding harmony by moving backward through the diatonic circle of fifths, adjusting the timing to create a strong match between the chords and the melody. For example, in the first A, I wrote the harmony in the following way:

- I established the V chord (G dominant seventh in C major) at the end of the section to create a half cadence
- I targeted the V chord moving through the diatonic circle of fifths, working backward to arrive at the V just in time
- in the diatonic circle of fifths, the V is preceded by the ii, the vi, and the iii
- in C major, the ii is D minor, the vi is A minor, and the iii is E minor

Step Two: Complete One A-Section Melody

The next step is to complete the music and lyrics for a single A section. The refrain gives important clues regarding what to include in the rest of the lyric:

- a word that rhymes with "wind"
- a situation that involves throwing caution to the wind
- a tone consistent with the Great American Songbook

The rhyme with "wind" is the most concrete place to start. As a first step, I brainstormed pure, assonant, and consonant rhymes with "wind," aiming for ten in each category:

Pure	Assonant	Consonant
1. chinned	1. trimmed	1. find
2. twinned	2. dimmed	2. sand
3. thinned	3. brimmed	3. land
4. skinned	4. limbed	4. pined
5. sinned	5. skimmed	5. pond
6. chagrined	6. winged	6. kind
7. rescind	7. been	7. lined
8. pinned	8. spin	8. signed
9. finned	9. win	9. fanned
10. grinned	10. lid	10. aligned

Next, I created possible lyrics that include the rhyming words while introducing the theme of taking chances. Each lyric must be concise enough to fit naturally into a four-measure phrase. It's worthwhile to brainstorm many possibilities here, as each of the three A sections will ultimately need similar lyrics. Here are seven lyrical ideas I came up with during the brainstorming process:

1. *If you want to make history, you can't be thin-skinned*

2. *Folks who don't place bets are folks who never win*

3. *We could go to sea before our sails are trimmed*

4. *You've got a brand-new car, then take her for a spin*

5. *Wise men seek adventure before the spirit's dimmed*

6. *Sometimes the sweetest fruit hangs from the furthest limb*

7. *The day has turned to evening, and now the skies are dim*

I based the first A section on #6 because I liked the parallel structure of "sweetest fruit" and "furthest limb." The playful metaphor of a fruit tree matches the tone of a typical Great American Songbook tune, and the image reminds me of the monkeys in Nat "King" Cole's "Straighten Up and Fly Right."

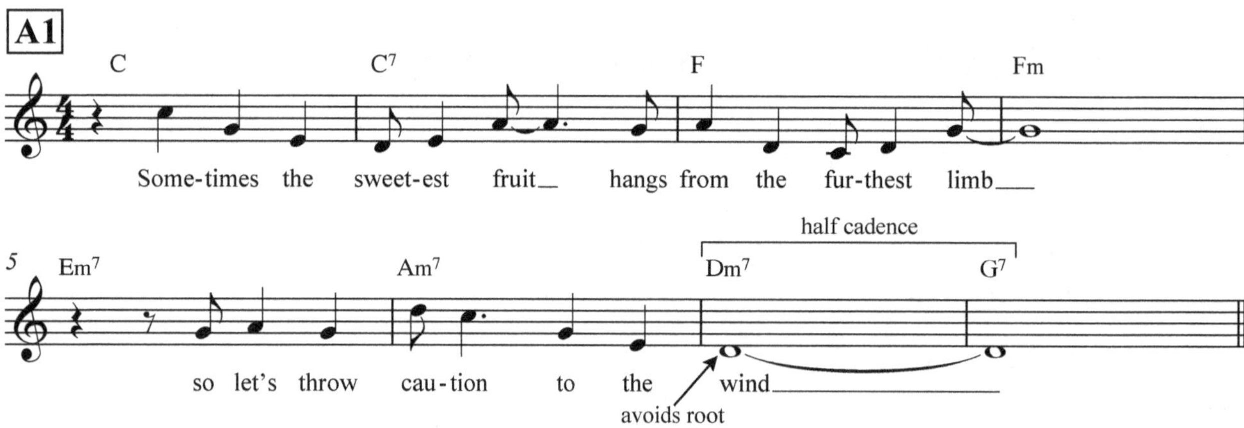

Analysis

Melody: AABA tunes commonly employ melodic sequences. In this melody, there is a sequence between the beginning of measure two ("sweetest fruit") and the end of measure three ("never win"). Notice the syncopation in the melody that creates a jazzy rhythmic feel.

Harmony: Songs in this style typically move outside of the diatonic key using secondary dominants and modal interchange. Both devices are included here: the C dominant seventh chord in measure 2 is the V/IV, a secondary dominant; the F minor chord in measure 4 is borrowed from the C minor key signature, an example of modal interchange.

Step Three: Complete The Other Two A Sections

Once the first A section is complete, two additional A-section lyrics are needed. I utilized two other phrases from my previous brainstorm and edited them to fit the melody of the first A section, maintaining the same accent pattern and number of syllables as the first lyric. Here are the lyrics for all three A sections:

First A: Sometimes the sweetest fruit hangs from the furthest limb
Second A: If you don't place a bet, you're never gonna win
Third A: Life is a Firebird so take it for a spin

The second A is based on my previous brainstorm, "*Folks who don't take chances are folks who never win.*" The rhythm of the second half ("are folks who never win") already matches the first A section rhythm perfectly. To make the first half match, I changed the subject from "folks" to "you" and started the phrase with "if."

The third A is based on the brainstorm, "*You've got a brand-new car, then take her for a spin.*" Replacing the generic phrase, "brand-new car" with the more evocative "Firebird" was primarily a matter of syllable count and accent pattern. Although other sports cars like "Mercedes" or "Ferrari" have the right number of syllables, their accent pattern doesn't complement the accent pattern of "sweetest fruit." Plus, the drama of the name "Firebird" creates an aura of danger and derring-do that fits the song's theme.

With the exception of the cadences, the melody and chords should remain identical for each of the three A sections. The next example shows a draft with all three A sections completed. The refrain is adjusted slightly (from "so" to "and") to match the phrasing in the last A.

Caution to the Wind

Jeremy Siskind

Step Four: Write the Bridge

The primary function of the bridge is to create contrast, providing relief from the musical repetition of the A sections. Before writing the bridge, reflect on elements of the A sections and what possible contrasts could be created in the bridge.

Starting Harmony:

>*A Sections:* The A sections start on the tonic chord (C major in the key of C major).
>
>*Contrast:* The bridge could start on other important chords in the key like the IV chord (F major) or the relative minor (vi) chord (A minor).

Phrase Length:

>*A Sections:* The A sections have two four-measure phrases.
>
>*Contrast:* Using shorter phrases, one or two measures long, would help create a clear contrast in the bridge.

Lyrical Perspective:

>*A Sections:* The lyrics in the A sections are very philosophical and impersonal.
>
>*Contrast:* The bridge lyric could add a personal dimension.

When brainstorming lyrics, I kept four goals in mind:

1. More personal, story-telling content, including "you" and/or "me"

2. Shorter lines to help create contrast in the musical phrasing

3. Relate back to the idea of taking chances

4. Include at least one rhyme (but the rhyme doesn't have to be with "wind")

I wrote four brainstorms:

1. *I'd hold you forever*
   If you'd agree
   To be bold and endeavor
   To take a chance on me

2. *When it's love dear, you just feel it*
   Don't think too deep
   If you love me, if it's real
   don't look before you leap

3. *My heart yearns for you*
   But my feelings are scrambled
   Still your eyes tell me
   You're worth the gamble

4. *What is love, my dear*
   If it's not taking chances
   How will our plot ever advance
   if you keep refusing my advances?

I chose #2 because I liked the inclusion of a second English idiom, "look before you leap." It functions as an effective payoff at the end of the bridge, a moment that often delivers a song's lyrical punchline. I chose to set it to music with short phrases:

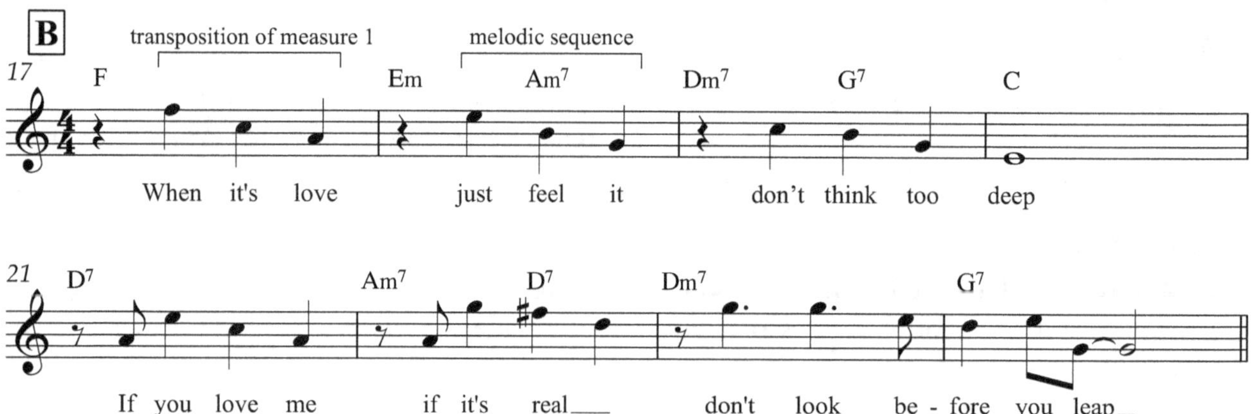

Analysis

Melody: The melody for the short phrases in 17-18 and 21-22 is inspired by the first three notes of the song and the theme of three descending notes in a row is repeated and sequenced throughout the section. There are two moments of word-painting, first in measure 20 where the melody goes down to reflect the word "deep," then in measure 24, where the melody leaps by a sixth for the word "leap."

Harmony: The bridge begins on the IV chord to create contrast. Although it starts on the IV chord, the overall *key* is still C major, and the rest of the first line moves through the diatonic circle of fifths to target C. The second line uses some secondary dominants (D dominant seventh is the V/V) before ultimately ending in a half cadence to target the tonic.

Now the first draft is complete! Look through this full version of "Caution to the Wind," noticing how an extra chord was added in measure 16 to lead into the bridge.

Caution to the Wind

Jeremy Siskind

Step Five: Edit

With the first draft complete, I sang and played it over and over, paying attention to my intuition regarding lyrics that stick out and musical choices that disrupt the flow. During the editing process, I strive to avoid becoming too attached to any phrase, chord, rhyme, or melody because changing even strong ideas is often necessary to improve a song.

Here are three elements that I determined could improve:

1. **Spot:** Last A section lyric

    Issue: it is impersonal and doesn't create a meaningful conclusion for the song

    > *Original:*   *Life is a Firebird*
    > *Let's take it for a spin*

    > *Fix:*   *Though if our lips should meet*
    > *My head would start to spin*

2. **Spot:** B section lyrics

    Issue: the extra syllables for the "ifs" in 21-22 feel rhythmically awkward and the rhyme between "real" and "feel" doesn't quite line up

    > *Original:*   *If it's love*
    > *Just feel it*
    > *Don't think too deep*
    > *If you love me*
    > *If it's real*
    > *Don't look before you leap*

    > *Fix:*   *Let down your*
    > *Defenses*
    > *Don't think too deep*
    > *You love me*
    > *I sense it*
    > *You don't have to look before you leap*

3. **Spot:** Melody at the beginning of the bridge

    Issue: the first note, F, is difficult for a vocalist to find

    > *Fix:*   start with an E, which is more closely related to the C major harmony; additionally, the first note in measure 18 would change to a D to maintain the sequence

To see the updated leadsheet and hear a full performance, visit the page for this chapter by scanning the QR code at the beginning of the chapter.

Takeaways

1. Popular idioms provide a good starting place to inspire lyrical ideas for Great American Songbook-style tunes.

2. Establish appropriate cadences first to guarantee that the AABA song will have a smooth sense of organization.

3. Work backward from the refrain to create the first A section, considering rhymes, tone, and story.

4. When writing a bridge, consider multiple methods of creating contrast including phrase length, starting chord, and lyrical perspective.

5. Once the first draft is complete, sing the song repeatedly to identify the weakest spots. Write alternatives that solve the problems you encounter, never considering any part of the song to be too important to change.

Practice

1. Choose 2 of the idioms listed at the beginning of this chapter and write 5 possible refrains for each, for a total of 10 possible refrains.

   Idiom 1:

   A.

   B.

   C.

   D.

   E.

   Idiom 2:

   A.

   B.

   C.

2. Create a melody for your refrain and include the appropriate cadences on the next staff.

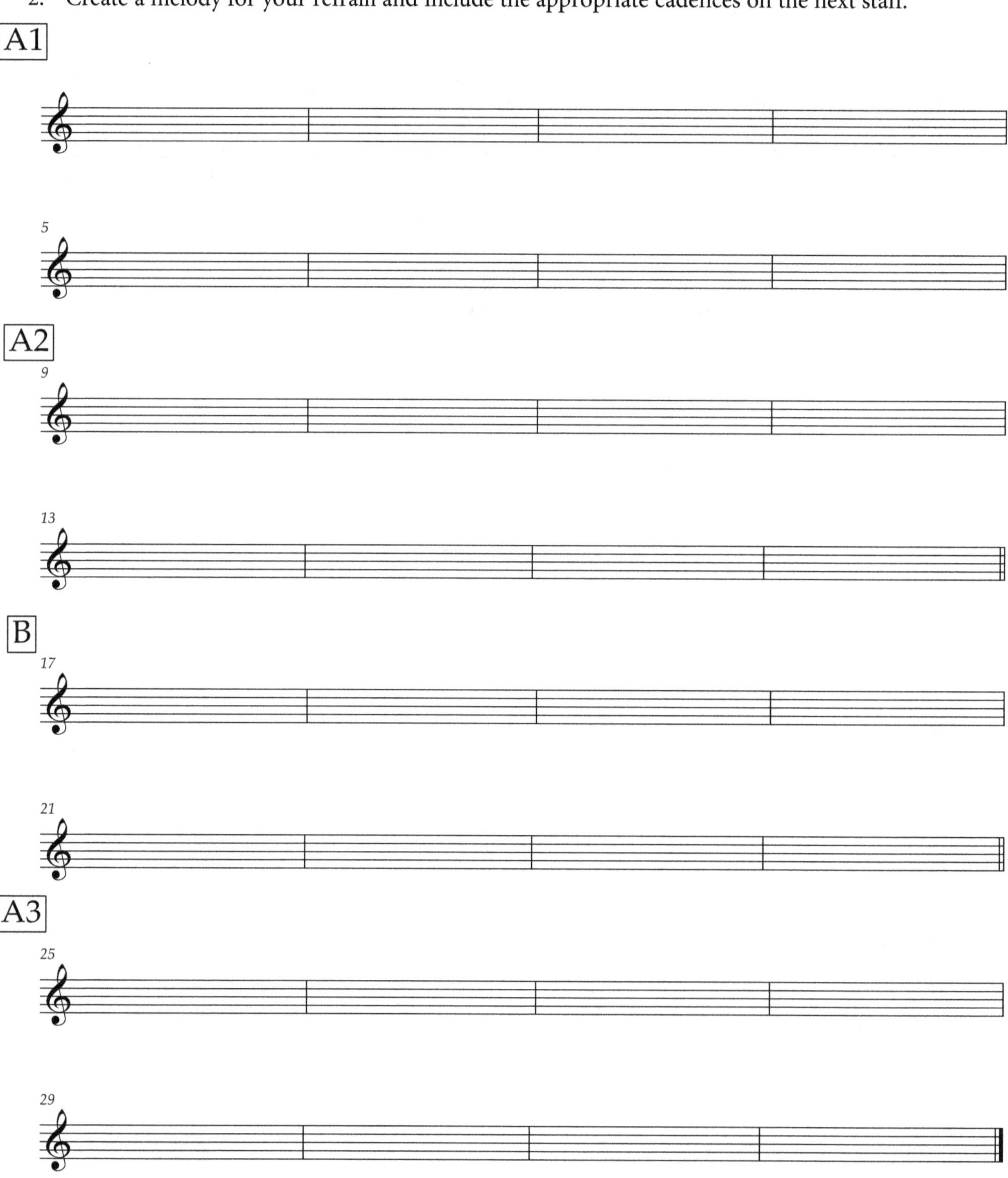

3. Choose your favorite refrain idea from #1 and brainstorm 10 pure, assonant, and consonant rhymes for the end of the refrain. Then write 5 possibilities for lines that rhyme with the end of the refrain.

10 Rhymes:

Pure	Assonant	Consonant
1.	1.	1.
2.	2.	2.
3.	3.	3.
4.	4.	4.
5.	5.	5.
6.	6.	6.
7.	7.	7.
8.	8.	8.
9.	9.	9.
10.	10.	10.

5 Lines:

A.

B.

C.

D.

E.

4. Complete your first A section with lyrics and music. If you are skilled at musical notation, write it on the staff below. Remember to end with a half cadence.

A1

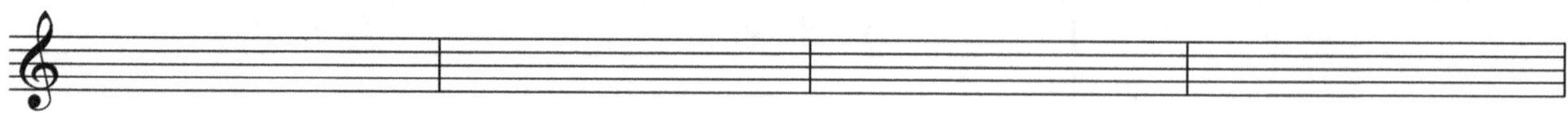

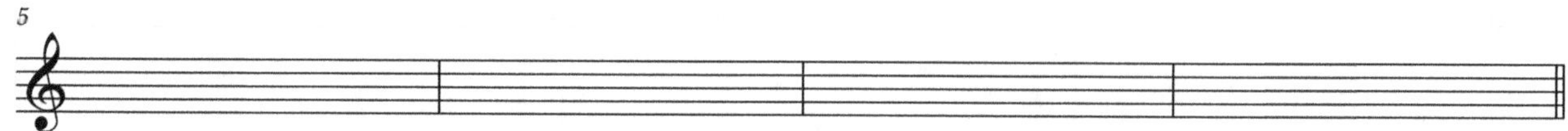

5. Using the first A section as a model, write lyrics for the second and third A sections. Remember to maintain the rhyme scheme, approximate syllable count, and stress pattern from the first A section.

Second A:

Last A:

6. Reflect on aspects of your A sections and consider how you could create contrast in the bridge. Then, brainstorm 5 lyrical ideas for your bridge.

Phrase Length
> *A Sections:*
> *Contrast:*

Starting Chord
> *A Sections:*
> *Contrast:*

Harmonic Rhythm

A Sections:

Contrast:

Lyrical Perspective

A Sections:

Contrast:

Lyrical Ideas:

1.

2.

3.

4.

5.

7. Using your favorite lyrical idea and ideas for contrast, complete the lyrics and the music for
the bridge. If you're comfortable with musical notation, write your bridge on the next staff.

8. Notate your complete song including all three A's and the bridge to create your first draft.

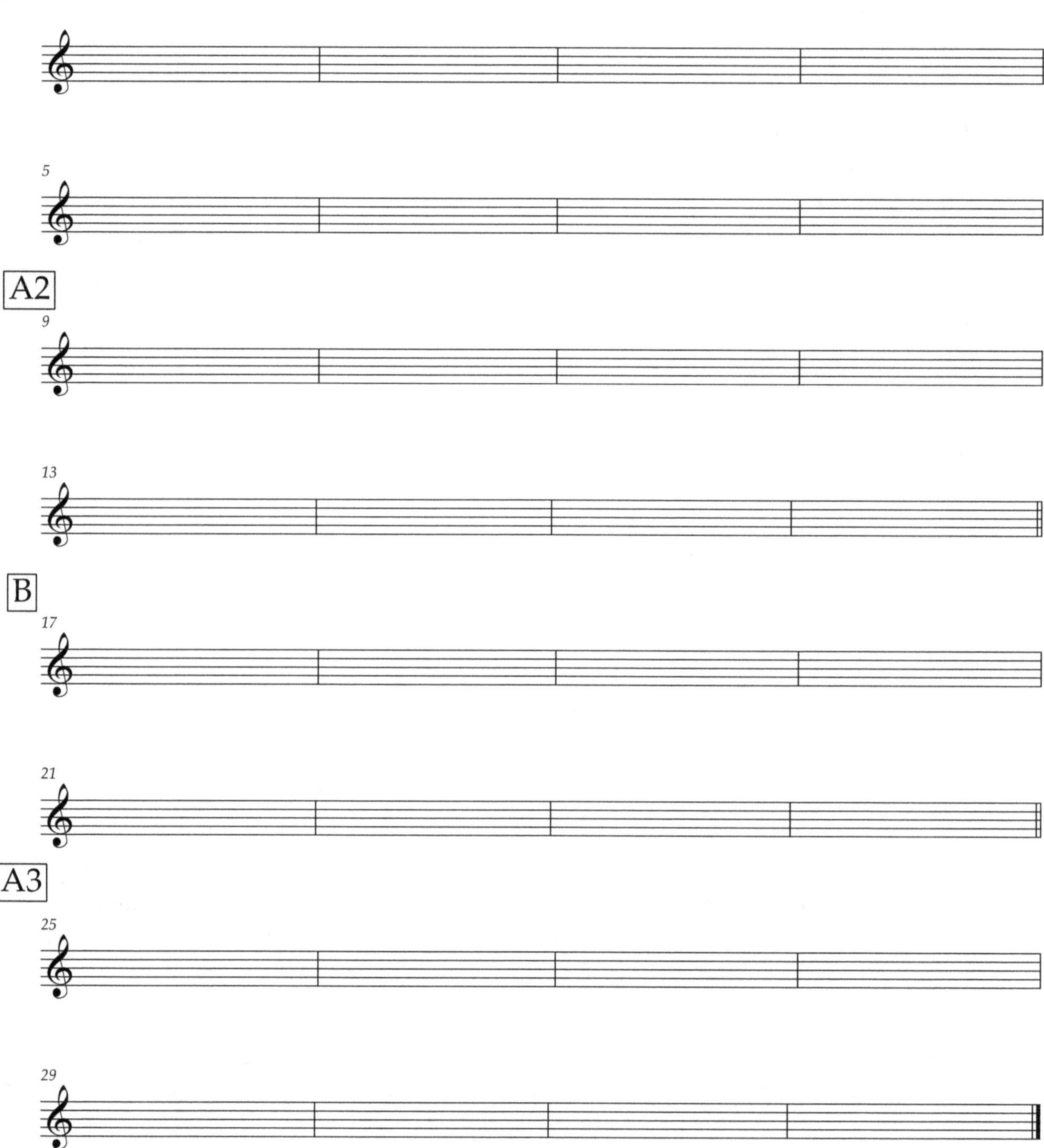

9. Sing and play your song repeatedly over multiple days. Then, select three weak elements and write alternate versions.

1. **Spot:**
   Problem:

   Alternate:

2. **Spot:**
   Problem:

   Alternate:

3. **Spot:**
   Problem:

   Alternate:

15. ABAC Form

According to the *Guinness Book of World Records*, Bing Crosby's 1942 version of "White Christmas" is the best-selling single of all time. Even beyond that staggering achievement, "White Christmas" has lived many lives. Written by a Jewish immigrant whose son died on Christmas Day, the song comforted US troops after Pearl Harbor, won an Academy Award for Best Original Song, inspired a 1956 film (*White Christmas*) that became the highest-grossing movie of all time, and even served as a secret signal to cue the American evacuation of Saigon.

The writer of "White Christmas," Irving Berlin, was a Russian immigrant with no formal musical training who became one of America's legendary composers. Due to his limited musical capabilities, he used a transposing piano, a jerry-rigged instrument called the "Buick," that mechanically shifted the keyboard. The device let Berlin keep his fingers resting comfortably on the black keys while transposing his melodies to different key centers. Berlin made no apologies for his lack of musical training. He advocated for clarity and tunefulness over complexity and cleverness, saying, "A simple melody will always linger. I mean the kind you pick out with one finger."

The writer of many other well-known songs like "God Bless America," "Puttin' on the Ritz," "Blue Skies," and "Cheek to Cheek," Berlin was as passionate about melodies as he was precise about musical forms. "White Christmas" and other Berlin songs follow ABAC form, a cornerstone of the Great American Songbook style. Learning to write in ABAC form helps songwriters develop precision and coherence in their craft.

ABAC Basics

Along with AABA form, **ABAC form** stands as one of the two pillars supporting the Great American Songbook. Like AABA, ABAC tunes typically consist of four eight-measure sections (A, B, A, and C) that combine to form a thirty-two-measure song. Well-known ABAC songs include "Fly Me to the Moon," "Moon River," "Someday My Prince Will Come," "When I Fall in Love," "My Romance," and "For Once in My Life."

In ABAC form, the two A sections don't come to a conclusive cadence but instead flow smoothly into the B or C section. Full cadences appear only at the song's midpoint (measure 16, marked with a double barline) and at the very end. Because the A sections never come to a stop, some musicians prefer to call this form **A-A Prime (A-A')**, a name that indicates two similar sixteen-measure sections – AB and AC ("prime," indicated by an apostrophe, indicates a varied repetition). Unlike AABA form, ABAC form has no bridge and the B section in ABAC form should not be described using that word.

The next graphic shows general frameworks for AABA and ABAC forms placed side by side to demonstrate the broad differences between them.

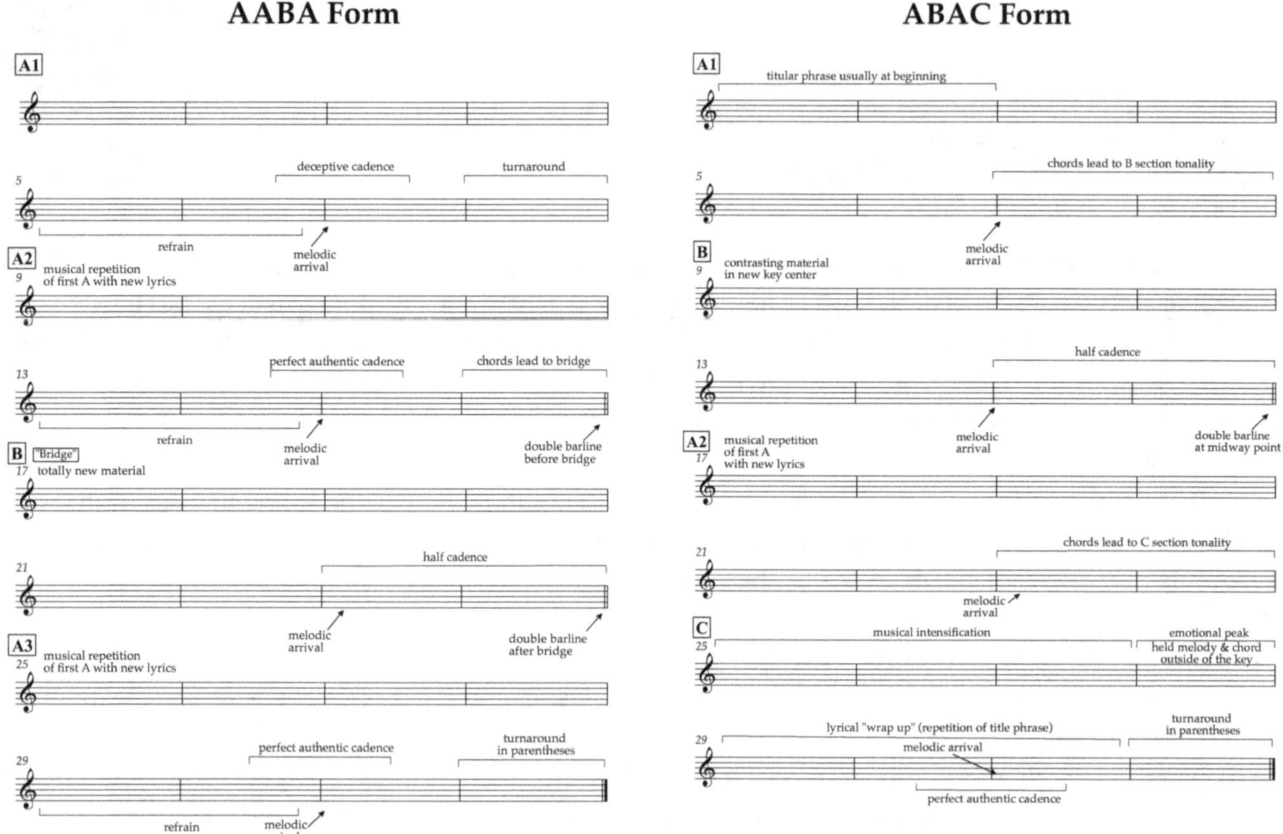

Like AABA songs, ABAC songs are generally played more than once through, with instrumentals replacing vocals during subsequent repetitions. For example:

- The famous Frank Sinatra recording of "Fly Me to the Moon" begins with Sinatra singing the thirty-two-measure form once through. Then, the entire form repeats: the band plays the first half (AB) of the tune before Sinatra returns with the lyrics for the second half (AC).

- Stevie Wonder's version of "For Once in My Life" similarly begins with Wonder singing the entire thirty-two measure ABAC form plus a repeated tag. On the repetition, the music moves up by a half step and Wonder plays a harmonica solo over the harmony for the first half (the AB) before singing the second half (AC).

Even with these repetitions, musicians still describe the song as being in ABAC form with thirty-two measures of music and the lyrics from the original statement are usually repeated exactly upon repetition.

Constructing an ABAC Song

Once you understand how each section functions and connects, you can build a coherent, satisfying ABAC song of your own. To guide you through the details of ABAC form, this section will use the classic 1924 song, "It Had to Be You" as an example. Written by Isham Jones and Gus Kahn, "It Had to Be You" had a Renaissance when it was featured prominently in the 1989 movie, When Harry Met Sally. Each section of the song appears separately after the corresponding text and the entire leadsheet is provided at the end of this section.

The First A Section

The first A section introduces the songs' musical and lyrical themes. In contrast to AABA songs, ABAC songs rarely end their A sections with a repeated "refrain." Instead, the first lyric commonly includes the song's title and signature lyric. Observe how popular ABAC songs begin with the title phrase:

Fly Me to the Moon (Bart Howard)
First Lyric: *Fly me to the moon and let me play among the stars*

For Once in My Life (Murden/Miller)
First Lyric: *For once in my life, I have someone who needs me*

Moon River (Mancini/Mercer)
First Lyric: *Moon River, wider than a mile*

Although A section melodies typically end with a long note on the penultimate (seventh) measure of each section, the harmony generally does not arrive at a conclusive cadence. Instead, the last few chords target the first measure of the B section, using a secondary dominant. In "It Had to Be You," the A section ends on the A dominant seventh chord, which will lead to a D chord in the B section. From a theory perspective, this is the "five of five" (V/V), because D is the fifth scale degree in the home key of G major.

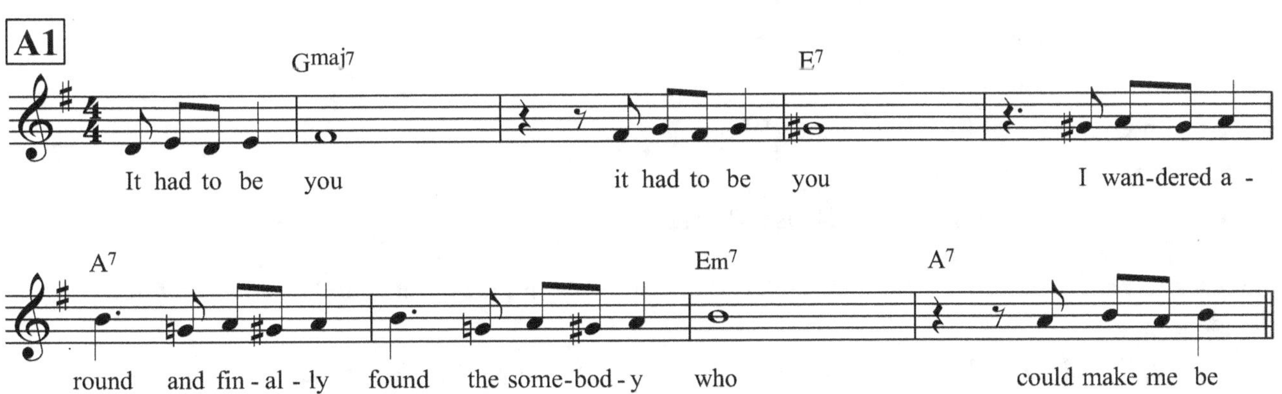

Melodic repetition and sequencing are hallmarks of the Great American Songbook style. Note the melodic repetition in the first eight measures of "It Had to Be You." A single melodic shape repeats five times – six, if you count the pickups to the B section – sequenced to start on different notes. The short-short-long phrase structure of the melody is often referred to as a **sentence.**

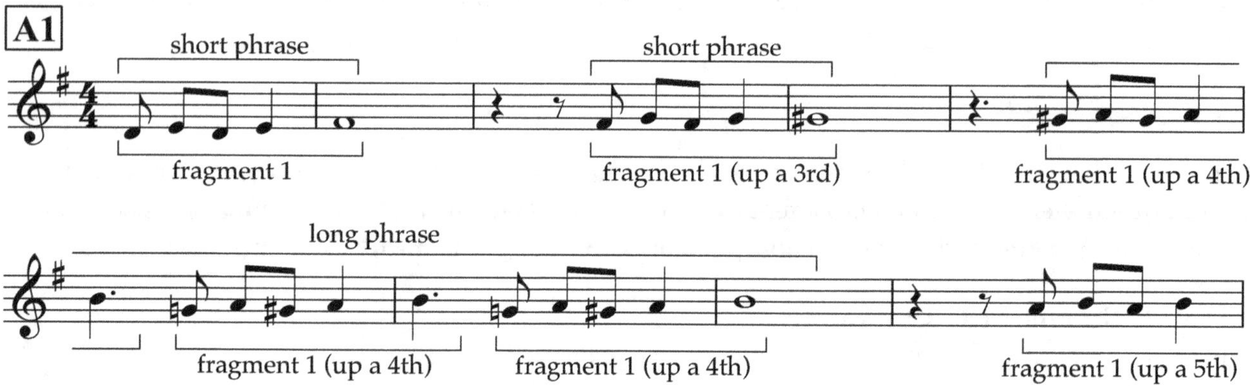

The B Section

Although it is not considered a bridge, the B section still needs to contrast strongly with the A section. B sections commonly differ from the A section in terms of phrase lengths, melodic shapes, rhyme schemes, and harmonic rhythm.

Perhaps most importantly, the harmony in the B section establishes a new center or ventures into unfamiliar harmonic territory. Some songs visit traditional key centers like the IV and vi in major or the III in minor. However, it's also relatively common for the B section to visit very distant key centers, like parallel keys a third away from the tonic. The songs in the next list move from a tonic major key to a major key a third away in the B section:

- Long Ago and Far Away (Kern/Gershwin)
- Like Someone in Love (Van Heusen/Burke)
- If I Were a Bell (Loesser)
- On Green Dolphin Street (Kaper/Washington)
- Autumn in New York (Duke)
- Here's that Rainy Day (Van Heusen/Burke)

The B section should end with an open-ended sound, preparing the audience to hear the recapitulation of the opening:

- The last note of the B section melody, often a held note in the penultimate measure, usually represents an unstable sound such as a note of the V chord.
- The harmony ends with a half cadence, preparing the ear for the I chord at the beginning of the next A section.

In "It Had to Be You," the harmony is the engine of contrast. The section begins on the V chord, visits the relative minor and spends two measures on the V/V before concluding with a half cadence. On the other hand, the melody is not very contrasting – it reuses fragment 1 from the A section, repeating the rhythms and phrasing introduced in the A section. To create a satisfying cadence, the melody comes to a rest in the seventh measure of the phrase, while the harmony reaches a half cadence.

The Second A Section

The second A section should approximately repeat the music from the first A with a new set of lyrics attached. Along with the repeated melody, the rhyme scheme of the first A section is usually replicated in the second A section. Although songwriters can write an entirely new set of lyrics, key words like sentence beginnings or the title phrase, are often retained from one A section to the next. The next three examples utilize different levels of repetition from one A section to the next:

My Romance (Rodgers/Hart)

A1	*My romance*	**A**
	Doesn't have to have a moon in the sky	**B**
	My romance	**A**
	Doesn't need a blue lagoon standing by	**B**

A2	*My romance*	**A**
	Doesn't need a castle rising in Spain	**B**
	Nor a dance	**A**
	To a constantly surprising refrain	**B**

Analysis: The title phrase repeats at the beginning of both A sections. The second lines also begin similarly (*doesn't have/doesn't need*).

For Once in My Life (Murden/Miller)

A1	*For once in my life I have someone who needs me*	**A**
	Someone I've needed so long	**B**
	For once, unafraid, I can go where life leads me	**A**
	And somehow, I know I'll be strong	**B**

A2	*For once in my life I won't let sorrow hurt me*	**A**
	Not like it hurt me before	**B**
	For once I have something I know won't desert me	**A**
	I'm not alone anymore	**B**

Analysis: Many elements from the first A repeat in the second A. Both start their first line with the title phrase and end the line with similar constructions (*needs me/hurt me*). Both start their third line with "for once" and end with similar constructions (*leads me/desert me*).

When I Fall in Love (Young/Heyman)

A1	*When I fall in love*	**A**
	It will be forever	**B**
	Or I'll never fall in love	**A**

A2	*When I give my heart*	**A**
	It will be completely	**B**
	Or I'll never give my heart	**A**

Analysis: These two stanzas are written in precise parallel structure. Only a few of the words are substituted from one section to the next: *fall* becomes *give*, *love* becomes *heart*, and *forever* becomes *completely*.

Moon River (Mancini/Mercer)

A1	*Moon River*	**A**
	Wider than a mile	**B**
	I'm crossing you in style	**B**
	Someday	**C**

A2	*Two drifters*	**A**
	Off to see the world	**B**
	There's such a lot of world	**B**
	To see	**C**

Analysis: Although it might not be readily audible to listeners, the first line of the A sections rhymes: "Moon River" and "two drifters." The rhyme helps maintain the same sonic palette between sections, which otherwise do not share words in common.

The last two measures of the A sections are often musically different because they lead to different musical destinations: the B and C sections. In fact, some second A sections change even earlier, entering a new key center for the last four measures. For instance, in the second A section of Vernon Duke's song, "Autumn in New York," the music is sequenced up a fourth in the second half. The change both leads to a new key center for the final eight measures and matches the word "pain" with a minor chord. The next example shows just the second half, the last four measures of each A section.

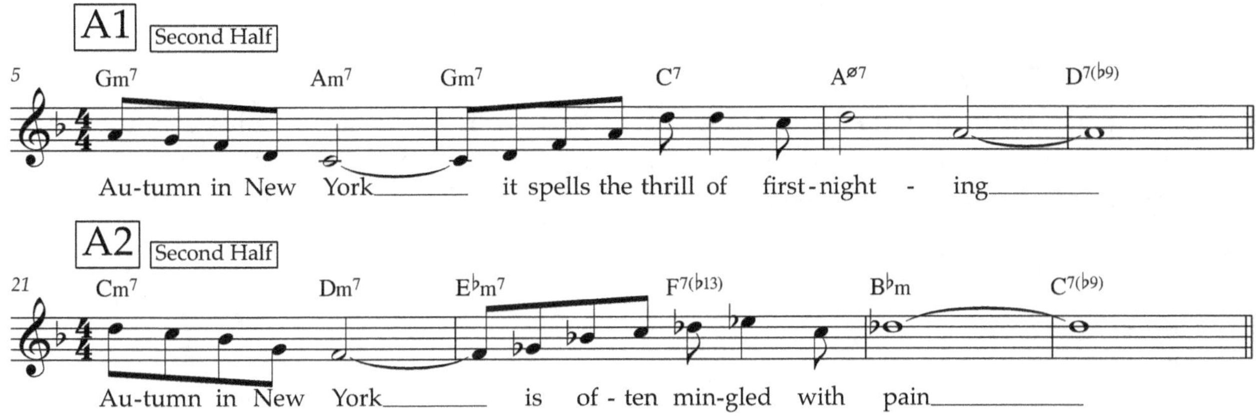

In the second A of "It Had to Be You," the music repeats exactly until the very last measure while the lyrics don't reprise any part of the first A section lyric. Although the first four rhyming words (*seen, mean, cross, boss*) maintain the original rhyme scheme, the final word is directed towards the end of the song and doesn't rhyme with any words in this section.

The C Section

The C section gives the songwriter a chance to shine. In just eight measures, the melody should ascend to a climax, the harmony should create tension before resolving neatly, and the melody should cleverly and concisely wrap up the lyrical content. To assist you in dissecting these tasks, this section is divided into two parts: one representing intensification and one representing resolution.

Measures 25-28: Intensification

Beginning the C Section

The first question facing a songwriter is how to start the C section. The C section usually starts in one of two ways – either it sequences material from the A section or it begins like the B section. The next two examples show the source material for the C section opening for "My Romance" and "When I Fall in Love."

My Romance (Rodgers/Hart)

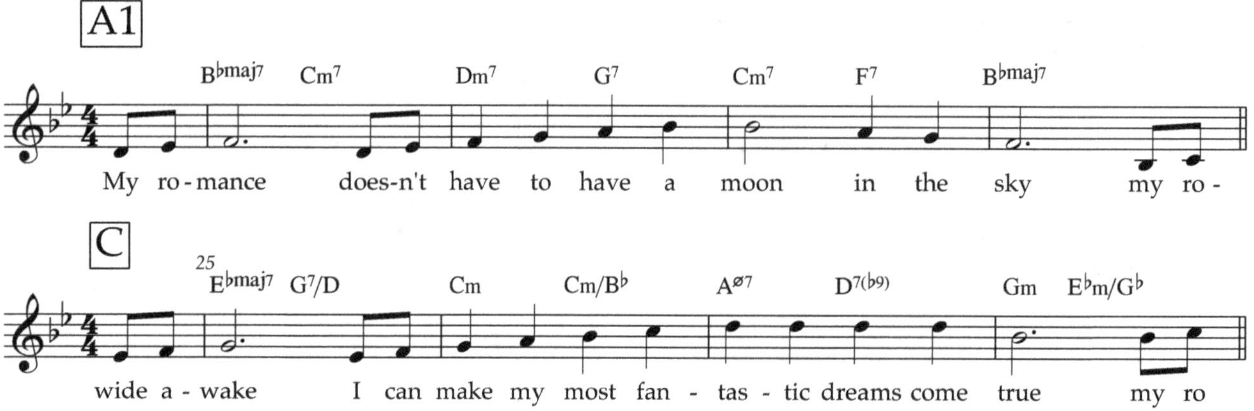

Analysis: The material in the C section sequences the material from the A section, starting up a step and continuing to a melodic peak.

When I Fall in Love (Young/Heyman)

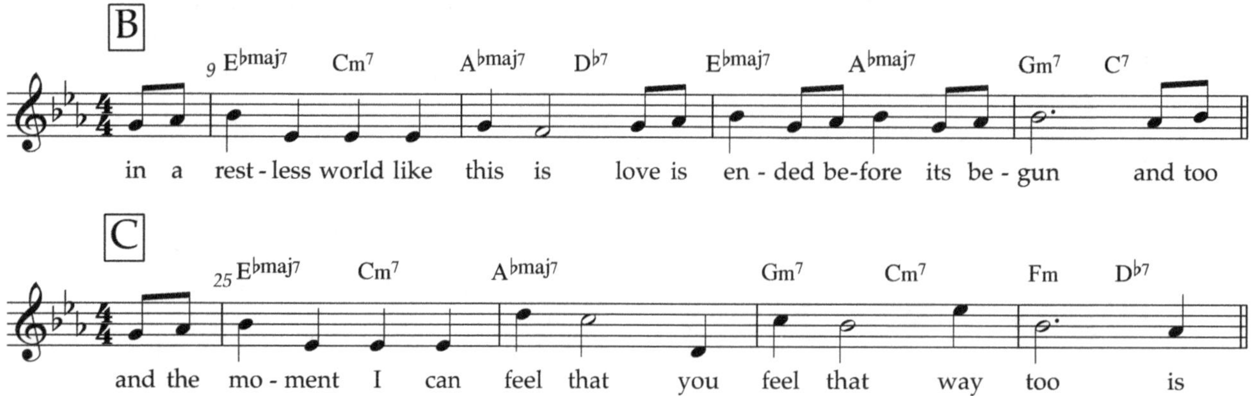

Analysis: The B and C section start musically identically, only diverging in the second measure as the C section moves towards a climax.

The Emotional Peak

The first four measures of the C section musically build towards an emotional peak in measure 28. The melody follows an ascending motion, arriving at a held note in the upper melodic range. Meanwhile, the bassline commonly moves downwards to move to a low note for the same measure.

The melodic arrival in measure 28 is often accompanied by a chord outside of the key – using either a secondary dominant or a chord borrowed from the parallel minor. The most common chords to use in a major key are:

Roman Numeral	In the Key of C
the minor iv	F minor
the half-diminished ii	D half diminished
the ♭VII dominant	B-flat dominant
The V/V dominant (II dominant)	D dominant
the ♭VI dominant	A-flat dominant
the ♭iii diminished	E-flat diminished

Reexamine the first four measures of the C section of "My Romance" and "When I Fall in Love" for the emotional peak, keeping in mind that "My Romance" is in B-flat major while "When I Fall in Love" is in E-flat major.

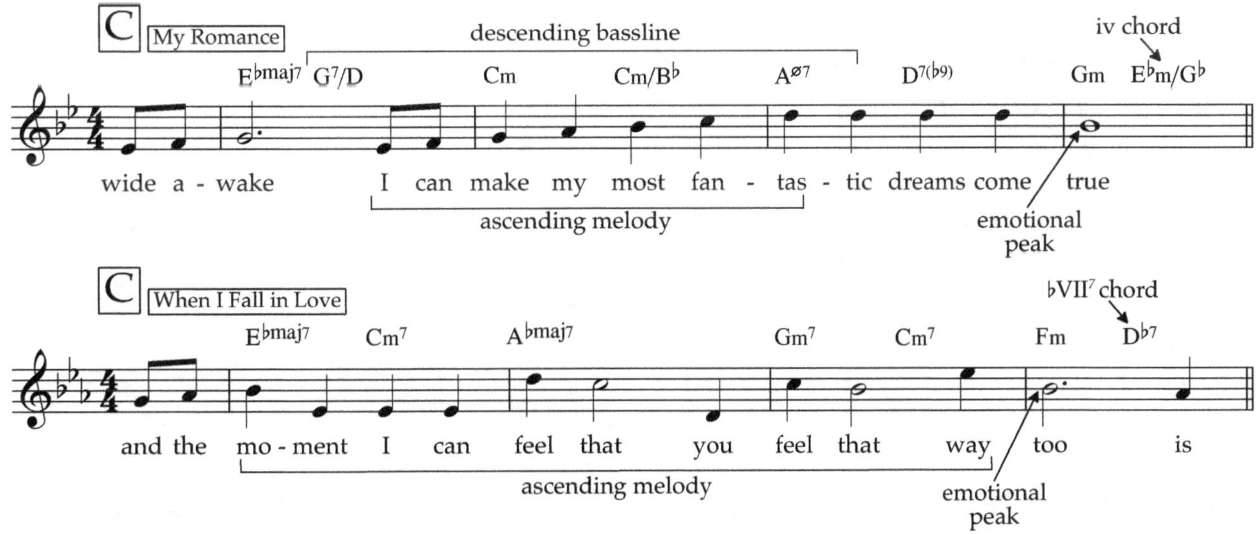

Lyrical Intensification

In measures 25-29, the lyrics should build towards the emotional peak while leaving the phrase open-ended – it will be completed in the last four measures. Here are some ways a songwriter can indicate a change in the last four measures:

- use of pivot words like *and, for, but, so, then,* etc.
- increased pace of rhyme or repetition
- use of hyperbole or superlative (*most, least, everything, nothing,* a thousand, *ever, never*)
- direct questioning or call to action

Here are some examples of lyrical intensifications:

It Had to Be You (Jones/Kahn)

> *For nobody else gave me a thrill*
> *For all your faults I love you still*

Analysis: use of pivot word ("for"), hyperbolic language ("nobody"), increased pace of rhymes ("thrill"/"still")

When I Fall in Love (Young/Heyman)

> *And the moment I can feel that*
> *You feel that way too*

Analysis: use of pivot word ("and"), hyperbolic language ("the moment"), increased pace of repetition ("feel that")

There Will Never Be Another You (Warren/Gordon)

> *Yes, I may dream a million dreams*
> *But how can they come true?*

Analysis: use of pivot word ("yes"), speedy repetition ("dream,"), hyperbolic language ("a million"), direct questioning ("how can they come true?")

How Deep Is the Ocean (Berlin)

> *And if I ever lost you,*
> *How much would I cry?*

Analysis: use of pivot word ("and"), hyperbolic language ("ever"), direct questioning ("How much would I cry?")

On the emotional peak itself, the word sung on the held note in measure 28 almost always rhymes with the last word of the song. It's no coincidence that "true" and "too," the lyrics at the climax of "My Romance" and "When I Fall in Love," rhyme with each other – they're placed strategically to rhyme with the word "you," the most common final word of an ABAC song.

Measures 29-32: Wrap Up

Following the emotional peak, the final four measures need to provide the "falling action." The last four measures should bring the themes to a satisfying conclusion with an appropriate cadence and a final lyrical flourish.

Musical Wrap-up

At the end of an ABAC song, the melody descends from the emotional peak and resolves with a perfect authentic cadence in the song's penultimate measure. The last measure should include a turnaround in parentheses that is used for every repetition other than the final one, when the song comes to rest on the stable chord in the penultimate measure.

Composers often return to the opening melodic theme to bookend the song and wrap up musical motifs. Notice how "When I Fall in Love" restates and continues the opening melody in the last four measures:

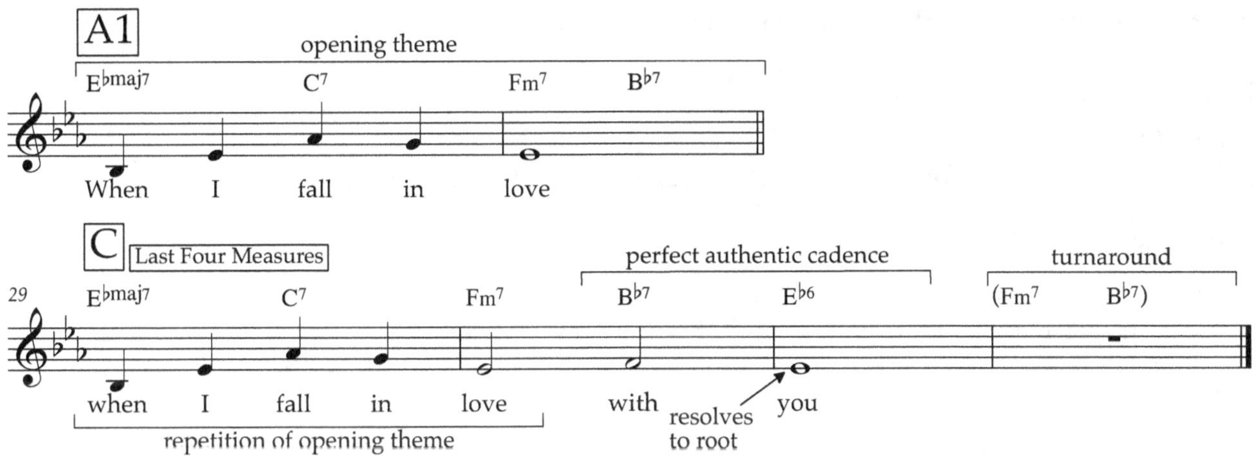

In "My Romance," the three-note ascending scale from the opening returns sequenced to a higher register to build excitement at the end of the song:

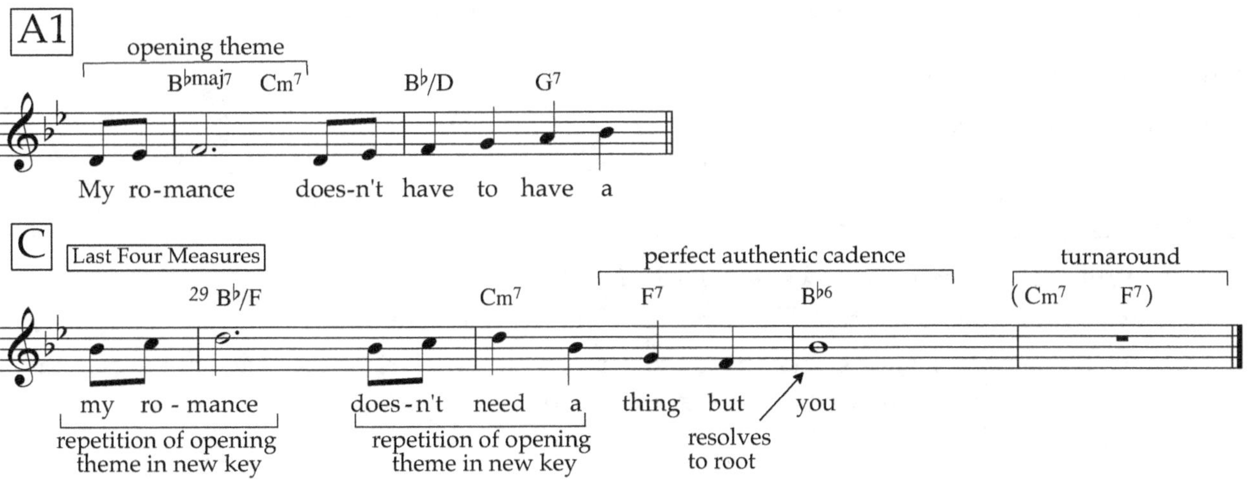

Lyrical Wrap-up

The final lyric should bring the song's story to a satisfying close. The most common way to end a song is to bookend the lyric by repeating the title phrase or the opening line, a device referred to in rhetorical studies as **epanalepsis.** Sometimes, two elements of a title phrase are brought back in reverse order, a device known as **chiasmus.**

Some of the other most common ways to bring closure to a lyric include:

- direct naming of a character ("you," "he," "me," etc.)
- antithesis or categories
- making a direct pledge or command
- asking a direct question

When I Fall in Love (Young/Heyman)

Final Lyric: *When I fall in love with you*
Analysis: Repetition of title phrase, direct naming of a character ("you")

My Romance (Rodgers/Hart)

Final Lyric: *My romance doesn't need a thing but you*
Analysis: Repetition/transformation of title phrase, direct naming of a character ("you")

White Christmas (Berlin)

Final Lyric: *May all your Christmases be white*
Analysis: Transformation of title phrase using chiasmus, direct wish

For Once in My Life (Murden/Miller)

Final Lyric: *For once in my life I have someone who needs me*
Analysis: Repetition of first lyric, direct naming of character ("me")

Moon River (Mancini/Mercer)

Final Lyric: *Moon River and me*
Analysis: Transformation of the title phrase, direct naming of character ("me")

Fly Me to the Moon (Howard)

Final Lyric: *In other words, I love you*
Analysis: Direct pledge, direct naming of character, "you"

How Deep Is the Ocean (Berlin)

Final Lyric: *How deep is the ocean, how high is the sky?*
Analysis: Repetition of title phrase, antithesis between "deep"/"high" and "ocean"/"sky"

The next example shows the entire C section lyric to demonstrate how lyricists can add antithesis in the last line to contrast with words introduced earlier in the C section:

All of Me (Marks/Simons)

You took the part
That once was my heart
So why not take all of me?

Analysis: Direct question, antithesis between *part/all* and *you/me*

It Had to Be You Analysis

Although the emotional peak of "It Had to Be You" arrives on a relatively low melody note for the word "still," the B-flat diminished seventh chord, the ♭iii diminished seventh, one of the typical chords for this moment, provides ample tension. The lyric repeats the title phrase twice in the final four measures before ending by directly naming a character, "you," on the final note in measure 31.

It Had to Be You

Isham Jones/Gus Kahn

With the inner workings of these four sections in mind, examine the entire thirty-two-measure leadsheet for "It Had to Be You," observing each of the landmarks discussed in the preceding material.

This page intentionally left blank

Embraceable You
George Gershwin/Ira Gershwin

"Embraceable You" is one of the classic Gershwin love songs. Its sophisticated harmony includes a **common-tone diminished seventh chord**, a diminished seventh chord based on the tonic (in this case, B-flat diminished seventh in the key of B-flat). The lyrics are notable for the multisyllabic rhymes (*embraceable/ irreplaceable, tipsy in me/gypsy in me*).

Studying each section through the lens of ABAC form reveals why "Embraceable You" endures as a timeless classic:

A Sections

Music: The A sections start on the tonic and consist of two four-measure melodic phrases, with the second phrase sequenced a fourth above the original. The two A sections are musically identical with the exception of the final chords, which reflect the upcoming sections.

Lyric: Although the title phrase isn't stated as the very first lyric, it appears very close to the opening. The two A sections do not repeat any lyrics but do share a common rhyme scheme. In the A sections, the final stressed syllable used for rhymes is the fourth-to-last syllable in each line. All subsequent syllables after the rhymed syllable simply repeat, as in "*charms* about you" and "*arms* about you."

B Section

Music: Contrasting the short phrases of the A section, the B section features two longer, four-measure phrases that share the same rhythm. The harmony starts in the relative minor key and cycles through different tonal centers before reaching a half cadence at the end of the section.

Lyrics: After the commands of the A section, the B section adds color and imagery. It reveals how the "embraceable you" brings out the speaker's playful side.

C Section

Music: Starting on the IV chord, the music comes to the emotional peak in measure 28 with a held high note on the word "do," which is sung over the V/V chord. In the last four measures, the melody returns to the three-note ascending scale of the opening theme. The melody extends the opening theme until it resolves to the root for a perfect authentic cadence.

Lyrics: The verb tense returns to the imperative and the speaker issues direct commands, "don't be a naughty baby" and "come to mama" which repeats twice in quick succession. The titular lyric returns in the last line to conclude the song.

Always

Irving Berlin

Irving Berlin's song "Always" was written as a wedding present for his wife. It feels like a lullaby or nursery rhyme due to its scalar melodies and the reassuring repetition of the titular word, "always."

What makes "Always" sound so satisfying? Examining each section helps to expose the underlying structure:

A Sections

Music: The A sections start on the I chord and repeat a similar four-measure melodic shape twice, modifying the melody to fit the changing chord progressions. In the second A section, the music is quite different from the first. The sections' second half moves to the key center of G minor and ascends to the melody's highest note.

Lyrics: Both A sections return to the repetition of "always" in the second half of each phrase. While the first A section generically makes promises of everlasting love, the second A section introduces the threat of struggle and adversity.

B Section

Music: Although the B section, unusually, starts with the same chord and melodic phrase as the A sections, it quickly moves to a distant new key center, a third away from the tonic. The melodic phrase is shorter than in the A's, repeating every two measures instead of every four. The last two measures of the B section move back to the tonic key using quick harmonic rhythm that creates momentum leading to the half cadence.

Lyrics: Reflecting the two-measure repetitions of the melody, the lyrics rhyme every two measures. Unusually, the B section includes the titular word, twice repeating "always" during the transition back to the A section.

C Section

Music: The melody, unusually, descends from the beginning of the C section to the end. The two-measure melodic sequence descends by a step with each repetition until the final statement of "always," which mimics earlier iterations, falling by a third. The harmony creates drama in measures 25-29 by using modal interchange (B-flat minor is the iv chord) and a secondary dominant (D dominant seventh is the V/ii).

Lyrics: The sequencing of words drawn from the same category (temporal measurements) helps to bring the piece to a satisfying close. The progression from "hour" to "day" to "year," and eventually to "always" ties the tune together while giving a new perspective to the titular word.

Practice

1. The next example shows the first eight measures of two Harold Arlen songs in ABAC form. Given the first eight-measure A section, write both music and lyrics for an appropriate B section. Remember to create contrasts in the harmony and phrasing. Then, listen to the original songs to compare your result to Arlen's.

2. The next example shows the first eight measures of two Jerome Kern songs in ABAC form. Given each (first) A section, create both music and lyrics for an appropriate C section. Remember that the C section typically includes the emotional peak in the first four measures and a return to the first lyric in the second four measures. Then, listen to the original songs to compare your result to Kern's.

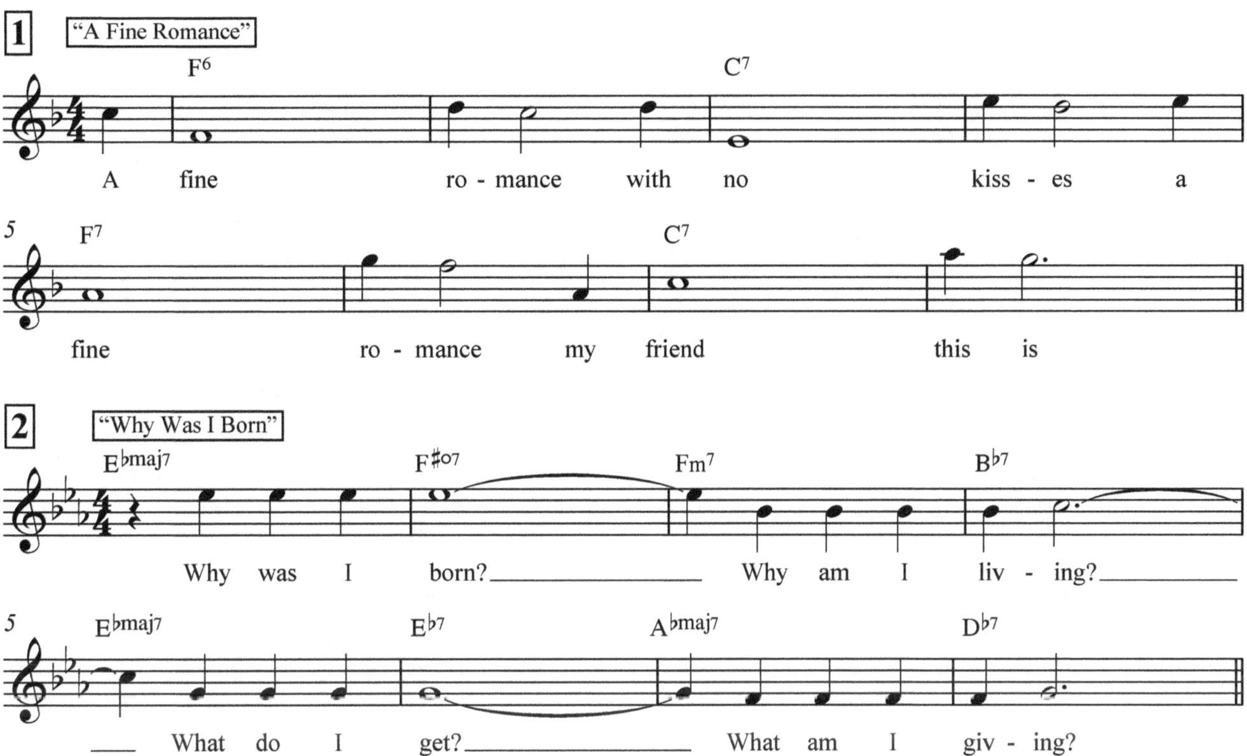

15A Writing an ABAC Song

Although ABAC songs demand the same precision as AABA songs, they require a slightly different strategy to deliver a satisfying payoff in the C section. Follow along with this chapter's seven-step process for writing an ABAC song.

Step One: Pursue Inspiration

To brainstorm, "spew" a paragraph about a personal subject. "Spewing" refers to writing for a set amount of time without filtering or editing. The goal of spewing is to produce a large quantity of raw material from which you can later select the most promising ideas.

 The prompts in the next list are drawn from 36 questions developed by psychologist Arthur Aron to encourage emotional closeness between friends or partners:

- Paint a picture of a scene that you cherish from your everyday life.
- When did you last cry?
- What would you save from your house in a fire?
- What is too serious to be joked apart?
- What do you value most in a friendship?
- What's your perfect day?
- How is your relationship with your mother?
- What's the best piece of advice you've ever gotten?

Here's what I wrote in response to the question about friendship, in about one minute:

Q: *What do you value most in a friendship?*

A: *The most important thing for a friendship is to be available in the moments when you're needed most. I suppose that being there in the hard moments requires a foundation of other moments: hangouts, get-togethers, and conversations in easier times, even though those don't really feel like the important stuff. It's almost as though we get together with friends in the easy times to establish firm foundations for when times are tough. Of course, nobody's thinking about it that way. We're just showing up to a barbeque or a game night or a beach day with our friends because it's going to be a good time. But, all the while, we're subconsciously building up our relationships so that we know who we can turn to in a difficult moment.*

Next, I distilled the paragraph into five lyrical ideas. These lyrics don't need to summarize the paragraph or include every detail. Instead, they should develop a core idea or draw on a few compelling words.

Here are five ideas drawn from my paragraph:

1. *You're here for the good times*

2. *But will you be here*
   For the hard times?

3. *Good times, we're here for good times*

4. *Won't you spend some time with me*
   I want to be the one to be
   By your side when the others leave

5. *Hours passing like clouds in the sky*
   With every hour that passes, I know that I
   Am getting closer and closer to you

6. *Laugh with me and play with me*
   But when times get tough
   Will you be there for me?

Step Two: Plan the Ending

ABAC forms typically end with a clever turn of phrase that transforms the song's first idea into a satisfying conclusion. Common devices include:

- naming a previously unnamed character (usually "you")
- reintroducing elements in an opposite order (chiasmus)
- juxtaposing opposite words (antithesis).

Could any of these devices work with the five ideas presented? Since all of these lyrics already speak directly to a "you," I focused on chiasmus and antithesis. I wrote possible concluding lines for each of the lyrics where I could imagine these devices working.

Chiasmus

Lyric 1

Original: *You're here for the good times*
But will you be here for the hard times?

Chiasmus: *You could make the hard times good*

Analysis: original has *good* then *hard*; the version with chiasmus has *hard* then *good*

Lyric 3

Original: *Won't you spend some time with me*
I want to be the one to be
By your side when the others leave

Chiasmus: *When others leave, I want to be the one by your side*

Analysis: original has "by your side" then "when the others leave"; the version with chiasmus says "when the others leave" then "by your side"

Antithesis

Lyric 2

Original: *Good times, we're here for good times*
Antithesis: *Bad times aren't so bad with good friends*
Analysis: *good* and *bad* are opposite words

Lyric 5

Original: *Laugh with me and play with me*
                But when times get tough will you be there for me?

Antithesis: *Laugh with me and cry with me too*

Analysis: *laugh* and *cry* are opposite words

Based on these potential endings, I chose #5 as the basis for my song because I like the parallel structure of "laugh with me" and "play with me." Plus, I think that adding the word "cry" at the end will create an appropriately poignant conclusion.

Step Three: Write an A Section

First, I wrote a melody for the A section lyric. I imagine the style as similar to a Burt Bacharach song – light, orchestral, and breezy.

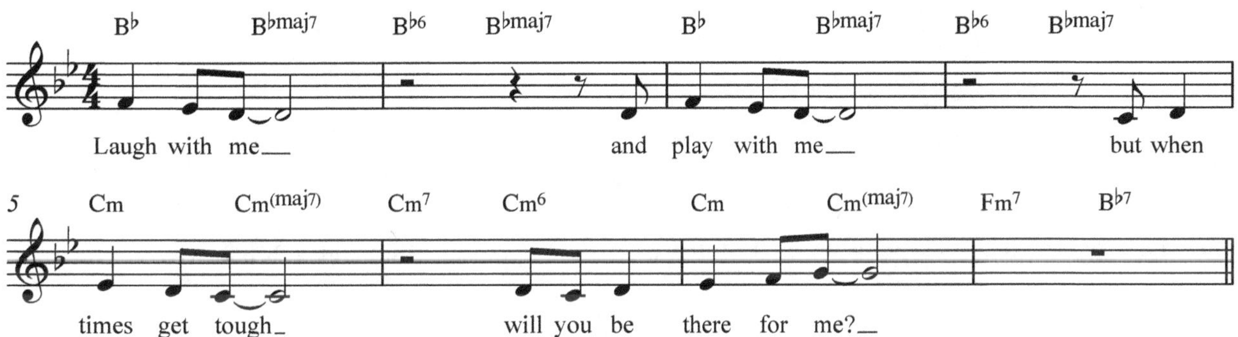

Analysis

Melody: With relatively few syllables in the lyrics, the melody is spacious, with many holds and rests. The three-syllable units of "laugh with me," "play with me," "times get tough" and "there for me" are all set with the same rhythm (a quarter note and two eighths) which repeats every two measures, creating a pleasant parallelism between the phrases. When there are additional syllables, they are added as pickups leading into the repeated rhythmic phrase.

Harmony: My song is written in B-flat major and spends four measures on the I chord and three measures on the ii chord. The changes in chord quality form a countermelody that generates motion: B♭-A-G-A for the I chord and C-B-B♭-A for the ii chord.

The first A section should not end with an authentic cadence. Instead, it should introduce the harmony of the B section by ending with a dominant chord that leads to a new key center. In my song, I used a V/IV, a B-flat dominant seventh chord, to target the IV chord, E-flat major.

Step Four: Write the Second A Section

The second A section presents new lyrics while maintaining the melody and harmony from the first. I brainstormed five lyrical approaches for my song, focusing on matching the three-syllable melodic motif in each line.

1. *Yell at me, get mad at me*

2. *Stay by my side, don't run and hide*

3. *Don't toy with me, don't fool with me*

4. *Don't worry me, don't bother me*

5. *Hand in hand, and eye to eye*

Examining these lines, elements from #1 and #5 could be combined using "mad" and "hand" as assonant rhymes. Here's how it looks after some editing:

> *Yell at me*
> *Get mad at me*
> *But when the road gets rough*
> *Walk hand in hand with me*

The new lyric fits the original melody well, requiring only a few additional pickup notes.

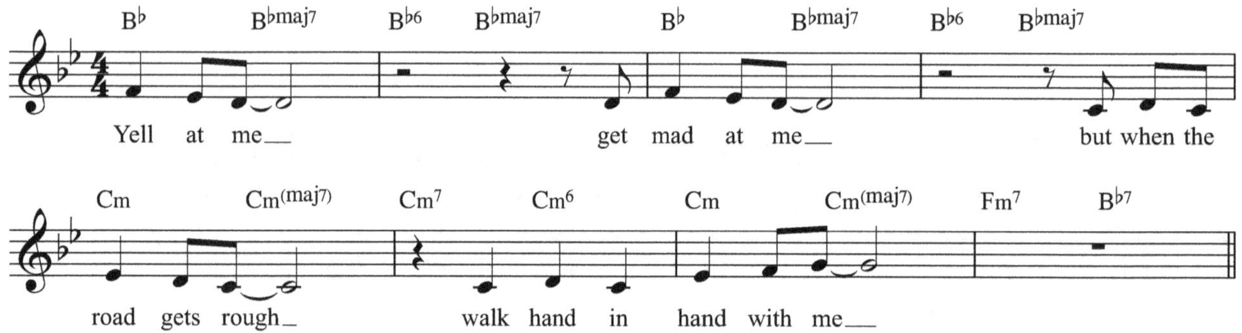

Step Five: Write the B Section

Before starting to write a B section, analyze the prominent features of the A section and consider how the B section could create a meaningful contrast. Here's the analysis for my song:

Phrasing: The A section has very few syllables, leading to short, choppy phrasing with long rests.
Contrast: The B section can focus on longer, flowing sentences.

Lyrical Style: My A section discusses friendship in a very general way, using the imperative verb tense to give commands.
Contrast: There's an opportunity to include a higher level of detail in the B section, including adjectives and vivid imagery.

Lyrical Content: The lyrics touch on both the joys of friendships and the perils. The question at the end of the first A looms large, "When times get tough, will you be there for me?"
Contrast: The B section could try to persuade or convince instead of questioning and commanding.

I brainstormed five ideas for a B section based on these possible contrasts:

1. *I want you there for the soft summer nights*

2. *Will you run away and hide your face*

3. *When the party's over and the dishes pile up*

4. *When I need a cry, will you sit down beside me*

5. *Don't hide your face when tears start falling*

I chose to develop #1 because of the vividness and sound play of "soft summer nights," and because it expresses desire instead of questioning. I developed the basic idea into a complete lyric, referencing all four seasons in two lines:

> *I want you there for soft summer nights and cold winter eves*
> *I want you there for blooming flowers and falling leaves*

I set the lyrics to music as follows:

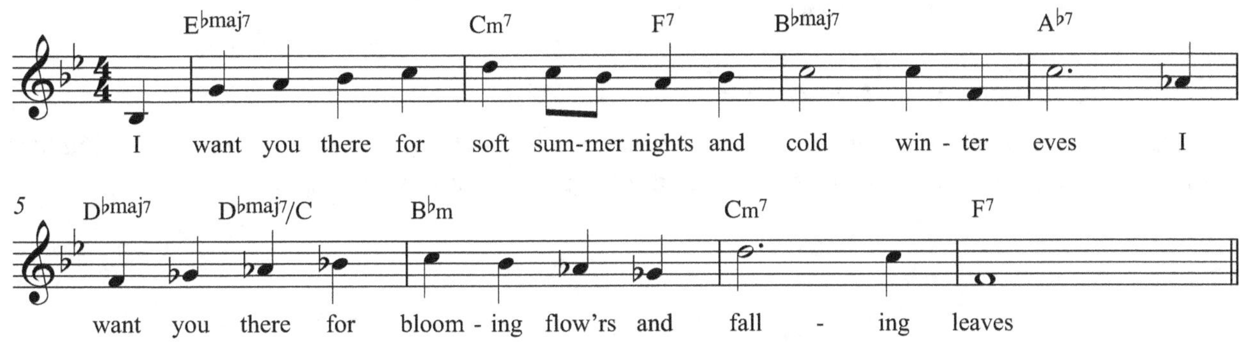

Analysis

Melody: Whereas there were many holds and rests in the A section, the B section has no rests at all. Reflecting the wordier lyrics, the B section melody is written in long, four-measure phrases that contrast with the two-measure phrases of the A. Because the A section melody stays within a very limited range, I created a much wider range for the B-section melody, which spans more than an octave between its lowest and highest notes. The melody for "falling leaves" descends to simulate falling.

Harmony: The first and last chord of the B section need to connect with the surrounding A sections. In my B section, the E-flat major chord (the IV) is the expected resolution of the B-flat seventh chord that ends the first A. The half-cadence ending using the F seventh chord (the V) leads back to the I chord for the start of the second A.

In between these preset harmonies, a songwriter can be playful and move far away from the home key during the B section. In my example, the harmony moves to D-flat major in the second half, a key center far removed from the B-flat major tonic.

Step Six: Complete the C Section

The C section is the most difficult but most rewarding part of the song to write. The first four measures intensify the song toward the climax, while the last four cleverly bring the song to a close by referencing elements from the opening.

In Step Two, I already invented a lyric for the final four measures, *"Laugh with me and cry with me too."* The line that precedes that one needs to heighten the tension and end with a rhyme for "too."

Fortunately, lots of words rhyme with "too." The words that resonated with this song's themes were *blue, few, through, view, you,* and *overdue.* I wrote a line for each possible rhyme, even when the lines didn't come naturally. I started each line with a transitional word like *and, for, but, because,* and *although* to heighten the stakes leading to the climax.

Blue: *'Though I want you when I'm happy I need you when I'm blue*
So laugh with me and cry with me too

Few: *'Though I don't need too many friends, you're one of the few*
Who can laugh with me and cry with me too

Through: *Although you don't come 'round often, I trust that you'll come through*
Come laugh with me and cry with me too

View: *And my heart smiles a little bit when you come into view*
So laugh with me and cry with me too

You: *'Though I don't like the crying, I like spending time with you*
So laugh with me and cry with me too

Overdue: *And every time you visit, your visit's overdue*
So laugh with me and cry with me too

I chose the first option with the word *blue* because it has an easy rhythmic flow and includes pleasing juxtapositions between the adjectives *happy* and *blue* and the verbs *want* and *need.*

Musically, the C section has a lot of landmarks to hit in just eight measures.

First Four Measures

Melody: The beginning of the melody often repeats the opening of the B section, then ascends to the highest note of the piece.

Harmony: The harmony usually starts on the same chord as the B section. As the melody goes up, the bassline often descends to create contrary motion. The chord in the fourth-measure climax should be a non-diatonic chord, commonly a result of modal interchange.

Last Four Measures

Melody: The melody from the last four measures often returns or references the melody of the A section to create a bookending effect. The melody ends in the penultimate measure, reserving the last measure for a "turn-around" written in parentheses that resets the harmony to the tonic chord for further repetitions.

Harmony: The piece needs to end with a perfect authentic cadence.

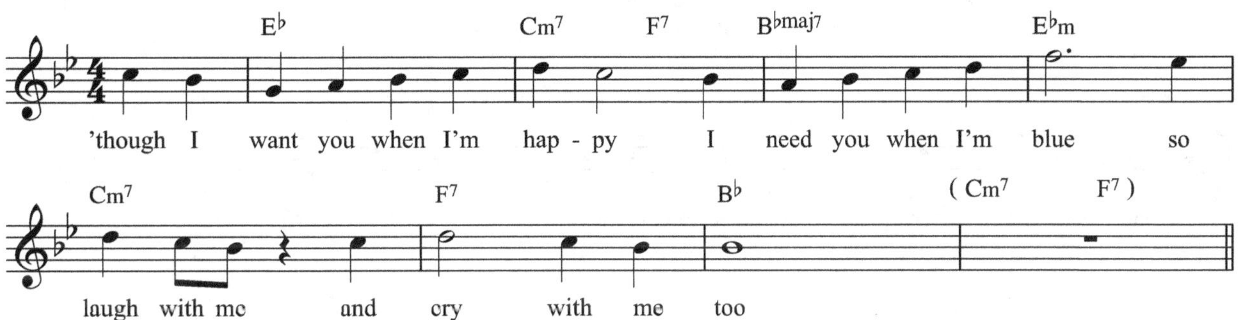

Analysis

Melody: The melody ascends to the highest note for the climax in the fourth measure. In the last four measures, the three-note descending pattern from the first four measures returns.

Harmony: The E-flat minor used for the climax is borrowed from the parallel minor key. The piece ends with a perfect authentic cadence before the turnaround, written in parentheses in the last measure.

Step Seven: Edit

Because the piece was written in sections, it's crucial to examine how the sections fit together. The next example shows a full version of the song written throughout this chapter:

Laugh with Me

Jeremy Siskind

My favorite editing strategy is to choose the three weakest parts of the song and propose an alternate version for each section. If the new version is better than the original, keep it; if the original is better, then don't change it.

I chose the following three problems to rewrite:

1. **Spot:** measures 7-8 and 23-24

   Issue: the chord progression is awkward; the C minor-major seventh doesn't naturally lead to the F minor

   Solution: If the melody notes are changed, the F minor chord can enter earlier. Here is the result for measures 7-8:

2. **Spot:** transition into second A (measures 16-17)

   Issue: entrance into new material feels sudden

   Solution: The word "so" could be added before the end of the B section to connect between the lyrics. A G-flat in the melody both creates color and connects to the previous key center of D-flat.

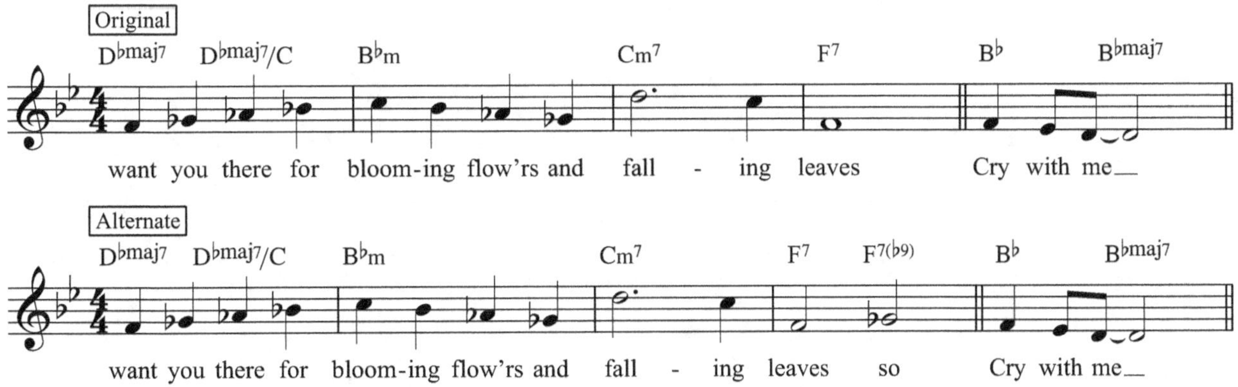

3. **Spot:** measures 13-14

    Issue: the sequence feels too obviously repetitive and leaping from G-flat is awkward.

    Solution: Two more notes could make a huge difference. Adding extra syllables in the fourth beats of both measures creates subtle variation.

In every case, I was able to come up with something that I think is better than my original. I could repeat this process of finding the three weakest elements over and over again to continue improving the song.

To see the updated leadsheet and hear a performance of the song, visit the chapter page by scanning the QR code at the beginning of the chapter.

Takeaways

1. "Spewing" can be a good way to brainstorm for your song. Pick prompts and write a full paragraph of uninterrupted thoughts for a minute, refraining from judgments about whether the writing is "good" or "useful."

2. Figure out the end before you start writing. ABAC songs need a strong and satisfying ending that refers back to the beginning of the tune. Common devices include introducing an absent "you," reintroducing elements in reverse order (chiasmus), and juxtaposing opposite words (antithesis).

3. Before writing your B section, reflect on the characteristics of the A sections. B sections should contrast in phrasing and lyrical content.

4. The C section needs to address multiple important structural landmarks. The first four measures build to a climax, and the last four measures provide a satisfying conclusion.

5. After putting the pieces of your song together, pay special attention to how the sections fit together and massage the transitions. Choose three weak spots and brainstorm an alternate possibility for each issue. If the solution is better than the original, replace the original with the alternate idea.

Practice

1. Choose two of the prompts listed at the beginning of the chapter and write a response for one minute without censoring yourself. Then, write five lyrical ideas based on something that sticks out to you from your paragraphs.

   Prompt 1

   Prompt 2

Lyrical Ideas:

1.

2.

3.

4.

5.

2. Invent concluding lines based on your five ideas. How many could be transformed to name a character directly, use antithesis, or employ chiasmus? Write the transformed lines in the spaces below:

Name a character (you):

Antithesis:

Chiasmus:

3. Select a lyric with a promising final line and write a full A section. If you are skilled with musical notation, write it on the staff below.

A1

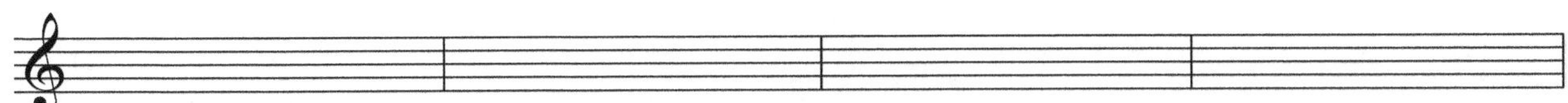

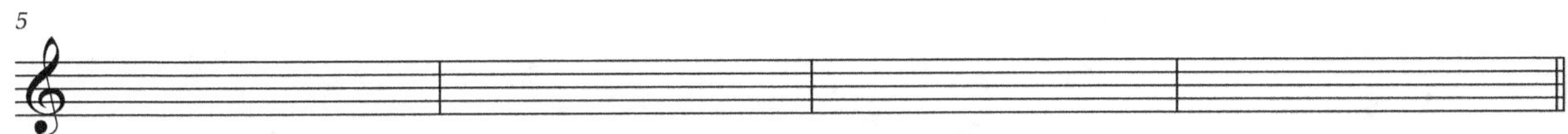

4. Brainstorm five lyrical ideas for a second A section based on your first A. Then, select your favorite idea and complete the lyrics for the section.

    1.

    2.

    3.

    4.

    5.

5. Write some characteristics of your A sections and reflect how they might change to create a contrast in your B section.

Phrasing

A section:

Contrast:

Lyrical Style

A section:

Contrast:

Lyrical Content

A section:

Contrast:

Harmony

A section:

Contrast:

6. Brainstorm five ideas for B section lyrics, then write a B section, notating it in the staff below
    if possible.

    1.

    2.

    3.

    4.

    5.

7. Brainstorm five strong rhymes for the last word of your concluding phrase, which you created for Step 2. Then, write a possible line for each rhyme that leads to the concluding phrase:

Rhymes:

Lyrics:

1.

2.

3.

4.

5.

8. Complete the music and lyrics for the C section. If you are skilled with musical notation, write it on the staff below.

C

9. Finally, complete the song, adding necessary transitions to create a natural flow between sections. If you are skilled with musical notation, you can write it on the staff below.

10. Choose three weak spots to edit, inventing an alternate version for each.

1. **Spot:**
   Issue:

   Solution:

2. **Spot:**
   Issue:

   Solution:

3. **Spot:**
   Issue:

   Solution:

16. List Songs

What if you tried to encapsulate the entire world in a song? In a sense, that's the idea of "Waters of March" (Portuguese title "Águas de março"), a song by bossa nova legend Antônio Carlos Jobim. Jobim, who wrote songs like "The Girl from Ipanema" and "Desafinado," wrote a lyric that presents objects, visions, scenes, and feelings one after the other, offering no explanatory links between them. Here are the first four lines of the English lyric of the song, which Jobim wrote himself alongside the Portuguese lyric:

> *A stick, a stone, it's the end of the road*
> *It's the rest of a stump, it's a little alone*
> *It's a sliver of glass, it is life, it's the sun*
> *It is night, it is death, it's a trap, it's a gun*

After nearly three stanzas of listing, the song arrives at its refrain:

> *And the riverbank talks of the waters of March*
> *It's the promise of life, it's the joy in your heart*

The refrain references the rainy season in Rio de Janeiro in which the city streets regularly flood, causing damage to homes and buildings while forcing residents inside. The list's dizzying scope and the refrain's cyclical theme combine to express how life so often tumbles far beyond our ability to grasp or control it.

Jobim's ambitious lyrical structure proved successful: in a 2001 poll from the newspaper *Folha de São Paulo*, "Águas de março" was voted Brazil's best song of all time. Jobim also provides a perfect example of a list song, a type of song in which the lyrics provide an inventory of objects, feelings, people, places, or anything else a songwriter can imagine. List songs provide a distinctive way for writers to explore stories and emotions while giving them an opportunity to dazzle and delight audiences with inventive language.

List Song Basics

List songs, also known as **catalog songs**, include a list in at least one of their sections. A list song is not a musical form like strophic or AABA, and list songs can be written in any song form, including those that have been presented in this book. There's no particular rule regarding how much of a song must be a list to qualify, but most list songs have at least one section that primarily presents an inventory.

Although list songs can exist in any genre, they are most commonly found in the Great American Songbook. Some well-known list songs written for musicals and movies include "You're the Top," "I Got Rhythm," "If I Were a Bell," "Everything Happens to Me," "If I Should Lose You," and "I Can't Get Started."

Elements of a List Song

List songs often serve as subtle platforms for persuasion. Each song has a central message to communicate and uses the list to convince the audience with abundant supporting evidence. With that in mind, every list song should have two elements: a list and a reason for the list.

The List

One feature that distinguishes a list from other forms of speech is lists' paratactic structure. **Parataxis** refers to presenting grammatical structures equally, without connecting them or drawing a relationship between them. For instance:

> **Paratactic:** *I've got rhythm, I've got music, I've got my gal*
> **Not Paratactic:** *I've got rhythm and I've also got music, and, best of all, I've got my gal*

While most items in a list are presented using parataxis, connecting words like "and" and "or" are commonly used to link items and clarify structure.

Without narrative connections, lists can easily become monotonous. Only well-organized, descriptive, and linguistically rich lists will hold an audience's attention. To that end, songwriters need to intentionally shape their lists to be delightful, virtuosic, or evocative. Some devices songwriters frequently use to make their lists appealing include:

- frequent or multisyllabic rhymes
- repeated sounds like alliteration, assonance, consonance, repeated syllables, and repeated words
- parallel structure
- antithesis and categories
- evocative, poetic language
- rapid-fire enumeration

To reinforce a list's paratactic structure, list songs' melodies often present list items using repeated or sequenced phrases. Notice how the melodic repetition at the beginning of "My Favorite Things" accentuates the repeated structure of the list. All four list items are presented using the same rhythm and final two notes, creating contrast only through the register of the first three notes.

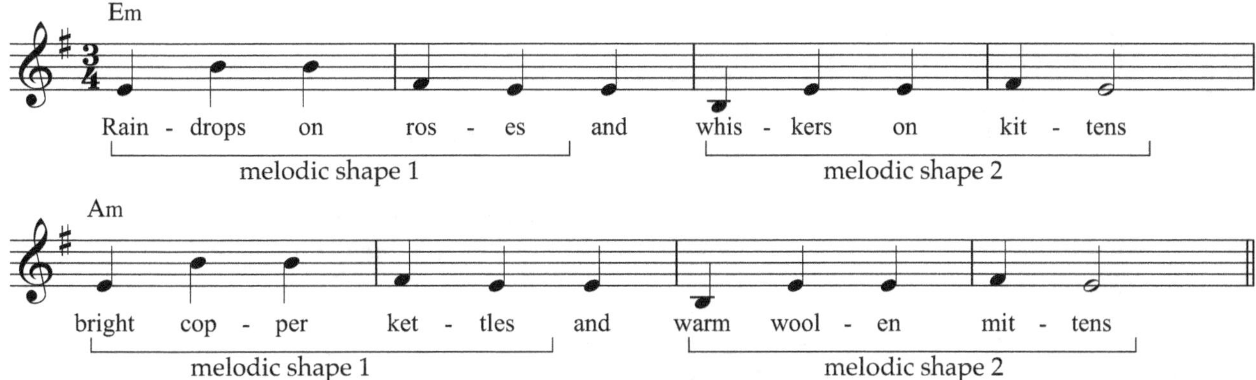

"I Got Rhythm" reinforces its list by using the same rhythm for each item of the list. To create contrast, Gershwin reverses the order of the notes for the second melodic phrase (F-G-B♭-C to C-B♭-G-F), a technique known as **retrograde**. In a song about rhythm, Gershwin had to do something interesting with the rhythm, so he builds all of the phrases for the list from dotted-quarter-note groups to form a cross-rhythm that rubs against the song's four-four meter.

Reason for the List

A list song shouldn't present just any list – nobody wants to hear a list of your favorite colors or weekly grocery needs. The reason for the list should be meaningful for the speaker, perhaps sharing something very important, deep, or personal to them. Songs can list cherished memories with a lost love, reasons for being alive, or ways to keep calm when facing danger.

In musical theater, the lists themselves often influence the plot. For instance, in *The Sound of Music*, Maria uses "My Favorite Things," to comfort the von Trapp children during a thunderstorm. The very act of listing beautiful and pleasing objects changes the children's mood, providing solace in a scary situation. Or, in *Mary Poppins*, the children sing a song called "The Perfect Nanny," listing the attributes they want in a caregiver, everything from "rosy cheeks, no warts" and "you must be kind, you must be pretty" to "sing songs, bring sweets." In a sense, the song initiates the musical's plot, summoning the magical Mary, who exactly meets their description.

The next examples show excerpted lyrics from four list songs along with analysis regarding what is being listed, the reason for the list, and how the list is shaped to maintain interest.

I Just Called to Say I Love You (Wonder)

Form: verse-chorus

Verse	**Chorus**
No New Year's Day to celebrate	*I just called to say I love you*
No chocolate covered candy hearts to give away	*I just called to say how much I care*
No first of spring	*I just called to say I love you*
No song to sing	*And I mean it from the bottom of my heart*
In fact, here's just another ordinary day	

What's being listed (verse): special holidays or celebrations
Reason for the list (chorus): to establish that the speaker's call is a spontaneous and pure outpouring of love
Shaping: frequent rhymes (*day/celebrate/away, spring/sing*), expressive details with alliteration (*chocolate covered candy hearts*), parallel structure (*no first of spring/no song to sing*)

What a Wonderful World (Thiele/Weiss)

Form: AABA

I see skies of blue
And clouds of white
The bright blessed day
The dark sacred night
And I think to myself
What a wonderful world

What's being listed (body of A section): beautiful elements of nature
Reason for the list (last two lines): encourage positive perspective and gratitude
Shaping: parallel structure (*skies of blue/clouds of white, bright blessed day/dark sacred night*), antithesis and categories (*blue/white, bright/dark, day/night*)

My Favorite Things (Rodgers/Hammerstein)

Form: AAB (a somewhat unusual form for the Great American Songbook)

A section	**B Section**
Raindrops on roses and whiskers on kittens	*When the dog bites*
Bright copper kettles and warm woolen mittens	*When the bee stings*
Brown paper packages tied up with strings	*When I'm feeling bad*
These are a few of my favorite things	*I simply remember my favorite things*
	And then I don't feel so sad

What's being listed (A section): things that delight the speaker
Reason for the list (B section): to feel better in a moment of sadness or fear
Shaping: multisyllabic rhymes (*kittens/mittens*); repeated sounds: alliteration (*raindrops/roses, paper/packages, warm/woolen, copper/kettles*), assonance (*whiskers/kittens*); parallel structure (*raindrops on roses/whiskers on kittens, bright copper kettles/warm woolen mittens*)

I Love Being Here with You (Schluger/Lee)

Form: AABA

I love the East, I love the West
And North and South, they're both the best
But I only want to go there as a guest
'Cause I love being here with you

What's being listed (body of A section): things that the speaker loves
Reason for the list (refrain of A section): to emphasize how much they like being with the audience
Shaping: antithesis/categories (*East*/*West*/*North*/*South*); frequent rhymes (*West*/*best*/*guest*); parallel structure (*I love the East*/*West*)

List Songs and Song Forms

Because including a list is a lyrical, not musical, device, list songs can be written in any musical form. Across different forms, the reason for the list typically appears in a climactic or repeated part of the form like the chorus or refrain, whereas the list's items populate sections with changing lyrics.

The next section details the most common ways that lists interact with common song forms. Each section includes an excerpt of an example from that form.

Strophic Form

Location of list: the body of the stanza
Location of reason: refrain

Blowin' in the Wind (Dylan)

How many roads must a man walk down
Before you call him a man?
How many seas must a white dove sail
Before she sleeps in the sand?

Yes, and how many times must the cannonballs fly
Before they're forever banned?
The answer, my friend, is blowin' in the wind
The answer is blowin' in the wind

What's being listed (body of the stanza, first six lines): questions regarding how long things must last before they change
Reason for the list (refrain, last two lines): open to interpretation; "blowin' in the wind" could mean that the answer to these questions is ephemeral and unattainable; or the answer to these questions depends on how hard the "winds of change" blow, i.e. how hard activists push for change

Verse-Chorus Form

Location of list: verses
Location of reason: chorus

If I Ain't Got You (Keys)

Verse
Some people live for the fortune
Some people live just for the fame
Some people live for the power, yeah
Some people live just to play the game

Chorus
Some people want it all
But I don't want nothing at all
If I ain't got you, baby

What's being listed (verse): common life goals and reasons for living
Reason for the list (chorus): the speaker prioritizes their beloved over all else

AABA

Location of list: body of A sections
Location of reason: refrain of A sections

They Can't Take That Away from Me (Gershwin/Gershwin)

A Section

The way you wear your hat
The way you sip your tea
The memory of all that
No, no, they can't take that away from me

What's being listed (body of A Sections): vivid memories of a person
Reason for the list (refrain, last line): give reassurance that even if someone is gone, their memories remain

ABAC

Location of list: A and B sections
Location of reason: C section

You're the Top (Porter)

A Section 1	**B Section**
You're the top	*You're a melody from a symphony by Strauss*
You're the Coliseum	*You're a Bendel bonnet*
You're the top	*A Shakespeare sonnet*
You're the Louvre Museum	*You're Mickey Mouse*

A Section 2	**C Section**
You're the Nile	*I'm a worthless check*
You're the Tower of Pisa	*A total wreck, a flop*
You're the smile	*But if, baby, I'm the bottom*
On the Mona Lisa	*You're the top*

List (A and B Sections): exceptional things
Reason for the List (C Section): compliment the beloved and compare them favorably to the speaker

Let's look closely at three complete examples to see how list songs achieve their effects.

We Didn't Start the Fire

Billy Joel

"We Didn't Start the Fire" is a 1989 song written in verse-chorus form. The verse presents a list in a semi-rapped, rapid-fire succession of eighth notes. The list is presented completely paratactically, with next-to-no commentary, connecting words, or adjectives adding color.

The song's relentless, colorless inventory has proved divisive among audiences and critics. On one hand, the song reached number one on the charts and received a Grammy nomination; on the other, it is now one of the most reviled songs in pop history, with even Joel himself expressing dislike for it. In various interviews, Joel has called the song "a terrible piece of music," and compared the melody to both "a dentist drill" and "a mosquito buzzing around your head."

Despite its mixed reception, it remains a quintessential example of a list song in verse-chorus form. The first verse, which begins the list, is shown in the next graphic:

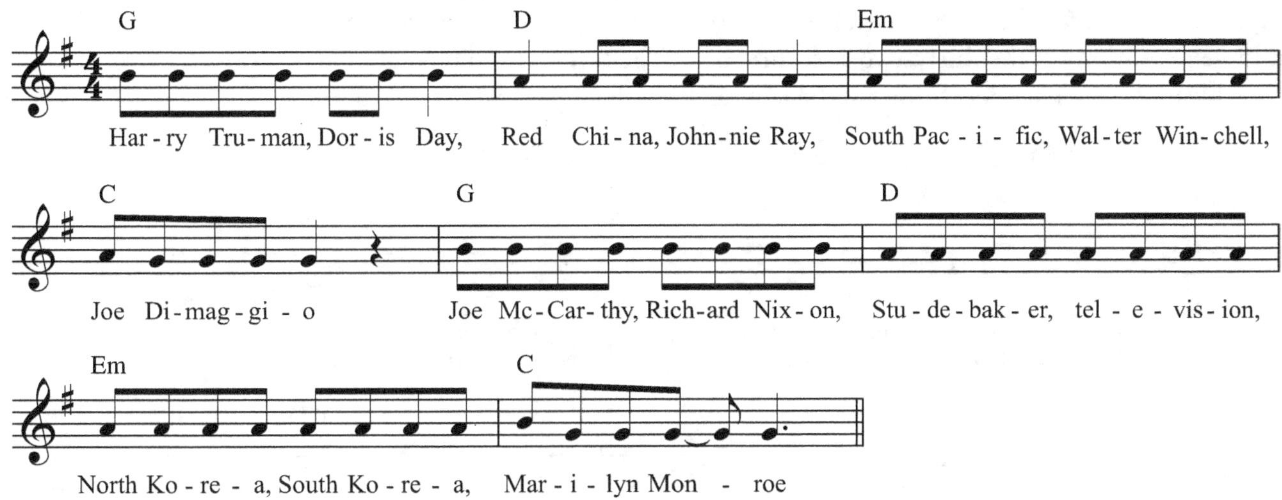

After another verse, Joel shares the reason for the list in the chorus:

How does this song fit into the rubric of lists, reasons, and shaping?

What's being listed (verse): major political, technological, and cultural events from the twentieth century
Reason for the list (chorus): Although it's somewhat open to interpretation, the "fire" probably refers to the state of society, particularly to societal unrest, in which the "we" is Joel's generation. In this framework, the song objects to the pattern in which each generation blames the younger generation for all of society's problems. By presenting this list, Joel argues that his generation is not solely responsible for the state of the world.
Shaping: interesting, multisyllabic rhymes like *Dimaggio/Marilyn Monroe*; virtuosic performance due to the list's breakneck pace
Melody: The melody stays almost entirely flat for the entirety of the list in order to allow the dense lyrics to be clearly articulated and understood. In the chorus, the melody creates contrast with a more varied shape using notes of the G major pentatonic scale.

Let's Do It (Let's Fall in Love)
by Cole Porter

Originally written for the 1928 musical, *Paris*, Cole Porter's AABA song presents an extended list during multiple repetitions of the thirty-two-measure form. The original song includes an introductory verse followed by as many as five repetitions of the form, although singers rarely sing all the verses.

The following leadsheet shows the first two verses of the song written beneath the melody:

The next two verses list insects and zoo animals, respectively, who "do it":

<table>
<tr><td>

Verse 3

The dragonflies in the reeds do it
Sentimental centipedes do it
Let's do it, let's fall in love

Mosquitos, heaven forbid, do it
Soon as every katydid do it
Let's do it, let's fall in love

The most refined ladybugs do it
When a gentleman calls
Moths in your rugs do it
What's the use of moth balls

Locusts in trees do it, bees do it
Even over-educated fleas do it
Let's do it, let's fall in love

</td><td>

Verse 4

The chimpanzees in the zoo do it
Some courageous kangaroos do it
Let's do it, let's fall in love

I'm sure giraffes on the sly do it
Heavy hippopotami do it
Let's do it, let's fall in love

Sloths who hang down from the twigs do it
Though the effort is great
Sweet guinea pigs do it--
Buy a couple and wait!

The world admits bears in pits do it
Even Pekingeses in the Ritz do it
Let's do it, let's fall in love

</td></tr>
</table>

An additional, rarely performed verse uses bird species as the subject (larks are crazy for a lark, and cuckoos in clocks are doing it). How can we dissect this song to better understand the list?

What's being listed (body of A sections, B sections): things that "fall in love," i.e. have sex
Reason for the list (refrain of A sections): to convince someone to fall in love/make love with the singer
How the list delights: Porter relishes wordplay and double entendre, playing with sounds and pushing boundaries in order to get a laugh. He infuses wit and humor into his lyrics in the following ways:

- alliteration and consonance (*in shallow shoals, English soles do it, courageous kangaroos, heavy hippopotami*)
- repeated syllables and polyptoton (*sentimental centipedes, Siam/Siamese, shad/shad roe, katy did/do it, moths/moth balls, oysters/Oyster Bay*)
- frequent and unexpected rhymes (*admits/pits/Ritz, shoals/soles/bowls*)
- speaking directly to the audience (*buy a couple and wait, think of Siamese twins, what's the use of moth balls*)
- inventive or mismatched descriptions (*lazy jellyfish, refined ladybugs, over-educated fleas, the privacy of bowls*)

Melody: The A section repeats a three-note descending motif that reflects the itemization of the list. During the A section, the descending melody employs a chromatic passing note to signal a light-hearted Great American Songbook style. The bridge even uses the three-note theme, starting on a different pitch and repeating it only twice – rather than three times – in each four-note phrase.

The next example shows a comparison between the use of the three-note descending theme in the A sections and the B section (bridge).

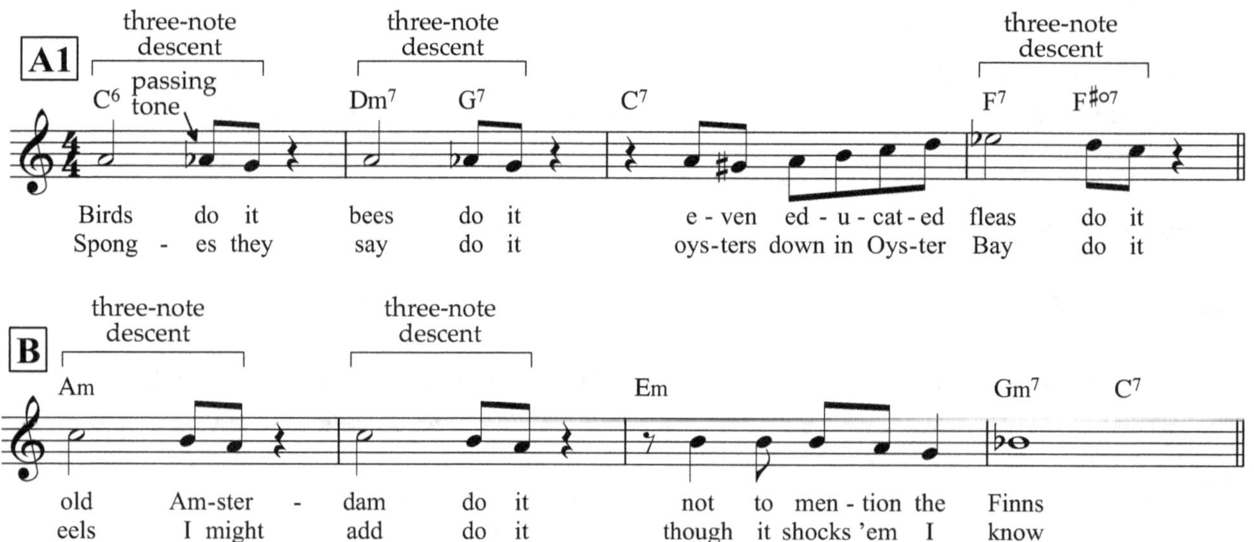

Porter always places his funniest jokes at the end of the bridge, directly talking to the audience or another character (like the waiter taking an order of "shad roe"). In this moment, Porter flattens his melody to a single recitation tone to ensure that his punchline is heard clearly. The next example shows the last four measures of the bridge:

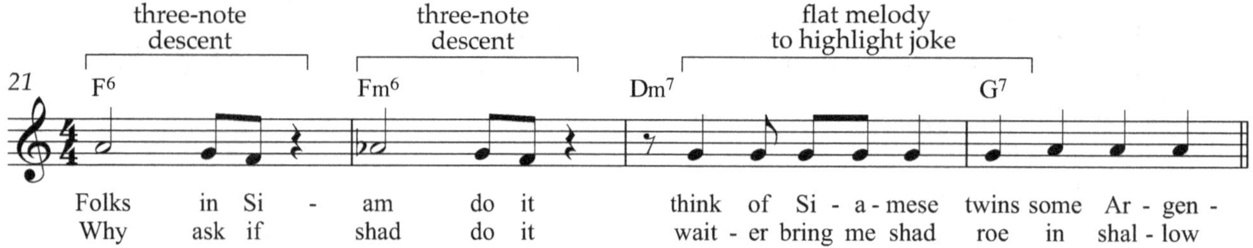

My Romance

Richard Rodgers/Lorenz Hart

"My Romance" is an ABAC song originally written for the 1935 musical, *Jumbo*. The song opens by listing what fanciful adventures the speaker insists are not needed in their love affair. Notice the longer, more descriptive list items in the first eight measures (the A section) contrasted with the shorter list items in the latter eight measures (the B section).

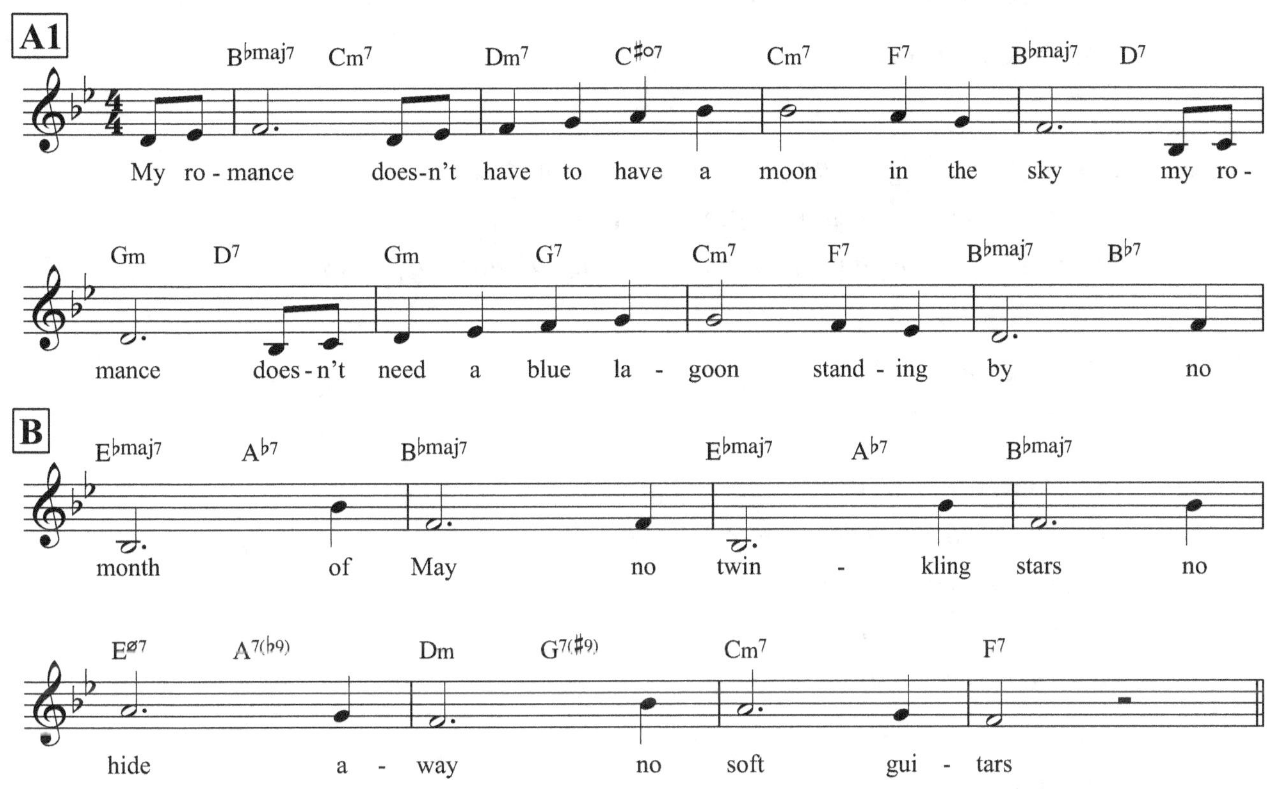

After the second A section continues with more items in the list ("a castle rising in Spain," "a dance to a constantly surprising refrain"), the lyric finally gives the reason for the list, and explains what the singer *does* need for a successful romance in the C section:

> *Wide awake*
> *I can make my most fantastic dreams come true*
> *My romance doesn't need a thing but you*

What's being listed: things not needed to enhance the speaker's romance
Reason for the list: affirm the beloved, reinforcing that *they* are the crucial element in the relationship
How the list delights: interesting adjectives and descriptors (*blue lagoon, twinkling stars, soft guitars*); assonance (*blue lagoon*) and alliteration (*month of May*); parallel structure (*My romance doesn't…*); frequent rhymes including internal rhymes (*moon/lagoon/sky/by, May/stars/hideaway/guitars*)
Melody: The melody best reflects the enumerative quality of the list in the B section, where the phrases become short and repetitive.

Practice

1. Identify what is being listed and the reason for the list in the following lyrical excerpts:

A. *It's the melancholy times that I'll miss most*
The quiet taxis in the rain
The still nights in a cold hotel
The leavetakings, the dial tones

What's being listed:
Reason for the list:

B. *I make a date for golf and you can bet your life it rains*
I try to throw a party and the guy upstairs complains
I guess I'll go through life just catching colds and missing planes
Everything happens to me

What's being listed:
Reason for the list:

C. *I've grown accustomed to her face*
She almost makes the day begin
I've grown accustomed to the tune
She whistles night and noon
Her smiles, her frowns
Her ups, her downs

What's being listed:
Reason for the list:

D. *I've flown around the world in a plane*
I've settled revolutions in Spain
The North Pole I have charted
But I can't get started with you

What's being listed:
Reason for the list:

E. *A tinkling piano in the next apartment*
Those stumbling words that told you what my heart meant
A fairground's painted swings
These foolish things remind me of you

What's being listed:
Reason for the list:

2. The next exercises present lists that could be turned into a song. For each list, name what is being listed, invent a reason for the list, then shape the items into a stanza more appropriate for song lyrics. You can add elements to the list, change the order of the items, and enhance the items with descriptions, as necessary. The first example is done for you.

A. **List:** your mouth, your cheek, your hair, your eyes, your neck, your chin
What it's listing: parts of your face
Reason for the list: things I love about you

Shaped Version: *Your melancholy mouth that gently teases me*
Your elegant neck that leads the way
Your eyes whose look gently appeases me
Your chin that nods to say "good day"

B. **List:** bedroom, bathroom, kitchen, attic, basement, hallway, living room, dining room, playroom
What's being listed:
Reason for the list:
Shaped Version:

C. **List:** dawn, dusk, sunrise, sunset, afternoon, morning, evening, bedtime
What's being listed:
Reason for the list:
Shaped Version:

D. **List:** the beach, a café, a grassy hill, a lookout point, an open field, a city street
What's being listed:
Reason for the list:
Shaped Version:

E. **List:** a rock star, an astronaut, a millionaire, president, a CEO, a great painter, an actor
What's being listed:
Reason for the list:
Shaped Version:

16A Writing a List Song

Scan Here for
Chapter 16A Page

A list song is defined by its lyrical content rather than its musical form. To create a list song, a songwriter can start with the list's purpose and items and then decide how to express them musically.

Step One: Choose a Reason for the List

A list song needs a strong reason for presenting the list's items. This reason should carry *high stakes*, that is, it should matter deeply to the singer. List songs often make an argument or underscore the intensity of a feeling.

Brainstorm ten possible subjects for a list song, focusing on ideas that genuinely matter to you. As you brainstorm ideas, consider what would be included in each list. I brainstormed ten possible list song ideas:

1. Technology is distracting (list different types of technologies)

2. California is a great state (list special aspects of California)

3. You and I could have so much fun together (list things we could do together)

4. I need more money (list bills and expenses)

5. I really want a dog (list what I would do with a dog)

6. I need a vacation (list places I want to go or things I want to do)

7. Jason is so hot (list characteristics that make him hot)

8. Autumn is our favorite season (list things we love about autumn)

9. Memories of my dad are painful (list painful memories)

10. I think about you all the time (list activities I'm doing while I think about you)

I chose to work with #4 ("I need more money") because I like the idea of writing about something other than love and relationships. Additionally, the idea has broad appeal because worrying about money is a nearly universal experience.

Step Two: Brainstorm List Items

During the brainstorming stage, write as many simple list items as possible – at least fifteen – without expanding on the items or worrying about rhyme. The more items you generate at this stage, the easier the eventual lyric-writing process will be. I listed twenty-five common bills and expenses:

1. electric bill
2. rent
3. save for a house
4. car payments
5. tithing
6. taxes
7. groceries
8. inflation
9. internet and phone
10. gifts
11. an engagement ring
12. bar tab
13. going out for brunch
14. an occasional nice bottle of wine
15. gas
16. broken appliance (air conditioner?)
17. course textbooks
18. monthly subscriptions
19. taking a date out
20. guitar lessons
21. car tuneup
22. credit card debt
23. new shoes
24. tolls
25. retirement savings

Step Three: Decide on a Musical Form

List songs can be written in any musical form: strophic, verse-chorus, AABA, and ABAC. Because the financial concerns that I want to include in my song feel contemporary, I chose a verse-chorus form. Typically, in a verse-chorus form, the verses present the list while the chorus expresses the reason for the list.

Step Four: Write a Section Based on the List

Write the section that lists your items, organizing the list and adding new elements to create rhyme and a natural rhythmic flow. At this stage, the list should be shaped to delight the audience, often using wordplay, frequent rhymes, repeated sounds, and/or rapid-fire delivery.

The lyrics for my first verse are shown below, alongside the list items that inspired each line:

Lyric	List Item
The electric bill arrived today	electric bill
With taxes I don't want to pay	taxes
Gas hit twenty dollars a gallon	gas
Go to church, you owe ten percent	tithing
Even God's got you paying rent	rent
Jesus, I could use compassion	

Because the subject matter is so sad and self-pitying, I set this verse in a minor key with bluesy harmonies. The music I wrote for this lyric is shown in the next example:

Analysis

Melody: The melody begins by arpeggiating a D minor triad over a wide range. It spans almost an octave and a half in just the first two measures. The A-flats in the melody are drawn from the D blues scale and add a bluesy sound. The first eight measures repeat starting in measure 9, with the notes in measures 13-15 adjusted to fit the changing harmony.

Harmony: The song is written in D minor. The stepwise bassline in the first three measures descends to form contrary motion against the ascending melody. The B-flat seventh chords match the A-flat in the melody, contributing to the bluesy undercurrent.

Step Five: Write More Lyrics for the First Section

Using the list items brainstormed during step two, write more lyrics that fit the first musical section. Because adding items to the list strengthens the song's argument, I chose to write two more verses, for a total of three.

The second verse focuses on possible romance, while the third verse uses fewer list items but leans into wordplay (a pun on *fix*, polyptoton with *pressed/pressure*).

Verse 2	List Item
Pay the rent the first of every month	rent
And careful not to fall in love	
Romantic gifts are just too expensive	gifts
See a diamond ring at the jewelry store	engagement ring
When you see the price, you'll say "love's a bore"	
And suddenly, you've come to your senses.	

<table>
<tr><td>

Verse 3

To buy a home feels out of reach

Not in this economy

Seems like I'll be renting forever

Something new breaks every day

The fix is in and you've gotta pay

I'm pressed for cash and feeling the pressure

</td><td>

List Item

save for a house

rent

broken appliance

</td></tr>
</table>

Step Six: Write a Musical Section for the Reason for the List

Now that the list is clearly established, write a musical section that gives the reason for the list.

In a verse-chorus song, the chorus typically presents the reason for the list. I wrote a chorus for my verse based on a line that I wrote for the verse but couldn't include. Although the phrase "Is there anything left for me?" didn't rhyme with any of the words in the verse, it clearly captured the underlying reason for the list. I wrote a chorus based on that phrase:

Analysis

Melody: In contrast with the wide-ranging melody of the verse, the chorus melody focuses on repeated notes (as in measures 1-2, 5-6, 13-14) that help the listener discern the lyrics for the rapid-fire eighth notes. The chorus has an internal AABA form, with the "A" theme repeating in measures 1, 5, and 13 and a contrasting section starting in measure 9. The repetition and simplicity of the melody are designed to create a memorable, catchy chorus.

Harmony: The chorus starts away from the tonic of D minor but returns to the tonic chord by the ending. In contrast to the bluesy minor sound of the verses, the chorus uses mostly major triads in its A sections. The combination of a descending melody and the cadential return to the minor key gives a feeling of a big, disappointed exhalation at the end, as the singer accepts that "there ain't anything left for me."

Step Seven: Write Complementary Musical Sections

Depending on your song's form, additional sections might be needed. These sections can connect between lyrical ideas, further expand upon the list items, or give an alternate perspective.

I wrote a pre-chorus and bridge to complete my song.

Writing a Pre-Chorus

Because the verse and the chorus don't naturally connect, I added a pre-chorus. Before writing it, I summarized the two existing sections to identify missing information or possible connective material.

Verse: there are so many things to pay for
Chorus: there is no money left for me

One possible missing element between these ideas is how the money is acquired – probably by working. I brainstormed five ideas for a pre-chorus that could fill in the missing material while connecting the verse and chorus:

1. *I'm working day and night*
   But everything's still tight

2. *In the office every day from nine to five*
   is this any way to feel alive?

3. *Some say we work to live*
   some say we live to work

4. *Work, work, work, work*
   when is it time for fun?

5. *Nine to five ain't cutting it no more*
   The bill collector's knocking
   Always knocking at my door

I formed a full pre-chorus lyric out of #1, creating chiasmus between line one and line three:

> *I work all night and I work all day*
> *Just to have enough to pay*
> *I work all day and I work all night*
> *But honey, money's always tight*

I wrote the following music to accompany the lyric:

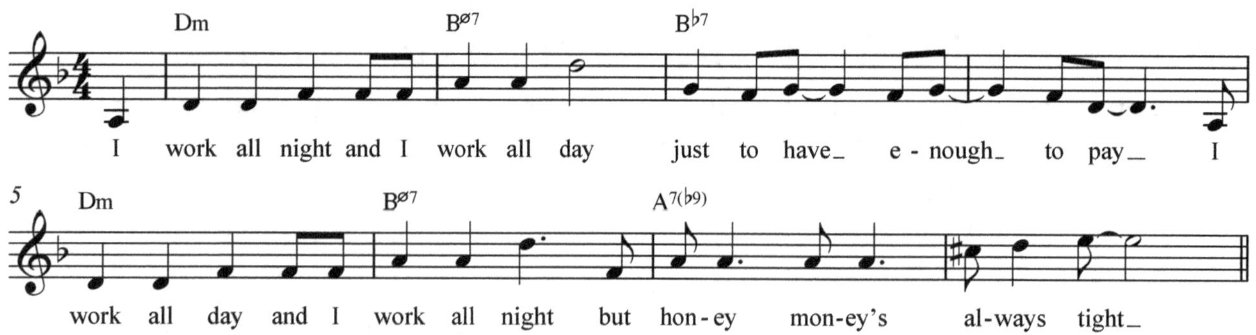

Analysis

Melody: The arpeggiated beginning of the pre-chorus melody returns to the opening melody of the verse. The ending of the melody rises to an unresolved note. The E ending the pre-chorus resolves by step to the D that begins the chorus.

Harmony: The chord progression starts on the tonic and ends with a tense half cadence, which increases energy leading to the chorus.

Writing a Bridge

The bridge typically provides an alternate perspective to the lyrics of the verse and chorus. Because this song maintains a consistently negative outlook, I decided to write a bridge that communicates positivity. My lyric imagines what I would do if I didn't have any financial pressures to worry about. The last few lines, however, snap the singer out of their daydream and back to reality.

Melody: The melody is written in quarter-note triplets to give the music a feeling of stretchy expansiveness, as though the melody is floating above the rhythm. The spaciousness of the phrasing (notice the measures of rest at the beginning of each four-measure phrase) and the downwards direction of the melody give the bridge melody the feeling of a relaxed exhale.

In the last four measures the character of the melody changes with the lyrical shift. The short phrase repeats after just two measures and the shape of the melody begins to climb rather than fall. With these changes, our "musical heart rate" is increasing, preparing us to enter back into the "real world" of the chorus.

Harmony: The harmonic rhythm slows down during the bridge to create a feeling of relaxation. The move to a distant key and the Lydian sound of the major seventh, sharp eleventh chords create the feeling of an oasis in the middle of a minor-key song.

Step Eight: Put the Song Together

With all of the sections complete, place them in order and add any necessary chords to connect between them. The next example shows a full first draft of my song, which I named "Is There Anything Left?" spread across multiple pages.

Is There Anything Left?

Jeremy Siskind

26
F
C
A7
is there an - y - thing left____ for me?

29
B♭
F
C
A7
They call it mak-ing a liv - ing but it feels like the death_ of me

33
Dm
Dm/C♯
Dm/C
G/B
Just a lit - tle bit more just a few more years and I'll be free

37
B♭
F
A7
but there ain't noth - ing left there ain't an - y - thing left____

40
Dm
To Coda
Verse 3
Dm
for me____________ Pay the rent the first_ of ev -

44
F7/C
B♭7
G7(♭9)
F/C
A/C♯
- 'ry month_ and care-ful not____ to fall in love___ ro - man - tic gifts are

48
Dm
G7
A7(♭9)
Dm
just too ex - pen - sive see a dia - mond ring_ at the

52
F7/C
B♭7
G7(♭9)
jew'l - ry store_ when you see the price you'll say love's a bore____ and

55
B♭
F
E⌀7
A7(♭9)
D.S. al Coda
sud - den - ly you've come to your sens - es I

Coda
Bridge
Dm
A♭maj7(♯11)
G♭maj7(♯11)
I could be on a trop - i - cal is - land
63
A♭maj7(♯11)
Dm7
Feel the breeze on my skin
67
A♭maj7(♯11)
G♭maj7(♯11)
I could swim in a lake by a cab - in
71
Fm
A♭
It ain't gon - na hap - pen
It ain't gon - na hap - pen
Chorus
75
F
B♭
F
Is there an - y - thing left
is there an - y - thing left
78
C
A7
B♭
for me?
They call it mak - ing a liv -
81
F
C
A7
Dm
- ing but it feels like the death of me
Just a lit - tle bit
85
Dm/C♯
Dm/C
G/B
B♭
more just a few more years and I'll be free
but there ain't noth - ing left
89
F
A7
Dm
there ain't an - y - thing left
for
me

Step Nine: Edit

The completed song only represents a first draft. After singing and playing the song multiple times, identify at least three moments that could be improved through editing. Write an alternate version of each to see if you can invent something better.

The next section shows how I dealt with the four weakest moments that I identified:

1. **Spot:** the beginning of the pre-chorus

    Issue: it sounds too similar to the beginning of the verse

    Solution: change the harmony at the beginning of the pre-chorus to help distinguish it from the verse

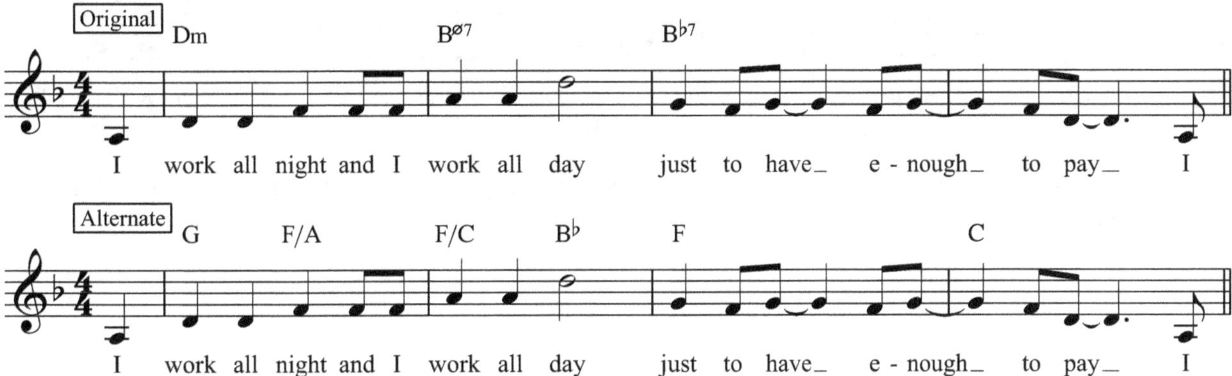

2. **Spot:** measures 9-11 of the chorus

    Issue: *"Just a little bit more, just a few more years"* should be in parallel structure to reflect the musical repetition in that spot

    Solution: lyric could be changed to:

    Give a few more months
    Give a few more years
    And you'll be free

3. **Spot:** third measure of the bridge melody

    Issue: the E-flat in the bridge melody sounds out of place

    Solution: the melody could focus on the B-flat major pentatonic scale to avoid the E-flat. The first phrase would look like the following:

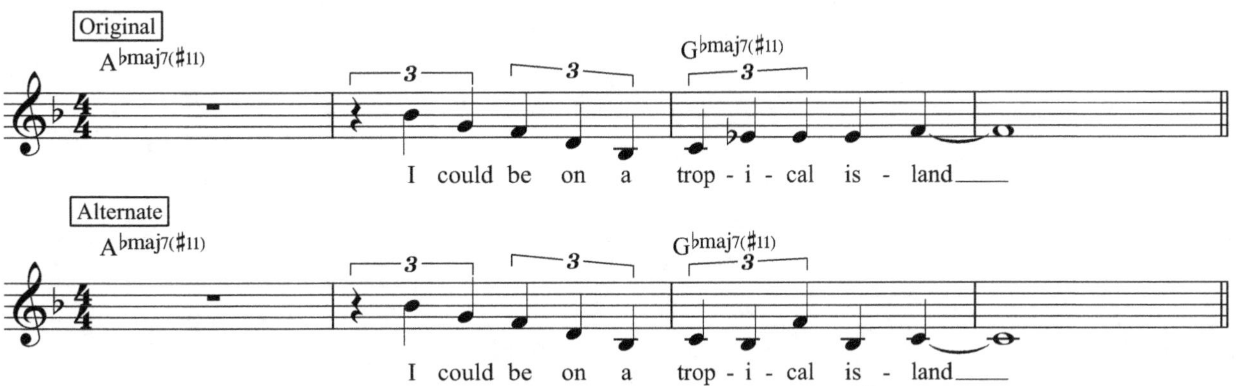

4. **Spot:** lead-in to the final chorus

> **Issue:** the bridge harmony creates an opportunity for a key change in the final chorus

> **Solution:** the final chorus could be transposed a whole-step higher:

To view the revised score and hear a full version of the song, visit the webpage for this chapter by scanning the QR code on the first page.

Takeaways

1. Brainstorm possible reasons for a list, focusing on making arguments or proving points that could have high stakes for the speaker.

2. Brainstorm many items for your list without considering rhyme or detail. That list will become strong raw material that you can use later in your song.

3. The section that presents the list should be written in a delightful way, adding new details that form rhyme, create vivid images, engage in wordplay, and support a musical rhythm.

4. The reason for the list should be rephrased and presented in a personal and expressive way, showing rather than telling.

5. When putting sections together, think deeply about transition points, adding chords or extra time to solidify the musical flow.

6. A song with all of the sections assembled is merely a first draft. After playing and singing the song multiple times, select at least three weak sections and write alternate versions of each.

Practice

1. Brainstorm 10 different reasons for a list that you could pursue.

   1.

   2.

   3.

   4.

   5.

   6.

   7.

   8.

   9.

   10.

2. Choose one and write a list of at least 15 items.

    1.   9.

    2.   10.

    3.   11.

    4.   12.

    5.   13.

    6.   14.

    7.   15.

    8.

3. Decide on a musical form. Write it below:

4. Write lyrics and music for a section that features the list. Write the lyrics below, choosing a few items and elaborating on them to form song lyrics.

5. Write additional lyrics for any repetition(s) of this section, maintaining the syllable count and musical accents to fit with the melody.

6. Write lyrics and music for the section that includes the reason for the list. Write the lyrics below, focusing on showing, rather than telling, the reason for the list.

7. Write other complementary sections, like a pre-chorus or bridge, as needed. Write the lyrics below in the space given.

8. Complete the song by putting it together and adding transitions and other missing sections.

9. Pick at least three of the weakest moments in the song and write alternate versions. If the new version is better than the original, replace the original with your edit.

1. **Spot:**
    Issue:

    Solution:

2. **Spot:**
    Issue:

    Solution:

3. **Spot:**
    Issue:

    Solution:

Glossary

AABA form (241) – musical structure consisting of three repeated musical sections separated by a contrasting section; usually thirty-two measures in length *(see song form)*

A-A Prime (A-A') (283) – alternate name for ABAC form that emphasizes the similarity of the two sixteen measure sections

ABAC form (283) – musical structure from the Great American Songbook which typically consists of four eight measure sections (A, B, A, and C)

adjectival simile (108) – simile in which the tenor is an adjective

adjectives – descriptive words that modify a noun, making a scene more vivid

adverbial simile (108) – simile in which the tenor is a verb

adverbs (130) – words commonly ending in *-ly* that can modify verbs, adjectives, or adverbs

aleatoric methods (123) – songwriting strategies that are derived from games of chance or randomness

alliteration (188) – repetition of consonant sounds at the beginning of nearby words

anadiplosis (194) – repetition of a word or phrase that links the end of one line to the beginning of the next line

analogy (113) – two-part metaphor, often stated in the form of "A is to B as C is to D"

anapest (12) – three-syllable metrical pattern of unstressed-unstressed-stressed

anaphora (231) – repetition of words at the beginning of consecutive lines

antanaclasis (193) – rhetorical device in which the same word is repeated but carries a different meaning

anticipate (213) – to play before the typical rhythmic placement, usually causing syncopation

antithesis (234) – the inclusion of two opposite words in close proximity to one another

arpeggiate (211) – to melodically outline a chord

assonance (188) – repetition of a vowel sound anywhere within nearby words

assonant rhyme (24) – type of rhyme in which only the vowel sounds are shared between two words' final stressed syllable

authentic cadence (98) – cadence that gives a traditional sense of finality, moving from the V to the I chord

bridge (145) – palate-cleansing section that disrupts the alternation between verses and choruses; B section of an AABA form

catalog song (322) – also known as a list song, includes a list in at least one musical section (see *list song*)

categories (236) – words that fit together logically but aren't exactly opposites

chiasmus (195) – rhetorical device in which two words or phrases are repeated in the reverse order of their original presentation

chorus (137) – the catchy, repetitive, singable part of a pop song that typically repeats the same lyrics with each repetition; in musical theater, the main part of the song that follows the verse

chromatic neighbor (217) – note a half-step away from a scale tone that decorates the scale tone

chromatic passing tone (217) – note that connects between whole steps by "filling in" the missing note in between

coin (131) – to invent a new word

common-tone diminished seventh chord (297) – a diminished seventh chord based on the tonic note, often used to create suspense before resolving to the tonic

conditional tense (127) – verb tense that indicates that something might happen in the future, usually using the words "would," "could," or "should"

confessional singer-songwriter tradition (124) – tradition in which the singer is assumed to be vulnerably telling their own story, usually using the first-person perspective

consonance (188) – repetition of a consonant sound anywhere within nearby words

consonant rhyme (24) – type of rhyme in which only the consonant sounds are shared between two words' final stressed syllable

dactyl (12) – three-syllable metrical pattern of stressed-unstressed-unstressed

dash (-) (11) – indication of stressed syllable in prosody

delay (212) – a strategy of writing melodic rhythms in which the composer places a rest on beat one and starts a melodic phrase after the beat

diatonic (91) – staying within a single major scale with no added flats or sharps

diatonic circle of fifths (93) – chord progression in which the roots of the chords descend by the interval of a fifth while staying within the key

diatonic melodies (207) – melodies that stay within the major scale without adding additional flats or sharps

diatonic seventh chords (176) – four-note chords that can be created by stacking every-other note of a single major scale

diatonic triads (91) – major, minor, and diminished triads staying within a major scale with no added flats or sharps

diminished fifth (93) – an interval consisting of six half-steps, the exact midpoint of the octave, also known as a tritone

diminished triad (92) – triad created by stacking two minor thirds, denoted with a superscript "o" sign; diminished triads are typically avoided

dominant chord (96) – chord based on the fifth scale degree which typically represents tension in typical schemes of tension and release

dorian mode (218) – seven-note scale that lowers the third and seventh of the parallel major scale

double chorus (146) – part of a musical form in which a chorus repeats twice

double refrain (67) – technique in which two portions of a stanza are repeated in each verse

elision (10) – removal of a syllable by replacing a vowel with an apostrophe

epanalepsis (197) – repetition of a word or phrase to bookend a stanza or a song

expressive leaps (211) – melodic intervals of more than a third that often simulate struggle or passion

extended metaphor (117) – a simile or metaphor that lasts for more than a couple of lines

feminine rhyme (27) – rhyme between two words or phrases that don't have a stress on the final syllable

fifth (92) – interval in which two notes are placed on non-adjacent lines or spaces and/or the third-to-bottom note of any chord that is stacked in thirds

first inversion (177) – inversion with the third on bottom

first-person perspective (124) – perspective in which the narrator is the protagonist and uses the "I" pronoun

first-person plural perspective (124) – perspective in which the narrator is a group of protagonists and uses the "we" pronoun

functional harmony (93) – harmony that strategically targets the tonic chord using traditional methods of tension and release, especially the circle of fifths

future tense (127) – verb tense in which the action is a prediction expected to happen in the future

gerund (127) – a verb ending in *-ing*

Great American Songbook (241) – songs from musicals and movies generally written between 1920 and 1960 by songwriters like George Gershwin, Cole Porter, Irving Berlin, Jerome Kern, and Richard Rodgers

half cadence (98) – a chord progression that gives the music a feeling of open-ended questioning by ending on the V chord

half step (206) – adjacent notes like E to F or C to D-flat

harmonic minor scale (95) – scale that lowers the third and sixth compared to the parallel major scale, notably retaining the leading tone

harmonic rhythm (98) – the pace at which chords change, for instance every measure, every beat, or every two beats

hemiola (140) – repeated rhythmic pattern that does not fit cleanly into the overall meter, especially groupings of three in four-four meter

homonym (193) – a word that has the same spelling and sound as another word but a different meaning

hook (138) – memorable part of a chorus that gets caught in the listener's head

iamb (11) – two-syllable metrical pattern of unstressed-stressed

imperative tense (127) – verb tense used to issue a command

implied vehicle (112) – in a simile or metaphor, a vehicle that is not explicitly mentioned

indirect object (126) – an object that exists in relation to a sentence's object

interlude (65) – instrumental section that introduces contrasting material

internal rhyme (30) – rhyme type in which one or both words are not followed by a musical pause

inversion (177) – rearranging of a chord so that notes other than the root are placed on bottom

leading tone (95) – note one half step below the tonic that resolves upwards to the root; leading tones are essential to defining a key center

list song (322) – a song that includes a list in at least one musical section (see *catalog song*)

lower chromatic neighbor (217) – notes that decorate scale tones from a half-step below

major pentatonic scale (207) – five-note scale consisting of the 1, 2, 3, 5, and 6 of a major scale

major scale (206) – a collection of seven notes organized in whole steps except for the half steps between the third and fourth and seventh and eighth scale degrees

major triads (92) – triads with a major third on bottom and a minor third on top, such as the I, IV, and V in a major scale

masculine rhyme (27) – rhyme between two words that have a stress on the final syllable

measure (13) – rhythmic division that defines stronger and weaker beats

melisma (10) – single syllable stretched across multiple notes

melismatic (10) – style of singing in which syllables are commonly stretched across multiple notes

melodic minor scale (95) – scale with different ascending/descending forms; when ascending, the scale lowers just the third as compared to the parallel major scale; when descending, the scale matches the natural minor scale

metaphor (107) – comparison of two unlike objects without using the words "like" or "as"

metonymy (118) – a device in which a representative symbol is used to replace a noun

metrical foot (11) – building-block pattern of stressed and unstressed syllables (see *poetic foot*)

minor pentatonic scale (209) – five-note scale consisting of the same pitches as the major pentatonic scale of the relative major

minor triads (92) – triads with a minor third on bottom and a major third on top, such as the ii, iii, and vi in a major scale

modal borrowing (182) – intermingling of chords from parallel major and minor keys (see *modal interchange*)

modal interchange (182) – intermingling of chords from parallel major and minor keys (see *modal borrowing*)

modes of the major scale (219) – seven-note scales built by starting the major scale from different scale degrees

monosyllabic (9) – consisting of a single syllable

multisyllabic rhyme (27) – type of rhyme in which more than one syllable share vowel and consonant sounds

musical emphasis (12) – melodic properties of strong rhythmic placement, longer hold, and higher pitch that complement stressed syllables

natural minor (95) – minor scale that lowers the third, sixth, and seventh as compared to the major scale; a natural minor scale shares the same notes as its relative major

ninth (177) – note equivalent of the second that is used to create extra color in seventh chords

non-functional harmony (94) – harmony that moves freely between chords without prioritizing traditional tension and release created primarily through the circle of fifths

nouns (123) – characters, settings, objects, and ideas

object (123) – part of the sentence that receives the verb's action

offbeats (13) – the "ands" between the beats in a measure

onomatopoeia (227) – lyrical device in which words simulate sounds

parallel keys (95) – major and minor keys based on the same tonic, for instance C major and C minor

parallel structure (230) – lyrical device in which grammatical structures are repeated with new words

pararhyme (34) – type of rhyme in which words share all of their consonant sounds but have different vowel sounds

parataxis (322) – rhetorical device in which items are presented equally without defining a relationship between them

past tense (127) – verb tense in which the action is completed

patter song (187) – a musical theater song whose rapid-fire, mostly-spoken lyrics focus on rhythm and wordplay

pedal point (179) – technique in which the bass remains the same while the chords change above

personification (117) – comparison in which the tenor is something non-human and the vehicle is a person

perspective (124) – determination of who is narrating the song or story

phoneme (188) – an individual sound within a word, such as a consonant or vowel

pickup (212) – a note or notes that precedes beat one

phrase (206) – complete musical statement that has a clear beginning and ending

plagal cadence (98) – chord progression moving from the IV chord to the I chord that indicates a bluesy or gospel tradition

poetic (225) – language that focuses on deep meaning, comparison, and emotion rather than clarity or literal expression

poetic foot (11) – building-block pattern of stressed and unstressed syllables (see *metrical foot*)

polyptoton (192) – syllabic repetition in which multiple words share the same root word with a repeated syllable

polysyllabic (9) – consisting of more than one syllable

portmanteau (132) – a word that combines two existing words to form a new word

post-chorus (147) – section that allows the energy of the chorus to dissipate and transition smoothly back into the verse

power chord (97) – a chord consisting of only the root and the fifth, omitting the third

pre-chorus (143) – musical section that creates an energetic buildup to the emotional peak of the chorus

present continuous tense (127) – tense that expresses an ongoing action, using a gerund form

present tense (127) – verb tense in which the action is happening currently

proper nouns (123) – distinctly named, unique entities, usually capitalized

prosody (11) – study of stressed and unstressed syllables in poems and songs

pure rhyme (24) – strongest kind of rhyme in which the vowel sound and final consonant sound are identical in a word's final stressed syllable

range (206) – distance between the highest and lowest note of a melody

recitation tone (210) – a flat melodic shape consisting of a single melodic note that is repeated for multiple words

refrain (66) – in strophic songs, a repeated lyric or phrase; in the Great American Songbook tradition, the refrain is frequently the "main part" of the song, excluding the verse

relative keys (209) – keys that share the same key signature like C major and A minor

repetitive rhyme (35) – type of rhyme in which rhymes are created by repeating a single word twice

retrograde (323) – compositional device in which melodic notes are presented in the opposite order in which they first appeared

rhyme (23) – pairing words that share similar sounds

rhyme scheme (31) – pattern of how often and where rhymes are placed

root (92) – note on which a chord is based, the lowest note when the triad is stacked in thirds

root position (177) – inversion with the root on bottom

scat syllables (131) – nonsense syllables meant to imitate the sound of another instrument

second inversion (177) – inversion with the fifth on bottom

second-person perspective (124) – perspective in which the narrator is the listener and the "you" pronoun is used

secondary dominant (180) – non-diatonic dominant seventh chord that targets a diatonic chord other than the tonic; secondary dominants target their chords from a fifth above

sentence (286) – a musical phrase structure consisting of a 1 + 1 + 2 ratio

seventh chords (176) – four-note chords that include the seventh scale degree which usually create a "jazzy" sound

sequence (215) – melodic strategy in which the same melodic shape repeats starting at a different place in the scale

sighing gesture (216) – a melodic figure that descends by step, typically at the end of a phrase

simile (107) – comparison of two unlike objects using the words "like" or "as"

slash (/) (11) – indication of stressed syllables in prosody

slash chords (178) – chords that place a note in the bass that is not part of the original chord

song form (241) – also known as AABA form, a musical structure consisting of three repeated musical sections separated by a contrasting section; usually thirty-two measures in length (see *AABA form*)

stanza (65) – set of lyrics that goes with a single musical section

stepwise basslines (179) – bass motions in which the bass note moves by half step or whole step

story song (66) – song in which characters progress and develop, with significant change occurring between the beginning and end

stressed syllable (11) – part of a word that receives rhythmic emphasis

strong beat (13) – beats one and three of a four-four measure

strophe (65) – a stanza of lyrics

strophic song (65) – song that consists of a single, repeated musical section

subject (123) – part of a sentence that performs the verb's action

syncopation (14) – emphasis on offbeats

synecdoche (118) – a device in which a part of something is used to represent the whole

syllable (9) – single rhythmic utterance

syntax (227) – sentence structure

tag ending (242) – ending device in which the last few measures are repeated, usually three times

tenor (107) – part of a simile or metaphor already in the song that is being described

tessitura (206) – a portion of an instrument or singer's possible range in which they can comfortably execute a passage

text setting (9) – the relationship between melody and lyrics

third inversion (177) – inversion with the seventh on bottom

third-person omniscient (47) – writing style in which the narrator can equally take the perspective of all characters, including entering their minds to share their thoughts

third-person perspective (124) – perspective in which the narrator is a third party and the "he," "she," or "they" pronouns are used

thirds (91) – interval created by combining two notes from a scale with only one note "skipped" in between, for instance the first and third or second and fourth; stacking thirds creates triads and seventh chords; the "third" of a chord is the second-to-bottom note of any chord that is stacked in thirds

tone (110) – how you want the song to feel to the listener

tonic (91) – the harmonic home of a piece and/or the first note of a scale

trochee (11) – two-syllable metrical pattern of stressed-unstressed

u shape (˘) (11) – indication of unstressed syllable in prosody

unstressed syllable (11) – part of a word that does not receive rhythmic emphasis

upper chromatic neighbor (217) – a note that decorates scale tones from a half-step above

upper extensions (176) – notes stacked above the triad, especially the ninth, eleventh, and thirteenth

vamp (94) – section that repeats until cued

vehicle (107) – part of a simile or metaphor introduced into a song to describe or qualify the tenor

verb (125) – action words that set a song's characters into motion

verb tense (127) – the way in which a verb indicates a story's temporal position

verse (65, 138) – musical section whose lyrics change each time it repeats; in musical theater, a prelude to the main part of the song that supplies the narrative background

verse-chorus form (137) – a category of songs in which a series of verses lead into and provide contrast with the emotional "pay-off" of a chorus

weak beats (13) – beats two and four of a four-four measure

whole step (206) – interval consisting of two half steps, such as C to D or F to G

word painting (226) – songwriting technique in which a song musically dramatizes what the lyric is describing

x (x) (11) – indication of unstressed syllable in prosody

Bibliography

Chapter 1: Getting Started

Light, Alan. *The Holy or the Broken: Leonard Cohen, Jeff Buckley, and the Unlikely Ascent of "Hallelujah."* New York: Atria Books, 2013.

Simon, Paul. "I Know What I Know." *American Songwriter.*
https://americansongwriter.com/paul-simon-on-songwriting-i-know-what-i-know/

Simon, Paul. "Song About the Moon." Official artist website.
https://www.paulsimon.com/track/song-about-the-moon-2/

"Songwriters on Songwriting: Bob Dylan." *Go Into the Story (The Black List).*
https://gointothestory.blcklst.com/songwriters-on-songwriting-bob-dylan-4b5ac314fd8

Jones, Lucy. "The Incredible Way Michael Jackson Wrote Music." *NME.*
https://www.nme.com/blogs/nme-blogs/the-incredible-way-michael-jackson-wrote-music-16799

Bon Iver. "Working on a Dream." *American Songwriter.*
https://americansongwriter.com/bon-iver-working-on-a-dream/2/

Chapter 3: Rhyme

"Eminem Rhymes the Word 'Orange.'" *60 Minutes Archive.* YouTube video.
https://www.youtube.com/watch?v=WgQI655FqtM

Chapter 4: Show, Don't Tell

Porter, Cole. "The Play: *Mexican Hayride.*" *The New York Times.*
https://archive.nytimes.com/www.nytimes.com/books/98/11/29/specials/porter-hayride.html

"I Love You." *JazzStandards.com.*
https://www.jazzstandards.com/compositions-1/iloveyou.htm

Chapter 5: Strophic Songs

"The Mystique of 'Parsley, Sage, Rosemary and Thyme.'" *McGill University Office for Science and Society.*
https://www.mcgill.ca/oss/article/environment-quirky-science-supplements/mystique-parsley-sage-rosemary-and-thyme

Chapter 7: Similes and Metaphors

"Metaphor and Meaning." *JSTOR.*
https://www.jstor.org/stable/435560

Chapter 8: The Lyricist's Toolbox

"How David Bowie, Thom Yorke, and Kurt Cobain Wrote Lyrics." *Far Out Magazine.*
https://faroutmagazine.co.uk/david-bowie-thom-yorke-kurt-cobain-lyrics-method/

"Ben Bridwell (Band of Horses)." *Songwriters on Process.*
https://www.songwritersonprocess.com/blog/2015/2/10/ben-bridwell-band-of-horses

Bon Iver. "Working on a Dream." *American Songwriter.*
https://americansongwriter.com/bon-iver-working-on-a-dream/2/

Chapter 9: Verse–Chorus Form

"The Science of Concerts." *Epigram.*
https://epigram.org.uk/the-science-of-concerts/

"Dopamine and Concert Highs." *EcoSalon.*
https://ecosalon.com/dopamine-and-concert-highs/

"Oxytocin." *Cleveland Clinic.*
https://my.clevelandclinic.org/health/articles/22618-oxytocin

Chapter 10: Harmony Beyond Major and Minor

"Harlan Howard." *Country Music Hall of Fame.*
https://www.countrymusichalloffame.org/artist/harlan-howard

Chapter 11: Repeated Sounds and Structures

"Only Murders in the Building: 'Which of the Pickwick Triplets Did It?'" Music video. Hulu. YouTube.
https://www.youtube.com/watch?v=Piv19tK4lH4

Chapter 12: Melody

Raksin, David. *David Raksin Conducts His Great Film Scores.* Liner notes. RCA Victor 1490-2-RG.

Chapter 13: Poetic Language

"About 'Somebody Told Me.'" *Reddit: r/TheKillers.*
https://www.reddit.com/r/TheKillers/comments/wvwgfk/about_somebody_told_me/

Chapter 14: AABA Form

"Sinatra Family Piano Finds New Home at UCLA." *UCLA Newsroom.*
https://newsroom.ucla.edu/stories/sinatra-family-piano-storied-legacy-finds-new-home-at-ucla

"Sammy Cahn." *Concord Music Publishing.*
https://concord.com/publishing-roster/sammy-cahn/

"Jimmy Van Heusen." *Palm Springs Life.*
https://www.palmspringslife.com/history/jimmy-van-heusen/

Chapter 15: ABAC Form

"The Songwriter's Craft." *Irving Berlin Official Website.*
  https://www.irvingberlin.com/the-songwriters-craft

"The Sad Story Behind 'White Christmas.'" *KUOW.*
  https://www.kuow.org/stories/sad-story-behind-white-christmas-america-s-favorite-christ-mas-carol

Guinness Book of Records. 2009 ed., pp. 14, 15, 169.

"The Fall of Saigon (1975): The Bravery of American Diplomats and Refugees." *National Museum of American Diplomacy.* April 29, 2021.

Chapter 15A: Writing an ABAC Form

Aron, Arthur, et al. "The Experimental Generation of Interpersonal Closeness: A Procedure and Some Preliminary Findings." *Personality and Social Psychology Bulletin* 23, no. 4 (1997): 363–377. https://doi.org/10.1177/0146167297234003

Chapter 16: List Songs

Nascimento, Elma Lia. "Calling the Tune." *Brazzil,* September 2001.
  https://www.brazzil.com/p08sep01.htm

"Song of the Week #51: 'Águas de Março.'" *Song of the Week Blog.*
  https://songoftheweekblog.wordpress.com/2013/09/01/song-of-the-week-51-aguas-de-marco-waters-of-march-tom-jobim/

"Why Billy Joel Hates 'We Didn't Start the Fire.'" *Ultimate Classic Rock.*
  https://ultimateclassicrock.com/billy-joel-we-didnt-start-the-fire-hate/